T0260070

Security, Privacy, and Digital Forensics in the Cloud

Security, Privacy, and Digital Forensics in the Cloud

Edited by

Lei Chen

Georgia Southern University, USA

Hassan Takabi

University of North Texas, USA

Nhien-An Le-Khac

University College Dublin, Ireland

This edition first published 2019

Published by John Wiley & Sons Singapore Pte Ltd, 1 Fusionopolis Walk, #07-01 Solaris South Tower, Singapore 138628, under exclusive license granted by Higher Education Press Limited Company for all media and languages excluding Chinese and throughout the world excluding Mainland China, and with non-exclusive license for electronic versions in Mainland China.

Registered Offices
John Wiley & Sons, Inc., 111 River Street, Hoboken, NJ 07030, USA
John Wiley & Sons Singapore Pte. Ltd, 1 Fusionopolis Walk, #07-01 Solaris South Tower, Singapore 138628

Editorial Office
The Atrium, Southern Gate, Chichester, West Sussex, PO19 8SQ, UK

For details of our global editorial offices, customer services, and more information about Wiley products visit us at www.wiley.com.

Wiley also publishes its books in a variety of electronic formats and by print-on-demand. Some content that appears in standard print versions of this book may not be available in other formats.

Library of Congress Cataloging-in-Publication Data

Names: Chen, Lei, 1978 July 28– editor. | Takabi, Hassan, 1982– editor. |
Le-Khac, Nhien-An, 1972– editor.
Title: Security, privacy, and digital forensics in the cloud / edited by Lei Chen,
Hassan Takabi, Nhien-An Le-Khac.
Description: Hoboken, NJ ; Singapore : John Wiley & Sons, 2019. |
Includes bibliographical references and index. |
Identifiers: LCCN 2018034906 (print) | LCCN 2018056741 (ebook) |
ISBN 9781119053408 (Adobe PDF) | ISBN 9781119053378 (ePub) |
ISBN 9781119053286 (hardcover)
Subjects: LCSH: Cloud computing–Security measures. | Digital forensic science.
Classification: LCC QA76.585 (ebook) | LCC QA76.585 .S4445 2019 (print) |
DDC 004.67/82–dc23
LC record available at https://lccn.loc.gov/2018034906

Cover Design: Wiley
Cover Image: © frankpeters/Getty Images

Set in 10/12pt Warnock by SPi Global, Pondicherry, India

10 9 8 7 6 5 4 3 2 1

Contents

List of Contributors

Farzaneh Abazari
School of Computer Engineering, Iran University of Science and Technology, Tehran, Iran

Irfan Ahmed
University of New Orleans, New Orleans, LA, USA

Morteza Analoui
School of Computer Engineering, Iran University of Science and Technology, Tehran, Iran

Nathalie Baracaldo
IBM Almaden Research Center, San Jose, CA, USA

Barry Cartwright
Simon Fraser University, Burnaby, BC, Canada

Paolina Centonze
Iona College, New Rochelle, NY, USA

Lei Chen
Georgia Southern University, Statesboro, GA, USA

Robert Craig
Walworth County Sheriff's Office, Elkhorn, WI, USA

Lucia De Marco
University College Dublin, Dublin, Ireland

Richard Frank
Simon Fraser University, Burnaby, BC, Canada

Frank Ferrese
Electrical and Computer Engineering, Temple University, Philadelphia, PA, USA

Mohammad GhasemiGol
Department of Computer Engineering, University of Birjand, Birjand, Iran

Joseph Glider
SAP Labs, Palo Alto, CA, USA

Jay Iyer
Office of CTO Security Business Group, Cisco Systems, San Jose, CA, USA

Patrick Kamongi
University of North Texas, Denton, TX, USA

M-Tahar Kechadi
University College Dublin, Dublin, Ireland

Ram Krishnan
University of Texas at San Antonio, San Antonio, TX, USA

Nhien-An Le-Khac
University College Dublin, Dublin, Ireland

Michel Mollema
Dutch National High Tech Crime Unit, Driebergen-Rijsenburg, The Netherlands

Farhan Patwa
University of Texas at San Antonio, San Antonio, TX, USA

James Plunkett
University College Dublin, Dublin, Ireland

Vassil Roussev
University of New Orleans, New Orleans, LA, USA

Steven Ryder
Europol, The Hague, The Netherlands

Ravi Sandhu
University of Texas at San Antonio, San Antonio, TX, USA

Sebastian Schlepphorst
University College Dublin, Dublin, Ireland

Avinash Srinivasan
Computer and Information Sciences, Temple University, Philadelphia, PA, USA

Hassan Takabi
Department of Computer Science and Engineering, University of North Texas, Denton, TX, USA

George R. S. Weir
University of Strathclyde, Glasgow, UK

Lanchuan Xu
Chengdu Railway Public Security Bureau, Chengdu, China

Saman Taghavi Zargar
Office of CTO Security Business Group, Cisco Systems, San Jose, CA, USA

Yun Zhang
University of Texas at San Antonio, San Antonio, TX, USA

Saman Zonouz
Rutgers University, New Brunswick, NJ, USA

Part I

Cloud Security and Privacy

1

Introduction to the Cloud and Fundamental Security and Privacy Issues of the Cloud

Hassan Takabi[1] *and Mohammad GhasemiGol*[2]

[1] *Department of Computer Science and Engineering, University of North Texas, Denton, TX, USA*
[2] *Department of Computer Engineering, University of Birjand, Birjand, Iran*

1.1 Introduction

Cloud computing is the most popular paradigm in the computer world that provides on-demand computing and storage capabilities to consumers over the Internet. However, these benefits may result in serious security issues such as data breaches, computation breaches, flooding attacks, etc. On the other hand, the whole IT infrastructure is under the control of the cloud provider, and cloud consumers have to trust the security-protection mechanisms that are offered by service providers. Therefore, security concerns should be considered to improve the assurance of required security for cloud customers.

The key security constructs in the cloud environment are information, identity, and infrastructure. Cloud information flows into the physical infrastructure from many users across different devices and geographies. The objective of information security is to protect information as well as information systems from unauthorized access, use, disclosure, disruption, modification, or destruction (Winkler 2011). In other words, at the heart of any information security system is the requirement to protect the confidentiality, integrity, and availability of data. It is important to thoroughly understand your organization's security policies in order to implement standards in a cloud environment that will form your security framework (Steiner and Khiabani 2012). Data governance concerns commonly arise in the areas of IP protection, regulatory governance, industry compliance requirements, and data mobility. A consistent set of policies is needed for compliance and governance across cloud platforms that IT may not always control. These policies are required for identifying sensitive information; controlling its transmission, storage, and use in the Cloud; and sharing it among users and devices. These policies must be consistently enforced across private and public clouds, and physical infrastructure. Traditionally, IT has used enterprise identity to control user access and entitlement to a variety of on-premises information and application assets. This principle must be extended to identities at cloud service providers, controlling what information employees can access in which clouds, from which devices, and in which locations.

Security, Privacy, and Digital Forensics in the Cloud, First Edition. Edited by Lei Chen, Hassan Takabi, and Nhien-An Le-Khac.

This chapter provides an introduction to the Cloud and its fundamental security and privacy issues. We start with a background of cloud computing and security issues in Section 1.2. In Section 1.3, we briefly discuss identity security in cloud computing. Cloud information security issues are investigated in Section 1.4. In Section 1.5, we discuss some cloud security standards. Finally, conclusions are drawn in Section 1.6.

1.2 Cloud Computing and Security Issues

The US National Institute of Standards and Technology (NIST) defines cloud computing as follows: "Cloud computing is a model for enabling ubiquitous, convenient, on-demand network access to a shared pool of configurable computing resources (e.g. networks, servers, storage, applications, and services) that can be rapidly provisioned and released with minimal management effort or service provider interaction. This cloud model is composed of five essential characteristics, three service models, and four deployment models (Mell and Grance 2011)."

NIST defines five major actors: cloud consumer, cloud provider, cloud auditor, cloud broker, and cloud carrier (Hogan et al. 2011):

- **Cloud consumer** – A person or organization that maintains a business relationship with and uses services offered by cloud providers.
- **Cloud provider** – A person, organization, or entity responsible for offering various services to cloud consumers.
- **Cloud auditor** – A party that can conduct independent assessments of cloud services, information system operations, performance, and security of cloud implementations.
- **Cloud broker** – An entity that manages the use, performance, and delivery of cloud services, and negotiates relationships between cloud providers and cloud consumers.
- **Cloud carrier** – The intermediary that provides connectivity and transport of cloud services from cloud providers to cloud consumers.

There are three service-delivery models and four deployment models in the cloud environment. As shown in Figure 1.1, cloud providers offer Infrastructure-as-a-Service (IaaS), Platform-as-a-Service (PaaS), and Software-as-a-Service (SaaS) as three fundamental services (Hashizume 2013; Mell and Grance 2011):

- **Infrastructure-as-a-Service** – IaaS is the most basic cloud service model, where cloud providers offer servers, storage, and network, typically in the form of virtual appliances. Consumers can deploy and run any software such as operating systems and applications. IaaS providers are responsible for the underlying infrastructure including housing, running, and maintaining these resources, while consumers are responsible for maintaining the operating system and their applications. Amazon Elastic Compute Cloud (EC2, http://aws.amazon.com/ec2)), Eucalyptus (http://www8.hp.com/us/en/cloud/helion-eucalyptus.html), and OpenNebula (http://opennebula.org) are some examples of IaaS providers.
- **Platform-as-a-Service** – In PaaS, providers offer environments for developing, deploying, hosting, and testing software applications. Typically, it includes programming languages, databases, libraries, and other development tools. Consumers are

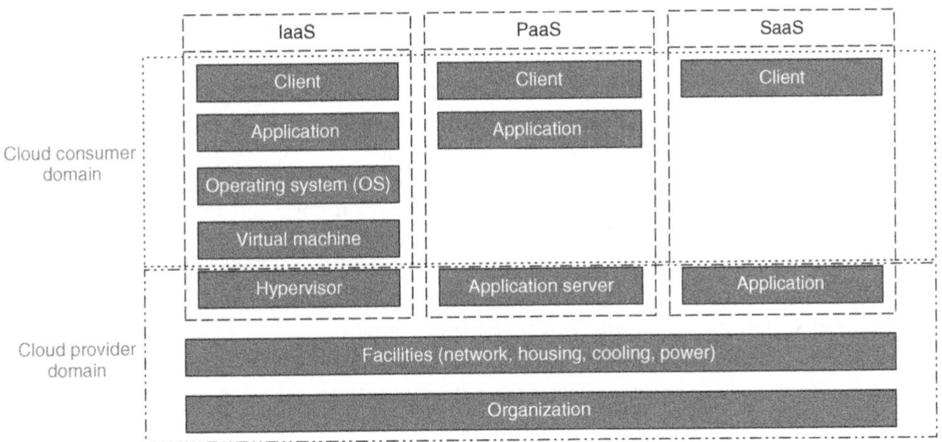

Figure 1.1 Cloud components in the different types of cloud services.

not responsible for the underlying infrastructure, operating systems, or storage, but they are responsible for their deployed applications. Examples of PaaS providers include Microsoft Azure (https://azure.microsoft.com/en-us), Force.com (http://www.force.com), and Google App Engine (https://cloud.google.com/appengine).

- **Software-as-a-Service** – In SaaS, cloud providers offer applications on demand that are hosted on the Cloud and can be accessed through thin clients. Consumers do not manage or control the underlying infrastructure. Some SaaS applications allow limited user-specific customization. Examples of SaaS providers include Salesforce.com's Customer Relationship Management (CRM, www.salesforce.com) and FreshBooks (www.freshbooks.com).

The four cloud deployment models are briefly described as follows (Mell and Grance 2011):

- **Public cloud** – A public cloud is deployed by an organization that offers various services to the general public over the Internet. The infrastructure is owned and managed by the service provider, and it is located in the provider's facilities. Cloud providers are responsible for the installation, management, provisioning, and maintenance of the cloud services. Users' data is stored and processed in the Cloud, which may raise security and privacy issues. It exists on the premises of the cloud provider.
- **Private cloud** – A private cloud is deployed for a single organization and is dedicated entirely to that organization's internal users. The private cloud resides in the organization's facilities; however, it can be hosted and managed by a third-party provider. The private cloud can be owned, managed, and operated by the organization, a third party, or some combination of them, and it may exist on or off premises, so that data security and availability can be controlled by each of them.
- **Community cloud** – A community cloud is deployed for a specific community of consumers from organizations that share common computing concerns. It may be owned, managed, and operated by one or more of the organization's members, a third party, or some combination of them, and it may exist on or off premises.

- **Hybrid cloud** – This is a combination of the previous types of clouds (private, public, or community) that remain unique entities but are bound together by standardized or proprietary technology that enables data and application portability. In order to ensure security, an organization should migrate some of its processes to a public cloud while remaining its critical process in-house.

Several characteristics of cloud computing that are mentioned in the literature are listed next (Hashizume 2013; Kizza and Yang 2014; Mell and Grance 2011):

- **Accessibility** – Cloud services can be accessed from anywhere at any time via browsers or APIs by different client platforms such as laptops, desktops, mobile phones, and tablets. Cloud services are network dependent, so the network (Internet, local area network [LAN], or wide area network [WAN]) has to work in order to access cloud services.
- **On-demand, self-service** – Traditionally, acquisition of computing services demanded perpetual ownership of software or computing hardware and sustainable technical support to help with computing services. Those models are being phased out because we have cloud computing as a flexible model: consumers of computing services are no longer restricted to rigid traditional models of ownership or boxed services. Now, a consumer is able to not only automatically provision any computing services and capabilities as needed but also determine the time to begin using provisioned services and how long to use them.
- **Rapid elasticity** – The ability to resize and dynamically scale virtualized computing resources such as servers, processors, operating systems, and others to meet the customer's on-demand needs is referred to as computing service *elasticity*. To meet elasticity demands on computing resources, the provider must make sure that there are abundant resources available to ensure that end users' requests are continually and promptly met. Amazon EC2 is a good example of a web service interface that allows the customer to obtain and configure capacity with minimal effort.
- **Resource pooling** – As noted in the NIST report, the provider's computing resources are pooled to serve multiple consumers using a multitenant model, with different physical and virtual resources dynamically assigned and reassigned according to consumer demand. These fluctuating and unpredictable customer demands are a result of new cloud computing flexibility, access, and ease of use.
- **Pay-as-you-go** – Depending on the pricing model, customers only pay for the services they consume (computing power, bandwidth, storage, number of users, etc.). Sometimes, services have a flat rate or are free of charge.
- **Versatility** – Cloud computing supports different types of services: IaaS, PaaS, and SaaS. Each service can provide various applications running at the same time.
- **Shared resources** – Cloud resources such as infrastructure, platform, and software are shared among multiple customers (multitenant), which enables unused resources to serve different needs for different customers.
- **Reliability** – Cloud computing supports reliability by adding redundant sites in case an error or attack occurs.
- **Performance** – Application performance can be better in the cloud because computing resources can be assigned to applications when workloads surge. The Cloud can be suitable for data-intense applications since they require multiple computing resources.

- **Ubiquitous network access** – The recent ubiquitous access to computer networks and services can be attributed to advances in the use of high-speed Internet and virtualization technology. Advances and development in these technologies have increased the options in the repertoire of computing services a customer can select from. With more options have also come the high degree of specialization and quality of services that customers expect.
- **Measured service** – The increase in the repertoire of services available to users has been enhanced by cloud services' elasticity, flexibility, and on-demand capabilities, thus allowing for these services to be metered. The concept of metered services allows customers to get the services they want when and for however long they need them. One of the most popular characteristics of cloud computing technology is measured or metered service for most, if not all, cloud services, including storage, processing, bandwidth, and active user accounts. This *pick-what-you-can-afford-to-pay-for* principle based on metering results in automatic control and optimization of cloud technology resource use based on the type of service. These statistics can be reported as needed, thus providing transparency for both the provider and consumer.

There are several benefits to adopting cloud computing; however, there are also some significant obstacles to its acceptance. One important issue is security, followed by privacy, standardization, and legal matters. Research in cloud computing security is a new area that is evolving rapidly. Cloud resources are centrally managed, so in theory security should be improved in this type of environment. But security in complex environments is hard to undertake, due to the fact data is stored and processed in unknown places, resources are shared by unrelated users, and other concerns. There are several security challenges that are specific for each delivery model, especially for public cloud adoption. Also, cloud computing inherits security issues from its underlying technologies and presents its own security challenges as well. This makes it even harder to secure the entire system. Most security measures have been developed to mitigate or stop parts of a system, but there is rarely a global security analysis of the complete cloud system (Hashizume 2013).

The following examples illustrate the need for cloud security (Pearson and Yee 2013):

- Hackers stole the credentials of Salesforce.com's customers via phishing attacks (2007).
- T-Mobile customers lost data due to the "Sidekick disaster" of the Microsoft cloud (2009).
- A botnet incident at Amazon EC2 infected customers' computers and compromised their privacy (2009).
- Hotmail accounts were hacked due to technical flaws in Microsoft software (2010).
- Amazon customer services were unavailable for multiple days, and data was lost due to a logical flaw in the cloud storage design (2011).

Numerous research studies address cloud computing security from various perspectives. (Juan Ferrer, 2013). *Jansen and Grance* organize the key security issues in cloud computing in the following categories: trust, architecture, identity management, software isolation, data protection, and availability (Jansen and Grance 2011). Cloud computing confers the highest level of trust to providers due to the level of insider access available to the provider and other users that share the infrastructure, and also due to providers' lack of transparency about their security practices.

Risk analysis is more important in IaaS due to due to the primary sources of vulnerabilities that exist in the hypervisor and virtual infrastructures, such as leaks of sensitive data through the virtual machines (VMs) and lack of intrusion and detection systems in virtual networking infrastructure. On the other hand, multitenancy is identified as the main source of threats for data protection, and it refers to the cloud characteristic of resource sharing. *Jansen and Grance* propose data encryption and data sanitization as a means to protect sensitive information. *Multitenancy* refers to the cloud characteristic of resource sharing. Compliance is also identified as a risk, because there is no way for users to track data location. With regard to availability, they present examples of distributed denial of service (DDoS) attacks and both permanent and temporal outages. They also believe that attacks on the cloud infrastructure will be more difficult to defend against and more common in the future.

Jensen et al. provide an overview of technical security issues of cloud computing environments. They consider diverse technology such as Web Services Security (WS-Security), Transport Layer Security (TLS), XML Signature, browser security, and integrity and binding issues, such as cloud malware-injection attacks and metadata-spoofing attacks based on exploiting Web Services Description Language (WSDL) vulnerabilities (Jensen et al. 2009). They also investigate *flooding* attacks, described as an attacker sending so many requests to the provider that the result is a denial of service in the provider's hardware. It has to be noted in this case that many public cloud providers already consider this possibility in their architectures by establishing a maximum amount of services a user can request simultaneously (e.g. Amazon Web Services (AWS) specifies that a user cannot launch more than 20 VMs at the same time, and Azure limits non-identified users to 100 operations per user per day). As enterprises move their computing environments with their identities, information, and infrastructure to the Cloud, they must be willing to give up some level of control.

Grobauer et al. investigate the specific vulnerabilities that are applicable in cloud computing and inherent to its essential characteristics including unauthorized access to management interfaces, Internet protocol vulnerabilities, data-recovery vulnerability, and metering and billing evasion (Grobauer et al. 2011).

Subashini and Kavitha elaborate on the various security issues of cloud computing due to its service-delivery models (Subashini and Kavitha 2011). Their work contains a very detailed analysis of SaaS; PaaS and IaaS are analyzed with a lower level of detail. On the other hand, cloud security can be analyzed at three levels: identity security, information security, and infrastructure security (Dokras et al. 2009; Tianfield 2012):

- **Identity security** – Identity security proposes end-to-end identity management, third-party authentication services, and federated identities in order to preserve integrity and confidentiality of data and applications while making access readily available to appropriate users. Identity security requires strong authentication and more granular authorization.
- **Information security** – Data needs its own security that travels with it and protects it while it's in transit and in the Cloud, by means of encryption techniques to protect data privacy and legal compliance. Sensitive data in the Cloud will require granular security, maintained consistently throughout the data lifecycle. Information security requires data isolation, more granular data security, consistent data security, effective data classification, information rights management, and governance and compliance.

- **Infrastructure security** – Infrastructure security includes securing not only the physical machines, but also storage area networks (SANs) and other hardware devices. It also considers securing and monitoring intangibles such as networks, end points, traffic flowing among computers, and software firewalls, to detect unauthorized users or employees. Infrastructure security requires inherent component-level security, more granular interface security, and resource lifecycle management.

1.3 Identity Security in the Cloud

End-to-end identity management, third-party authentication services, and federated identity are key elements of cloud security. Identity security preserves the integrity and confidentiality of data and applications while making access readily available to appropriate users. Support for these identity-management capabilities for both users and infrastructure components is a major requirement for cloud computing, and identity must be managed in ways that build trust. The following are required (Dokras et al. 2009):

- **Strong authentication** – Cloud computing must move beyond weak username-and-password authentication if it is going to support the enterprise. This means adopting techniques and technologies that are already standard in enterprise IT, such as strong authentication (multifactor authentication with one-time password technology), federation within and across enterprises, and risk-based authentication that measures behavior history, current context, and other factors to assess the risk level of a user request. Additional tiering of authentication is essential to meet security service-level agreements (SLAs), and utilizing a risk-based authentication model that is largely transparent to users will reduce the need for broader federation of access controls.
- **More granular authorization** – Authorization can be coarse-grained within an enterprise or even a private cloud. But in order to handle sensitive data and compliance requirements, public clouds need granular authorization capabilities (such as role-based controls and information rights management [IRM]) that can be persistent throughout the cloud infrastructure and the data's lifecycle.

1.4 Information Security in the Cloud

SysAdmin, Audit, Network, Security (SANS) defines information security as processes and methodologies that are intended to protect sensitive information or data from unauthorized access, disclosure, modification, or use (https://www.sans.org/information-security). The form of the protected data or information can be electronic, printed, or other forms (Putri 2011). Information security encompasses security attributes such as the following:

- **Confidentiality** – This attribute is concerned with protecting sensitive information from unauthorized disclosure.
- **Integrity** – This attribute is concerned with accuracy, completeness, and validity of information in regard to business requirement and expectations.

- **Availability** – This attribute is concerned with information being operational and accessible whenever it is required by the business process, now as well as in the future. Further, the information must be inaccessible to unauthorized users.
- **Accountability** – This attribute is concerned with from responsibility. An organization is obligated to be answerable for its actions (Ko et al. 2011a).
- **Nonrepudiation** – This attribute is concerned with the ability to prevent users from denying responsibility for the actions they performed.

Security in general is related to the important aspects of confidentiality, integrity, and availability; they thus are building blocks to be used in designing secure systems. These important aspects of security apply to the three broad categories of assets that need to be secured: data, software, and hardware resources. The cloud infrastructure presents unique security challenges that need to be considered in detail.

1.4.1 Confidentiality

Confidentiality refers to only authorized parties or systems having the ability to access protected data. The threat of data compromise increases in the Cloud, due to the greater number of parties, devices, and applications involved, which leads to an increase in the number of points of access. Delegating data control to the Cloud inversely leads to an increase in the risk of data compromise, because the data becomes accessible to more parties. A number of concerns emerge regarding the issues of multitenancy, data remanence, application security, and privacy. Several aspects of the information system (IS) are shared, including memory, programs, networks, and data. Cloud computing is based on a business model in which resources are shared (i.e. multiple users use the same resource) at the network level, host level, and application level. Although users are isolated at a virtual level, hardware is not separated. With a multitenant architecture, a software application is designed to virtually partition its data and configuration so that each client organization works with a customized virtual application instance.

Multitenancy is similar to multitasking in operating systems. In computing, multitasking is a method by which multiple tasks, also known as *processes*, share common processing resources such as a CPU. Multitenancy, like multitasking, presents a number of privacy and confidentiality threats. Object reusability is an important characteristic of cloud infrastructures, but reusable objects must be carefully controlled lest they create a serious vulnerability. Data confidentiality could be breached unintentionally, due to data remanence. *Data remanence* is the residual representation of data that has been in some way nominally erased or removed. Due to virtual separation of logical drives and lack of hardware separation between multiple users on a single platform, data remanence may lead to the unintentional disclosure of private data. But in addition, a malicious user may claim a large amount of disk space and then scavenge for sensitive data. Data confidentiality in the Cloud is correlated to user authentication. Protecting a user's account from theft is an instance of a larger problem of controlling access to objects, including memory, devices, software, etc. *Electronic authentication* is the process of establishing confidence in user identities that are electronically presented to an information system. Lack of strong authentication can lead to unauthorized access to users account on a cloud, leading to a breach in privacy.

Software confidentiality is as important as data confidentiality to overall system security. It refers to trusting that specific applications or processes will maintain and handle the user's personal data in a secure manner. In a cloud environment, the user is required to delegate "trust" to applications provided by the organization owning the infrastructure. Software applications interacting with the user's data must be certified not to introduce additional confidentiality and privacy risks. Unauthorized access can become possible through the exploitation of an application vulnerability or lack of strong identification, bringing up issues of data confidentiality and privacy.

In addition, the cloud provider is responsible for providing secure cloud instances, which should ensure users' privacy. *Privacy* refers to the desire of a person to control the disclosure of personal information. Organizations dealing with personal data are required to obey to a country's legal framework that ensures appropriate privacy and confidentiality protection. The Cloud presents a number of legal challenges regarding privacy issues related to data stored in multiple locations in the Cloud, which additionally increases the risk of confidentiality and privacy breaches. Instead of data being stored on the company's servers, data is stored on the service provider's servers, which could be in Europe, Asia, or anywhere else. This tenet of cloud computing conflicts with various legal requirements, such as European laws that require that an organization know where the personal data in its possession is at all times (Zissis and Lekkas 2012).

1.4.2 Integrity

A key aspect of information security is integrity. *Integrity* means that assets can be modified only by authorized parties or in authorized ways and refers to data, software, and hardware. *Data integrity* refers to protecting data from unauthorized deletion, modification, or fabrication. Managing an entity's admittance and rights to specific enterprise resources ensures that valuable data and services are not abused, misappropriated, or stolen. By preventing unauthorized access, organizations can achieve greater confidence in data and system integrity. Additionally, such mechanisms offer greater visibility into determining who or what may have altered data or system information, potentially affecting their integrity (accountability). *Authorization* is the mechanism by which a system determines what level of access a particular authenticated user should have to secure resources controlled by the system. Due to the increased number of entities and access points in a cloud environment, authorization is crucial for assuring that only authorized entities can interact with data.

A cloud computing provider is trusted to maintain data integrity and accuracy. The cloud model presents a number of threats, including sophisticated insider attacks on these data attributes. *Software integrity* refers to protecting software from unauthorized deletion, modification, theft, or fabrication. Deletion, modification, or fabrication can be intentional or unintentional. For instance, a disgruntled employee may intentionally modify a program to fail when certain conditions are met or when a certain time is reached. Cloud computing providers implement a set of software interfaces or application programming interfaces (APIs) that customers use to manage and interact with cloud services. In addition to the previously mentioned threats, the security of cloud services depends heavily on the security of these interfaces, because an unauthorized user gaining control of them could alter, delete, or fabricate user data. In the Cloud, responsibility for the protection of the software's integrity is transferred to the software's owner or administrator. Hardware and network integrity is an additional issue that needs to be addressed by cloud providers, because they are burdened with protecting the underlying hardware from theft, modification, and fabrication (Zissis and Lekkas 2012).

1.4.3 Availability

Availability refers to the property of a system being accessible and usable upon demand by an authorized entity. System availability includes a system's ability to carry on operations even when authorities misbehave. The system must be able to continue operations even in the event of a security breach. Availability refers to data, software, and hardware being available to authorized users upon demand. There is a heavy reliance on the ubiquitous network's availability when users can access hardware infrastructure on demand. The network is now burdened with data retrieval and processing. Cloud computing services place a heavy reliance on the resource infrastructure and network availability at all times.

1.4.4 Accountability

The concept of *accountability* is present in finance and public governance, and is becoming more integrated into business regulatory programs as well as emerging privacy and data-protection frameworks globally. Accountability can decrease regulatory complexity in global business environments, which is especially helpful in the European Union (EU) due to the complex matrix of national laws that makes compliance with data-protection legislation especially difficult. Further, as the scale of data in the Cloud increases, data processing becomes more sophisticated, and cloud supply chains become more complex, the need for a coherent approach that works from the end user throughout the supply chain and that integrates the legal and regulatory dimensions effectively and efficiently becomes even more pressing (Pearson et al. 2012).

Academics and practitioners have different views and interpretations of the accountability concept. For example, accountability in computer science has been referred to as a limited and imprecise requirement that is met via reporting and auditing mechanisms (Cederquist et al. 2005; Doelitzscher 2014); while *Yao et al.* consider accountability a way of making the system accountable and trustworthy by a combination of mechanisms (Yao et al. 2010). *Muppala et al.* refer to accountability as the adherence to accepting ownership and responsibility toward all actions in a standardized way, as regulated by an acknowledged organization such as the Organization for Economic Cooperation and Development (OECD), which published privacy guidelines in 1980 (Muppala et al. 2012). And *Ko et al.* consider accountability as only one component of trust in cloud computing (Ko et al. 2011b, pp. 432 – 444).

In addition, the Centre for Information Policy Leadership identifies accountability "in relation to privacy as the acceptance of responsibility for personal information protection. An accountable organization must have in place appropriate policies and procedures that promote good practices which, taken as a whole, constitute a privacy management program. The outcome is a demonstrable capacity to comply, at a minimum, with applicable privacy laws. Done properly, it should promote trust and confidence on the part of consumers, and thereby enhance competitive and reputational advantages for organizations" (https://www.priv.gc.ca/media/2102/gl_acc_201204_e.pdf; Al-Rashdi et al. 2015).

Castelluccia et al. believe accountability offers three capabilities (Castelluccia et al. 2011):

- **Validation** – It allows users to verify at a later time whether the system has performed data processing as expected.
- **Attribution** – In case of a fault, users can assign responsibility.
- **Evidence** – It can produce evidence that can be used to convince a third party when a dispute arises.

Accountability is often confused with fault tolerance or responsibility. *Fault tolerance* is defined as the ability of a system to respond gracefully to an unexpected hardware or software failure. What makes accountability different from fault tolerance is that it does not attempt to mask faults, but it provides evidence and may detect arbitrary faults (Kamel 2010).

Customers of an accountable cloud can check whether the cloud is performing as agreed. If a problem occurs, the customer and the provider can use the evidence to decide who is responsible; and, if a dispute arises, they can present the evidence to a third party, such as an arbitrator or a judge. However, existing accountability techniques fall short of the requirements for cloud computing in several ways. Since clouds are general-purpose platforms, the provider should be able to offer accountability for any service customers may choose to run; this rules out application-specific techniques like Certified Accountable Tamper-evident Storage (CATS) and Repeat and Compare (Michalakis et al. 2007; Yumerefendi and Chase 2007). On the other hand, an application-independent technique such as PeerReview (Haeberlen et al. 2007) requires software modifications and assumes that the behavior of the software is deterministic, neither of which seems realistic in a cloud computing scenario. Finally, even if these limitations are overcome, these techniques can only detect violations of a single property (correctness of execution); they were not designed to check other properties of interest in the Cloud, such as conformance to SLAs, protection of confidential data, data durability, service availability, and so on (Haeberlen 2010).

1.4.5 Nonrepudiation

Nonrepudiation means ensuring that a traceable legal record is kept and is not changed by a malicious entity. A loss of nonrepudiation would result in the questioning of a transaction that occurred. A simple example of nonrepudiation is signing a contract. The signer cannot claim they did not agree to a contract, because there is evidence that they did agree. The difference is that a signature can be forged, but good encryption cannot.

Repudiating interactions (mainly during transmission of data or on storage) is often counteracted by preventing authorized access in the first place. Techniques are therefore often used to address access-control requirements and are classified as such. Among others, they include the exchange of public keys (PKI), certificates, or (proxy) signatures. The SaaS Application Security model for Decentralized Information Flow Control (DIFC, or SAS-DIFC) as proposed in (Tingting and Yong 2013), aims to guarantee information security in SaaS applications. Trusted code in this approach controls the dissemination of private data, so that the right user at the right location will receive what belongs to them. It also offers monitoring mechanisms for user-aware monitoring. Denying another user access to private data that is currently being accessed or transmitted is an issue of guaranteeing integrity and privacy, which research papers connect to nonrepudiation in their proposals of solutions (Höner 2013). *Kumar* and *Subramanian* say that a homomorphic distribution verification protocol (classified under "Integrity") enforces nonrepudiation implicitly (Kumar and Subramanian 2011).

1.4.6 Key Considerations in Information Security

The key considerations identified in this section for protecting information in cloud deployments are as follows:

- Understanding provider security practices and controls is essential for public and community cloud offerings.
- Encryption and digital signatures are the primary means of confidentiality and integrity protection for data stored or transmitted in a public or community cloud.
- Without appropriate protections, data may be vulnerable while being processed in a public or community cloud.
- Deleted data may remain in persistent storage when the storage is released back to the cloud vendor as a shared, multitenant resource.
- Existing internal applications may need analysis and enhancement to operate securely in a public or community cloud.
- Data replication provided by a cloud provider is not a substitute for backing up to another independent provider or out of the Cloud.
- Privacy protection responsibilities should be reviewed if considering moving personally identifiable information (PII) to the Cloud.
- Cloud identity and access management (IdAM) capabilities vary widely. Integration of cloud and enterprise IdAM mechanisms may be challenging.

1.4.7 Information Security Analysis in Some Clouds

In this section, Amazon AWS, Force.com, Google App Engine, GoGrid, Rackspace, and Microsoft Azure are compared regarding information security concerns (Mietto and Vitorino 2010):

- **Amazon AWS** – As part of normal operation, data stored in Amazon Elastic Block Store (EBS), Amazon S3, or Amazon SimpleDB is redundantly stored in multiple physical locations. On the initial write, by storing objects multiple times across multiple availability zones, Amazon S3 and Amazon SimpleDB provide object durability. In the event of device unavailability or detected bit rot, further replication is actively done. AWS procedures include a decommissioning process when a storage device has reached the end of its useful life. The process is designed to prevent customer data from being exposed to unauthorized individuals. As part of the decommissioning process, AWS uses the techniques detailed in U.S. Department of Defense (DoD) 5220.22-M (U.S. Department of Defense 1995) or NIST 800-88 (Kissel et al. 2006) to destroy data. In accordance with industry-standard practices, a hardware device is degaussed or physically destroyed if the device cannot be decommissioned.

- **Force.com** – Force.com guarantees that customer data is protected with physical security, application security, user authentication, and data encryption. It also ensures the latest standard-setting security practices and certifications, including ISO 27001, Sarbanes-Oxley Act (SOX), SysTrust certifications, protection from third-party vulnerabilities, and world-class security specification SAS 70 Type II. It provides secure point-to-point data replication for data backups: backup tapes for customer data never leave provider facilities – no tapes are ever in transport. Salesforce.com uses 1024-bit Rivest–Shamir–Adleman (RSA) public keys and 128-bit Verisign Secure Sockets Layer (SSL) certification to ensure that the strongest encryption products protect customer data and communications. The lock icon in the browser indicates that data is fully shielded from access while in transit. Using Redundant Array of Independent Disks (RAID) and multiple data paths, customer data is stored on carrier-class disk storage. On a nightly basis, all customer data is automatically backed up to a primary tape library, up to the last committed transaction. On a regular basis, to guarantee their integrity, backup tapes are cloned and moved to fire-resistant, secure, off-site storage.
- **Google App Engine** – A distributed NoSQL data-storage service is provided by App Engine with transactions and a query engine. The distributed datastore grows with data just as a distributed web server grows with traffic. Two different data-storage options are available for customers and are differentiated by their availability and consistency guarantees. The App Engine datastore is not like a traditional relational database. Here, data objects, or *entities*, have a set of properties; using these properties, queries can retrieve entities of a given kind, filtered and sorted. Any of the supported property value types can be property values. Datastore entities are *schemaless*, and data entity structures are enforced and provided by customers' application code. The datastore uses optimistic concurrency control and is strongly consistent. If other processes are trying to update the same entity simultaneously, an entity update occurs in a transaction that is retried a fixed number of times. To ensure the integrity of customer data, the customer application can execute multiple datastore operations in a single transaction, which either all fail or all succeed. Using *entity groups*, transactions are implemented across the distributed network. Entities are manipulated through a transaction within a single group. For efficient execution of transactions, the same group's entities are stored together. When the entities are created, the application can assign them to groups. In case of errors or system failure, Google can recover data and restore accounts, because it keeps multiple backup copies of customers' content. When a customer asks to delete messages and content, Google makes a reasonable effort to remove deleted information from its systems as quickly as is practicable (Zahariev 2009).
- **GoGrid** – GoGrid offers disaster-recovery and backup solutions, including i365 EVault SaaS for online data protection. For small and medium-sized businesses, a cost-effective recovery and backup solution is EVault SaaS. It provides efficient, reliable, secure protection of an organization's critical data through the Internet. It automatically backs up server, desktop, and laptop data from across the customer's organization. The customer can configure the retention schedule and monitor backups using a web browser. Customer data is reduplicated, compressed, encrypted, and then transmitted to a vault in one of i365's top-tier data centers.

- **Rackspace** – For secure collaboration, disaster recovery, and data access, Rackspace provides Cloud Drive. Cloud Drive automatically backs up any file type or file size, with no restrictions. Here, files are kept secure using admin-controlled keys and Advanced Encryption Standard (AES-256) encryption.
- **Microsoft Azure** – To minimize the impact of hardware failures, Microsoft Azure replicates data within the Azure Storage Fabric to three separate nodes. Microsoft Azure Storage Fabric is used as the main data management channel to provide unlimited storage capacity that is highly optimized for storing data within the recovery points of the data source (Maturana et al. 2014). By creating a second storage account to provide hot-failover capability, customers can leverage the geographically distributed nature of the Microsoft Azure infrastructure. To synchronize and replicate data between Microsoft facilities, customers can create custom roles. Customers can also create customized roles to extract data from storage for off-site private backups. Strict hardware-disposal processes and data-handling procedures are followed by Microsoft operational personnel after a system's end of life. Assets are classified to determine the strength of security controls to apply. To determine the required protections, a defense-in-depth approach is taken. For example, when data assets reside on removable media or are involved in external network transfers, they fall into the moderate impact category and are subject to encryption requirements. High-impact data, in addition to those requirements, is also subject to encryption requirements for network transfers, storage, and the internal system. The Security Development Lifecycle (SDL) cryptographic standards list the acceptable and unacceptable cryptographic algorithms, and all Microsoft products must meet those standards. For example, symmetric encryption is required for keys longer than 128 bits. When using asymmetric algorithms, keys of 2048 bits or longer are required (Calder et al. 2011).

1.5 Cloud Security Standards

Although some security requirements may be unique to the cloud implementation, it is important that requirements for cloud security are consistent with appropriate standards, such as International Organization for Standardization (ISO) 27001 and ISO 27002, if you are to leverage a large body of practical experience, best practices, and reviews. Further, all aspects of security should be captured in a cloud security policy, which is best developed as a formal document that has the complete approval and blessing of management. A security policy should be seen as the foundation from which all security requirements derive. It should not detail technical or architectural approaches (as these may change more frequently than the policy); rather, the policy should set forth the underlying requirements from an organizational or business standpoint. For instance, the security policy should explain the need for using standards-based encryption via a formally evaluated commercial product, rather than spelling out the use of Transport Layer Security, Secure Sockets Layer, or another specific means of communication security (Winkler 2011).

The security standards and regulatory organizations that have the most direct effect on cloud computing security are PCI DSS, FISMA, and HIPAA (Kajiyama 2013):

- The **Payment Card Industry Data Security Standard (PCI DSS)** provides a framework for cloud providers to host applications that require a robust payment card data security process (https://www.pcisecuritystandards.org/documents/PCI_DSS_v3-2-1.pdf). By choosing a PCI DSS-compliant cloud provider, developers can easily build applications with a secure credit card payment system without using a third-party merchant account provider. PCI DSS is a worldwide information security standard that applies to organizations that hold, process, or exchange cardholder information. Cardholder data includes the primary account number, expiration date, name as it appears on the card, card verification value (CVV), CVV2, and magnetic stripe. This standard helps prevent credit card fraud through increased controls around data and its exposure to compromise. PCI DSS includes requirements for security management, policies, procedures, network architecture, and software design. PCI DSS compliance includes a self-assessment questionnaire (PCI DSS SAQ) that acts as a validation tool. The SAQ includes a series of yes-or-no questions about security posture and practices and depends on the business scenario. The PCI Security Standards Council published new guidelines regarding the PCI DSS Virtualization section to provide guidance on the use of virtualization in accordance with the PCI DSS (https://www.pcisecuritystandards.org/documents/Virtualization_InfoSupp_v2.pdf). They explain how PCI DSS applies to virtual environments, including evaluating the risks of a virtualized environment, implementing additional physical access controls for host systems and securing access, isolating security processes that could put card data at risk, and identifying which virtualized elements should be considered "in scope" for the purposes of PCI compliance.
- The **Federal Information Security Management Act (FISMA)** requires federal agencies to develop, document, and implement an agency-wide program to provide information security for the information and information systems (https://csrc.nist.gov/csrc/media/publications/sp/800-53/rev-4/archive/2013-04-30/documents/sp800-53-rev4-ipd.pdf). FISMA-accredited cloud providers auto-comply with the regulations that federal agencies are required to follow for data security.
- The **Health Insurance Portability and Accountability Act (HIPAA)** requires every healthcare provider and organization that handles protected healthcare information (PHI) to adhere to strict information security guidelines that assure the protection of patient privacy. Even though HIPAA does not directly impose these guidelines on cloud providers, if a company chooses to store protected healthcare information in the Cloud, the service provider must either be HIPAA compliant or provide secure infrastructure and policies that satisfy the HIPAA standards and requirements. Sometimes the standard also describes technical security measures that can be implemented to reach security objectives (implement a firewall, encrypt network traffic, have locks on doors, etc.).
- The **Cloud Security Alliance Cloud Controls Matrix (CSA CCM)** is a list of controls collected from a range of different international Information Security Management System (ISMS) standards, such as ISO 27001, PCI DSS, SOC 2, and others. In this way, the CCM provides a framework for showing compliance to a range of different standards.
- **Service Organization Control 2 (SOC 2)** is a predefined set of security and privacy requirements. A SOC 2 report can be used to provide customers an overview of security and privacy measures in place.

- The **Tier standard** is a set of requirements for security, protection, and resilience measures for data centers. A Tier 1, 2, or 3 certification can provide customers the assurance that the data center in question is resilient in the face of attacks or disasters.
- **Information Technology Infrastructure Library (ITIL)** is a standard for managing service delivery. By asserting compliance to ITIL, the provider can assure the customer that service-delivery processes are set up in a structured and predictable way.
- **Safe Harbor** is a streamlined process for U.S. companies to comply with EU Directive 95/46/EC on the protection of personal data. Intended for organizations within the EU or U.S. that store customer data, the Safe Harbor Principles are designed to prevent accidental information disclosure or loss. U.S. companies can opt into the program as long as they adhere to the seven principles outlined in the Directive. The process was developed by the U.S. Department of Commerce in consultation with the EU.
- **SAS 70** is a widely recognized auditing standard developed by the American Institute of Certified Public Accountants (AICPA) (http://sas70.com/sas70_overview.html). Service organizations or service providers must demonstrate that they have adequate controls in place when they host or process data belonging to their customers. SAS 70 certifies that a service organization has had an in-depth audit of its controls (including control objectives and control activities). SSAE 16 effectively replaced SAS 70 as the standard for reporting on service organizations beginning June 15, 2011.
- The **Statement on Standards for Attestation Engagements (SSAE) No. 16** is an attestation standard issued by the Auditing Standards Board (ASB) of AICPA (http://ssae16.com/SSAE16_overview.html). Specifically, SSAE 16 is an attestation standard geared toward addressing engagements conducted by auditors on service organizations for purposes of reporting on the design of controls and their operating effectiveness. SSAE 16 engagements on service organizations result in the issuance of either a SSAE 16 Type 1 or Type 2 Report. A Type 1 report is technically known as a "Report on Management's Description of a Service Organization's System and the Suitability of the Design of Controls." A Type 2 Report is technically known as a "Report on Management's Description of a Service Organization's System and the Suitability of the Design and Operating Effectiveness of Controls."
- **International Standards for Assurance Engagements (ISAE) No. 3402** is a standard put forth by the International Auditing and Assurance Standards Board (IAASB), a standard-setting board within the International Federation of Accountants (IFAC) (http://isae3402.com/ISAE3402_overview.html). It is a global standard for assurance reporting on services organizations to demonstrate customers have an adequate internal control system to protect data and sensitive information belonging to the customers. In ISAE 3402, there are two crucial components: the service organization must produce a description of its system and must provide a written statement of assertion. SAAE 16 and ISAE 3402 are essentially similar standards; they are the convergence of auditing standards for reporting on controls at service organizations. Since 2011, ISAE 3402 (international standard) and SSAE 16 (American standard) have been used instead of SAS 70.
- The **ISO 9001:2008** audit standard sets out the criteria for a quality-management system and is the only standard in the category that can be certified in a business, although this is not a requirement (https://www.iso.org/standard/46486.html). It is implemented by more than one million companies and organizations in over 170

countries. The standard is based on a number of quality-management principles including a strong customer focus, the motivation and involvement of top management, the process approach, and continual improvement. Using ISO 9001:2008 helps ensure that customers get consistent, good-quality products and services, which in turn yields many business benefits. Certification is a confirmation of the requirements of ISO 9001:2008, which guarantees the company's disciplined approach to the management and quality of products and services.

- **ISO/IEC 27001:2005** is an information security standard (https://www.iso.org/standard/42103.html). It specifies the requirements for establishing, implementing, operating, monitoring, reviewing, maintaining, and improving a documented ISMS within the context of the organization's overall business risks. It is designed to ensure the selection of adequate and proportionate security controls that protect information assets and give confidence to interested parties.
- **ISO 31000:2009** was published as a standard on the November 13, 2009, and provides a standard for the implementation of risk management (https://www.iso.org/standard/43170.html). It gives generic guidelines for the design, implementation, and maintenance of risk-management processes throughout an organization. ISO 31000:2009 is applicable and adaptable for "any public, private or community enterprise, association, group, or individual." As a family of risk-management standards, it provides a generic best-practice structure and guidance to all operations concerned with risk management.
- **Control Objectives for Information and related Technology (COBIT)** is a model (framework) for the management of Information and Communication Technology (ICT), created in 1992 by the American Information Systems Auditor (Information Systems Audit and Control Association [ISACA]) and the IT Governance Institute (ITGI). COBIT provides managers, auditors, and users of IT systems with a reference grid: the structure of the IT processes and a series of theoretical and practical tools related to the processes, with the aim of assessing whether effective governance of the IT function (IT governance) is in place or to provide guidance to restore it. COBIT has achieved the status of internationally recognized standard; the EU has set COBIT as one of three standards that can be used to ensure the security of information systems.
- The **NIST Special Publication 800-53** standard, titled "Recommended Security Controls for Federal Information Systems and Organizations," was co-developed by the Computer Security Division of NIST, DoD, and the U.S. intelligence community, as well as the industrial control system community. It benefited from extensive public review and comments. It represents the best practices and guidance available today, not only for the government but for private enterprises as well. The purpose of SP 800-53 is to achieve information system security and effective risk management, in part by providing a common information security language for all information systems and by providing consistent and repeatable guidelines for selecting and specifying standard security controls. In 2013, NIST presented the SP 800-53, Revision 4 to update the content of the security controls catalogue and the guidance for selecting and specifying security controls for federal information systems and organizations (https://csrc.nist.gov/csrc/media/publications/sp/800-53/rev-4/archive/2013-04-30/documents/sp800-53-rev4-ipd.pdf). Many of the changes arose from particular security issues and questions, including, for example, application security, cloud

computing, insider and advanced persistent threats, and firmware integrity. The controls and enhancements are distributed throughout the control catalogue in several families and provide specific security features that are required to support new computing technologies and approaches.

- **Federal Information Processing Standard (FIPS) Publication 140-2** is a U.S. government security standard that specifies the security requirements for cryptographic modules protecting sensitive information. To support customers with FIPS 140-2 requirements, for example, Medidata private cloud VPN endpoints and TLS-terminating load balancers operate using FIPS 140-2 validated algorithms. Operating in FIPS 140-2 compliance mode requires comparable capabilities on the user's browser side of the connection.

1.6 Conclusion

We investigated the Cloud and its fundamental security and privacy issues to improve the assurance of required security for cloud customers. Cloud security principles encompass three categories: identity, information, and infrastructure. Identity security maintains the confidentiality and integrity of data and applications while allowing appropriate users to readily access services. Information security includes security attributes such as confidentiality, integrity, availability, accountability, and nonrepudiation that are used in designing secure systems. In this chapter, we discussed identity security requirements and information security attributes. We also compared some clouds with regard to information security concerns. Finally, we introduced some of the security standards and regulatory organizations that are suitable for cloud computing security.

References

Al-Rashdi, Zahir, Dick, Martin, and Storey, Ian. (2015). A conceptual framework for accountability in cloud computing service provision. Paper presented at the 26th Australasian Conference on Information Systems.

Castelluccia, C., Druschel, P., Hübner, S. et al. (2011). *Privacy, accountability and trust: challenges and opportunities. ENISA* www.enisa.europa.eu.

Cederquist, J.G., Conn, R, Dekker, Mac, Etalle, Sandro, and Den Hartog, J.I. (2005). An audit logic for accountability. Paper presented at the Sixth IEEE International Workshop on Policies for Distributed Systems and Networks.

Calder, B., Wang, Ju, Ogus, A. et al. (2011). Windows Azure Storage: a highly available cloud storage service with strong consistency. In: *Proceedings of the Twenty-Third ACM Symposium on Operating Systems Principles.*

Doelitzscher, Frank. (2014). Security audit compliance for cloud computing. Doctoral dissertation. Plymouth University.

Dokras, Satchit, Hartman, Bret, and Mathers, Tim. (2009). The role of security in trustworthy cloud computing. White paper, RSA, The Security Division of EMC.

Faatz, D and Pizette, L. (2010). Information security in the clouds. MITRE Corporation Technical Report Case.

Grobauer, B., Walloschek, T., and Stöcker, E. (2011). Understanding cloud computing vulnerabilities. *IEEE Security and Privacy* 9 (2): 50–57.

Haeberlen, A., Kouznetsov, P., and Druschel, P. (2007). PeerReview: Practical accountability for distributed systems. *ACM SIGOPS operating systems review* 41 (6): 175–188.

Haeberlen, A. (2010). A case for the accountable cloud. *ACM SIGOPS Operating Systems Review* 44 (2): 52–57.

Hashizume, K. (2013). *A Reference Architecture for Cloud Computing and its Security Applications*. Florida Atlantic University.

Hogan, M., Liu, F., Sokol, A., and Tong, J. (2011). NIST cloud computing standards roadmap. *NIST Special Publication* 35: 6–11.

Höner, Patrick. (2013). Cloud computing security requirements and solutions: a systematic literature review. Bachelors thesis. University of Twente.

Jansen, W. and Grance, T. (2011). Guidelines on security and privacy in public cloud computing. *NIST Special Publication* 800 (144): 10–11.

Jensen, Meiko, Schwenk, Jörg, Gruschka, Nils, and Iacono, Luigi Lo. (2009). On technical security issues in cloud computing. Paper presented at CLOUD'09, the IEEE International Conference on Cloud Computing.

Juan Ferrer, Ana M. (2013). Analysis of security of cloud systems: Comparative Analysis of Security features between Amazon Web Services and Windows Azure. Working Paper Series; WP00-000. IN3 Working Paper Series. IN3 (UOC).

Kajiyama, Takahiko. (2013). Cloud computing security: how risks and threats are affecting cloud adoption decisions. Doctoral dissertation. San Diego State University.

Kamel, Brahim. (2010). Cloud Computing: Accountability. Doctoral dissertation. University of Bologna.

Kissel, R., Scholl, M., Skolochenko, S. et al. (2006). *NIST Special Publication 800-88 Revision 1: Guidelines for Media Sanitization*. NIST.

Kizza, J.M. and Yang, L. (2014). Is the cloud the future of computing? In: *Cloud Technology: Concepts, Methodologies, Tools, and Applications*, 2149–2164. IGI Global.

Ko, Ryan K.L., Jagadpramana, Peter, Mowbray, Miranda et al. (2011a). TrustCloud: A framework for accountability and trust in cloud computing. Paper presented at the IEEE World Congress on Services.

Ko, R.K.L., Lee, B.S., and Pearson, S. (2011b). Towards achieving accountability, auditability and trust in cloud computing. In: *International Conference on Advances in Computing and Communications*, 432–444. Springer.

Kumar, P.S. and Subramanian, R. (2011). Homomorphic distributed verification protocol for ensuring data storage security in cloud computing. *Information – An International Interdisciplinary Journal* 14 (10): 3465–3476.

Maturana, F.P., Asenjo, J.L., Philip, N.S. et al. (2014). Merging agents and cloud services in industrial applications. *Applied Computational Intelligence and Soft Computing* 2014: 1–8.

Michalakis, Nikolaos, Soulé, Robert, and Grimm, Robert. (2007). Ensuring content integrity for untrusted peer-to-peer content distribution networks. In: Proceedings of the 4th USENIX Conference on Networked Systems Design and Implementation.

Mietto, Antonio Alberto Gati and Vitorino, Aurelio Jose. (2010). Information security in cloud computing. Paper presented at the International Conference on Information Systems and Technology Management.

Mell, Peter and Grance, Tim. (2011). The NIST definition of cloud computing. National Institute of Standards and Technology (NIST).

Muppala, J.K., Shukla, D., and Patil, S.K. (2012). Establishing trust in public clouds. *Journal of Information Technology and Software Engineering* 2: e107.

Pearson, Siani, Tountopoulos, Vasilios, Catteddu, Daniele et al. (2012). Accountability for cloud and other future internet services. Paper presented at the IEEE 4th International Conference on Cloud Computing Technology and Science (CloudCom).

Pearson, S. and Yee, G. (2013). *Privacy and Security for Cloud Computing*. London: Springer-Verlag.

Putri, N.R. (2011). *Enhancing Information Security in Cloud Computing Services Using Sla Based Metrics*. Blekinge Institute of Technology.

Steiner, T. and Khiabani, H. (2012). *An Introduction to Securing a Cloud Environment*. SANS Institute https://www.sans.org/reading-room/whitepapers/cloud/introduction-securing-cloud-environment-34052.

Subashini, S. and Kavitha, V. (2011). A survey on security issues in service delivery models of cloud computing. *Journal of Network and Computer Applications* 34 (1): 1–11.

Tingting, Liu and Yong, Zhao. (2013). A decentralized information flow model for SaaS applications security. Paper presented at the Third International Conference on Intelligent System Design and Engineering Applications (ISDEA).

Tianfield, Huaglory. (2012). Security issues in cloud computing. Paper presented at the IEEE International Conference on Systems, Man, and Cybernetics (SMC).

U.S. Department of Defense (1995). National Industrial Security Program Operating Manual. https://biotech.law.lsu.edu/blaw/dodd/corres/pdf2/p522022m.pdf.

Winkler, V.J. (2011). *Securing the Cloud: Cloud Computer Security Techniques and Tactics*. Elsevier.

Yao, Jinhui, Chen, Shiping, Wang, Chen, Levy, David, and Zic, John. (2010). Accountability as a service for the cloud. Paper presented at the IEEE International Conference on Services Computing (SCC).

Yumerefendi, A.R. and Chase, J.S. (2007). Strong accountability for network storage. *ACM Transactions on Storage (TOS)* 3 (3): 11.

Zahariev, A. (2009). Google app engine. Helsinki University of Technology.

Zissis, D. and Lekkas, D. (2012). Addressing cloud computing security issues. *Future Generation Computer Systems* 28 (3): 583–592.

2

Cloud Infrastructure Security

Mohammad GhasemiGol

Department of Computer Engineering, University of Birjand, Birjand, Iran

2.1 Introduction

Cloud infrastructure consists of servers, storage, network, management and deployment software, and platform virtualization. Therefore, cloud infrastructure security is the most important part of cloud security, and any attacks to the cloud infrastructure will cause a large amount of service disruption. On the other hand, virtualization is an important underlying technology in cloud infrastructures that provides dynamic resource allocation and service provisioning, especially in Infrastructure-as-a-Service (IaaS). With this technology, multiple operating systems (OSs) can co-reside on the same physical machine without interfering with each other (Xiao and Xiao 2013). However, virtualization is the source of a significant security concern in cloud infrastructure. Because multiple VMs run on the same server, and because the virtualization layer plays a considerable role in the operation of a VM, a malicious party has the opportunity to attack the virtualization layer. A successful attack would give the malicious party control over the all-powerful virtualization layer, potentially compromising the confidentiality and integrity of the software and data of any VM (Keller et al. 2010).

Although infrastructure security is more relevant to customers of IaaS, similar consideration should be given to providers' Platform-as-a-Service (PaaS) and Software-as-a-Service (SaaS) environments, since they have ramifications for customers' threat, risk, and compliance management. When discussing public clouds, the scope of infrastructure security is limited to the layers of infrastructure that move beyond the organization's control and into the hands of service providers (i.e. when responsibility for a secure infrastructure is transferred to the cloud service provider [CSP], based on the Service Provider Interface [SPI] delivery model) (Mather et al. 2009).

This chapter discusses cloud security from an infrastructure perspective. The rest of the chapter is organized as follows: cloud infrastructure security is discussed in Section 2.2. In Section 2.3, we focus on the role of the hypervisor security in the Cloud. We analyze the infrastructure security in several existing cloud platforms in Section 2.4. Section 2.5 discusses some countermeasure to protect cloud infrastructure against various threats and vulnerabilities. Finally, conclusions are drawn in Section 2.5.

Security, Privacy, and Digital Forensics in the Cloud, First Edition. Edited by Lei Chen, Hassan Takabi, and Nhien-An Le-Khac.

2.2 Infrastructure Security in the Cloud

Cloud infrastructure consists of servers, storage, network, management and deployment software, and platform virtualization. Hence, infrastructure security can be assessed in different areas. In this section, we look at the network level, host level, and application level of infrastructure security and the issues surrounding each level with specific regard to cloud computing. At the network level, although there are definitely security challenges with cloud computing, none of them are caused specifically by cloud computing. All of the network-level security challenges associated with cloud computing are exacerbated by cloud computing, not caused by it. Likewise, security issues at the host level, such as an increased need for host-perimeter security (as opposed to organizational entity-perimeter security) and secured virtualized environments, are exacerbated by cloud computing but not specifically caused by it. The same holds true at the application level. Certainly there is an increased need for secure software development life cycles due to the public-facing nature of (public) cloud applications and the need to ensure that application programming interfaces (APIs) have been thoroughly tested for security, but those application-level security requirements are again exacerbated by cloud computing, not caused by it.

Therefore, the issues of infrastructure security and cloud computing are about understanding which party provides which aspects of security (i.e. does the customer provide it, or does the CSP provide it?) – in other words, defining trust boundaries. With regard to infrastructure security, an undeniable conclusion is that trust boundaries between customers and CSPs have moved. When we see poll after poll of information executives (e.g. CIOs) and information security professionals (e.g. CISOs) indicating that security is their number-one concern related to cloud computing, the primary cause for that concern is altered trust boundaries. To be more specific, the issue is not so much that the boundaries have moved, but more importantly that customers are unsure where the trust boundaries have moved. Many CSPs have not clearly articulated those trust boundaries (e.g. what security is provided by the CSP versus what security still needs to be provided by the customer), nor are the new trust boundaries reinforced in operational obligations such as service-level agreements (SLAs).

Although CSPs have the primary responsibility for articulating the new trust boundaries, some of the current confusion is also the fault of information security personnel. Some information security professionals, either fearing something new or not fully understanding cloud computing, are engaging in fear, uncertainty, and doubt (FUD) with their business customers. Similar to confusion over moved trust boundaries is the fact that the established model of network tiers or zones no longer exists. That model has been replaced with domains, which are less precise and afford less protection than the old model. (Domain names are used in various networking contexts and application-specific naming and addressing purposes based on the Domain Name System [DNS].) If we can no longer trust the network (organizational) perimeter to provide sufficient protection and are now reliant on host perimeter security, what is the trust model between hosts?

An analogy to this problem exists and was dealt with 20 years ago: Secure Telephone Unit (STU) IIIs used by the U.S. Department of Defense (DoD) and the intelligence community. In that model, each STU-III unit (a host) was responsible for its own "perimeter security" (i.e. the device's electronic components were tamper resistant), and each device had a secure authentication mechanism (i.e. a dongle with an identity written on it, protected and verified by asymmetric encryption and Public Key Infrastructure [PKI]). Additionally, each device would negotiate a common level of authorization (classification level) based on an attribute included with the identity in the dongle.

Today, we have no such model in cloud computing. The STU-III model simply is not viable for cloud computing, and there is no trusted computing platform for virtual machine (VM) environments. Therefore, host-to-host authentication and authorization is problematic in cloud computing, since much of it uses virtualization. Today the use of federated identity management is focused on trust, identity, and authentication of people. The identity management solutions of today do assist in managing host-level access; however, no viable solution addresses the issue of host-to-host trust. This issue is exacerbated in cloud computing because of the sheer number of resources available. Conceptually similar to the trust-boundary problem at the application level is ensuring that one customer's data is not inadvertently provided to another, unauthorized customer. Data has to be securely labeled to ensure that it remains separated among customers in a multitenancy environment. Today, data separation in cloud computing is logical, not physical, as was the case previously, and there are valid concerns about the adequacy of that logical separation (Mather et al. 2009).

2.2.1 Infrastructure Security: The Network Level

When looking at the network level of infrastructure security, it is important to distinguish between public clouds and private clouds, as we explained in Chapter 1. With private clouds, there are no new attacks, vulnerabilities, or changes in risk specific to this topology that information security personnel need to consider. Although your organization's IT architecture may change with the implementation of a private cloud, your current network topology probably will not change significantly. If you have a private extranet in place (e.g. for premium customers or strategic partners), for practical purposes you probably have the network topology for a private cloud in place already. The security considerations you have today apply to a private cloud infrastructure, too. And the security tools you have in place (or should have in place) are also necessary for a private cloud and operate in the same way.

However, if you choose to use public cloud services, changing security requirements will require changes to your network topology. You must address how your existing network topology interacts with your cloud provider's network topology. There are four significant risk factors in this use case:

- Ensuring the confidentiality and integrity of your organization's data in transit to and from your public cloud provider
- Ensuring proper access control (authentication, authorization, and auditing) to whatever resources you are using at your public cloud provider
- Ensuring the availability of the Internet-facing resources in a public cloud that are being used by your organization, or have been assigned to your organization by your public cloud provider
- Replacing the established model of network zones and tiers with domains

We will discuss each of these risk factors in the sections that follow.

2.2.1.1 Network-Level Mitigation

Given the factors discussed in the preceding sections, what can you do to mitigate these increased risk factors? First, note that network-level risks exist regardless of what aspects of cloud computing services are being used (e.g. SaaS, PaaS, or IaaS). The primary determination of risk level therefore is not which services are being used, but rather whether your organization intends to use or is using a public, private, or hybrid cloud. Although some IaaS clouds offer virtual-network zoning, they may not match an internal private cloud environment that performs stateful inspection and other network security measures.

If your organization is large enough to afford the resources of a private cloud, your risks will decrease, assuming you have a true private cloud that is internal to your network. In some cases, a private cloud located at a cloud provider's facility can help meet your security requirements but will depend on the provider's capabilities and maturity. You can reduce risks related to confidentiality by using encryption: specifically, by using validated implementations of cryptography for data in transit. Secure digital signatures make it much more difficult, if not impossible, for someone to tamper with your data, and this ensures data integrity. Availability problems at the network level are far more difficult to mitigate with cloud computing unless your organization is using a private cloud that is internal to your network topology. Even if your private cloud is a private (i.e. nonshared) external network at a cloud provider's facility, you will face increased risk at the network level. A public cloud faces even greater risk. But let's keep some perspective: greater than what?

Even large enterprises with significant resources face considerable challenges at the network level of infrastructure security. Are the risks associated with cloud computing actually higher than the risks enterprises are facing today? Consider existing private and public extranets, and take into account partner connections when making such a comparison. For large enterprises without significant resources, or for small to medium-size businesses (SMBs), is the risk of using public clouds (assuming that such enterprises lack the resources necessary for private clouds) really higher than the risks inherent in their current infrastructures? In many cases, the answer is probably no: there is not a higher level of risk.

2.2.2 Infrastructure Security: The Host Level

When reviewing host security and assessing risks, you should consider the context of cloud service delivery models (SaaS, PaaS, and IaaS) and deployment models (public, private, and hybrid). Although there are no known new threats to hosts that are specific to cloud computing, some virtualization security threats such as VM escape, system-configuration drift, and insider threats by way of weak access control to the hypervisor carry into the public cloud computing environment. The dynamic nature (elasticity) of cloud computing can bring new operational challenges from a security-management perspective. The operational model motivates rapid provisioning and fleeting instances of VMs. Managing vulnerabilities and patches is therefore much harder than just running a scan, because the rate of change is much greater than in a traditional data center.

In addition, the fact that the Cloud harnesses the power of thousands of compute nodes, combined with the homogeneity of the OS employed by hosts, means threats can be amplified quickly and easily. This is referred to as the *velocity of attack* factor in the Cloud. More importantly, you should understand the trust boundary and the responsibilities that fall on your shoulders to secure the host infrastructure you manage. And you should compare this with providers' responsibilities in securing the part of the host infrastructure the CSP manages.

2.2.2.1 SaaS and PaaS Host Security

In general, CSPs do not publicly share information related to their host platforms, host OSs, and processes in place to secure the hosts, since hackers can exploit that information when they try to intrude into the cloud service. Hence, in the context of SaaS (e.g. Salesforce.com, Workday.com) or PaaS (e.g. Google App Engine, Salesforce.com's Force.com) cloud services, host security is opaque to customers, and the responsibility of securing the hosts is relegated to the CSP. To get assurance from the CSP about the security hygiene of its hosts, you should ask the vendor to share information under a non-disclosure agreement (NDA) or simply demand that the CSP share the information via a controls-assessment framework such as SysTrust or International Organization for Standardization (ISO) 27002. From a controls-assurance perspective, the CSP has to ensure that appropriate preventive and detective controls are in place and must do so via a third-party assessment or ISO 27002 type assessment framework.

Since virtualization is a key enabling technology that improves host hardware utilization, among other benefits, it is common for CSPs to employ virtualization platforms, including Xen and VMware hypervisors, in their host computing platform architecture. You should understand how the provider is using virtualization technology and the provider's process for securing the virtualization layer. Both the PaaS and SaaS platforms abstract and hide the host OS from end users with a host abstraction layer. One key difference between PaaS and SaaS is the accessibility of the abstraction layer that hides the OS services the applications consume. In the case of SaaS, the abstraction layer is not visible to users and is available only to developers and the CSP's operations staff, whereas PaaS users are given indirect access to the host abstraction layer in the form of a PaaS API that in turn interacts with the host abstraction layer. In short, if you are a SaaS or PaaS customer, you are relying on the CSP to provide a secure host platform on which the SaaS or PaaS application is developed and deployed by the CSP and you, respectively.

In summary, host security responsibilities in SaaS and PaaS services are transferred to the CSP. The fact that you do not have to worry about protecting hosts from host-based security threats is a major benefit from a security management and cost standpoint. However, as a customer, you still own the risk of managing information hosted in the cloud services. It's your responsibility to get the appropriate level of assurance regarding how the CSP manages host security hygiene.

2.2.2.2 IaaS Host Security

Unlike with PaaS and SaaS, IaaS customers are primarily responsible for securing the hosts provisioned in the Cloud. Given that almost all IaaS services available today employ virtualization at the host layer, host security in IaaS should be categorized as follows:

- **Virtualization software security** – The software layer sits on top of bare metal and provides customers with the ability to create and destroy virtual instances. Virtualization at the host level can be accomplished using any of the virtualization

models, including OS-level virtualization (Solaris containers, BSD [Berkeley Software Distribution] jails, Linux-VServer), paravirtualization (a combination of the hardware version and versions of Xen and VMware), or hardware-based virtualization (Xen, VMware, Microsoft Hyper-V). It is important to secure this layer of software that sits between the hardware and the virtual servers. In a public IaaS service, customers do not have access to this software layer; it is managed by the CSP.
- **Customer guest OS or virtual server security** – The virtual instance of an OS that is provisioned on top of the virtualization layer and is visible to customers from the Internet: e.g. various flavors of Linux, Microsoft, and Solaris. Customers have full access to virtual servers.

2.2.3 Infrastructure Security: The Application Level

Application or software security should be a critical element of your security program. Most enterprises with information security programs have yet to institute an application security program to address this realm. Designing and implementing applications targeted for deployment on a cloud platform requires that existing application security programs reevaluate current practices and standards. The application security spectrum ranges from standalone single-user applications to sophisticated multiuser e-commerce applications used by millions of users. Web applications such as CMSs, wikis, portals, bulletin boards, and discussion forums are used by small and large organizations. Many organizations also develop and maintain custom-built web applications for their businesses using various web frameworks (PHP, .NET, J2EE, Ruby on Rails, Python, etc.). According to SANS (Northcutt et al. 2008), until 2007, few criminals attacked vulnerable websites because other attack vectors were more likely to lead to an advantage in unauthorized economic or information access. Increasingly, however, advances in cross-site scripting (XSS) and other attacks have demonstrated that criminals looking for financial gain can exploit vulnerabilities resulting from web programming errors as new ways to penetrate important organizations. Here, we will limit our discussion to web application security: web applications in the Cloud accessed by users with a standard Internet browser, such as Firefox, Internet Explorer, or Safari, from any computer connected to the Internet.

2.2.4 Hypervisor Security in the Cloud

Before the discussion of data and application security in the Cloud, we first need to focus first on security and the role of the hypervisor and then the servers on which user services are based. A hypervisor is also called a virtual machine manager (VMM), which is one of many hardware-virtualization techniques allowing multiple OSs to run concurrently on a host computer. The hypervisor is piggybacked on a kernel program, itself running on the core physical machine running as the physical server. The hypervisor presents to the guest OSs a virtual operating platform and manages the execution of the guest OSs. Multiple instances of a variety of OSs may share the virtualized hardware resources. Hypervisors are very commonly installed on server hardware, with the function of running guest OSs that themselves act as servers. The security of the hypervisor therefore involves the security of the underlying kernel program and the underlying physical machine, the physical server, and the individual virtual OSs and their anchoring VMs.

The key feature of the cloud computing model is the concept of virtualization. Virtualization gives the Cloud the near-instant scalability and versatility that makes cloud computing so desirable a computing solution for companies and individuals. The core of virtualization in cloud computing is the easy process of minting VMs on demand with the hypervisor. The hypervisor allocates resources to each VM it creates and also handles the deletion of VMs. Since each VM is initiated by an instance, the hypervisor is a bidirectional conduit into and out of every VM. The compromise of either, therefore, creates a danger to the other. However, most hypervisors are constructed in such a way that there is a separation between the environments of the sandboxes (the VMs) and the hypervisor. There is just one hypervisor, which services all virtual sandboxes, each running a guest OS. The hypervisor runs as part of the native monolithic OS, side-by-side with the device drivers, file system, and network stack, completely in kernel space. So, one of the biggest security concerns with a hypervisor is the establishment of covert channels by an intruder. According to the Trusted Computer Security Evaluation Criteria (TCSEC), a covert channel is created by a sender process that modulates some condition (such as free space, availability of some service, or wait time to execute) that can be detected by a receiving process. If an intruder succeeds in establishing a covert channel, either by modifying file contents or through timing, it is possible for information to leak from one VM instance to another (Violino 2010).

Also, since the hypervisor is the controller of all VMs, it becomes the single point of failure in any cloud computing architecture. That is, if an intruder compromises a hypervisor, the intruder has control of all the VMs the hypervisor has allocated. This means the intruder can create or destroy VMs at will. For example, the intruder can perform a denial of service attack by bringing down the hypervisor, which then brings down all VMs running on top of the hypervisor.

The processes for securing virtual hosts differ greatly from processes used to secure their physical counterparts. Securing virtual entities like a hypervisor, virtual OSs, and corresponding VMs is more complex. To understand hypervisor security, let us first discuss the environment in which the hypervisor works. Recall that a hypervisor is part of a virtual computer system (VCS). In his 1973 thesis in the Division of Engineering and Applied Physics, Harvard University, Robert P. Goldberg defines a VCS as a hardware-software duplicate of a real computer system in which a statistically dominant subset of the virtual processor's instructions execute directly on the host processor in native mode. He also gives two parts to this definition, the environment and implementation (Goldberg 1973):

- **Environment** – The VCS must simulate a real computer system. Programs and OSs that run on the real system must run on the virtual system with identical effect. Since the simulated machine may run at a different speed than the real one, timing-dependent processor and I/O code may not perform exactly as intended.
- **Implementation** – Most instructions being executed must be processed directly by the host CPU without recourse to instruction-by-instruction interpretation. This guarantees that the VM will run on the host with relative efficiency. It also compels the VM to be similar or identical to the host, and forbids tampering with the control store to add new order code.

In the environment of VMs, a hypervisor is needed to control all the sandboxes (VMs). Generally, in practice, the underlying architecture of the hypervisor determines if there is true separation between the sandboxes. Goldberg classifies two types of hypervisor (Goldberg 1973):

- **Type-1 (or native, bare-metal)** hypervisors run directly on the host's hardware to control the hardware and to manage guest OSs. All guest OSs then run on a level above the hypervisor. This model represents the classic implementation of VM architectures. Modern hypervisors based on this model include Citrix XenServer, VMware ESX/ESXi, and Microsoft Hyper-V. The most common commercial hypervisors are based on a monolithic architecture. The underlying hypervisor services all virtual sandboxes, each running a guest OS. The hypervisor runs as part of the native monolithic OS, side-by-side with the device drivers, file system and network stack, completely in kernel space.
- **Type-2 (or hosted)** hypervisors run just above a host OS kernel such as Linux, Windows, and others. With the hypervisor layer as a distinct second software level, guest OSs run at the third level above the hardware. The host OS has direct access to the server's hardware, such as host CPU, memory, and I/O devices, and is responsible for managing basic OS services. The hypervisor creates VM environments and coordinates calls to CPU, memory, disk, network, and other resources through the host OS. Modern hypervisors based on this model include KVM and VirtualBox.

The discussion so far highlights the central role of the hypervisor in the operations of VM systems and points to its central role in securing all VM systems. Before we look at what can be done to secure it, let us ask what security breaches can happen to the hypervisor. Some malicious software, such as rootkit, masquerades as hypervisors in self-installation phases.

Neil MacDonald, vice president, distinguished analyst, and a Gartner Fellow Emeritus at Gartner Research, based in Stamford, CT, published his observation about hypervisors and their vulnerabilities in his blog post "Yes, Hypervisors Are Vulnerable" (MacDonald 2011). His observations are summarized here (Kizza and Yang 2014):

- The virtualization platform (hypervisor/VMM) is software written by human beings and will contain vulnerabilities. Microsoft, VMware, Citrix, and others, all will and have had vulnerabilities.
- Some of these vulnerabilities will result in a breakdown in isolation that the virtualization platform was supposed to enforce.
- Bad guys will target this layer with attacks. The benefits of compromising this layer are simply too great.
- While there have been a few disclosed attacks, it is just a matter of time before a widespread publicly disclosed enterprise breach is tied back to a hypervisor vulnerability.

There have been a growing number of virtualization vulnerabilities. Published papers have so far shown that the security of hypervisors can be undermined. As far back as 2006, *King and Chen* demonstrated the use of a type of malware called a *virtual-machine based rootkit* (VMBR), installing a VM monitor underneath an existing OS and hoisting the original OS into a VM (King and Chen 2006).

In their study, the authors demonstrated a malware program that started to act as its own hypervisor under Windows. We know that the hypervisor layer of virtualization, playing the core role in the virtualization process, is very vulnerable to hacking because it's the weakest link in the data center. Therefore, attacks on hypervisors are on the rise. Data from the IBM X-Force *2010 Mid-Year Trend and Risk Report* (Young 2010) shows that every year since 2005, vulnerabilities in virtualization server products (the hypervisors) have overshadowed those in workstation products, an indication of hackers' interest in the hypervisors. The report further shows that 35% of server virtualization vulnerabilities allow an attacker to "escape" from a guest VM to affect other VMs or the hypervisor. Note that the hypervisor in a type-1 environment is granted CPU privilege to access all system I/O resources and memory. This makes it a security threat to the whole cloud infrastructure. Just a single vulnerability in the hypervisor could result in a hacker gaining access to the entire system, including all guest OSs. Because malware runs below the entire OS, there is a growing threat of hackers using malware and rootkits to install themselves as a hypervisor below the OS, thus making them more difficult to detect. In a type-2 hypervisor configuration, the microkernel architecture is designed specifically to guarantee a robust separation of application partitions. This architecture puts the complex virtualization program in the user space, so every guest OS uses its own instantiation of the virtualization program. In this case, therefore, there is complete separation between the sandboxes (VMs), thus reducing the risks exhibited in type-1 hypervisors. An attack on a type-2 hypervisor can bring down only one virtual box, no more, and cannot bring down the cloud infrastructure as is the case with a type-1 hypervisor. According to *King and Chen*, overall, VM-based rootkits are hard to detect and remove because their state cannot be accessed by software running in the target system. Further, VMBRs support general-purpose malicious services by allowing such services to run in a separate OS that is protected from the target system (King and Chen 2006).

2.3 Infrastructure Security Analysis in Some Clouds

In this section, we analyze the infrastructure security in Force.com, Amazon AWS, Google App Engine, and Microsoft Azure.

2.3.1 Force.com

Force.com is targeted toward corporate application developers and independent software vendors. Unlike other PaaS offerings, it does not expose developers directly to its own infrastructure. Developers do not provision CPU time, disk, or instances of running OSs. Instead, Force.com provides a custom application platform centered around the relational database, one resembling an application server stack you might be familiar with from working with .NET, J2EE, or LAMP. Although it integrates with other technologies using open standards such as Simple Object Access Protocol (SOAP) and Representational State Transfer (REST), the programming languages and metadata representations used to build applications are proprietary to Force.com. This is unique among the PaaS products but not unreasonable when examined in depth. Force.com operates at a significantly higher level of abstraction than the other PaaS products, promising dramatically higher productivity to developers in return for their investment and trust in a single-vendor solution.

The Force.com platform architecture includes a database, a workflow engine, and user interface design tools. The platform includes an Eclipse-based integrated development environment (IDE) and a proprietary programming language called Apex. Apex has Java-like syntax. The database is a relational database. It is not possible to run any Java or .NET programs on the Force.com platform – developers must use Apex to build applications. Force.com includes a tool called the *builder* for building web applications quickly. Builder provides a user interface to create objects, fields within objects, and relationships between fields. Once a user creates these objects, the builder automatically creates a web interface with create, update, and delete operations. Using the builder allows developers to build simple to moderate applications without writing any significant amount of code and in a reasonably short time. The platform also provides a rich reporting environment for plotting bar graphs and pie charts (Padhy et al. 2011).

Multitenancy is an abstract concept, an implementation detail of Force.com, but one with tangible benefits for developers. Customers access shared infrastructure, with metadata and data stored in the same logical database. The multitenant architecture of Force.com consists of the following features:

- **Shared infrastructure** – Every customer (or tenant) of Force.com shares the same infrastructure. You are assigned a logical environment within the Force.com infrastructure. At first, some might be uncomfortable with the thought of handing their data to a third party where it is comingled with that of competitors. Salesforce's whitepaper on its multitenant technology includes the technical details of how it works and why your data is safe from loss or spontaneous appearance to unauthorized parties (http://developerforce.s3.amazonaws.com/whitepapers/WP_Force-MT_101508_PRINT.pdf).
- **Single version** – There is only one version of the Force.com platform in production. The same platform is used to deliver applications of all sizes and shapes, used by 1–100,000 users, running everything from dog-grooming businesses to the Japanese national post office.
- **Continuous, zero-cost improvements** – When Force.com is upgraded to include new features or bug fixes, the upgrade is enabled in every customer's logical environment with zero to minimal effort required.

Salesforce.com addresses application security by combining the strengths of multitenancy with modern development and management processes to minimize security vulnerabilities and maximize performance and usability. To achieve high scalability and performance, the database behind Salesforce.com customer relationship management (CRM) products is a single instance shared by thousands of customers. The application ensures that users see only the data to which they have assigned privileges:

- Every record of the database contains the customer's orgID.
- During login, the authenticated user is mapped to their org and access privileges according to the sharing model.
- Every request to the database is formed by the application and is limited to the user's orgID and privileges.

- Every row returned from the database is then validated against the orgID.
- An error in the query process does not return any data to the client.

The software development life cycle (SDLC) used by Salesforce.com incorporates security as a core consideration. Before a product can be considered "done," it must meet security requirements as well as functional requirements. To ensure high-quality code, security is part of each of the design, code, test, and release phases of the SDLC.

Salesforce can roll out new releases with confidence because it maintains a single version of its infrastructure and can achieve broad test coverage by leveraging tests, code, and configurations from the company's production environment. Customers help maintain and improve Force.com in a systematic, measurable way as a side effect of using it. This deep feedback loop between Force.com and its users is impractical to achieve with on-premises software.

Salesforce is hosted from dedicated spaces in top-tier data-center facilities. Its data centers are low-profile and designed as anonymous buildings without any company signage. The exterior walls of the facilities are bullet resistant. Concrete bollards are positioned around the facility perimeter to provide further security protection. All facilities maintain multiple transit access routes and are within close proximity to local law enforcement and fire/emergency services. All data centers selected are at core Internet hubs with diverse physically protected routes into the facility. In addition to securing the data center locations, it is critical that all facilities maintain robust critical infrastructure to support Salesforce.com through the following services:

- Next-generation uninterruptible power supply (UPS) systems (N + 1)
- N + 1 cooling infrastructure
- Fire-detection and -suppression system
- Multi-gigabit IP transit for external customer service
- Access to thousands of global Internet peering points
- Private peering with key carriers
- Diverse physically protected secure paths into facilities, for redundancy

All infrastructure is redundant and fault tolerant across components, including network, application servers, and database servers.

The Salesforce CRM suite of applications is powered entirely by Linux and Solaris systems, built with an automated process that ensures compliance to standardized build specifications, including removal of unnecessary processes, accounts, and protocols and use of non-root accounts to run services. Monitoring and validation of host security includes:

- File-integrity monitoring for unexpected changes to the system configuration
- Malicious software detection on application servers
- Vulnerability detection and remediation, including internal and external scanning and patching
- Forwarding of all host logs to a centralized log-aggregation and event-correlation server for review and alerting

Access to Salesforce.com is via the public Internet, and connections are secured via Secure Sockets Layer (SSL) / Transport Layer Security (TLS). Salesforce.com contracts with multiple carriers to provide the connectivity and bandwidth to host business-critical data.

The database in Salesforce.com is hardened according to industry and vendor guidelines, and is accessible only by a limited number of Salesforce.com employees with DBA access. Customers do not have direct database or OS-level access to the Salesforce environment. Customer passwords for the Salesforce CRM are hashed via SHA 256 before being stored in the database. Customers can specify that certain field types use encryption. These custom fields are encrypted by the application before being saved to the database and can be configured to mask the display of their contents according to user access.

Customer data is mirrored, backed up locally, and also mirrored over an encrypted network (Advanced Encryption Standard [AES] 128) to a 100% full-scale replica disaster-recovery data center. Salesforce's information security management system follows ISO 27002 practices and is certified to the ISO 27001 standard. The Computer Security Incident Response Team (CSIRT) runs in parallel with site operations to provide monitoring and incident response. The CSIRT consists of senior-level security analysts and manages a variety of tools and third-party resources that include:

- Intrusion Detection Systems (IDS)
- Security Event Management (SEM)
- Threat monitoring
- Perimeter monitoring
- External Certificate Authority

Briefly, Force.com is the proven cloud infrastructure that powers Salesforce CRM apps. It provides data encryption using AES-128 in transfer. It also includes a multitenant kernel, ISO 27001-certified security, proven reliability, real-time scalability, a real-time query optimizer, transparent system status, real-time upgrades, proven integration, real-time sandbox environments, integration, and global data centers with built-in disaster recovery. Force.com's security policies, procedures, and technologies have been validated by the world's most security-conscious organizations, including some of the largest financial services firms and leading security technology organizations. Customers' data is protected with comprehensive physical security, data encryption, user authentication, and application security as well as the latest standard-setting security practices and certifications, including:

- World-class security specifications.
- SAS 70 Type II, SOX, ISO 27001, and third-party vulnerability and SysTrust certifications.
- Secure point-to-point data replication for data backup: backup tapes for customer data never leave the facilities, and no tapes are ever in transport.

2.3.2 Amazon AWS

The AWS global infrastructure includes the facilities, network, hardware, and operational software (e.g. host OS, virtualization software, etc.) that support the provisioning and use of these resources. This global infrastructure is designed and managed according to security best practices as well as a variety of security compliance standards. AWS customers are assured that they are building web architectures on top of some of the most secure computing infrastructure in the world.

AWS compliance enables customers to understand the robust controls in place at AWS to maintain security and data protection in the Cloud. As systems are built on top of AWS cloud infrastructure, compliance responsibilities are shared. By tying together governance-focused, audit-friendly service features with applicable compliance or audit standards, AWS compliance enablers build on traditional programs, helping customers to establish and operate in an AWS security control environment. The IT infrastructure that AWS provides to its customers is designed and managed in alignment with security best practices and a variety of IT security standards, including:

- SOC 1/SSAE 16/ISAE 3402 (formerly SAS 70)
- SOC 2
- SOC 3
- FISMA, DIACAP, and FedRAMP
- DOD CSM Levels 1–5
- PCI DSS Level 1
- ISO 9001/ISO 27001
- ITAR
- FIPS 140-2
- MTCS Level 3

In addition, the flexibility and control that the AWS platform provides allows customers to deploy solutions that meet several industry-specific standards, including:

- Criminal Justice Information Services (CJIS)
- Cloud Security Alliance (CSA)
- Family Educational Rights and Privacy Act (FERPA)
- Health Insurance Portability and Accountability Act (HIPAA)
- Motion Picture Association of America (MPAA)

AWS's data centers are state of the art, utilizing innovative architectural and engineering approaches. The data centers are housed in nondescript facilities. Physical access is strictly controlled both at the perimeter and at building ingress points by professional security staff utilizing video surveillance, intrusion-detection systems, and other electronic means. Authorized staff must pass two-factor authentication a minimum of two times to access data center floors. All visitors and contractors are required to present identification and are signed in and continually escorted by authorized staff.

AWS only provides data center access and information to employees and contractors who have a legitimate business need for such privileges. When an employee no longer has a business need for these privileges, their access is immediately revoked, even if they continue to be an employee of Amazon or AWS. All physical access to data centers by AWS employees is logged and audited routinely.

Automatic fire-detection and -suppression equipment has been installed to reduce risk. The data center electrical power systems are designed to be fully redundant and maintainable without impact to operations, 24 hours a day, and seven days a week. Climate control is required to maintain a constant operating temperature for servers and other hardware, which prevents overheating and reduces the possibility of service outages. Data centers are conditioned to maintain atmospheric conditions at optimal levels. Personnel and systems monitor and control temperature and humidity at appropriate levels. AWS monitors electrical, mechanical, and life-support systems and equipment so that any issues are immediately identified. Preventative maintenance is performed to maintain the continued operability of equipment. When a storage device has reached the end of its useful life, AWS procedures include a decommissioning process that is designed to prevent customer data from being exposed to unauthorized individuals. AWS uses the techniques detailed in DoD 5220.22-M ("National Industrial Security Program Operating Manual," http://www.dss.mil/documents/odaa/nispom2006-5220.pdf) or NIST 800-88 ("Guidelines for Media Sanitization," https://ws680.nist.gov/publication/get_pdf.cfm?pub_id=50819) to destroy data as part of the decommissioning process. All decommissioned magnetic storage devices are degaussed and physically destroyed in accordance with industry-standard practices.

Amazon's infrastructure has a high level of availability and provides customers with the features to deploy a resilient IT architecture. AWS has designed its systems to tolerate system or hardware failures with minimal customer impact. Data center business continuity management at AWS is under the direction of the Amazon Infrastructure Group. Data centers are built in clusters in various global regions. All data centers are online and serving customers; no data center is "cold." In case of failure, automated processes move customer data traffic away from the affected area. Core applications are deployed in an N + 1 configuration, so that in the event of a data center failure, there is sufficient capacity to enable traffic to be load-balanced to the remaining sites.

AWS provides the flexibility to place instances and store data within multiple geographic regions as well as across multiple availability zones within each region. Each availability zone is designed as an independent failure zone. This means availability zones are physically separated within a typical metropolitan region and are located in lower-risk flood plains (specific flood zone categorization varies by region). Availability zones are all redundantly connected to multiple tier-1 transit providers. Distributing applications across multiple availability zones provides the ability to remain resilient in the face of most failure modes, including natural disasters or system failures. The Amazon Incident Management team employs industry-standard diagnostic procedures to drive resolution during business-impacting events. Staff operators provide 24x7x365 coverage to detect incidents and to manage their impact and resolution.

The AWS network has been architected to permit customers to select the level of security and resiliency appropriate for their workload. To enable customers to build geographically dispersed, fault-tolerant web architectures with cloud resources, AWS has implemented a world-class network infrastructure that is carefully monitored and managed. Network devices, including firewall and other boundary devices, are in place to monitor and control communications at the external boundary of the network and at key internal boundaries within the network. These boundary devices employ rule sets, access control lists (ACLs), and configurations to enforce the flow of information to specific information system services.

ACLs, or traffic-flow policies, are established on each managed interface, and manage and enforce the flow of traffic. ACL policies are approved by Amazon Information Security. These policies are automatically pushed using AWS's ACL-Manage tool, to help ensure these managed interfaces enforce the most up-to-date ACLs. AWS has strategically placed a limited number of access points to the Cloud to allow for more comprehensive monitoring of inbound and outbound communications and network traffic. These customer access points are called *API endpoints*, and they allow secure HTTP access (HTTPS), which allows customers to establish a secure communication session with storage or compute instances within AWS. To support customers with Federal Information Processing Standard (FIPS) cryptographic requirements, the SSL-terminating load balancers in AWS GovCloud (U.S.) are FIPS 140-2-compliant. In addition, AWS has implemented network devices that are dedicated to managing interfacing communications with Internet service providers (ISPs). AWS employs a redundant connection to more than one communication service at each Internet-facing edge of the AWS network. These connections each have dedicated network devices.

Customers can connect to an AWS access point via HTTP or HTTPS using Secure Sockets Layer (SSL), a cryptographic protocol that is designed to protect against eavesdropping, tampering, and message forgery.

For customers that require additional layers of network security, AWS offers the Amazon Virtual Private Cloud (VPC), which provides a private subnet within the AWS cloud, and the ability to use an IPsec virtual private network (VPN) device to provide an encrypted tunnel between the Amazon VPC and the customer's data center. For more information about VPC configuration options, refer to the Amazon Virtual Private Cloud (https://aws.amazon.com/vpc).

Logically, the AWS Production network is segregated from the Amazon Corporate network by means of a complex set of network security/segregation devices. AWS developers and administrators on the corporate network who need to access AWS cloud components in order to maintain them must explicitly request access through the AWS ticketing system. All requests are reviewed and approved by the applicable service owner.

Approved AWS personnel then connect to the AWS network through a bastion host that restricts access to network devices and other cloud components, logging all activity for security review. Access to bastion hosts require SSH public-key authentication for all user accounts on the host. It should be noted that all communications between regions is across public Internet infrastructure; therefore, appropriate encryption methods must be used to protect sensitive data.

AWS utilizes a wide variety of automated monitoring systems to provide a high level of service performance and availability. AWS monitoring tools are designed to detect unusual or unauthorized activities and conditions at ingress and egress communication points. These tools monitor server and network usage, port-scanning activities, application usage, and unauthorized intrusion attempts. The tools have the ability to set custom performance-metric thresholds for unusual activity.

Systems within AWS are extensively instrumented to monitor key operational metrics. Alarms are configured to automatically notify operations and management personnel when early warning thresholds are crossed on key operational metrics. An on-call schedule is used so personnel are always available to respond to operational issues. This includes a pager system so alarms are quickly and reliably communicated to operations personnel.

AWS security-monitoring tools help identify several types of denial of service (DoS) attacks, including distributed, flooding, and software/logic attacks. When DoS attacks are identified, the AWS incident-response process is initiated. In addition to the DoS prevention tools, redundant telecommunication providers at each region as well as additional capacity protect against the possibility of DoS attacks.

The AWS network provides significant protection against traditional network security issues, and customers can implement further protection. The following are a few examples:

- **Distributed denial of service (DDoS) attacks** – AWS API endpoints are hosted on large, Internet-scale, world-class infrastructure that benefits from the same engineering expertise that built Amazon into the world's largest online retailer. Proprietary DDoS mitigation techniques are used. Additionally, AWS's networks are multihomed across a number of providers to achieve Internet access diversity.
- **Man-in-the-middle (MITM) attacks** – All of the AWS APIs are available via SSL-protected endpoints that provide server authentication. Amazon EC2 Amazon Machine Images (AMIs) automatically generate new SSH host certificates on first boot and log them to the instance's console. Customers can then use the secure APIs to call the console and access the host certificates before logging in to the instance for the first time. Amazon encourages customers to use SSL for all interactions with AWS.
- **IP spoofing** – Amazon EC2 instances cannot send spoofed network traffic. The AWS-controlled, host-based firewall infrastructure will not permit an instance to send traffic with a source IP or MAC address other than its own.
- **Port scanning** – Unauthorized port scans by Amazon EC2 customers are a violation of the AWS Acceptable Use Policy. Violations of the AWS Acceptable Use Policy are taken seriously, and every reported violation is investigated. When unauthorized port scanning is detected by AWS, it is stopped and blocked. Port scans of Amazon EC2 instances are generally ineffective because, by default, all inbound ports on Amazon EC2 instances are closed and are only opened by customers. Strict management of security groups by customers can further mitigate the threat of port scans. If customers configure the security group to allow traffic from any source to a specific port, then that specific port will be vulnerable to a port scan. In these cases, customers must use appropriate security measures to protect listening services that may be essential to their application from being discovered by an unauthorized port scan. For example, a web server must clearly have port 80 (HTTP) open to the world, and the administrator of this server is responsible for the security of the HTTP server software, such as Apache. Customers may request permission to conduct vulnerability scans as required to meet specific compliance requirements. These scans must be limited to customer instances and must not violate the AWS Acceptable Use Policy.
- **Packet sniffing by other tenants** – It is not possible for a virtual instance running in promiscuous mode to receive or "sniff" traffic that is intended for a different virtual instance. While customers can place their interfaces into promiscuous mode, the hypervisor will not deliver any traffic to them that is not addressed to them. Even two virtual instances that are owned by the same customer located on the same physical host cannot listen to each other's traffic. Attacks such as Address Resolution Protocol (ARP) cache poisoning do not work within Amazon EC2 and Amazon VPC. Amazon EC2 does provide ample protection against one customer inadvertently or maliciously attempting to view another's data, but as a standard practice, customers should encrypt sensitive traffic.

In addition to monitoring, regular vulnerability scans are performed on the host OS, web application, and databases in the AWS environment using a variety of tools. Also, AWS Security teams subscribe to newsfeeds for applicable vendor flaws and proactively monitor vendors' websites and other relevant outlets for new patches.

AWS has established formal policies and procedures to delineate the minimum standards for logical access to AWS platform and infrastructure hosts. AWS conducts criminal background checks, as permitted by law, as part of pre-employment screening practices for employees and commensurate with the employee's position and level of access. The policies also identify functional responsibilities for the administration of logical access and security.

AWS Security has established a credentials policy with required configurations and expiration intervals. Passwords must be complex and are forced to be changed every 90 days. AWS's development process follows secure software development best practices, which include formal design reviews by the AWS Security team, threat modeling, and completion of a risk assessment. Static code analysis tools are run as part of the standard build process, and all deployed software undergoes recurring penetration testing performed by carefully selected industry experts. Security risk assessment reviews begin during the design phase, and the engagement lasts through launch to ongoing operations.

Routine, emergency, and configuration changes to existing AWS infrastructure are authorized, logged, tested, approved, and documented in accordance with industry norms for similar systems. Updates to AWS's infrastructure are done to minimize any impact on customers and their use of the services. AWS will communicate with customers, either via email or through the AWS Service Health Dashboard, when service use is likely to be adversely affected.

AWS applies a systematic approach to managing change so that alterations to customer-impacting services are thoroughly reviewed, tested, approved, and well-communicated. The AWS change-management process is designed to avoid unintended service disruptions and to maintain the integrity of service to the customer. Changes are typically pushed into production in a phased deployment starting with lowest-impact areas. Deployments are tested on a single system and closely monitored so impacts can be evaluated. Service owners have a number of configurable metrics that measure the health of the service's upstream dependencies. These metrics are closely monitored, with thresholds and alarming in place. Amazon's Corporate Applications team develops and manages software to automate IT processes for UNIX/Linux hosts in the areas of third-party software delivery, internally developed software, and configuration management. The Infrastructure team maintains and operates a UNIX/Linux configuration-management framework to address hardware scalability, availability, auditing, and security management. By centrally managing hosts through the use of automated processes that manage change, Amazon is able to achieve its goals of high availability, repeatability, scalability, security, and disaster recovery. Systems and network engineers monitor the status of these automated tools on a continuous basis, reviewing reports to respond to hosts that fail to obtain or update their configuration and software.

Internally developed configuration-management software is installed when new hardware is provisioned. These tools are run on all UNIX hosts to validate that they are configured and that software is installed in compliance with standards determined by the role assigned to the host. This configuration-management software also helps to regularly update packages that are already installed on the host. Only approved personnel enabled through the permissions service may log in to the central configuration-management servers.

2.3.3 Google App Engine

Google security policies provide a series of threat-prevention and infrastructure-management procedures. Malware poses a significant risk to today's IT environments. An effective malware attack can lead to account compromise, data theft, and possibly additional access to a network. Google takes these threats to its networks and its customers very seriously and uses a variety of methods to address malware risks.

This strategy begins with manual and automated scanners that analyze Google's search index for websites that may be vehicles for malware or phishing. (More information about this process is available at https://webmasters.googleblog.com/2008/10/malware-we-dont-need-no-stinking.html.) The blacklists produced by these scanning procedures have been incorporated into various web browsers and Google Toolbar to help protect Internet users from suspicious websites and sites that may have become compromised. These tools, available to the public, operate for Google employees as well. In addition, Google makes use of anti-virus software and proprietary techniques in Gmail, on servers, and on workstations to address malware.

Google's security-monitoring program analyzes information gathered from internal network traffic, employee actions on systems, and outside knowledge of vulnerabilities. At multiple points across Google's global network, internal traffic is inspected for suspicious behavior, such as the presence of traffic that might indicate botnet connections. This analysis is performed using a combination of open source and commercial tools for traffic capture and parsing. A proprietary correlation system built on top of Google technology also supports this analysis. Network analysis is supplemented by examining system logs to identify unusual behavior, such as unexpected activity in former employees' accounts or attempted access of customer data. Google Security engineers place standing search alerts on public data repositories to look for security incidents that might affect the company's infrastructure. They review inbound security reports and monitor public mailing lists, blog posts, and web bulletin-board systems. Automated network analysis helps determine when an unknown threat may exist and escalates to Google Security staff. Network analysis is supplemented by automated analysis of system logs.

Google employs a team that has the responsibility to manage vulnerabilities in a timely manner. The Google Security Team scans for security threats using commercial and in-house-developed tools, automated and manual penetration efforts, quality assurance (QA) processes, software security reviews, and external audits. The vulnerability-management team is responsible for tracking and following up on vulnerabilities. Once a legitimate vulnerability requiring remediation has been identified by the Security Team, it is logged, prioritized according to severity, and assigned an owner. The vulnerability-management team tracks such issues and follows up until they can verify that the vulnerability has been remediated. Google also maintains relationships and interfaces with members of the security research community to track reported issues in Google services and open source tools. Under Google's Vulnerability Reward Program (http://www.google.com/about/company/rewardprogram.html), security researches receive rewards for the submission of valid reports of security vulnerabilities in Google services.

Google has an incident-management process for security events that may affect the confidentiality, integrity, or availability of its systems or data. This process specifies courses of action and procedures for notification, escalation, mitigation, and documentation. Staff are trained in forensics and handling evidence in preparation for an event, including the use of third-party and proprietary tools. Testing of incident response plans is performed for identified areas, such as systems that store sensitive customer information. These tests take into consideration a variety of scenarios, including insider threats and software vulnerabilities.

The Google Security Team is available 24x7 to all employees. When an information security incident occurs, Google's Security staff respond by logging and prioritizing the incident according to its severity. Events that directly impact customers are treated with the highest priority. An individual or team is assigned to remediating the problem and enlisting the help of product and subject experts as appropriate. Google Security engineers conduct post-mortem investigations when necessary to determine the root cause for single events and trends spanning multiple events over time, and to develop new strategies to help prevent recurrence of similar incidents.

Google employs multiple layers of defense to help protect the network perimeter from external attacks. Only authorized services and protocols that meet Google's security requirements are permitted to traverse the company's network. Unauthorized packets are automatically dropped. Google's network security strategy is composed of the following elements:

- Control of the size and make-up of the network perimeter. Enforcement of network segregation using industry standard firewall and ACL technology.
- Management of network firewall and ACL rules that employs change management, peer review, and automated testing.
- Restricting access to networked devices to authorized personnel.
- Routing of all external traffic through custom front-end servers that help detect and stop malicious requests.
- Creating internal aggregation points to support better monitoring.
- Examination of logs for exploitation of programming errors (e.g. XSS) and generating high-priority alerts if an event is found.

Google provides many services that use Hypertext Transfer Protocol Secure (HTTPS) for more secure browser connections. Services such as Gmail, Google Search, and Google+ support HTTPS by default for users who are signed into their Google accounts. Information sent via HTTPS is encrypted from the time it leaves Google until it is received by the recipient's computer.

Based on a proprietary design, Google's production servers are based on a version of Linux that has been customized to include only the components necessary to run Google applications, such as those services required to administer the system and serve user traffic. The system is designed for Google to be able to maintain control over the entire hardware and software stack and support a secure application environment. Google's production servers are built on a standard OS, and security fixes are uniformly deployed to the company's entire infrastructure. This homogeneous environment is maintained by proprietary software that continually monitors systems for binary modifications. If a modification is found that differs from the standard Google image, the system is automatically returned to its official state. These automated, self-healing mechanisms are designed to enable Google to monitor and remediate destabilizing events, receive notifications about incidents, and slow down potential compromise on the network. Using a change-management system to provide a centralized mechanism for registering, approving, and tracking changes that impact all systems, Google reduces the risks associated with making unauthorized modifications to the standard Google OS.

Google App Engine provides DoS protection and SSL on all App Engine applications. Hardware security features are undisclosed, but all have successfully completed a SAS 70 Type II audit.

2.3.4 Microsoft Azure

Microsoft Azure can provide businesses with on-demand infrastructure that can scale and adapt to changing business needs. Customers can quickly deploy new VMs in minutes, and with pay-as-you-go billing, they aren't penalized when they need to reconfigure VMs. Microsoft Azure VMs even offer a gallery of preconfigured VM images to choose from so customers can get started as quickly as possible. Customers can also upload or download virtual disks, load-balance VMs, and integrate VMs into their on-premises environment using virtual networks.

Microsoft Azure is Microsoft's cloud computing platform and infrastructure for building, deploying, and managing applications and services through its global network of data centers.

Virtualization in Azure is based on the Hyper-V hypervisor, and supported OSs are Windows, some Linux distributions (SUSE Linux Enterprise Server, Red Hat, Enterprise Linux versions 5.2–6.1, and CentOS 5.2–6.2), as well as UNIX Free BSD. Hyper-V is a hypervisor-based virtualization technology that was first introduced for x64 versions of Windows Server 2008. Isolation is supported in terms of logical units of isolation, called *partitions*. Host nodes run root or parent partitions enabled by supported version of Windows Server Operating System (2008, 2008 R2, or 2012). The root partition is the single one that has direct access to the hardware devices, and it creates child partitions by API calls. Improvements to Windows Server 2012 Hyper-V (http://download.microsoft.com/download/a/2/7/a27f60c3-5113-494a-9215-d02a8abcfd6b/windows_server_2012_r2_server_virtualization_white_paper.pdf) include the following:

- Multitenant VM isolation through private virtual LANs (PVLANs). A PVLAN is a technique used to isolate VMs that share a VLAN. Isolated mode means ports cannot exchange packets with each other at layer 2. Promiscuous ports can exchange packets with any other port on the same primary VLAN ID. Community ports on the same VLAN ID can exchange packets with each other at layer 2.
- Protection against a malicious VM stealing IP addresses from other VMs using ARP spoofing, provided by Hyper-V Extensible Switch.
- Protection against Dynamic Host Configuration Protocol (DHCP) snooping and DHCP guard, by configuring ports that can have DHCP servers connected to them.
- Isolation and metering though virtual port ACLs that enable customers to configure which MAC addresses can (and cannot) connect to a VM.
- Ability to trunk traditional VLANs to VMs. Hyper-V Extensible Switch trunk mode allows traffic from multiple VLANs to be directed to a single network adapter in a VM that could previously receive traffic only from one VLAN.
- Ability to monitor traffic from specific ports flowing through specific VMs on the switch.

An interface scripting environment allows control and automated deployment and workload management in Microsoft Azure. Authentication is over SSL for security, and it can use the user's certificate or generate a new one.

Microsoft Azure Virtual Network provides the following capabilities:

- Creation and management of virtual private networks in Microsoft Azure with the user's defined address space to connect with cloud services (PaaS) and VMs. The address space follows the RFC 1918 specification, and public addresses are not allowed in the virtual network.
- Cross-site connectivity over IPsec VPN between the virtual network and on-premises network to enable a hybrid cloud and securely extend the on-premises data center (https://docs.microsoft.com/en-us/azure/vpn-gateway/vpn-gateway-about-vpn-devices). This feature can be enabled by a VPN device or use the Routing and Remote Access Service (RRAS) on Windows Server 2012. Microsoft Azure has validated a set of standard site-to-site S2S VPN devices in partnership with device vendors, in order to ensure its compatibility.

Microsoft Azure defined site-to-site VPNs can be either static or dynamic:

- Static routing VPNs are policy based. Policy-based VPNs encrypt and route packets through an interface based on a customer-defined policy. The policy is usually defined as an access list.
- Dynamic routing VPNs are route based. Route-based VPNs depend on a tunnel interface specifically created for forwarding packets. Any packet arriving on the tunnel interface is forwarded through the VPN connection.

Microsoft Azure recommends using dynamic routing VPNs when possible. Different features are available for dynamic and static routing VPNs.

Microsoft Azure blob storage is used to store unstructured binary and text data. This data can be accessed over HTTP or HTTPS. Based on the user's preferences, data can be encrypted through the .NET Cryptographic Service Providers libraries. Through them, developers can implement encryption, hashing, and key management for storage and transmitted data. Azure Drive is a feature of Azure that provides access to data contained in an NTFS-formatted virtual hard disk (VHD) persisted as a page blob in Azure Storage. A single Azure instance can mount a page blob for read/write access as an Azure Drive. However, multiple Azure instances can mount a snapshot of a page blob for read-only access as an Azure Drive. The Azure Storage blob lease facility is used to prevent more than one instance at a time from mounting the page blob as an Azure Drive. When mounting a drive, the application has to specify credentials that allow it to access the page blob in the Microsoft Azure blob service. Microsoft Azure Drive supports two authorization schemes, account and key, as well as Shared Access Signatures (SAS).

The Azure Storage Service supports association of access permissions with a container through public access control. This allows public read access to the container and the blobs in it or public read access only to the blobs in the container and not to the container itself. The latter would, for example, prohibit unauthenticated listing of all the blobs in the container. The Azure Storage Service also supports shared-access signatures, which can be used to provide a time-limited token allowing unauthenticated users to access a container or the blobs in it. Shared access can be further managed through container-level access policy.

By default, storage accounts are configured for geo-redundant storage (GRS), meaning blob data is replicated both within the primary location and to a location hundreds of miles away (geo-replication).

In addition, durability for Microsoft Azure Storage is achieved through replication of data. The replication mechanism used is Distributed File System (DFS), where data is spread out over a number of storage nodes. The DFS layer stores the data in what are called *extents*. This is the unit of storage on disk and the unit of replication, where each extent is replicated multiple times. Typical extent sizes range from approximately 100 MB to 1 GB. When storing a blob in a blob container, entities in a table, or messages in a queue, the persistent data uses one or more extents.

Microsoft Azure offers SQL Database, which is based on Microsoft SQL Server. It offers two types of access control, SQL authentication and a server-side firewall that restricts access by IP address:

- **SQL authentication** – SQL Database only supports SQL Server authentication: the user's accounts with strong passwords and configured with specific rights.
- **SQL Database firewall** – Lets the user allow or prevent connections by specifying IP addresses or ranges of IPs.

Along with access control, SQL Database only allows secure connections via SQL Server's protocol encryption through the SSL protocol. SQL Database supports Transparent Data Encryption (TDE). It performs real-time I/O encryption and decryption of data and log files. For encryption, it uses a database encryption key (DEK), stored in the database boot record for availability during recovery. TDE protects data stored in the database and enables software developers to encrypt data by using AES and Triple Data Encryption Algorithm (3DES) encryption algorithms without changing existing applications.

Microsoft Azure provides the following (Singh 2015):

- **Identity and access** – Monitor access patterns to identify and mitigate potential threats. Help prevent unauthorized access with Azure multifactor authentication. End users have self-service identity management.
- **Network security** – Azure VMs and data are isolated from undesirable traffic and users. However, customers can access them through encrypted or private connections. Firewalled and partitioned networks help protect against unwanted traffic from the Internet. Customers can manage VMs with encrypted remote desktops and Windows PowerShell sessions, and can keep traffic off the Internet by using Azure ExpressRoute, a private fiber link between the client and Azure.
- **Data protection** – Azure provides technology safeguards such as encryption, and operational processes about data destruction maintain confidentiality. Encryption is used to help secure data in transit between data centers and clients, as well as between and at Microsoft data centers, and clients can choose to implement additional encryption using a range of approaches. If customers delete data or leave Azure, Microsoft follows strict industry standards that call for overwriting storage resources before reuse, as well as physically disposing of decommissioned hardware.
- **Data privacy** – Microsoft allows to specify the geographic areas where client's data is stored. Furthermore, data can be replicated within a geographic area for redundancy. To limit Microsoft access to and use of customer data, Microsoft strictly controls and

permits access only as necessary to provide or troubleshoot service. Client data is never used for advertising purposes.

- **Threat defense** – Integrated deployment systems manage security updates for Microsoft software, and clients can apply update-management processes to VMs. Microsoft provides continuous monitoring and analysis of traffic to reveal anomalies and threats. Forensic tools dissect attacks, and clients can implement logging to aid analysis. Clients can also conduct penetration testing of applications being run in Azure (legal permissions are required).
- **Compliance programs** – These include ISO 27001, SOC1, SOC2, FedRAMP, UK G-Cloud, PCI DSS, and HIPAA.

2.4 Protecting Cloud Infrastructure

In this section, we discuss several ways to protect the cloud infrastructure (Faatz and Pizette 2010).

2.4.1 Software Maintenance and Patching Vulnerabilities

Protecting software infrastructure in the Cloud is an essential activity for maintaining an appropriate security posture. For cloud providers and traditional IT alike, it involves activities such as securely configuring OSs and network devices, ensuring software patches are up to date, and tracking the discovery of new vulnerabilities.

The good news in terms of basic infrastructure security, such as configuration and patching, is that cloud providers may do a better job than most client organizations currently accomplish. The European Network and Information Security Agency (ENISA) observes, "... security measures are cheaper when implemented on a larger scale. Therefore, the same amount of investment in security buys better protection" (Catteddu and Hogben 2012. Large cloud providers will benefit from these economies of scale.

Cloud providers have an additional benefit: their systems are likely to be homogeneous, which is fundamental to delivering commodity resources on demand. Hence, a cloud provider can configure every server identically. Software updates can be deployed rapidly across the provider's infrastructure. As a contrasting example, suppose that a large federal agency has observed that each of its servers is unique; every server has at least one deviation from defined configuration standards. This heterogeneity adds to the complexity of maintaining infrastructure security (Faatz and Pizette 2010).

Homogeneity also has a potential downside: it ensures that the entire infrastructure has the same vulnerabilities. An attack that exploits an infrastructure vulnerability will affect all systems in a homogeneous cloud. The characteristic that makes routine maintenance easier may increase the impact of a targeted attack. A potential area for future research would be to employ an instance of a completely different technology stack for the express purpose of validating the integrity of the initial homogeneous infrastructure.

Although it may be easier for cloud providers to maintain infrastructure security, government clients should ensure that they understand the provider's standards for configuring and maintaining the infrastructure used to deliver cloud services.

While some security information is proprietary and sensitive, many providers are starting to share more information in response to customer needs. For example, Google recently published a set of white papers providing general information about its security operations and procedures (https://services.google.com/fh/files/misc/security_whitepapers_march2018.pdf).

2.4.2 The Technology Stack

The hardware and software stack, whether it is commercial off-the-shelf, government off-the-shelf, or proprietary, has an impact on the soundness of the provider's security practices and how readily the government can understand them. For example, Google and some other providers use proprietary hardware and software to implement their clouds. The proprietary cloud infrastructure may be as secure as or more secure than the cloud infrastructure constructed of commodity hardware and commercial software; however, there is no standard for comparison. If a cloud vendor is using a proprietary infrastructure, it may be difficult for the government to assess the platform's vulnerabilities and determine security best practices. There are no commonly accepted secure configurations standards and no public source of vulnerability information for these proprietary infrastructures. As a potential mitigation and best practice, government clients should understand the provider's disclosure policy regarding known vulnerabilities, administrative practices, security events, etc. They also should have relevant reporting contractually specified.

Similar to the community and public cloud providers, government organizations implementing private cloud solutions may find it easier and faster to maintain secure configurations and timely patching. Unlike physical servers, virtual servers do not have to be configured or patched individually. Instead, the VM images are configured and patched. Measuring compliance also can be simplified by checking the VM images rather than running measurement agents on each virtual server.

2.4.3 Disaster Recovery

In addition to maintaining the currency of software and expeditiously plugging vulnerabilities, cloud computing providers must be able to quickly recover from disaster events. For the government client organization, cloud computing can both simplify and complicate disaster-recovery planning. Because most major cloud providers operate several geographically dispersed data centers, a single natural disaster is unlikely to affect all centers. For example, Amazon EC2 describes its geographic resiliency as follows: "By launching instances in separate Availability Zones, you can protect your applications from failure of a single location" (https://docs.aws.amazon.com/AWSEC2/latest/UserGuide/using-regions-availability-zones.html). Some level of disaster recovery is inherent in a well-designed, large-scale, cloud computing infrastructure.

That said, circumstances might force a cloud provider to discontinue operations. Currently, most cloud service offerings are unique to each provider and may not be easily portable. An application built for the Google Apps platform will not run on Microsoft's Azure platform. Hence, clients may need to develop alternative hosting strategies for applications deployed to the Cloud. If dictated by system requirements for uptime and availability, organizations can develop processes to continue operations without access to community or public cloud-based applications.

For a private cloud, technologies such as virtualization can be employed to help with disaster recovery. Given that virtualized images frequently can be deployed independent of the physical hardware, virtualization provides an inherent continuity of operations capability (i.e. virtualized applications can be easily moved from one data center to another).

2.4.4 Monitoring and Defending Infrastructure

The challenge of monitoring and defending cloud-based systems depends on the service model and may increase due to shared control of the IT stack. Monitoring and defending systems consists of detecting and responding to inappropriate or unauthorized use of information or computing resources. Much like Microsoft Windows, which has been the dominant desktop OS and target of choice for malware, large public clouds and community clouds also are high-value targets. Penetrating the substrate of a public or community cloud can provide a foothold from which to attack the applications of all the organizations running on the Cloud.

Audit trails from network devices, OSs, and applications are the first source of information used to monitor systems and detect malicious activity. Some or all of these sources may not be available to a cloud client. With SaaS, all audit trails are collected by the cloud provider. With PaaS, application audit trails may be captured by the client, but OS and network audit trails are captured by the provider. With IaaS, a government organization may capture audit trails from the virtual network, virtual OSs, and applications. The provider collects the audit trails for the physical network and the virtualization layer. Correlation of events across provider-hosted VMs may be difficult, and the ability to place intrusion-detection sensors in the VMs may be similarly constrained.

To date, most cloud providers have focused on monitoring and defending the physical resources they control. Unlike their clients, cloud providers have the technical ability to collect audit-trail information and place intrusion-detection sensors in the infrastructure where their clients cannot. Although they can do this, cloud providers may not be willing or able to share that data. In clouds that host multiple tenants, the provider would need to protect the privacy of all its customers, which complicates the ability to share information. As noted by *Buck and Hanf*, SLAs that specify the exact types of information that will be shared are essential (Buck and Hanf 2010).

2.4.5 Incident Response Team

The government client's incident response team will need to learn the response capabilities offered by the cloud provider, ensure appropriate security SLAs are in place, and develop new response procedures that couple the cloud provider information with its own data. Given the difficulty of obtaining provider infrastructure information, a government client's incident response team may need to rethink how it detects some types of malicious activity. For example, an incident response team that provides proactive services such as vulnerability scanning may not be allowed to perform these functions on systems and applications deployed in the Cloud. A cloud provider's terms of use may prohibit these activities, as it would be difficult to distinguish legitimate client-scanning actions from malicious activities. Standard incident response actions may not be possible in the Cloud. For example, a government client's incident response team that proactively deletes known malicious e-mail from users' inboxes may not have this ability in a cloud-based SaaS email system. Given these challenges, it is essential that the appropriate contractual relationship with SLAs be established.

If the organization is creating a private cloud, there are new challenges that are different from many of the community and public cloud issues. The virtualization layer presents a new attack vector, and many components (e.g. switches, firewalls, intrusion-detection devices) within the IT infrastructure may become virtualized. The organization's security operations staff must learn how to safely deploy and administer the virtualization software, and how to configure, monitor, and correlate the data from the new virtual devices.

While cloud computing may make some aspects of incident detection and response more complex, it has the potential to simplify some aspects of forensics. When a physical computer is compromised, a forensic analyst's first task is to copy the state of the computer quickly and accurately. Capturing and storing state quickly is a fundamental capability of many IaaS clouds. Instead of needing special-purpose hardware and tools to capture the contents of system memory and copy disks, the forensic analyst uses the inherent capabilities of the virtualization layer in the IaaS Cloud. Leveraging this capability requires the incident response team to develop procedures for capturing and using this state information and, in the case of community and public clouds, develop and maintain a working relationship with the cloud provider.

2.4.6 Malicious Insiders

Clouds, whether public, community, or private, create an opportunity for malicious insiders. All three cloud deployment models create a new class of highly privileged insiders: cloud infrastructure administrators. OSs have long had privileged users such as the UNIX root user and the Microsoft Windows administrator. The risk associated with these users often has been managed using a variety of techniques (e.g. limiting the number of platforms on which a person can have privileged access). The cloud approach to providing computing resources may create users with broad privileged access to the entire underlying cloud infrastructure. Given this risk, mitigating controls and access restrictions must be maintained, because an unchecked, malicious cloud infrastructure administrator has the potential to inflict significant damage. For public and community clouds, it is important to understand how the vendor reduces the risk posed by cloud administrators. Organizations operating private clouds need to consider what operational and monitoring controls can be used to reduce this risk.

Public and community IaaS clouds significantly increase the number of people who are insiders or "near insiders." Multiple organizations will have VMs running on the same physical machine. Administrators of these neighbor VMs will have privileged access to those VMs – an excellent starting point for launching an attack. Using Amazon's EC2 IaaS offering [16], demonstrated the ability to map the cloud infrastructure and locate specific target VMs (Ristenpart et al. 2009). Having located the target, the researchers were able to reliably place a VM that they controlled on the same physical server. This capability enables a variety of VM-escape or side-channel attacks to compromise the target. Hence, in multitenant IaaS, neighbors are similar to malicious insiders.

The key considerations identified in this section for monitoring and protecting computing and communications infrastructure in cloud deployments are as follows:

- Large public clouds are high-value targets.
- Incident response teams must develop procedures (with contractual backing) for working with a cloud provider.
- Cloud infrastructure simplifies forensic capture of system state.
- Cloud virtualization technology may create a new class of highly privileged users with broad access to the cloud infrastructure.
- Cloud neighbors pose a threat similar to malicious insiders.
- Cloud service providers, through their homogeneous environments and economies of scale, may be able to provide better infrastructure security than many government organizations currently achieve.
- Assessing the security posture of providers is complicated if proprietary hardware or software is used.
- Many large-scale cloud providers operate multiple, geographically dispersed data centers.
- Unique cloud service offerings that are not easily portable make recovery from provider failure challenging.

2.5 Conclusion

There are many security issues related to cloud computing. Some reflect traditional web application, networking, and data-hosting problems and others are related to cloud-specific characteristics such as virtualization and multitenancy. In general, the security concerns of the cloud environment can be categorized into three groups: identity, information, and infrastructure. Cloud infrastructure security is a critical aspect of cloud security, and any attacks to the cloud infrastructure will cause significant service disruption. In this chapter, we briefly explained identity and information security, and discussed how cloud infrastructure security is investigated at three levels: network, host, and application. We also discussed other security issues to provide a high level of insight to cloud security.

References

Buck, Kevin and Hanf, Diane. (2010). Cloud SLA considerations for the government consumer. MITRE Corporation technical paper.

Catteddu, Daniele and Hogben, G. (2012). Cloud computing: benefits, risks and recommendations for information security. European Network and Information Security Agency technical report.

Faatz, D and Pizette, L. (2010). Information security in the clouds. MITRE Corporation technical paper.

Goldberg, Robert P. (1973). Architectural principles for virtual computer systems. PhD thesis. Harvard University.

Keller, Eric, Szefer, Jakub, Rexford, Jennifer et al. (2010). NoHype: virtualized cloud infrastructure without the virtualization. Paper presented at the ACM SIGARCH Computer Architecture News.

King, Samuel T and Chen, Peter M. (2006). SubVirt: implementing malware with virtual machines. Paper presented at the 2006 IEEE Symposium on Security and Privacy.

Kizza, J.M. and Yang, L. (2014). Is the cloud the future of computing? In: *Security, Trust, and Regulatory Aspects of Cloud Computing in Business Environments*, 57. IGI Global.

Ko, Ryan KL, Jagadpramana, Peter, Mowbray, Miranda et al. (2011). TrustCloud: A framework for accountability and trust in cloud computing. Paper presented at the 2011 IEEE World Congress on Services (SERVICES).

MacDonald, Neil. (2011). Yes, hypervisors are vulnerable. Gartner Blog.

Mather, T., Kumaraswamy, S., and Latif, S. (2009). *Cloud Security and Privacy: An Enterprise Perspective on Risks and Compliance.* O'Reilly Media, Inc.

Northcutt, S., Skoudis, E., Sachs, M. et al. (2008). *Top Ten Cyber Security Menaces for 2008.* SANS Institute: SANS Press Room.

Padhy, R.P., Patra, M.R., and Satapathy, S.C. (2011). X-as-a-Service: cloud computing with Google App Engine, Amazon Web Services, Microsoft Azure and Force.com. *International Journal of Computer Science and Telecommunications* 2 (9).

Ristenpart, Thomas, Tromer, Eran, Shacham, Hovav et al. (2009). Hey, you, get off of my cloud: exploring information leakage in third-party compute clouds. Paper presented at the 16th ACM conference on Computer and Communications Security.

Singh, T. (2015). Security in public cloud offerings: issues and a comparative study of Amazon Web Services and Microsoft Azure. *International journal of Science Technology & Management (IJSTM)* 6 (1).

Violino, B. (2010). *Five cloud security trends experts see for 2011.* CSO Security and Risk.

Xiao, Z. and Xiao, Y. (2013). Security and privacy in cloud computing. *IEEE Communications Surveys & Tutorials* 15 (2): 843–859.

Young, R. (2010). IBM X-force mid-year trend & risk report. IBM technical report.

3

Confidentiality of Data in the Cloud

Conflicts Between Security and Cost

Nathalie Baracaldo[1] *and Joseph Glider*[2]

[1] *IBM Almaden Research Center, San Jose, CA, USA*
[2] *SAP Labs, Palo Alto, CA, USA*

3.1 Introduction

Data confidentiality has been and remains a large concern for online and especially cloud-resident data. Information, once naturally protected by limited or no network connectivity outside of the information owner's domain, is now potentially vulnerable to theft or corruption resulting from any of a growing set of possible attacks. This chapter describes the trends of the last 20 years that have increased data-confidentiality concerns, technologies that have been used to address these concerns, conflicts between those technologies and the cost-reduction measures that cloud providers put in place, and some possible approaches to reconciling the confidentiality technologies with cost-reducing features.

Section 3.2 of this chapter presents some background on cloud storage systems and reasons data-confidentiality concerns have grown over the past 20 years. Then, Section 3.3 discusses concrete confidentiality issues and adversaries of cloud storage systems. Section 3.4 presents some common techniques used to protect confidentiality in current cloud storage systems, and Section 3.5 shows why these protection techniques often conflict with data-reduction methods, resulting in an increase of costs. Then, Sections 3.6 and 3.7 provide an overview and comparison of potential solutions and develop in more detail one such possible solution. Finally, Section 3.8 looks at future directions for cloud storage confidentiality.

3.2 Background

To understand the new confidentiality issues that arise when outsourcing data to cloud storage providers, we first overview the history of how they came to be. As recently as the year 2000, most access to data was physically restricted. Personal data was often on paper or perhaps on home computers that had limited access to public networks such as the Internet. Cellular phones contained no or very little personal data, perhaps

Security, Privacy, and Digital Forensics in the Cloud, First Edition. Edited by Lei Chen, Hassan Takabi, and Nhien-An Le-Khac.

limited to a set of phone numbers of contacts. Enterprise and government data was generally restricted to be accessed within the logical confines of the entity that owned the data, with only carefully controlled exceptions such as backups stored offsite, or information shared via private network connections with business or project partners.

In the early part of the 2000s, storage service providers (SSPs), offering storage capacity subscription services for enterprise, began to emerge. However, they ran into major obstacles balancing cost, performance, and security. For cost reasons, SSPs preferred to have multiple or many customers running on the same storage systems; but customers, for performance and security reasons, preferred to have their data isolated from others' in separate storage systems or different partitions within the same storage system. Ultimately, no satisfactory business model was found, and SSPs didn't find a successful path to profitability.

Some companies such as IBM and HP became managed storage providers (MSPs) for enterprise clients, managing storage located either in customer premises or sometimes in an MSP data center. The business model for this service was based on the MSP providing management and maintenance services less expensively than the client could,[1] and this storage services model has had success in the market. However, the basic premise of this service has been that the set of Internet technology (IT) equipment used by a client is entirely owned by the client, and therefore as long as networks connecting the MSP IT equipment and the client's IT equipment are kept secure, confidentiality and privacy of the client data is as assured as with an on-premises private data center.

Starting in the mid-to-late 2000s, a number of trends have dramatically changed the landscape of data privacy. The Internet became widely available and then almost ubiquitous. Mobility of data, with smartphones and tablets and more recently with many other types of electronic devices, has caused more and more personal data, some of it sensitive, to be network accessible. Most pronounced, the advent of cloud services—the new generation of application service providers (ASPs) and SSPs—has attracted a large amount of personal and business data such as cloud backups, music, and photo archives coming from mobile devices, peer-to-peer file sharing, e-mail, and social networks. Consumers and enterprise clients alike have found that cloud storage systems are a good choice for archiving and backups as well as primary storage. Cloud storage providers such as Amazon Web Services (AWS), Microsoft Azure, Dropbox, and Google Drive simplify data management for these tenants by offering an online service that abstracts and simplifies storage system configuration. Using these environments is especially beneficial for businesses that are looking to reduce their costs, want to deploy new applications rapidly, or do not want to maintain their own computational infrastructure.

In addition, the attraction of having data online and available to customers or the public has been quickly recognized by government organizations as well as businesses. As a result, a much larger volume of data kept by small and large organizations has increasingly become potentially exposed, and there has been an explosion of data breaches, as documented by yearly updates of the *Verizon Data Breach Investigation Report* (Verizon 2018), resulting in the exposure of confidential data (PCWorld 2010;

1 MSP providers achieve cost reductions by leveraging optimized processes and practices to manage more storage and more clients per administrator.

GigaOm 2012), temporary or permanent loss of availability (Metz 2009), or data corruption. There have been cases where client data was exposed to and leaked by cloud provider employees who had physical access to the storage medium, and also where cloud tenants gained access to other tenants' data after having been assigned physical storage resources previously assigned to another tenant (e.g. after that other tenant had canceled its cloud storage subscription).

While consumers might have been (and some or many still are) unwary about the issues associated with exposing their private data, enterprises and government organizations have generally been more aware and more cautious about allowing their data to be cloud resident, rightly worrying that they might lose control of the privacy of their data when they trust it to be stored in the Cloud. Personal health-related data is one such class of data. Healthcare organizations have increasingly made patients' healthcare records available online, and patients find great value in being able to access their own records; but keeping that data private has been a major concern, leading to government regulations such as the Health Insurance Portability and Accountability Act (HIPAA). Regulations in other industries, including the Gramm-Leach-Bliley Act (GLBA), the Payment Card Industry Data Security Standard (PCI DSS), and the European Union's General Data Protection Regulation (GDPR) have had a large impact on how that data is stored.

Given the continuing pattern of security incidents and breaches, some organizations have tended to use cloud computing infrastructure only for data and projects that are considered nonsensitive (Chow et al. 2009, pp. 85–90). Security of data stored in cloud storage systems needs to be improved, to reduce reluctance and thereby increase cloud storage adoption. Therefore, one of the largest concerns of cloud storage providers is finding a way to assure potential clients that their data will, under the care of the cloud provider, be accessible only to entities authorized by the client.

Improving the privacy of data in cloud storage environments often comes at higher cost. For instance, the capacity of cloud providers to achieve economies of scale often comes from sharing infrastructure among multiple tenants. To completely avoid threats related to multitenancy, special security provisions need to be in place. In the extreme case, the infrastructure is not shared (e.g. private cloud), while in other cases cloud data centers are strictly divided by tenant or data is encrypted by the tenant. In all these cases, the need for confidentiality increases the cost for both tenants and cloud providers. Costs may also increase because cloud administrators are required by tenants to perform all types of maintenance tasks, such as backing up data, yet they are not fully trusted and therefore must not be able to access the data in plaintext.

Clearly, there is a tension between providing better privacy and maintaining reasonable cost levels. Achieving low cost is a primary requirement for cloud storage systems: cloud providers' ability to compete and even their survival depends on being able to offer storage services at the lowest cost. There have been several price wars in the years since cloud storage started to gain traction, and cost will continue to be a primary consideration for customers.

Although maintaining privacy while managing costs is not an easy task, we believe that it is possible to find a way to achieve both. We highlight the challenges related to reconciling confidentiality and cost caused by outsourcing data storage to the Cloud, and study in detail the challenges and possible solutions for using data-reduction techniques such as compression and deduplication (a technique where multiple files contain some or all of the same content, to store only one copy of the duplicate content) to reduce the amount of required disk capacity, while maintaining confidentiality of data encrypted by tenants.

3.3 Confidentiality: Threats and Adversaries

Data confidentiality is one of the primary security requirements for cloud storage systems. From the time customers first store their data and even past the time they stop using the cloud provider, customers want assurances that other tenants, cloud provider administrators, and Internet users at large will not have unauthorized access to their data:

- **Confidentiality goals**—Tenants require that data stored in the Cloud should be accessible only by authorized entities (the data owner and delegates), both *at rest*, when data is stored in persistent media, and *in flight*, when it is transmitted to/from the cloud provider's storage system. Additionally, once a tenant decides to cancel its subscription to a storage provider (called *tenant offboarding)*, its information should remain inaccessible. We call this property *secure offboarding*. Finally, tenants also require that data deleted upon tenant request should not be accessible by any entity.
  Adversaries—Providing confidentiality is not an easy task in cloud storage systems. In this environment, multiple adversaries may try to gain unauthorized access to data stored in a cloud provider infrastructure. These include *curious cloud administrators, malicious tenants, law enforcement,* and *external adversaries* that can monitor, probe, and try to infiltrate the system:
  - *Curious cloud administrators* are particularly dangerous because they have legitimate access to software and physical infrastructure of the system to troubleshoot and maintain the infrastructure. However, they are not trusted to read confidential information stored by tenants. Curious cloud administrators may use their privileges to obtain access to confidential information. Additionally, *physical access* to the storage media may allow them to circumvent all the software-based access-control mechanisms and directly access tenant data written to disk.
  - In multitenant cloud storage environments, *malicious tenants* may be present. These adversaries try to obtain data from other tenants, taking advantage of their legitimate remote access to storage media. They may try to poke the system to retrieve data from their currently assigned disk space, hoping the physical space was previously assigned to other tenants and still contains private information.
  - For some tenants, one risk of storing information is the possibility of *law enforcement* examining their stored data. This adversary is personified by law enforcement agencies that require the use of court orders to gain access to the content of all storage servers, media, key repositories, and other components of the cloud storage system. Some cloud tenants may consider them adversaries that may try to retrieve confidential data and metadata stored in the cloud environment that may reveal confidential information and private usage patterns.
  - *External adversaries* have no legitimate access to the system and may try to remotely compromise it. These adversaries try to escalate their privileges to gain access to confidential information or compromise the integrity or availability of the storage system.

All these adversaries may try to compromise the confidentiality of data belonging to tenants. In the following section, we present existing mechanisms to prevent leakage of confidential information.

3.4 Achieving Data Confidentiality in Cloud Storage Systems

Tenant offboarding and disk-space reassignment open windows of opportunity to compromise the confidentiality of tenants by curious cloud administrators, malicious tenants, and law enforcement, especially if the cloud provider does not follow appropriate procedures. Securely erasing data from a storage system minimizes this opportunity but relies on the capabilities and cooperation of the cloud provider. It is not enough to remove the pointers to the occupied space and mark it as free for usage, as is the general practice for most file systems; if this is the only procedure followed, the next user given access to the space, with sufficient technical skills, may be able to see the data written by the previous user of the physical space.

Instead, cloud providers today can use an expensive (in time required and use of system resources) process that physically overwrites, one or multiple times, the sectors holding the data (Joukov et al. 2006, pp. 61–66; Wei et al. 2011). However, not only is this type of procedure expensive, but it also may be difficult or impossible for the cloud provider to physically erase the data. For example, certain types of storage devices such as solid state disk (SSD) cause writes to the same logical space to actually write the new blocks to new physical space and free for reuse the physical space where the previous version of the data was stored, defeating the efforts of the cloud provider to ensure that data is truly erased. Furthermore, placing special controls in SSD to ensure that previously stored data is immediately physically erased would be prohibitive in terms of system lifetime: the SSD would wear out enormously faster, because Flash devices can only endure a certain number of write cycles. Any log-structured storage system, where data written to the same logical location is never written directly over the old data in the logical location (e.g. ZFS [zfs 2018], BTRFS [btr 2018]) will have similar concerns.

Because secure erasure by a cloud provider is costly in time and resources and in some cases practically impossible, cryptographic approaches are preferred.

3.4.1 Cryptographic Solutions

Encrypting data is becoming a popular approach for tenants that want to use cloud storage infrastructure without compromising the confidentiality or privacy of their data and to avoid possible jurisdiction problems (Microsoft 2017). There are two approaches: *stage encryption* and *end-to-end encryption.*

3.4.1.1 Stage Encryption

Multiple systems opt for encrypting data before sending it to the Cloud using transport encryption (e.g. Transport Layer Security [TLS]), to achieve in-flight confidentiality and delegate the responsibility of data-at rest encryption (a.k.a. server-side encryption) to the cloud provider. These schemes are easy to implement because popular protocols like Secure Sockets Layer (SSL) and TLS can be used to protect data during its transmission. Once the encrypted data arrives at the cloud provider, it is decrypted; it is again encrypted before storing it to disk. This latter encryption may be performed by self-encrypting drives or by performing encryption at higher virtual data object levels such as by volume, directory, or file. In this way, if an adversary gains access to the physical storage medium, they cannot obtain any information. Examples of cloud storage systems that use this type of methodology are IBM Cloud Object Storage (Cleversafe 2018) and HGST Active Archive System (Amplidata 2018), which can receive transport-encrypted data and in turn store objects encrypted.

This scheme is useful when a component in the cloud provider infrastructure needs to access plaintext data sent by a tenant (e.g. for antivirus checking). In addition, stage encryption thwarts malicious tenants that have been reassigned disk space previously used by a targeted tenant. However, this method is not capable of stopping attackers such as curious cloud administrators and law-enforcement adversaries that can gain access to the data while it is in plaintext or possibly gain access to the keys with which the data at rest was encrypted. Additionally, because cloud providers may have access to the encryption keys used to store the data, the process of offboarding does not guarantee that a tenant's data is no longer available. As long as the provider has the keys, data may still be accessible to both curious cloud administrators and law-enforcement adversaries. Finally, tenants need to accept the encryption mechanisms of the cloud storage systems, which may not be as secure as needed. For example, in 2011, Dropbox was accused of using a single encryption key to encrypt all files in the system. This effectively meant that all registered users were sharing the same encryption key to encrypt their information, resulting in a large risk related to an attacker gaining access to the single key.

3.4.1.2 End-to-End Encryption

This scheme is often used today by tenants storing data that is required to be handled so as to meet privacy and confidentiality compliance regulations, to ensure not only that data is kept confidential, but also that keys are properly controlled and auditable. To achieve this objective, the tenants themselves must be able to control and safeguard encryption keys for the data at all times.

For this purpose, data is encrypted before it is sent to the cloud storage provider, achieving both in-flight and at-rest confidentiality. The advantage of this scheme is that no cooperation from the cloud provider is required. Provided that data is encrypted with a semantically secure cryptosystem and that each tenant is the only entity with access to its encryption keys, neither malicious tenants, curious administrators, nor law enforcement adversaries (unless the law-enforcement adversary gains access to the client's keys) can compromise the confidentiality of the information stored in the Cloud. This is true because all data stored in the Cloud is encrypted, and the only way to obtain its plaintext is by gaining access to the encryption keys that are in possession of the tenant. Furthermore, this mechanism ensures a smooth offboarding process, because only data encrypted with tenant keys is left with the cloud provider.

Additionally, end-to-end encryption allows key management to be easier and more effective for tenants. To remove all traces of information from storage media even in the presence of law-enforcement court orders to obtain cryptographic key material, tenants that use end-to-end encryption can securely erase their target keys whenever they want, to securely erase information. In contrast, when stage encryption is used, tenants often cannot control when encryption keys are deleted. An interested reader may refer to (Boneh and Lipton 1996, pp. 91–96; Di Crescenzo et al. 1999, pp. 500–509; Perlman 2005; Mitra and Winslett 2006, pp. 67–72; Tang et al. 2010; Cachin et al. 2013) where multiple cryptographic key management schemes to achieve secure data deletion are presented.

Tenants' business requirements may also result in the use of multiple encryption keys and end-to-end encryption facilitates this type of management. It is often the case for tenants to have multiple users that do not necessarily trust each other. For instance, a CEO may not want to share information with all employees of her company. This requires use of multiple keys to encrypt data according to tenants' business requirements, ensuring that only authorized users can obtain data in plaintext. Stage encryption limits tenants' ability to control isolation of their data. For example, it can be limiting for Amazon server-side encryption tenants to assign an encryption key per container to achieve isolation between different users. In comparison, end-to-end encryption allows users to assign encryption keys flexibly to fit whatever access control policy is required, like the ones presented in (Sahai and Waters 2005; Goyal et al. 2006, pp. 89–98; Bethencourt et al. 2007).

Unfortunately, end-to-end encryption introduces several drawbacks and costs. Tenants need to maintain servers and software infrastructure to assign, protect, and maintain encryption keys. This means tenants need to be in charge of maintaining a key repository, making sure it runs in a nonvulnerable server, and ensuring that uniquely authorized users can access it. Additionally, tenants need to ensure that their key repository can scale and does not limit the throughput of the system. To achieve these objectives, a skilled security administrator needs to be hired, and servers need to be provisioned, which clearly increases tenants' costs. End-to-end encryption also inhibits the cloud provider from performing any useful computation over the data. For example, searching for a particular record in a dataset cannot be performed by the cloud provider, nor can analytics be run, nor can algorithms such as compression be employed to decrease subscription costs by reducing the amount of space required to store the data. To alleviate these problems, a few research efforts are being conducted: to perform searchable encryption (Boneh et al. 2004, pp. 506–522) and to improve the efficiency of homomorphic encryption, which is a methodology that allows computation of certain operations over encrypted data without revealing the encryption keys to untrusted parties (Gentry 2009). Unfortunately, these methods are currently too slow to be used in real-world scenarios.

End-to-end encryption is a popular choice to protect data confidentiality because it does not require the cooperation of cloud providers. In the following section, we overview the impact of using this technique on the amount of storage capacity required and later present how cloud storage systems can recapture the cost savings.

3.5 Reducing Cloud Storage System Costs through Data-Reduction Techniques

Cloud storage providers offer a variety of storage services to their clients to allow for different levels of performance (e.g. solid-state drive [SSD] vs. hard disk drive [HDD]); provide reliability (e.g. across availability zones or regions, different levels of Redundant Array of Independent Disks [RAID] or erasure code); and offer different ways of accessing the data, such as object protocol (Amazon S3), file protocol (e.g. Google Drive), and block protocol (e.g. Amazon Elastic Block Store [EBS]). Cloud storage tenants can choose among these options to match the level and type of service required for their applications.

Regardless of the differences between the many types of storage and storage services deployed in the Cloud, their cloud presence implies a common set of requirements and concerns.

To lower costs, storage systems are increasingly including data-reduction capabilities in order to decrease as much as possible the amount of storage capacity needed to store tenants' data (EMC 2018; IBM 2018a). Using these techniques often leads to a reduction of 20–70% of disk-capacity utilization (Constantinescu et al. 2011, pp. 393–402) and lowers costs due not only to less capital costs but also to less operating costs related to data-center real estate, power consumption, and cooling (Russell 2010).

Tenants are also increasingly using encryption as a primary tool to build confidentiality assurance. Data is more and more being encrypted within customer premises (and keys are likewise being stored in customer premises) before being uploaded to cloud storage. In another use case, customers with compute and storage at a cloud provider may encrypt the data in the virtual machine (VM) or application server at the cloud provider before storing the data (e.g. Cryptfs [Zadok et al. 1998], IBM Spectrum Scale [IBM 2018b]). In either case, the tenant is assured that the data is only seen in plaintext in the tenant's server or virtual machine, and further that the tenant controls the keys to the data, such that the data will be unreadable if the physical medium is stolen or allocated to another tenant during or after the time the tenant is an active user of the cloud provider.

Unfortunately, data-reduction techniques lose some or all of their effectiveness when operating on encrypted data. Impacted techniques include *thin provisioning, zero-elimination, compression*, and *deduplication.*

Thin provisioning refers to the ability of a storage system to store only the actual data that is written. As an example, this technique is used by file systems to implement *sparse files*: an extremely large file is allocated but only small sections of it are written, in which case the storage system allocates only a small amount of space. In this case, a problem emerges when an application attempts to read from an area of a sparse file that wasn't written. The expected storage system response is to return zeroes; however, when data is encrypted, the storage system cannot return the encrypted version of zeroes. It doesn't know the data is encrypted, and even if it did, it would have no knowledge of encryption keys and other information needed to encrypt and subsequently return encrypted zeroes. This results in difficulties leveraging thin provisioning.

Likewise, many storage systems have the ability to detect large runs of written zeroes or other fill characters and choose to store them in a way that dramatically reduces the capacity needed. However, encrypted fill patterns are not detectable as a fill pattern, and therefore the storage system cannot optimize the capacity needed to store the data blocks containing fill pattern.

Compression is another technology that is impacted. Compression is effective on patterns discovered in streams of data, but encrypted data has very high entropy and therefore compression is not able to effectively reduce capacity required to store the data.

Finally, deduplication is not effective when applied over encrypted data. The term *deduplication* refers to the capability of detecting the same or similar content (often blocks of 4 KB or more) and storing only the one copy and perhaps differences relative to that copy. However, semantically secure encryption ensures that encrypting the same data multiple times result in a different ciphertext (initialization vectors are used to ensure that the same plaintext results in different ciphertexts to avoid inference attacks). Therefore, storage systems cannot determine that the same information is being stored.

3.6 Reconciling Data Reduction and Confidentiality

We now present several existing methods to allow end-to-end encryption to be employed while preserving the benefits achieved from data reduction. All of them have inherent trade-offs. We classify them in two main categories depending on where data-reduction techniques are performed.

There are two ways to arrange a data storage stack such that data can be encrypted close to the source while also being stored encrypted with tenant-controlled keys, in a compressed and deduplicated form. The first method (called client data reduction [CDR]) is to compress and deduplicate the data before the data is encrypted at the tenant side in the application server. The second approach is to encrypt data in the application server and leverage *trusted execution technology* downstream in the cloud storage to apply compression and deduplication without leaking confidential data. We call this second approach Trusted Decrypter (TD).

Both of these solutions are potentially applicable, but they have trade-offs at three levels: *hardware resource* and *performance*, *application storage software*, and *security*.

At the hardware resource level, the CPU cycles and memory to perform deduplication and compression using CDR may be costly, especially as many servers would need to be provisioned to accommodate the extra resource requirement. On the other hand, a shared resource such as a TD-enabled storage system can be a more efficient place to provision the hardware resources needed to perform compression and deduplication, as long as latency and throughput concerns are addressed and the resulting storage system is still cost-effective.

At the application software level, supporting CDR compression and deduplication in many environments requires extra software being installed, configured, and maintained across many servers to enable storage-efficiency functions to be applied before data is encrypted. In addition, many tenants would find it difficult to understand how to make purchasing and provisioning decisions about CDR-enabled application servers to accommodate the heavy resource requirements of data-reduction functions. Having instead a shared embedded compression/deduplication function available in a TD-enabled storage system can provide benefit by taking away the administration burden from the cloud provider.

Concerning security, providing upstream data-reduction functions in CDR-enabled application servers ensures that the security provided by encryption in the application server is intact. In contrast, the TD downstream decryption has the potential to introduce security exposures that limit the use cases for such a method. We note, however, that there are side-channel attacks (described later) that can be exploited in CDR-enabled systems that cannot operate in TD-enabled systems.

Because of these trade-offs, neither method is the single preferred option, and a choice of solution will be made based on specifics about operations within individual cloud providers and the service levels they want to provide. In the following section, we overview existing techniques in each area and contrast their security.

3.6.1 Existing Techniques

Compression and deduplication are two of the most popular techniques used to reduce the amount of data stored in a system (Constantinescu et al. 2011, pp. 393–402). Each of these operations has a different level of security challenges. Compression algorithms typically do not require data sharing, and it is possible to achieve good compression ratios by using file-based compression. In contrast, deduplication may use information already stored in the system, which results in an implicit sharing of data among entities storing their information in the same deduplication-enabled system. For this reason, deduplication results in more security concerns than compression.

From the security perspective, performing deduplication at the client side creates problems. In particular, adversaries authorized to send write requests to the storage system may compromise the confidentiality of other tenants by using the deduplication system as an oracle to determine whether a particular piece of data is already stored in the system and later gain illegitimate access to previously stored data (Harnik et al. 2010). To perform this attack, the adversary sends a claim to the storage system stating that they want to store a file or block with a given hash value. In client-side deduplication, when the hash matches an already-stored block or file, the data is never sent to the storage server. The deduplication system receives a hash claim and proceeds to add the adversary as an entity accessing the deduplicated data. Later, the adversary can request the deduplicated data. Therefore, by claiming ownership of the file, an adversary can obtain access to previously stored data that matches a claimed hash value.

Using the deduplication system as an oracle may have negative and tangible consequences in real cloud storage systems. Dropbox uses a file-based deduplication system that stores a file only if it has not been previously stored by any other user in the system. In this scenario, by claiming a hash value, an adversary may be able to obtain access to previously stored information, which clearly violates the confidentiality of other users storing files in the system.

To avoid this pitfall, Halevi et al. proposed a methodology called *proofs of ownership* (PoWs) (Halevi et al. 2011, pp. 491–500) to efficiently determine whether a user has a particular piece of data without having the user send a complete copy of the data to the server. In this approach, the user claims to have a file and sends its hash. Then, the deduplication system challenges the user to verify that it has the file the user claims to have. Different approaches to solve this challenge have been proposed in the literature (Halevi et al. 2011, pp. 491–500; Di Pietro and Sorniotti 2013). In general, the client needs to compute multiple hash values of subcontents of the claimed data. An adversary that does not have the claimed data cannot answer the challenge correctly, and hence the attack is thwarted.

By using proofs of ownership, tenants can have some assurance that the deduplication table can't be used as an oracle to leak their stored information. However, this scheme still leaks some information about the data stored. It has been shown that monitoring the amount of bandwidth required to upload data to a cloud storage server can be used to detect whether the data being uploaded was previously stored. This side-channel attack arises because when deduplication is possible, the data is not transmitted, whereas when the write request is the first to store a piece of data, all data needs to be transmitted, thus increasing the time it takes to complete the operation.

Other solutions use convergent encryption to perform deduplication (Bellare et al. 2012). Convergent encryption is currently used by multiple cloud storage services such as Freenet (Project 2018), among others. Convergent encryption is a cryptographic primitive in which any entity encrypting the same data will use the output of a deterministic function of the plaintext as the key. In this way, identical plaintext values will encrypt to identical ciphertexts, regardless of who encrypts them. Convergent encryption offers a weaker notion of security for encrypted data than the one provided by conventional symmetric cryptosystems (Bellare et al. 2012). In particular, it is susceptible to offline brute-force dictionary attacks, and it is not secure unless encrypted data is unpredictable in nature. Because common data has predictable patterns, like headers, convergent encryption is not ideal to ensure protection against leakage of confidential data. To mitigate such leakage problems, multiple variations to pure convergent-based deduplication have been proposed.

A methodology that uses convergent encryption and a threshold cryptosystem was presented in (Stanek et al. 2013). Popular data is assumed not to be confidential, and uncommon data confidential. When data is popular, it is only encrypted using convergent encryption, whereas unpopular data is additionally encrypted with threshold encryption. Once unpopular data becomes popular, the outer encryption layer is removed. This approach is not appropriate when popular data is confidential. A scheme to perform deduplication at the client side was presented in (Rashid et al. 2012, pp. 81–87), where deduplication units are encrypted before being sent to the cloud provider for storage. This work assumes that the deduplication information is stored in the client side and that all data in an organization is encrypted with the same key. This is not appropriate, because it would result in all the individuals in an organization having access to all information in the tenant side, violating the least-privilege principle; compromise of the encryption key would result in the leakage of all stored information.

DupLESS (Bellare et al. 2013) is another scheme related to convergent encryption that makes use of an external key server (KS) to help generate keys in combination with convergent encryption, as opposed to using the hashes of the deduplicated data as keys. Each tenant is assigned a secret. Similarly, the KS holds its own secret. When a tenant needs to store data, it contacts the KS to generate the key for uploading the data. An oblivious pseudo-random function (PRF) protocol (Naor and Reingold 2004, pp. 231–262) is used between the KS and tenants. This protocol ensures that the KS can cryptographically mix both secrets to compute the deduplication key without learning anything about the data tenants want to upload or the generated keys, while tenants learn nothing about the KS's secret. As long as the KS is not compromised, DupLESS provides more security than standard convergent-based deduplication systems. When the KS is compromised, DupLESS is equivalent to standard convergent-based deduplication systems. One drawback of this scheme is that it requires a trusted third party to maintain the keys, which increases the cost. Additionally, the KS's secret is identical for all tenants, which is subject to collusion attacks of the KS and other tenants. To alleviate this problem, a similar approach that uses multiple trusted parties to compute the key was presented in (Duan 2013). This system relies on peer-to-peer (P2P) networks to maintain a shared secret. Thus, to obtain the shared secret, at least a threshold number of collaborators must be compromised. One problem with this approach is that it is not clear what the incentives are for P2P nodes to provide this service, for them to act honestly, and for tenants to trust them.

One of the few efforts concerning data compression uses a methodology based on distributed source-coding theory to perform compression over encrypted data (Johnson et al. 2004, pp. 2992–3006). Unfortunately, this method is only efficient for encrypted data in the case of an ideal Gaussian source. The compression rate is reduced for more general and common data distributions such as those encountered in cloud computing scenarios. Additionally, this approach does not support deduplication and has not been widely studied to determine its security properties. Similarly, at the time of writing of this book, an algorithm to combine compression and encryption was presented in (Kelley and Tamassia 2014). However, this methodology is in its infancy and still needs to be studied by the security community before it can be widely trusted and adopted.

The Trusted Decrypter framework provides data-reduction capabilities downstream of where data is encrypted. The framework consists of a small trusted module and several secure data-reduction algorithms that leverage trusted execution technology to provide confidentiality guarantees to tenants. The framework provides for data confidentiality by encrypting data close to the source with a key uniquely owned and controlled by the tenant, ensuring that none of the tenant's data is accessible to the cloud provider and that secure offboarding from the cloud provider is easy and effective. Additionally, the framework generally requires no changes in the tenant's applications and minimum changes in the component encrypting tenant data, making it easier to integrate into current systems. For these reasons, in the following sections, a Trusted Decrypter architecture is presented and evaluated.

3.7 Trusted Decrypter

This section explores aTrusted Decrypter architecture. We present an overview of the architecture, a detailed description with an emphasis on security, and the results of some experiments showing the overheads and performances.

3.7.1 Overview

Driven by the requirement of enabling data reduction on encrypted data, maintaining an acceptable level of confidentiality through the lifetime of the data, and reducing as much as possible management overhead for tenants, in this section we present the Trusted Decrypter (TD) architecture originally published in (Baracaldo et al. 2014, pp. 21–32). This architecture was designed for tenants that require their data to be encrypted prior to its upload to the cloud storage provider. It provides confidentiality while the data is transmitted from the client to the cloud provider, when the data is stored in the cloud provider, and after the data is erased from the cloud provider. Additionally, the architecture allows secure offboarding, ensuring that reallocation of storage space from one user (tenant) to the other does not reveal any confidential information.

An overview of the TD framework is presented in Figure 3.1. The tenant side portrays the standard components of an IT system that uses an outsourced storage system, while the cloud storage provider offers a shared storage service. All messages exchanged between the system entities are exchanged over secure channels that provide perfect forward secrecy.

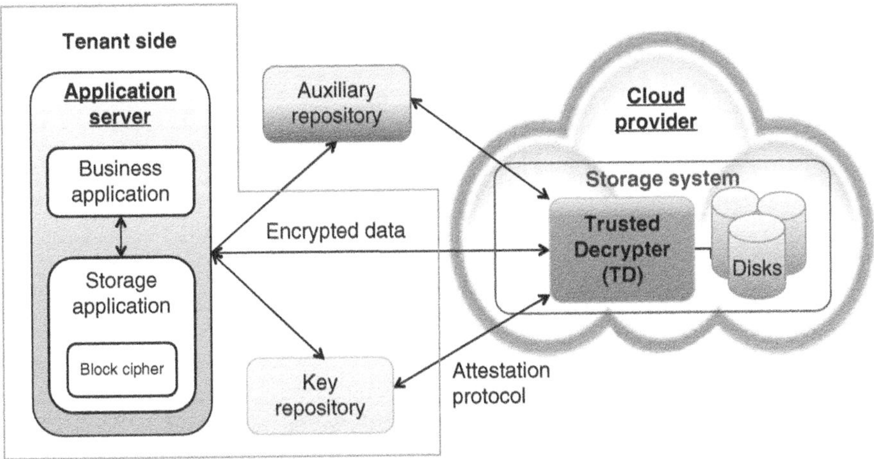

Figure 3.1 Overview of the Trusted Decrypter framework. On the tenant's side, as is typically the case, a *business application* such as a word processor generates data that is encrypted by a *storage application*. Additionally, each tenant manages its own *key repository*. The *auxiliary repository* can be hosted by the tenant or by the cloud provider. On the *cloud provider* side, all data-reduction operations are performed, and the stored data is stored to disk.

The tenant side consists of the following components: a *business application* (BA) that generates and processes data; the BA uses the services of a *storage application* (SA) to commit data to persistent storage and a key repository (KeyRep) that maintains the master keys used during encryption. The SA in turn uses the storage services offered by the storage system of the cloud provider to store data. To comply with the tenant's security requirements, the SA encrypts data prior to outsourcing it. Tenants may encrypt their data using one or more keys, which is a relevant requirement especially given tenants that consist of one or more *users* (e.g. the employees of a company) and require each user to be assigned their own master encryption key. The TD also includes an *auxiliary repository* (AuxRep) used to maintain encryption metadata for each block of uploaded data; this metadata is referred as *auxiliary information* and can be hosted by the tenant or by the cloud provider. Thus, every time the SA encrypts data, it updates the AuxRep with the corresponding auxiliary information. The encryption support is provided either natively by the hypervisor or by software running inside the VM or client machine.

The cloud storage provider consists of the *Trusted Decrypter* (TD) and the *storage media* (e.g. disks, tapes) used to store data. Storage requests sent by clients are received and processed by the TD. Depending on the type of request, the TD performs the appropriate data-reduction operations: for write requests, the TD decrypts the received data using the tenant key, compresses it, deduplicates it, re-encrypts it with the tenant key, and sends it to persistent storage. For read requests, the TD retrieves the compressed and/or deduplicated data from disk, decrypts it, decompresses it, inverts the deduplication process, re-encrypts it using the original context and keys, and sends the result back to the requesting user. The user is not aware of this process, because it receives the data exactly as it was originally written. Throughout its operation, the TD contacts both the AuxRep and KeyRep to fetch the appropriate information to decrypt and re-encrypt data according to the received requests.

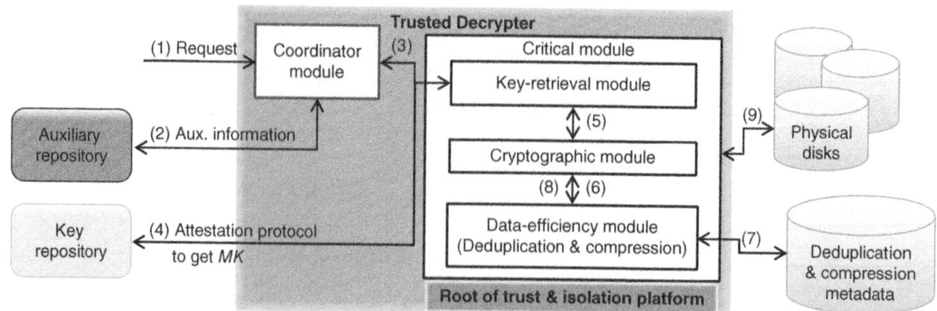

Figure 3.2 Detailed design of the *Trusted Decrypter*.

As shown in Figure 3.2, the TD consists of a *critical module* (CritMod) and a *coordinator module* (CoMod). The first module is in charge of all security-sensitive tasks, whereas the second performs all those that are not. For this reason, the critical module is secured with the aid of the *root of trust and isolation platform*. The root of trust and isolation platform is used to allow the TD to attest to remote third parties the integrity of the platform and to restrict untrusted processes from accessing confidential information while it is in memory. Special security provisions and implementations are discussed in Sections 3.7.3 and 3.7.4, respectively. As long as these provisions are in place, the TD can be trusted by tenants.

The CritMod has several subcomponents: the *key-retrieval module*, the *cryptographic module*, and the *data-efficiency module*. The key-retrieval module, through an attestation protocol, retrieves the key specified in the auxiliary information from the KeyRep. Upon the successful outcome of the attestation process, the key is retrieved and is used by the cryptographic module. The KeyRep is trusted to uniquely provide cryptographic keys to a trusted TD. The CritMod is always responsible for decrypting data coming into the TD and re-encrypting data leaving the TD, and the data-efficiency module is responsible for efficiency-related data-stream transformations according to whether data is being read or written. The AuxRep can be hosted by either the cloud provider or the tenant, because the information it maintains (initialization vectors and type of encryption algorithm used) is by definition public.

3.7.2 Secure Data-Reduction Operations

Although having a trusted component is necessary, and its design is challenging in itself, it does not solve all the security problems. In fact, when multiple entities in the system use different keys, as is the case with corporate environments, performing deduplication and storing data in a way that maintains its confidentiality is a challenging task.

First, we present an overview of the cryptographic schemes used by tenants and data-reduction methodologies used by the cloud storage provider. Then, we present the details of the secure data-reduction operations performed by the TD.

3.7.2.1 Preliminaries

We begin by looking at *data encryption performed in the tenant*. The SA uses a symmetric cryptosystem. For simplicity of description, in the following, the explicit mention of the initialization vector (IV) is omitted and simply denoted by $\{m\}_K$: the encryption of message m with key K. In addition, the terms *wrap* and *unwrap* are used to refer to encryption and decryption of keys (as opposed to data blocks). The SA encrypts individual blocks of fixed size.

The SA encrypts data using hierarchically organized keys. The hierarchy can be modeled with two-level trees: at the root of the hierarchy of keys, users have their own *master* encryption keys (MK): these keys belong to and are used by a particular user of a tenant, and each key is stored and managed by the KeyRep of the owning user. Master keys are only used to wrap (a set of) leaf keys. The keys that are directly used to encrypt user data represent the set of leaves of the tree. Leaf keys are stored (in wrapped form) together with the metadata about the data they encrypt, on persistent storage. The number of such leaf keys and the amount of data they encrypt can vary from system to system, ranging from one leaf key per sector through one per volume to a single leaf key for all volumes. There is a one-to-many mapping of leaf keys to sectors, and the concept of *file* is used to identify sets of sectors encrypted with the same leaf key. A *file-encryption key* (FK) is the leaf key used to encrypt the sectors of the file. The FK is *wrapped* with the MK of the owner of the file ($\{FK\}_{MK}$). This wrapped FK is stored as part of the metadata of the encrypted file.

This encryption approach, called *indirect encryption*, has multiple benefits in key management. The lifetime of MKs increases because they are used only to encrypt FKs as opposed to encrypting multiple potentially long files in their totality (NIST 2012). Additionally, when a MK is replaced (rekeying process), it is only necessary to rewrap FKs rather than re-encrypt all data. Finally, if a FK is compromised, the attacker will only have access to that file, whereas not using indirect encryption would result in the compromise of all files encrypted with the same MK.

For each encrypted block, the SA stores an auxiliary information entry $I = \langle LBA, ID_{MK}, \{FK\}_{MK}, algInfo \rangle$ in the AuxRep, where: *LBA* is the lookup key for each entry and represents the address of the encrypted page, ID_{MK} is the identifier of the master encryption key *MK* of the tenant-user that issues the request, *FK* is the ephemeral key used to encrypt all sectors in the page, and *algInfo* contains information related to the encryption algorithm and mode of operation.

Now we consider *data-reduction techniques used by the Cloud Storage Provider*. The following discussion is centered on fixed-size deduplication in the cloud storage provider side because of its suitability to primary storage systems; however, the concepts presented here can be easily extended to variable-size or file-based deduplication. In fixed-size deduplication, a fixed amount of input data, called a *chunk*, is processed in such a way as to ensure that no duplicate chunks are stored (Quinlan and Dorward 2002). For each chunk, a digest is computed and stored in a *deduplication table* (DedupTB) together with the physical block address (PBA) where data is stored. In Section 3.7.4, we discuss the trade-offs of sharing deduplication tables among different tenants (cross-tenant deduplication) as opposed to having a separate deduplication table for each tenant. Both compression and deduplication require an *indirection table* (IndTB), which maps logical block addresses (LBAs) into PBAs. This table is typically used by storage systems to keep track of the place where a given a data identifier is physically stored.

3.7.2.2 Detailed Secure Data-Reduction Operations

We now show how the TD handles *read, write, deletion, offboarding,* and *rekeying* requests. Designing these operations is challenging, due to the conflicting requirements: on the one hand, encryption protects user data from being accessed by any other entity; on the other, deduplication intrinsically requires sharing the content of common blocks. Additionally, every deletion operation must ensure that its requester is no longer able to retrieve the content, whereas the same content must still be accessible by other users that share it as a result of deduplication.

The descriptions that follow are simplified to focus on the most fundamental aspects of how data is transformed on its way to the disk, ignoring details such as placement on disk, I/O to multiple volumes, and length of I/O requests. A real implementation will need to consider many such details, which are presented in (Baracaldo et al. 2014, pp. 21–32). In the following, we present the general concepts.

3.7.2.3 Write Requests

Write requests are initiated by the storage application sending a (write) request identifier together with an input data buffer and LBA to the coordinator module. The latter retrieves the auxiliary information indexed by the LBA and is then able to sort the request based on the ID_{MK} specified in the auxiliary information entry. As shown in Figure 3.3a, grouping by ID_{MK} allows the system to speed up data-reduction operations since the MK of each user needs to be fetched only once, even for large amounts of data. The request buffer is then sliced into chunks.

Once a full input chunk—whose FK is wrapped by the same MK—is gathered, the following steps are followed, as shown in Figure 3.3b. First, the MK is retrieved, chunks are decrypted, and the plaintext is hashed. The digest is used as a lookup key to verify whether the chunk is unique or a duplicate. When the chunk cannot be deduplicated, the compression algorithm is invoked, generating the compressed plaintext. The

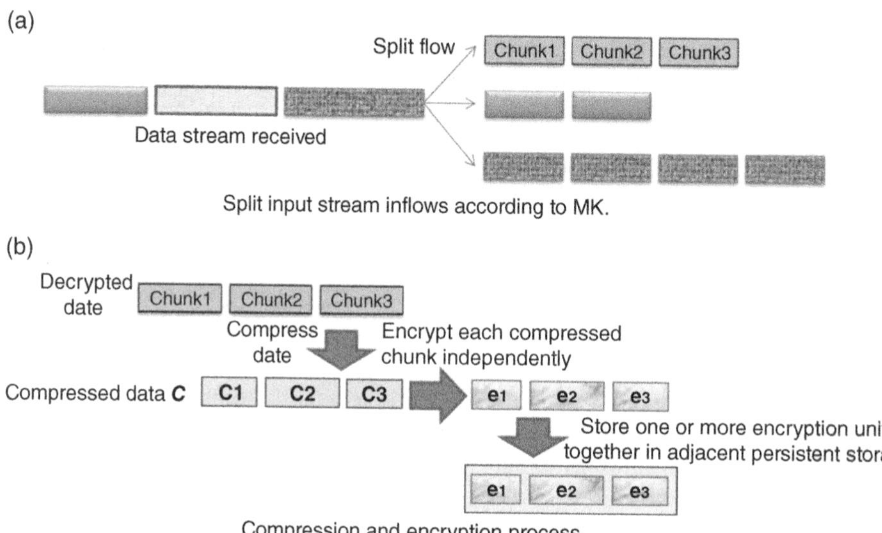

Figure 3.3 Processing a *write* request. In Figure 3.3a, the data stream is received and split according to its MK. Then, in Figure 3.3b, the data is decrypted. When chunks cannot be deduplicated, they are compressed and then each chunk is independently encrypted with its own randomly generated K_{aux}. Finally, one or more encryption units are stored together in adjacent persistent storage. (a) Split input stream inflows, according to MK. (b) Compression and encryption process.

compressed chunk is encrypted with a freshly generated auxiliary key K_{aux}, resulting in an *encryption unit.* Before acknowledging the write operation, the TD updates both indirection and deduplication tables. For every encryption unit, an entry in the indirection table is created, indexed by the original LBA. The new entry contains: (i) the PBA of the chunk in persistent storage; (ii) the auxiliary key used to encrypt the unit in its wrapped form ($\{K_{aux}\}_{MK}$); and (iii) the identifier of the master key ID_{MK} used in the wrapping process. Finally, the deduplication table is updated.

When a chunk can be deduplicated, a lookup in the deduplication table returns LBA^*, which is the location where the original chunk was written to. The TD then consults the indirection table entry indexed by LBA^*. This lookup returns the address (PBA^*) for that unit, the wrapped auxiliary key ($\{K^*_{aux}\}_{MK^*}$), and the identifier of the master key used in the wrapping (ID_{MK^*}). The CritMod contacts the KeyRep to obtain MK^*, and uses it to obtain the plaintext version of the auxiliary key K^*_{aux}. The latter is then rewrapped with the master key specified in the auxiliary information entry associated with the current write request (ID_{MK}) to produce a new wrapped version of the auxiliary key $\{K^*_{aux}\}_{MK}$. Finally, a new entry in the indirection table is created, indexed by the LBA of the current request, containing the PBA of the original copy of the chunk (PBA^*) and the new wrapped version of the auxiliary key ($\{K^*_{aux}\}_{MK}$) and the identifier of the MK (ID_{MK}).

As described, whenever a duplicate write comes in, the master key used to protect the original write needs to be retrieved in order to perform the subsequent unwrapping and rewrapping operations. A possible alternative to this step entails wrapping the auxiliary key with (one or more) master keys generated and maintained by the TD. This way, future write requests have no dependency on master key(s) owned and managed by the clients.

3.7.2.4 Read Requests

A read request is triggered when a tenant sends a (read) request that contains an LBA. First, the TD retrieves the auxiliary information entry associated with the LBA, to retrieve the wrapped version $\{FK\}_{MK^*}$ of the ephemeral key FK used by the client when sending the LBA to the storage system and the identifier of the master key used in the wrapping process, ID_{MK^*}. The TD then retrieves the associated entry in the indirection table and uses its content to retrieve the appropriate master key MK; with the MK, the wrapped auxiliary key is unwrapped. The PBA is used to read the encrypted unit from persistent storage; the encrypted unit is decrypted and decompressed to obtain the uncompressed plaintext page. The ephemeral key, FK, originally used to encrypt the page—stored in wrapped form in the associated auxiliary information entry—is then unwrapped. Finally, the uncompressed chunk is re-encrypted using the FK, and the result is returned to the client.

3.7.2.5 Rekeying Requests

One of the important use cases for the system is allowing clients to change their master keys. A rekeying request is initiated by the client, which sends the identifier of two master keys, ID_{MK_old} and ID_{MK_new}, requesting that all auxiliary keys currently wrapped with ID_{MK_old} be unwrapped and rewrapped with ID_{MK_new}. The TD can honor this request by scanning all entries in the indirection table and perform the rewrap operation when necessary. Notice that no bulk re-encryption needs to take place.

3.7.2.6 File Deletion

The user of the storage application may decide at any time to erase a file. Typically, file-deletion operations only entail the removal of file-system metadata (e.g. removal of a directory entry and marking the inode as free). Nevertheless, the storage applications have two ways of notifying the TD that a file has been deleted and—as a consequence—that the LBAs used to store its content can be reclaimed: implicitly, by issuing a new write request for the same LBA; or explicitly, by issuing a command requesting the TD to reclaim the LBAs holding the deleted file. The TD handles these requests by erasing the indirection table entries associated with the unmapped or overwritten LBAs. In addition, for the case of deduplicated chunks, (i) the TD needs to handle a reference counter for the original chunk, to be able to decide whether the PBA of the original chunk can be reused; and (ii) if the original LBAs are unmapped but its reference counter is greater than zero, the TD needs to ensure that the DedupTB entry pointing to the deleted chunk is removed, and if required by the deduplication design, a DedupTB entry is added for another chunk with the same content.

3.7.2.7 Offboarding Requests

Offboarding requests are a special case of file-deletion requests, wherein the set of unmapped or overwritten LBAs spans entire volumes or large portions thereof. These requests are assumed to take place when a tenant no longer requires the services of the storage provider. To honor these requests, the TD proceeds to erase all metadata that belongs to the tenant, and to remove from cache any keys possibly in use. After this step completes, data is no longer accessible by the cloud provider or the TD, since neither has access to the master keys required to decrypt it. Deduplicated chunks can be handled as described in section 3.7.2.6.

3.7.2.8 Secure Data Deletion

Secure data deletion, as described in (Cachin et al. 2013), can be achieved by tenants with a combination of: (i) file deletion (or offboarding) requests that remove the wrapped version of auxiliary keys used to encrypt the chunks of the deleted file; (ii) generation of a new master key (ID_{MK_new}); and (iii) rekeying requests to rewrap all auxiliary keys previously wrapped with ID_{MK_old}. ID_{MK_old} is the master key used to wrap the auxiliary key that encrypts the set of deleted chunks. Finally, the tenant can request its KeyRep to destroy ID_{MK_old}. After this step is completed, the previously unmapped chunks can no longer be decrypted.

The special case of deleting deduplicated chunks needs to be discussed: deduplication inevitably creates a trade-off between the abilities to erase data and to use storage space efficiently. A deduplicated page is clearly still accessible even after the aforementioned secure deletion steps are taken, because multiple cryptographic paths exist to decrypt the relevant auxiliary keys. While a complete analysis of this trade-off is out of the scope of this section, we present a few relevant arguments in Section 3.7.4.

3.7.3 Securing the Critical Module

Since the CritMod has momentary access to users' data in plaintext and to the master keys, the security of the overall scheme depends on whether the storage-access adversary is able to compromise it. Different implementations of the CritMod are possible:

their ability to meet the security requirements of the scheme depends on the assumptions about the surrounding context. For example, a plain software implementation that does not use hardware security modules (see Section 3.7.4. for details) can be considered secure only if the appropriate physical, procedural, and regulatory controls strengthen the limited technical controls available to restrict access to the TD process.

Implementations that leverage trusted execution environments (TEEs) can count on stronger technical controls, enabling the (trusted) TD process to run on an untrusted platform. The properties of this solution can be summarized as follows: (i) no other process in the hosting machine, not even a privileged one, can access the memory of the CritMod; (ii) the TD metadata does not leave the CritMod in plaintext form; (iii) data provided by the user is always stored in encrypted form; and (iv) once a deletion request from a tenant to erase its keys from the system is received, the CritMod should erase all the corresponding keys in use and all its corresponding metadata in IndTB and DedupTB. Unfortunately, TEEs cannot guarantee that the TD process cannot be exploited by supplying a sequence of inputs that subvert its control flow. To ensure against this type of threat, the code of the CritMod needs to be verified before deployment to ensure that it does not contain any backdoors or vulnerabilities. This can be achieved by automatic tools such as (CBMC 2018), inspecting the code manually, following secure software development procedures, and making the code of the CritMod public.

Another property of TEE-based solutions is their ability to execute remote attestation protocols, by means of which the CritMod code can authenticate to the KeyRep, thus establishing the root of trust necessary to allow the exchange of master keys. This allows an attestation protocol to take place when the key-retrieval module fetches master keys from a KeyRep. This occurs when the function GetKey is invoked. During the attestation protocol, the key-retrieval module contacts the KeyRep, which replies with a challenge to verify whether the CritMod can be trusted. Only when the attestation protocol is successful does the KeyRep send the requested key to the CritMod. If the process is successful, the CritMod can perform the storage operations. For efficiency reasons, master keys may temporarily be cached so as to only occasionally incur the overhead of attestation. The attestation process requires previous certification of the code, which means the KeyRep needs to be configured with the expected measurements of the CritMod, so that its integrity can be verified. In order for the attestation protocol to work properly, it is necessary to provision the root of trust and isolation platform with a private and a public key, so that the platform can attest the current state of the system to the KeyRep. The key-provisioning process needs to be performed in a secure way to ensure that the KeyRep and the TD administrators do not collude during the setup process; otherwise, a *cuckoo attack* (Parno 2008) could be performed, causing the KeyRep to inadvertently leak keys. In a cuckoo attack, if an attacker manages to set a bogus certificate of the TD in the KeyRep, the KeyRep will inadvertently leak the keys.

Finally, the TD needs to preserve the confidentiality and integrity of the deduplication and indirection tables. These objectives can be enforced technically (e.g. with secure hardware) and organizationally (e.g. with appropriate processes and workflows) while the entries reside in the main memory of the TD, and cryptographically when the TD commits the entries to persistent storage (e.g. by encrypting them with cryptographic material that never leaves the CritMod). This protection will be effective against a storage-access adversary, but not effective against a law-enforcement adversary.

3.7.4 Security Analysis

3.7.4.1 Data Confidentiality

First, we discuss how the confidentiality objective is addressed. An adversary cannot access data while in flight: this follows from our assumption of mutually authenticated secure channels providing perfect forward secrecy. We assume that mutual authentication provides sufficient means to thwart impersonation attacks on both the client side and the cloud side.

Once data reaches the TD, it is re-encrypted using an auxiliary key and then stored encrypted on the storage media. The auxiliary key exists in wrapped form in the indirection table, and occasionally in the main memory of the CritMod. Consider an adversary who is able to access the persistent storage physically or remotely and can subvert the operating system environment where the TD is hosted (e.g. obtain root privileges); henceforth, we refer to this adversary as a *storage-access adversary* (this adversary covers the curious administrator and malicious tenant presented in Section 3.3). This adversary can gain access to the chunks on disk, but these are encrypted with auxiliary keys. In light of the security provisions for the CritMod, we assume that this adversary cannot compromise the CritMod, either by subverting the integrity of its control flow or by accessing security-sensitive data and metadata in plaintext, which may temporarily be present in the main memory of the CritMod. Admittedly, this is a strong assumption, and it is by no means straightforward to implement. The ways of achieving this in practice are outside of the scope of this chapter and represent a security engineering challenge more than they do a research one (see Section 3.7.3 for a more detailed discussion of the subject). Auxiliary keys are present in plaintext in the memory of the TD and wrapped with a master key in the indirection table entries. We assume that—by means of a combination of technical, procedural, and regulatory controls—this adversary has no access to plaintext in the main memory of the TD. Indirection table entries are similarly protected. Additionally, even when in possession of plaintext indirection table entries, this adversary wouldn't be able to unwrap the auxiliary keys; they are wrapped by tenant master keys, and the latter are stored in the key repository, which is controlled by the tenant and is trusted to provide keys uniquely to key owners or a properly attested and authenticated CritMod.

Consider a more powerful adversary, which we call a *law-enforcement adversary*, who can access the content of the storage media, can compel tenants to reveal the cryptographic material stored in the KeyRep, and can request the storage provider to produce the content of the internal metadata of the TD (e.g. the indirection table). The only assumption we make is that the law-enforcement adversary cannot access master keys that have been destroyed after an explicit user request. It is apparent that—based on their capabilities—this adversary can compromise the confidentiality of user data. However, note that the same is also true in the absence of the TD. This type of adversary is, however, unable to access data that has been securely deleted by means of a sequence of rekeying operations and destruction of master keys in the KeyRep. This is true because this adversary can recover chunks encrypted by a set of auxiliary keys and then wrapped with a master key MK_{old}; however, the latter is assumed to be unrecoverable after the tenant has requested its destruction to its KeyRep. This adversary is also unable to recover data stored on the same storage medium as the targeted client but encrypted by another tenant whose keys have not been revealed to the adversary.

3.7.4.2 Data Confidentiality in the Presence of Deduplication

Deduplication represents a threat to confidentiality because it offers an oracle that can be consulted to discover whether the same content has already been uploaded, as described in (Halevi et al. 2011, pp. 491–500). An adversary can consult this oracle in an online fashion by colluding with a malicious tenant, whereas the law-enforcement adversary has direct access to the deduplication table and therefore has offline access to this oracle.

This vulnerability exists in every system that supports deduplication, and it is neither thwarted nor worsened by the existence of the TD. However, cross-tenant deduplication can increase the scope of the vulnerability since the oracle may be consulted by malicious tenants that want to compromise the confidentiality of a victim tenant's data. Avoiding this breach of confidentiality can be achieved by restricting deduplication to be intra-tenant only.

Focusing on the law-enforcement adversary, while this adversary cannot revert secure deletion, traces of deleted chunks may still be part of the system in the form of duplicates of the deleted chunks. However, the mere existence of a deduplicated page, disconnected from its original context (the ordered sequence of chunks that formed the deleted file), doesn't constitute significant leakage to a law-enforcement adversary: LBAs can be reused, and the tenant can always claim that all remaining chunks have no relation to the deleted page. Also, if cross-tenant deduplication is not allowed, tenant offboarding in conjunction with the destruction of master keys is effective, as no traces of existing data can be gathered. However, it is clear that if cross-tenant deduplication were allowed, a law-enforcement adversary could collude with another tenant and use deduplication as an effective way of establishing a connection between existing chunks before and after deletion, using the colluding tenant as a mean of circumventing deletion for a set of sensitive chunks. The law-enforcement adversary would indeed be able to use the colluding tenant to issue write requests for a set of sensitive chunks. If deduplication takes place, and if no duplicates are found after secure deletion is committed, the law-enforcement adversary could deduce that such chunks did exist and were the subject of secure deletion. This type of attack is extremely effective, but only for chunks with low conditional entropy. Avoiding this breach of confidentiality is another reason to disable cross-tenant deduplication in a TD system.

3.7.4.3 Security Impact of Different Technologies

There are different implementation possibilities for the CritMod, and their impact on the security of our framework varies. The alternatives vary according to the amount of trust that is initially placed in different components of the system and in the hardware required to ensure secure execution. In general, the smaller the size of the code that needs to be trusted, also known as the *trusted code base* (TCB), the more secure it is. We classify the isolation techniques as *hardware-based isolation* (HBI) and *virtualized-based isolation* (VBI). HBI solutions such as SecureBlue++ (Boivie 2012), (Lie et al. 2000; Suh et al. 2003, pp. 160–171; Williams and Boivie 2011; Intel 2018b), and Software Guard Extensions (SGX) (Intel, 2018a) use special hardware instructions to isolate critical applications from other processes that run in the same host, whereas VBI solutions such as TrustVisor (McCune et al. 2010, pp. 143–158), Overshadow (Chen et al. 2008, pp. 2–13), and (Vasudevan et al. 2012) depend on virtualization to provide isolation between trusted and untrusted code. Filtering out approaches that do not allow multithreading and simultaneous instances, because they would not allow the required performance, the TD could be implemented using HBI or VBI approaches with TPM.

HBI solutions are more secure than VBI solutions because they only rely on the critical application and the hardware itself. Furthermore, SecureBlue++ allows remote attestation and provides a higher level of assurance than other approaches: it permits continuous software-integrity protection, not only at boot-time. Among VBI solutions, TrustVisor has the smallest hypervisor, but it emulates the TPM operations in software to improve their performance. Overshadow has a larger TCB and requires the use of a TPM, making it less secure. In contrast, the implementation cost is larger for HBI solutions because they are not widely available, while VBI solutions do not require specialized hardware.

3.7.5 TD Overhead and Performance Implications

A prototype of the TD (see Figure 3.4) was implemented to understand its feasibility and measure the overhead. The tenant side was represented by the IBM Spectrum Scale with encryption support enabled (IBM 2018b), generating encrypted files and transmitting them to the cloud storage provider. Spectrum Scale was modified to store the encryption auxiliary information in AuxRep via User Datagram Protocol (UDP) messages. The key repository KeyRep was hosted in an IBM Security Key Lifecycle Manager (https://www.ibm.com/support/knowledgecenter/en/SSWPVP). The cloud storage provider was built as a network block device (NBD) (nbd 2018). The AuxRep was built as part of nbd-server. Advanced Encryption Standard (AES128) was used for encryption, and the prototype was implemented using C++.

The experiments were performed on a machine with an Intel Xeon L5640@2.27 GHz CPU with 18 GB of RAM, an IBM 42D0747 7200 RPM SATA HDD, an OCZ Vertex 2 SATA SSD, and a 64-bit operating system. For cryptographic operations, results were averaged across 50 independent repetitions of the measurements. To obtain the measurements of the disk accesses, 10 000 random accesses were performed to a file of 16 GB. The data presented is the average of all the repetitions. In our experiments, it was assumed that the master key used to encrypt the data was cached in the system. All figures of results are in logarithmic scale.

More details about the system and measurements made can be found in (Baracaldo et al. 2014, pp. 21–32). However, we summarize the most important results here. The measurements focused on the main concern of TD data-path performance and the cryptographic operations relative to the other data-path latencies, such as access to

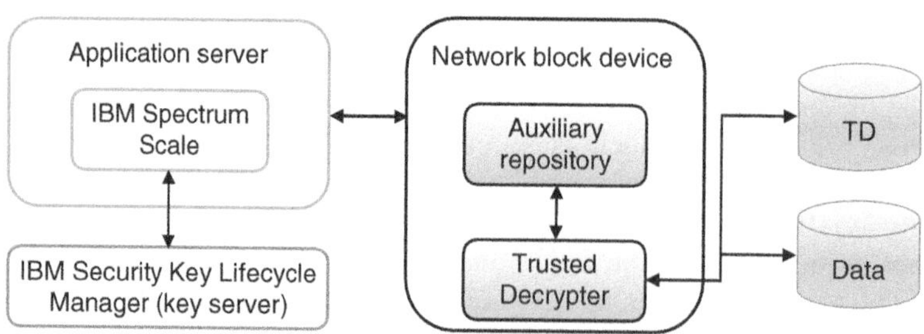

Figure 3.4 TD prototype system.

the storage medium. It was assumed that overheads and latencies for fetching keys and auxiliary information can be optimized by caching algorithms and therefore will not be generally seen as a significant contributor to TD overhead.

Figure 3.5 shows the relative time consumed by the various cryptographic operations relative to the read to the HDD storage medium, for a range of typical primary storage system chunk sizes. It confirms that encrypting and decrypting data incur the most latency, by about a factor of 10, and are about a factor of 30–100 less than the actual HDD storage medium accesses.

Figure 3.6 suggests that the aggregate overhead related to cryptographic operations is very small relative to HDD access times, as also indicated in Figure 3.5. For SSD, the overhead, with the low level of instruction-set acceleration present in the prototype, is on the same order of magnitude as the access to the storage medium.

Not shown here are overheads related to a base data-reduction system: compressing the data and the hash calculations normally associated with generating deduplication signatures. Those calculations are also substantial: compression and decompression calculations generally take on the order of 1.5–3 times (per byte) the overhead of AES encryption, and Secure Hash Algorithm (SHA-1) calculations (often used for deduplication signatures) often take on the order of 2–3 times more overhead than AES

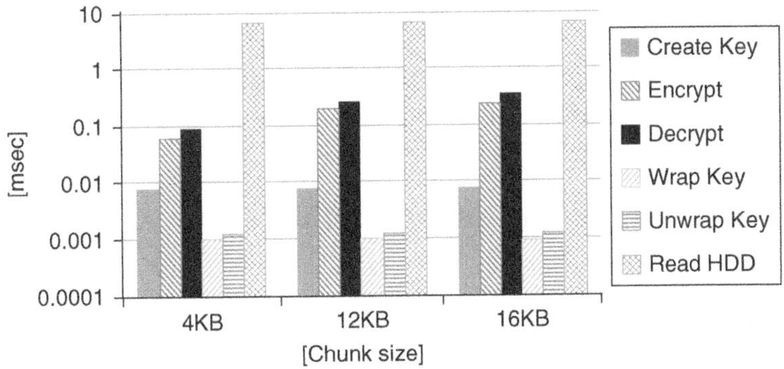

Figure 3.5 Overhead of data-path operations for read requests.

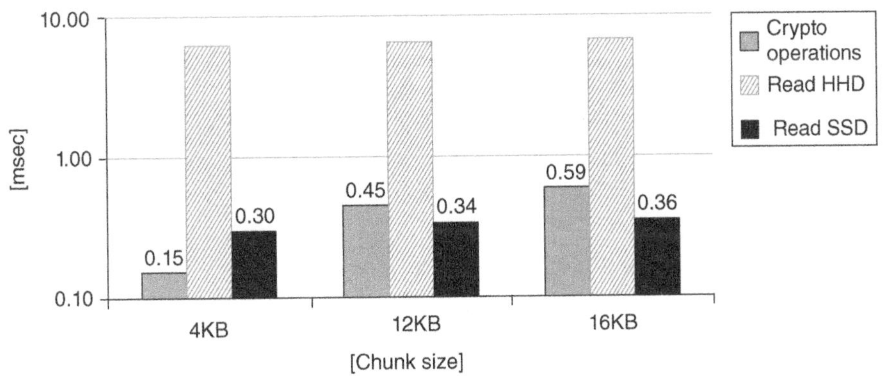

Figure 3.6 Comparing overheads for reads to HDD and SSD.

calculations for encryption/decryption (although the signature is only calculated on write operations). This suggests that the overhead of TD-related crypto operations will likely be even less substantial than these charts suggest, even for SSD.

In addition, increasingly capable hardware acceleration is being provided for compression/decompression calculations, for encryption/decryption calculations, and for secure hash calculations such as SHA-1 and SHA-2. For example, hardware accelerators such as Intel QuickAssist Technology (Intel 2018c) have compression and crypto engines, and instruction support such as Intel SSE4 (Intel 2017) is continuing to accelerate crypto, compression, and hashing algorithms.

Therefore, the data-path overhead for a TD operating in an HDD storage system today looks very reasonable. For SSD, the extra overhead imposed by TD is significant, but within the same order of magnitude as the compression and deduplication functions. However, since SSD is quite expensive relative to HDD, the extra cost to provide more compute resource in the TD-enabled storage system per byte of SSD storage is likely to be practical, still providing an affordable TD-enabled SSD storage platform. It appears that the TD data-path overheads are practical for HDD and SSD storage systems and will only become more practical over the next several generations as hardware continues to enhance compute resources for crypto operations.

Another area of overhead could be that associated with the TEE for the TD. The overhead incurred by these mechanisms is the price paid for achieving complete process isolation as well as providing tenants with verifiable trust assurance of the state of the TD provided by their storage provider. Hardware methods such as SGX and SecureBlue++ will incur very little overhead and will be the most secure; they hold great promise for TD-enabled storage systems with the highest security guarantees.

3.8 Future Directions for Cloud Storage Confidentiality with Low Cost

Multiple challenges need to be met to achieve full confidentiality at an affordable price in cloud storage systems.

3.8.1 Hardware Trends

Encryption and data-reduction computation costs are decreasing but still significant in servers in terms of CPU cycles and memory-bandwidth usage. In addition, the latency introduced by encryption can be very significant for some use cases. Processor instructions designed to speed up cryptographic or compression calculations, other types of hardware acceleration, and decreasing cost of cores in CPUs will increasingly mitigate this problem.

3.8.2 New Cryptographic Techniques

In the short term, cost-savings solutions such as those detailed in this chapter will help reduce cost by reducing capacity needed. In the long term, cryptographic techniques to perform computations over encrypted data, without revealing plaintext to untrusted third parties such as cloud storage providers, will be feasible and will allow data reduction on encrypted data. Homomorphic encryption (Gentry 2009) is one promising encryption method that still needs to be improved to achieve faster computation times. Designing such systems is one of the research tracks that can significantly improve the security of cloud systems.

3.8.3 Usability of Cryptographic Key Management

Key management today is difficult, is expensive to set up and maintain, and, once set up, is not easy enough for users. Key managers are often targeted by attackers who intend to steal data, as was the case in a recent security incident that targeted Amazon Web Services (CRN 2017). Operations such as distribution of keys, storage, and rekeying operations are still difficult to perform.

Usability of key management as well as other items related to seamless and integrated use of encryption by users will need to be improved to drive adoption rates. Efforts such as (Cachin et al. 2013) try to automate this process while achieving secure deletion. Federated key management spanning on-premises and multiple clouds will also be an enabler for the Trusted Decrypter and other similar systems, as long as those systems are designed carefully with strong security.

3.8.4 Trusted Execution Environments

Increasing the capabilities and availability of trustworthy execution environments and decreasing the costs associated with them will allow wider adoption of architectures such as Trusted Decrypters and will remove inhibitors to wider adoption. Trusted execution technologies and process-isolation techniques are mechanisms that can help protect and provide guarantees to tenants, as is the case in the TD architecture presented in Section 3.7. Current hardware components for trusted execution environments are not widely available in CPUs and servers. Although TPMs are generally available in many CPUs, their key-storage space is limited. And secure computing hardware such as Intel SGX (Intel 2018a) is not yet commonly used. Additionally, some challenges still need to be addressed for trusted execution environment technologies to be fully practical. Processes like key provisioning in cloud environments should be performed carefully to avoid man-in-the middle attacks (Parno 2008). New mechanisms to automate this process and avoid such pitfalls are needed.

Application software needs to be updated and patched often, causing the signatures of the system to change. Systems to distribute correct and up-to-date signature values in a secure way are necessary to avoid false positives.

In Section 3.7, we presented some methodologies to achieve data confidentiality through process isolation. Hypervisor-based process-isolation technologies seem to be a fast and more economical way to go forward. However, these solutions still have a large trusted code base that must be trusted. New ways to minimize the risk of trusting compromised hypervisors are needed.

Containers rather than hypervisors to isolate tenants are in wide use, and systems like Cloud Foundry (www.cloudfoundry.org), Amazon Web Services (https://aws.amazon.com), and Bluemix (https://www.ibm.com/cloud) effectively use containers to isolate tenants. A container is an isolated process belonging to a tenant. Each tenant is assigned a container, and multiple tenants share the same operating system. One of the main advantages of this system is that provisioning a new container is much faster than starting a VM image, allowing clients to bring up new applications faster. Using this type of isolation clearly increases the risk of exposure of tenants. Potential adversaries may share the same operating system and may try to compromise the system to obtain access to sensitive data of other tenants or to launch a denial of service attack (Zhang et al., 2014, pp. 990–1003; Catuogno and Galdi 2016, pp. 69–76). Research efforts to mitigate the risk of information leakage imposed by containers are currently underway (Gao et al. 2017, pp. 237–248; Henriksson and Falk 2017).

3.8.5 Privacy and Side-Channel Attacks

Existing systems do not offer confidentiality and privacy of metadata, such as filenames and folder paths, stored in the Cloud. In the systems presented in this chapter, it is assumed that such metadata is not confidential and can be freely shared with cloud storage providers. Sometimes, just getting to know the existence of a particular filename may allow adversaries to infer information about the victim. For example, if a file is named *companyA-acquisition-budget.xls*, an adversary may know that the tenant is at least analyzing the possibility of acquiring *companyA*. Protecting the confidentiality of storage systems' metadata is a complex problem that still needs to be studied by the research community. To the best of our knowledge, the problem of achieving data-reduction techniques and maintaining confidentiality of data has not been studied in the presence of confidential metadata.

During our analysis of data-reduction-enabled cloud storage systems, we presented multiple side-channel attacks: e.g. an adversary observing the bandwidth used, to determine if a particular piece of data was stored, can infer whether that piece of data was previously stored in the storage system. There are many more side-channel threats that are relevant to cloud storage systems. For example, side-channel threats occur when adversaries can observe patterns of data usage to infer tenants' intentions, even if data is encrypted (Van Dijk and Juels 2010, pp. 1–8). Private information retrieval (Chor et al. 1998) and oblivious storage (Stefanov et al. 2011; Goodrich et al. 2012, pp. 157–167; Chan et al. 2017, pp. 660–690) are techniques that obfuscate usage patterns to thwart these types of attacks; however, they can cause performance and cost issues (e.g. lower performance due to lower cache-hit rates in storage systems and lower "real" throughput achieved per storage system and network). Given these costs, novel and more efficient techniques to deal with these privacy side-channel attacks are necessary.

More research to identify and deter new and existing side-channel attacks is needed. In particular, additional cost savings from multitenant deduplication will be enabled once there is no concern about side-channel attacks.

3.9 Conclusions

Cloud storage systems have become increasingly popular, but their success depends on their ability to protect the confidentiality of the information stored by tenants while offering low-cost services. In this chapter, we overviewed some of the techniques commonly used to maintain data confidentiality and showed how these techniques can reduce the efficacy of traditionally used data-reduction techniques such as compression and deduplication, increasing costs for both tenants and cloud storage providers. To restore cost savings, we presented multiple techniques that alleviate this problem without compromising cloud data confidentiality. We detailed the Trusted Decrypter architecture as a feasible way to reconcile data-reduction techniques and confidentiality in the near future. In the long term, we expect that cloud storage systems will continue to evolve by leveraging increasingly faster and less expensive hardware to facilitate cryptographic and compression operations to protect data confidentiality without large overheads. We also anticipate that new cryptographic techniques to perform data reduction over encrypted data will become feasible. There is a long journey for these new cryptographic techniques to be considered secure by the community and provide adequate performance at low cost before they can be adopted in real systems. However, their development will play a positive role in cloud storage providers' ability to offer low-cost, secure data services.

References

Amplidata (2018). Himalaya. http://amplidata.com/himalaya.

Baracaldo, N., Androulaki, E., Glider, J., and Sorniotti, A. (2014). Reconciling end-to-end confidentiality and data reduction in cloud storage. *Proceedings of the 6th Edition of the ACM Workshop on Cloud Computing Security* (CCSW'14), 21–32. New York: ACM.

Bellare, M., Keelveedhi, S., and Ristenpart, T. (2012). Message- locked encryption and secure deduplication. Technical report. Cryptology ePrint Archive, Report 2012/631. http://eprint.iacr.org.

Bellare, M., Keelveedhi, S., and Ristenpart, T. (2013). Dupless: server-aided encryption for deduplicated storage. In: *Proceedings of the 22nd USENIX Conference on Security*, 179–194. USENIX Association.

Bethencourt, J., Sahai, A., and Waters, B. (2007). Ciphertext-policy attribute-based encryption. IEEE Symposium on Security and Privacy, 321–334.

Boivie, R. (2012). SecureBlue++: CPU support for secure execution. IBM Research Report.

Boneh, D. and Lipton, R. J. (1996). A revocable backup system. USENIX Security, 91–96.

Boneh, D., Di Crescenzo, G., Ostrovsky, R., and Persiano, G. (2004). Public key encryption with keyword search. In: *Advances in Cryptology-Eurocrypt 2004*, 506–522. Springer.

btr (2018). Btrfs filesystem for Linux. https://btrfs.wiki.kernel.org/index.php/Main_Page.

Cachin, C., Haralambiev, K., Hsiao, H.-C., and Sorniotti, A. (2013). Policy-based secure deletion. (accepted for publication). *Proceedings of the 20th ACM Conference on Computer and Communications Security*. ACM.

Catuogno, L. and Galdi, C. (2016). On the evaluation of security properties of containerized systems. *International Conference on Ubiquitous Computing and Communications and 2016 International Symposium on Cyberspace and Security (IUCC-CSS)*, 69–76. IEEE.

CBMC (2018). Bounded model checking for ansi-c. http://www.cprover.org/cbmc.

Chan, T. H. H., Guo, Y., Lin, W. K., and Shi, E. (2017). Oblivious hashing revisited, and applications to asymptotically efficient ORAM and OPRAM. *International Conference on the Theory and Application of Cryptology and Information Security*, 660–690). Springer, Cham.

Chen, X., Garfinkel, T., Lewis, E.C. et al. (2008). Overshadow: a virtualization-based approach to retrofitting protection in commodity operating systems. *SIGARCH Comput. Archit. News* 36 (1): 2–13.

Chor, B., Kushilevitz, E., Goldreich, O., and Sudan, M. (1998). Private information retrieval. *J. ACM* 45 (6): 965–981.

Chow, R., Golle, P., Jakobsson, M. et al. (2009). Controlling data in the cloud: outsourcing computation without outsourcing control. In: *Proceedings of the 2009 ACM Workshop on Cloud Computing Security*, 85–90. ACM.

Cleversafe (2018). Cleversafe data storage product portfolio. https://www.ibm.com/cloud/object-storage.

Constantinescu, C., Glider, J., and Chambliss, D. (2011). Mixing deduplication and compression on active data sets. *Data Compression Conference (DCC)*, 393–402.

CRN (2017). The 10 biggest data breaches of 2017 (so far). https://www.crn.com/slide-shows/security/300089736/the-10-biggest-data-breaches-of-2017-so-far.htm/pgno/0/2.

Di Crescenzo, G., Ferguson, N., Impagliazzo, R., and Jakobsson, M. (1999). How to forget a secret. In: *STACS 99*, 500–509. Springer.

Di Pietro, R. and Sorniotti, A. (2013). Proof of ownership for deduplication systems: a secure, scalable, and efficient solution. Technical report, Research Report IBM RZ 3854.

Duan, Y. (2013). Distributed key generation for secure encrypted deduplication. *IACR Cryptology ePrint Archive*, (2013): 807.

EMC (2018). Emc vnx deduplication and compression. https://www.emc.com/collateral/hardware/white-papers/h8198-vnx-deduplication-compression-wp.pdf.

Gao, X., Gu, Z., Kayaalp, M., Pendarakis, D., and Wang, H. (2017). Container leaks: emerging security threats of information leakages in container clouds. *2017 47th Annual IEEE/IFIP International Conference on Dependable Systems and Networks (DSN)*, 237–248. IEEE.

Gentry, C. (2009). A fully homomorphic encryption scheme. PhD thesis. Stanford University.

GigaOm (2012). iCloud breach highlights some hard truths about the consumer. https://gigaom.com/2012/08/05/icloud-breach-highlights-some-hard-truths-about-the-consumer-cloud.

Goodrich, M. T., Mitzenmacher, M., Ohrimenko, O., and Tamassia, R. (2012). Privacy-preserving group data access via stateless oblivious ram simulation. *Proceedings of the Twenty-Third Annual ACM-SIAM Symposium on Discrete Algorithms*, 157–167. SIAM.

Goyal, V., Pandey, O., Sahai, A., and Waters, B. (2006). Attribute-based encryption for fine-grained access control of encrypted data. Proceedings of the 13th ACM Conference on Computer and Communications Security, 89–98. ACM

Halevi, S., Harnik, D., Pinkas, B., and Shulman-Peleg, A. (2011). Proofs of ownership in remote storage systems. *Proceedings of the 18th ACM Conference on Computer and Communications Security*, 491–500. ACM.

Harnik, D., Pinkas, B., and Shulman-Peleg, A. (2010). Side-channels in cloud services: deduplication in cloud storage. *IEEE Secur. Priv.* 8 (6): 40–47.

Henriksson, O. and Falk, M. (2017). *Static Vulnerability Analysis of Docker Images*. Karlskrona, Sweden: Blekinge Institute of Technology.

IBM (2018a). IBM v7000. http://www-03.ibm.com/systems/storage/storwize.

IBM (2018b). IBM Spectrum Scale, version 5 release 1, advanced administration guide. Chapter 15.

Intel (2017). Processors - define sse2, sse3 and sse4. http://www.intel.com/support/processors/sb/CS-030123.htm.

Intel (2018a). Intel SGX. https://software.intel.com/en-us/sgx.

Intel (2018b). Software guard extensions programming reference.

Intel (2018c). Intel QAT. https://www.intel.com/content/www/us/en/architecture-and-technology/intel-quick-assist-technology-overview.html.

Johnson, M., Ishwar, P., Prabhakaran, V. et al. (2004). On compressing encrypted data. *IEEE Trans. Signal Process.* 52 (10): 2992–3006.

Joukov, N., Papaxenopoulos, H., and Zadok, E. (2006). Secure deletion myths, issues, and solutions. In: *Proceedings of the 2nd ACM workshop on Storage Security and Survivability*, 61–66. ACM.

Kelley, J. and Tamassia, R. (2014). Secure compression: theory & practice. Cryptology ePrint Archive, Report 2014/113. http://eprint.iacr.org.

Lie, D., Thekkath, C., Mitchell, M. et al. (2000). Architectural support for copy and tamper resistant software. *ACM SIGPLAN Not.* 35 (11): 168.

McCune, J. M., Li, Y., Qu, N., Zhou, Z., Datta, A., Gligor, V., and Perrig, A. (2010). Trustvisor:eEfficient tcb reduction and attestation. *Proceedings of IEEE Symposium on Security and Privacy*, 143–158.

Metz, C. (2009). Lightning strikes amazon cloud (honest). www.theregister.co.uk/2009/06/12/lightning_strikes_amazon_cloud.

Microsoft (2017). Microsoft cluster shared volumes. https://technet.microsoft.com/en-us/library/dn383585.aspx.

Mitra, S. and Winslett, M. (2006). Secure deletion from inverted indexes on compliance storage. Proceedings of the 2nd ACM Workshop on Storage Security and Survivability, 67–72. ACM.

Naor, M. and Reingold, O. (2004). Number-theoretic constructions of efficient pseudo-random functions. *J. ACM* 51 (2): 231–262.

nbd (2018). Network block device (nbd). http://nbd.sourceforge.net.

NIST (2012). Recommendation for key management part 1: general (revision 3). NIST Special Publication: 800–857.

Parno, B. (2008). Bootstrapping trust in a "trusted" platform. *Proceedings of the 3rd Conference on Hot Topics in Security*, 9:1–9:6. USENIX Association.

PCWorld (2010). Microsoft cloud data breach heralds things to come. https://www.pcworld.com/article/214775/microsoft_cloud_data_breach_sign_of_future.html.

Perlman, R. (2005). File system design with assured delete. *Third IEEE International Security in Storage Workshop, 2005. SISW'05*, 83–88 IEEE.

Project, T. F. (2018). Freenet. https://en.wikipedia.org/wiki/Freenet.

Quinlan, S. and Dorward, S. (2002). Venti: a new approach to archival data storage. *Proceedings of the 1st USENIX Conference on File and Storage Technologies*.89–102

Rashid, F., Miri, A., and Woungang, I. (2012). A secure data deduplication framework for cloud environments. *2012 Tenth Annual International Conference on Privacy, Security and Trust (PST)*, 81–87. IEEE.

Russell, D. (2010). Data deduplication will be even bigger in 2010. Gartner.

Sahai, A. and Waters, B. (2005). Fuzzy identity-based encryption. Advances in Cryptology EUROCRYPT, Lecture Notes in Computer Science, 457–473.

Stanek, J., Sorniotti, A., Androulaki, E., and Kencl, L. (2013). A secure data deduplication scheme for cloud storage. Technical report, Research Report IBM RZ 3852.

Stefanov, E., Shi, E., and Song, D. (2011). Towards practical oblivious ram. *arXiv preprint arXiv:1106.3652.*

Suh, G. E., Clarke, D., Gassend, B., van Dijk, M., and Devadas, S. (2003). Aegis: architecture for tamper-evident and tamper-resistant processing. *Proceedings of the 17th Annual International Conference on Supercomputing,* 160–171.

Tang, Y., Lee, P.P., Lui, J.C., and Perlman, R. (2010). Fade: secure overlay cloud storage with file assured deletion. In: *Security and Privacy in Communication Networks,* 380–397. Springer.

Van Dijk, M. and Juels, A. (2010). On the impossibility of cryptography alone for privacy-preserving cloud computing. *Proceedings of the 5th USENIX Conference on Hot Topics in Security (HotSec'10),* 1–8. Berkeley, CA: USENIX Association.

Vasudevan, A., Parno, B., Qu, N., Gligor, V. D., and Perrig, A. (2012). Lockdown: towards a safe and practical architecture for security applications on commodity platforms. *Proceedings of the 5th International Conference on Trust and Trustworthy Computing,* 34–54. Springer

Verizon (2018). 2018 data breach investigations report. https://www.verizonenterprise.com/resources/reports/rp_DBIR_2018_Report_en_xg.pdf.

Wei, M., Grupp, L. M., Spada, F. E., and Swanson, S. (2011). Reliably erasing data from flash-based solid state drives. *Proceedings of the 9th USENIX Conference on File and Storage Technologies,* 8:1–8:13. USENIX

Williams, P. and Boivie, R. (2011). Cpu support for secure executables. *Proceedings of the 4th International Conference on Trust and Trustworthy Computing,* 172–187. Springer

Zadok, E., Badulescu, I., and Shender, A. (1998). Cryptfs: A stackable vnode level encryption file system. http://filesystems.org/docs/cryptfs.

zfs (2018). Zfs on Linux. http://zfsonlinux.org.

Zhang, Y., Juels, A., Reiter, M. K., and Ristenpart, T. (2014). Cross-tenant side-channel attacks in paas clouds. *Proceedings of the 2014 ACM SIGSAC Conference on Computer and Communications Security,* 990–1003. ACM.

4

Access Control in Cloud IaaS

Yun Zhang, Ram Krishnan, Farhan Patwa, and Ravi Sandhu

University of Texas at San Antonio, San Antonio, TX, USA

4.1 Introduction

Cloud computing is revolutionizing the way businesses obtain IT resources. *Cloud computing* refers to Internet-based computing that provides on-demand access to a shared pool of configurable computing resources (Hassan 2011), such as networks, servers, storages, applications, services, etc. Instead of having an application installed on a local PC, applications are hosted in the Cloud. Cloud computing allows users and organizations to conveniently and rapidly get computing resources with minimal management effort, helping organizations avoid focusing on upfront infrastructure costs. Rapid maturity of both commercial and open source cloud platforms greatly contributes to the wider acceptance and application of cloud computing in industry.

Infrastructure-as-a-Service (IaaS) is a cloud service model (Mell and Grance 2011) in which a cloud service provider (CSP) offers compute, storage, and networking resources as a service to its tenants. *Tenant* refers to an organization that is a customer of a CSP. Traditionally, IaaS providers maintain strict separation between tenants, for obvious reasons. Thus their virtual resources are strongly isolated. For instance, in OpenStack (http://openstack.org), a tenant user does not have the capability to access resources outside its domain. *Domain* refers to the administrative boundary of that tenant. Similarly, in AWS (http://aws.amazon.com) and Microsoft Azure (https://azure.microsoft.com), *tenant* refers to an account—an administrative boundary. Users from one account (tenant) by default have no rights to access resources outside that account.

In this chapter, we will introduce the basic cloud access-control models for the dominant IaaS cloud platforms, including the open source cloud platform OpenStack, and two commercial cloud platforms: AWS and Microsoft Azure. We provide a formal characterization of the access-control models of these three cloud platforms. For each of the platforms, we also specify novel ways to construct intertenant secure information and resource sharing. The chapter outline is as follows. In Section 4.2, we present some background knowledge: more details of cloud services and the idea of information and resource sharing. In Sections 4.3, 4.4, and 4.5, we introduce the cloud access-control models for OpenStack, AWS, and Azure, respectively. For each of those platforms, we

Security, Privacy, and Digital Forensics in the Cloud, First Edition. Edited by Lei Chen, Hassan Takabi, and Nhien-An Le-Khac.

first give a formal access-control model specification, and then we extend the access-control model to include the capability of handling information and resources sharing across tenants. We also give a formal specification of the respective administrative models of information and resources sharing. Section 4.6 concludes the chapter.

4.2 Background

Cloud computing has three service models: Infrastructure-as-a-Service (IaaS), Platform-as-a-Service (PaaS), and Software-as-a-Service (SaaS). PaaS offer a development environment to application developers. SaaS offers application and software to end users. We focus on IaaS for two reasons: (i) IaaS is one of the most-adopted cloud service models today (as compared to PaaS and SaaS), and (ii) IaaS is the foundation of the Cloud, with characteristics such as elasticity, self-service, etc. By gaining insights into issues related to sharing at this lower level of abstraction, we can also develop better models for higher levels of abstraction of cloud computing, such as PaaS and SaaS.

Note that in the context of IaaS, the unit of sharing consists of virtual resources such as objects in a storage volume, virtual machines (VMs), etc. For models, we mainly focus on administrative aspects. Administrative models are concerned with managing which users and what resources are to be shared, setting up and tearing down platforms for sharing, etc. Examples include a tenant administrator creating a shared secure isolated domain, adding users and resources to and removing them from that domain, inviting other tenants to join the domain, etc.

While cloud technology provides significant convenience to business systems, it also gives great potential to facilitate cyber-collaborations among organizations. In a cloud community, organizations can share cybersecurity information with other members through a cybersecurity committee to make informed decisions about the community's security governance. In most cases, organizations maintain their group of security specialists, who manage security policies, conduct security audits, and investigate security-related events. A community also maintains a group of external security experts who help organizations with security issues. When a cybersecurity incident occurs, the cybersecurity committee members start an incident-response group with a cross-organization security team including organizations' internal security specialists and external security experts, as illustrated in Figure 4.1. Security information about this incident is shared within the incident response group.

Models for information sharing in IaaS are lacking. The concept we used to build our models for sharing comes from Group-Centric Secure Information Sharing (g-SIS) (Krishnan et al. 2009), which presents a method to control access among a group of users and objects that is well suited to the collaborative community scenario. In particular, g-SIS enables sharing using copies of the original information, versus traditional sharing that gives access to original information and resources (Cohen et al. 2002; Pearlman et al. 2002; Shands et al. 2000). Sharing by copy gives additional security protection, since access to the copies can be provided in a tightly controlled environment.

We present access-control models in a way that fits our best understanding. We abstract a necessary set of components to describe an access-control model. Based on the cloud platform access-control model, we build models for secure information and resource sharing. Then we formalize the administrative model. When we discuss the

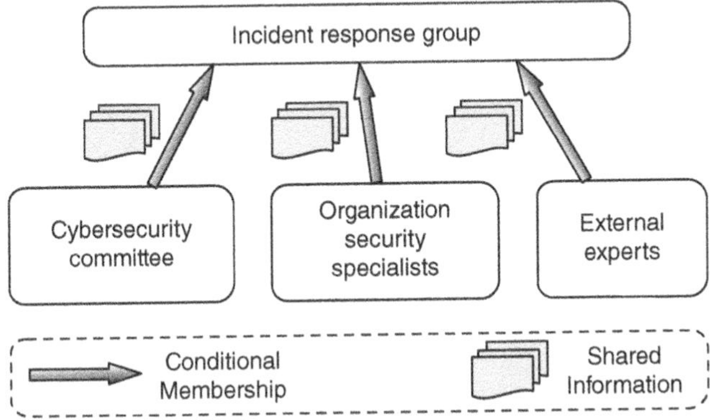

Figure 4.1 Community cyber-incident response governance.

models, we assume one organization has only one tenant in the cloud community. In the discussion of models for sharing, we simply ignore the group entity from cloud access-control models, since it is essentially a convenience to group users and can easily be incorporated in a more complete description. Instead, we use the term *group* to mean a group of organizations.

4.3 Access Control in OpenStack Cloud IaaS

In this section, we will introduce an access-control model for the OpenStack cloud IaaS platform and demonstrate its flexibility by extending it to include information and resource sharing. The content of this section has been published in (Zhang et al. 2015a). From the cloud provider's perspective, each tenant is an independent customer of the Cloud. From an organization's perspective, in general a single organization may have a single or multiple tenants in a single cloud. For simplicity, we assume here that each organization from the cloud community has exactly one tenant.

4.3.1 OpenStack Access-Control Model

A core OpenStack access control (OSAC) model was presented in (Tang and Sandhu 2014), based on the OpenStack Identity API v3 and Havana release. This model comprises nine entities: users, groups, projects, domains, roles, services, object types, operations, and tokens. Hierarchical multitenancy (HMT) (http://openstack.org) is a new feature added to OpenStack since the Juno release. We enhance the OSAC model with HMT, resulting in the OSAC-HMT model shown in Figure 4.2. In this and other figures in this chapter, the arrows denote binary relations, with the single arrowhead indicating one side and double arrowheads many sides.

Users represent people who are authenticated to access OpenStack cloud resources, while *groups* are sets of users. HMT does not change user/group management, which is handled at the domain level:

- **Domains and projects**—*Projects* are resource containers through which users access cloud services such as VMs, storage, networks, identity, and so on. Each project

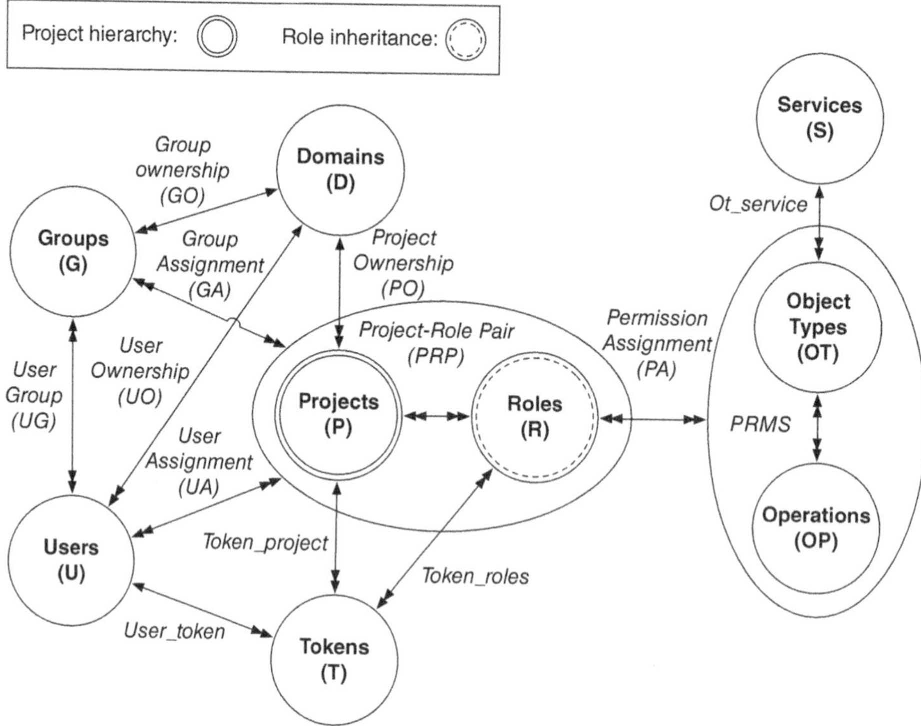

Figure 4.2 OpenStack Access Control (OSAC) model with HMT.

defines a boundary of cloud resources. *Domains* are administrative boundaries of collections of projects, users, and groups. Each domain contains multiple projects, users, and groups. Conversely, each project, user, and group is "owned" by a single domain. However, they can be assigned to multiple projects, which can be distributed in different domains. That is, the ownership of users and projects can be defined by assigning them to a domain. Note that users in a domain are powerless unless they are assigned to a project with a particular role. Typically, domains are created by a CSP for its tenants. A domain admin is an administrative user of that domain (tenant).

- **Project hierarchy**—The *project hierarchy* enables the resources to be divided into smaller management units, giving tenants more power to control their cloud resources. A domain can have multiple projects in it, each of which is a root project for a hierarchical project tree. A child project has only one parent project. Basically, child projects are a further division of resources of a parent project.
- **Roles**—*Roles* are global in that each role is applicable to every project. Roles are used to specify access levels of users to services in specific projects in a given domain. Roles and their associated permissions are defined by the CSP. Note that users are assigned to projects with a specific set of roles. For instance, by assigning a role of Member to a user, the user receives all operational rights over the resources in a project; by assigning a role of Admin to a user, the user receives admin rights over a project. The accesses defined by roles are enforced by a policy engine in the cloud based on policy files where the roles are defined.

- **Role inheritance**—Without a project hierarchy, a user is explicitly assigned to a project with a role. With a project hierarchy, a user needs to be able to be assigned to a child project, which is enabled by inherited role assignment. By assigning an inherited role to a user in a parent project, the user will automatically have the role in child projects.
- **Object types and operations**—An *object type and operation* pair defines actions that can be performed by end users on cloud services and resources. The concept of object types allows different operations to be specified for different services. For example, in the Nova compute service, an object type is VM, and operations on VM include start, stop, etc.
- **Token**—*Tokens* define the scope of resources that users are authenticated to access. Users authenticate themselves to the Keystone service and obtain a token that they then use to access different services. The token contains various information, including the user's domain and user's roles for specified projects. A token must be scoped to a target project on which the action is performed. Inherited roles allow tokens to be granted for child projects, giving access to the child projects.

We formalize the OSAC-HMT model next. Part of it is the same as the OSAC model (Tang and Sandhu 2014).

Definition 4.1 OSAC-HMT Model Components

- U, G, P, D, R, S, OT, and OP are finite sets of existing users, groups, projects, domains, roles, services, object types, and operations, respectively, in an OpenStack cloud system. We require two roles, so $\{admin, member\} \subseteq R$.
- User Ownership (UO) is a function UO: $U \rightarrow D$, mapping a user to its owning domain. Equivalently viewed as a many-to-one relation $UO \subseteq U \times D$.
- Group Ownership (GO) is a function GO: $U \rightarrow D$, mapping a group to its owning domain. Equivalently viewed as a many-to-one relation $GO \subseteq G \times D$.
- Object Type Owner (OTO) is a function OTO: $OT \rightarrow S$, mapping an OT to its owning service. Equivalently viewed as a many-to-one relation $OTO \subseteq OT \times S$.
- $UG \subseteq U \times G$ is a many-to-many relation assigning users to groups, where the user and group must be owned by the same domain.
- $PRP = P \times R$ is the set of project-role pairs.
- $PERMS = OT \times O$ is the set of permissions.
- $PA \subseteq PERMS \times R$ is a many-to-many permission-to-role assignment relation.
- $UA \subseteq U \times PRP$ is a many-to-many user-to-project role assignment relation.
- $GA \subseteq G \times PRP$ is a many-to-many group-to-project role assignment relation.
- Project Hierarchy (PH) is a function PH: $P \rightarrow P$, mapping a project to its parent project. Equivalently viewed as a many-to-one relation $PH \subseteq P \times P$. This is required to be a forest of rooted trees.
- Role Inheritance (RI) allows users' roles to be inherited from domain to project and from parent project to child project, as discussed earlier.
- user_tokens is a function $U \rightarrow 2^T$, mapping a user to a set of tokens; correspondingly, token user is a function token user $T \rightarrow U$, mapping a token to its owning user.
- token_project is a function token project: $T \rightarrow P$, mapping a token to its target project.

- token_roles is a function token roles: $T \rightarrow 2^R$, mapping a token to its set of roles. Formally, token_roles(t) = $\{r \in R \mid (\text{token\_user}(t),(\text{token\_project}(t),r)) \in UA\} \cup (\bigcup_{g \in user\_groups(token\_user(t))} \{r \in R \mid (g, (\text{token\_project}(t), r)) \in GA\})$.
- avail_token_perms is a function avail token perms: $T \rightarrow 2^{PERMS}$, mapping the permissions available to a user through a token. Formally, avail_token_perms(t) = $\bigcup_{r \in token\_roles(t)} \{perm \in PERMS \mid (perms,r) \in PA\}$.

4.3.2 Secure Information and Resource-Sharing Model in OpenStack

In this section, we present a model for sharing in OpenStack; we call it the Hierarchical Multitenancy OpenStack Access Control Model with Secure Isolated Domain extension (OSAC-HMT-SID model). In our discussion, we assume that a user belongs to one organization in the community, which is consistent with the user home-domain concept in OpenStack. The concept of a *home domain* requires that a user can belong to only one domain in OpenStack. OpenStack allows a user to be assigned to projects across domains and access those projects separately using the appropriate tokens.

The OSAC-HMT-SID model extends the OSAC-HMT model to include secure isolated domain (SID) (Zhang et al. 2014) functionality. We build the OSAC-HMT-SID model on top of the OSAC-HMT model. We will present the OSAC-HMT-SID model in a way that covers only the additional components compared to the OSAC-HMT model. Figure 4.3 shows the OSAC-HMT-SID model. We use circles to represents entities that can be created multiple times in OpenStack, whereas rectangles represent entities that can be created only once. The additional entity components included in the model are SID, Expert User (EU), Core Project (CP), Secure Isolated Project (SIP), and Open Project (OP):

- **Secure Isolated Domain (SID)**—A SID (Zhang et al. 2014) is a special domain that holds the security information for cross-organization security collaboration in the community cloud. It provides an administrative boundary for cybersecurity information and resource collecting, resource passing, analyzing and exporting results, as well as providing a secure isolated environment for cybersecurity collaborations among organizations.
- **Security Project (SP)**—SPs are hierarchical projects particularly used to collect, store, and analyze cybersecurity information for one organization. A SP provides the same capability of utilizing cloud resources as a normal project. Organizations keep their security information and resources in the SPs, with their security staff/users assigned to the corresponding level of project in the SP hierarchy. This separates an organization's regular projects from its SPs.
- **Core Project (CP)**—A CP is a shared project that holds the community cybersecurity committee (Sandhu et al. 2011). Each organization in the community has at least one user in the security committee, with one as an admin user of the CP and the rest as regular member users. The CP holds all SIPs that are designed for cyber-incident response and cybersecurity collaboration.
- **Open Project (OP)**—An OP is a project where users share public cybersecurity information and resources (Sandhu et al. 2011). Information published in an OP is public to every user who is subscribed to the project.
- **Secure Isolated Project (SIP)**—A SIP (Zhang et al. 2014) is a special project with constraints over its user membership, information, and resource utilization. The SIP

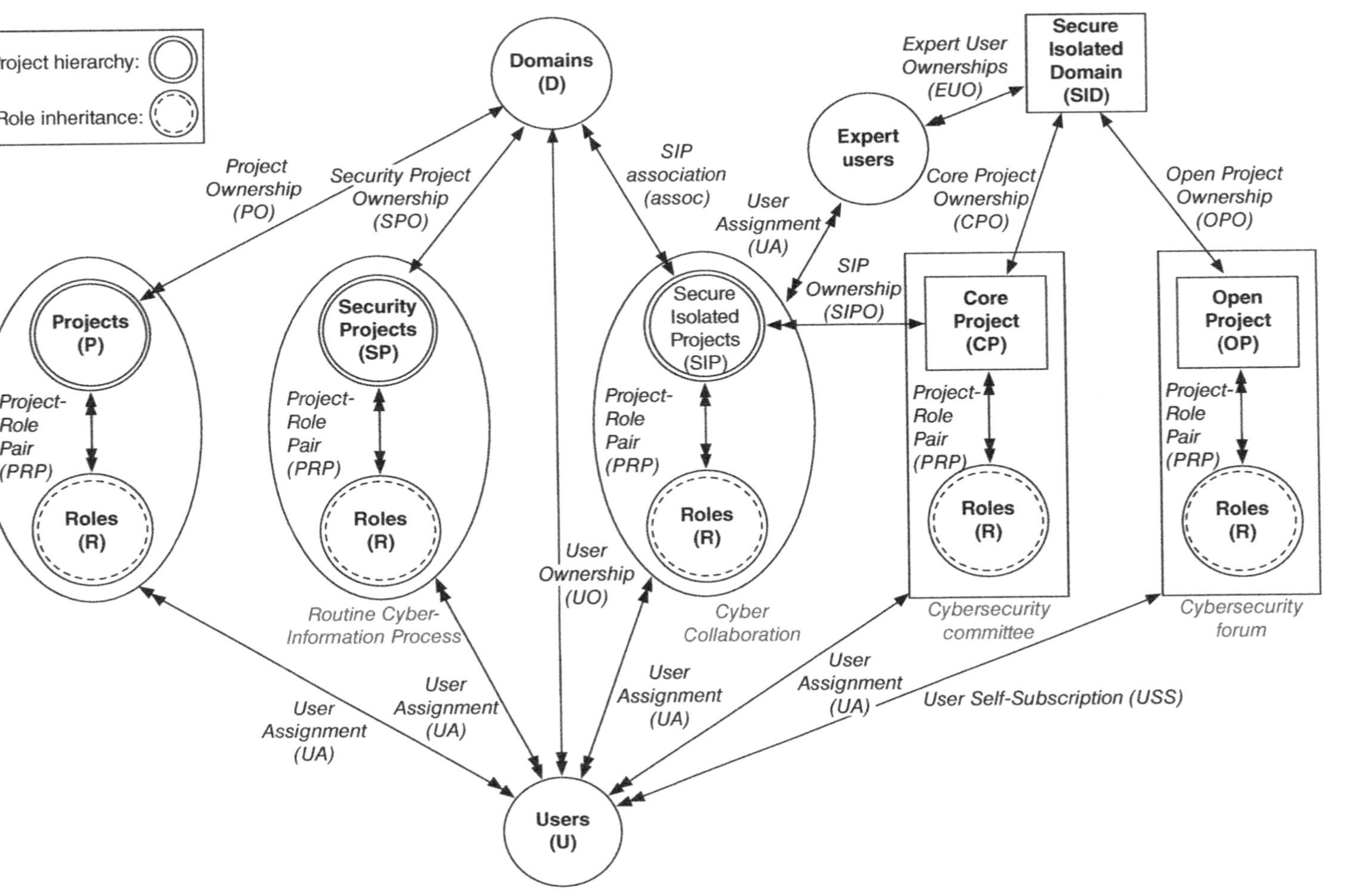

Figure 4.3 Hierarchical multitenancy OSAC model with SID extension (OSAC-HMT-SID) (ignoring the group, token, and services components).

provides a controlled environment for organizations to collaborate on security incidents.

- **Expert Users (EU)**—To get outside community professionals involved, EUs (Sandhu et al. 2011) are introduced to the SID. EUs originally don't belong to the community. They bring expertise from different cybersecurity categories. For instance, they may come from an IT consultant company that focuses on specific cyber attacks. Or they may be cybersecurity law-enforcement officers specializing in cybercrime. The involvement of EUs helps organizations handle cyber collaborations more effectively.

Following are the formalized concepts we just introduced, as well as the relationships among them.

Definition 4.2 OSAC-HMT-SID Model Components in Addition to OSAC-HMT

- SID is an implicitly existing SID, which is transparent to users. SID owns EU, CP, OP, and SIP, correspondingly represented by Expert User Ownership (EOU), CP Ownership (CPO), Open Project Ownership (OPO), and Secure Isolated Project Ownership (SIPO).
- SP, SIP, EU, and SO are finite sets of SPs, SIPs, EUs, and Swift Objects (SOs).
- Security Project Ownership (SPO) is a function SPO: SP $\rightarrow$ D, mapping a SP to its owning domain. Equivalently viewed as a one-to-one relation SPO $\subseteq$ D.
- Swift Object Ownership (SOO) is a function SOO: SO $\rightarrow$ P, mapping a SO to its owning project. Equivalently viewed as a many-to-one relation SOO $\subseteq$ SO $\times$ P.
- User Self Subscription (USS) is a function USS $\subseteq$ U $\times$ {<OP, *member*>}, a many-to-one user-to-project role assignment relation for the Member role in the single OP.
- SIP association (assoc) is a function assoc: SIP $\rightarrow 2^D$, mapping a SIP to all its member domains/organizations.

4.3.2.1 Administrative OSAC-HMT-SID Model

The administrative aspects of OSAC-HMT-SID are discussed informally next. A formal specification is given in Table 4.1.

Creation of the SID, CP, OP, and SP: A SID with a CP and OP is part of the community cloud functionality the CSP provides to its customers on behalf of organizations responding collaboratively to cyber incidents. The SID, CP, and OP are created when the community cloud is set up. Each domain has one corresponding SP. The creation of a SP is automatically done with the creation of a domain.

Initial user assignment for the SID, CP, OP, and SP: The SID has no admin users assigned on the domain level. The admin users of the CP come from an organization's domain. When a domain is created, the cloud admin assigns a domain admin user as an admin of the CP. We assume there is only one admin user for each domain. Domain admins assign admin users for their SPs. The OP doesn't have an admin user assigned to it. Each user in the Cloud can self-subscribe or unsubscribe as a member of the OP.

Create a SIP: Let *uSet* denote a set of domain admin users. A group of organizations comes together to create a SIP. Each organization in the group has equal administrative power over the SIP. The creation of the SIP succeeds based on agreement among the organizations. Organization membership in the SIP is established with the

Table 4.1 OSAC-HMT-SID administrative model.

Operation	Authorization Requirement	Update
SipCreate(uSet, sip) /* *A subset of Core Project/domain admin users together create a sip* */	∀ u ∈ uSet.(u ∈ U ∧ [u, <CP, admin>] ∈ UA) ∧ sip ∉ SIP	assoc(sip) $\cup_{u \in uSet}$ UO(u) SIP′ = SIP ∪ {sip} UA′ = UA ∪ uSet × {<sip, admin>}
SipDelete(uSet, sip) /* *The same subset of Core Project/domain admin users together delete a sip* */	∀ u ∈ uSet.(u ∈ U ∧ (u, <sip, admin>) ∈ UA ∧ (u, <CP, admin>) ∈ UA) ∧ assoc.(sip) = $\cup^{u \in uSet}$ UO(u) ∧ sip ∈ SIP	assoc(sip) = NULL SIP′ = SIP − {sip} UA′ = UA − uSet × {<sip, admin>}
ExpertUserCreate(coreadmin, eu) /* *Core Project admin users can create an expert user* */	coreadmin ∈ U ∧ (coreadmin, <CP, admin>) ∈ UA ∧ eu ∉ EU	EU′ = EU ∪ {eu}
ExpertUserDelete(coreadmin, eu) /* *Core Project admin users can delete an expert user* */	coreadmin ∈ U ∧ (coreadmin, <CP, admin>) ∈ UA ∧ eu ∈ EU	EU′ = EU − {eu}
ExpertUserList(adminuser) /* *Admin users of Core Project and SIPs can list expert users* */	adminuser ∈ U ∧ (∃ proj) {proj ∈ ({CP} ∪ SIP) ∧ (adminuser, <proj, admin>) ∈ UA}	
ExpertUserAdd(adminuser, r, eu, proj) /* *Core Project/sip admin can add an expert user to Core Project/sip* */	adminuser ∈ U ∧ proj ∈ ({CP} ∪ SIP) ∧ (adminuser, <proj, admin>) ∈ UA ∧ eu ∈ EU ∧ r ∈ R	UA′ = UA ∪ (eu, [proj, r])
ExpertUserRemove(adminuser, r, eu, proj) /* *Core Project/sip admin can remove an expert user from Core Project/sip* */	adminuser ∈ U ∧ proj ∈ ({CP} ∪ SIP) ∧ (adminuser, <proj, admin>) ∈ UA ∧ eu ∈ EU ∧ r ∈ R ∧ (eu, [proj, r]) ∈ UA	UA′ = UA − (eu, [proj, r])
UserAdd(adminuser, r, u, sp, p) /* *CP/Sip admin can add a user from their home domain Security Project to CP/sip* */	adminuser ∈ U ∧ (adminuser, <p, admin>) ∈ UA ∧ p ∈ ({CP} ∪ SIP) ∧ r ∈ R ∧ u ∈ U ∧(u, <sp, r>) ∈ UA ∧ SPO(sp) = UO(adminuser)	UA′ = UA ∪ (u, [p, r])
UserRemove(adminuser, r, u, sp, p) /* *CP/Sip admin can remove a user from the Core Project/sip* */	adminuser ∈ U ∧ (adminuser, <p, admin>) ∈ UA ∧ p ∈ ({CP} ∪ SIP) ∧ r ∈ R ∧ u ∈ U ∧ (u, <sp., r>) ∈ UA ∧ SPO(sp) = UO(adminuser) ∧ (u, [p, r]) ∈ UA	UA′ = UA − (u, [p, r])
OpenUserSubscribe(u, member, OP) /* *Users subscribe to Open Project* */	u ∈ U ∧ (u, <OP, member>) ∉ USS	USS′ = USS ∪ (u, <OP, member>)
OpenUserUnsubscribe(u, member, OP) /* *Users unsubscribe from Open Project* */	u ∈ U ∧ (u, <OP, member>) ∈ USS	USS′ = USS − (u, <OP, member>)
CopyObject(u, so1, sp., so2, p) /* *Copy object from Security Project to Core Project/SIP* */	so1 ∈ SO ∧ sp. ∈ SP ∧ so2 ∉ SO ∧ SOO(so1) = sp ∧ UO(u) = SPO(sp) ∧ u ∈ U ∧ (∃ r ∈ R) {(u, <sp, r>) ∈ UA ∧ (u, <p, r>) ∈ UA)} ∧ p ∈ ({CP} ∪ SIP)	SO′ = SO ∪ {so2} SOO(so2) = p
ExportObject(adminuser, so1, p. so2 sp) /* *Export object from Core Project/SIP to Security Project* */	adminuser ∈ U ∧ (adminuser, <p, admin>) ∈ UA ∧ p ∈ ({CP} ∪ SIP) ∧ so1 ∈ SO ∧ SOO(so1) = p ∧ so2 ∉ SO ∧ sp ∈ SP ∧ (adminuser, <sp., admin>) ∈ UA	SO′ = SO U {so2} SOO(so2) = sp

creation of the SIP. The size of the group ranges from one organization to the total number of organizations held in the community cloud. The group of organizations sets up a SIP by sending the SIP-creation request to the cloud admin. Users who are allowed to issue a SIP-creation command are admin users in CPs, who are domain admins as well. When a SIP is created, the users who issued the SIP-creation command automatically become the admin users of the SIP.

Delete a SIP: After the collaboration is finished, a SIP needs to be securely deleted. The delete command is issued by the same set of admin users (*uSet*) who issued the SIP-creation command. All information and resources are securely deleted. All users assigned to the SIP are removed from it. Removing information and resources guarantees no information and resources will leak after the SIP has been deleted. Removing users guarantees no users will have access to information and resources that belonged to a SIP.

Create/Delete an EU: New EUs are created when additional cyber expertise is needed, such as when a consultant company is introduced to the community or a new cybersecurity agent is involved with one of the collaboration groups. CP admin users send the EU-creation command to the cloud admin. he cloud admin returns the new EU and adds the user to the EU list. CP admin users can request to delete an EU. After the EU is deleted, the user will lose all access to any information and resources in the community cloud.

List EUs: CP and SIP admin users can list EUs in the SID. EUs are important human resources for cyber-collaboration activities. By listing the EUs in the SID, collaborative groups with SIPs can easily add experts to their SIPs.

Add/remove an EU: An EU is visible to all projects in the SID except the OP. Project admins in the SID can add EUs to their projects due to collaboration. After the cyber collaboration is done, project admins can remove EUs from their projects.

Add/remove a user to/from a CP/SIP: Admin users of a CP/SIP can add/remove users of their home SPs to/from CP or the corresponding SIP due to the need for collaboration. The removed user will lose access to information and resources that they had during collaborations in the CP/SIP.

Subscribe/unsubscribe a user to the **OP:** Every user in the OP is a normal member user. They can share cyber data but have no control over other users. Users subscribe/unsubscribe themselves to/from the OP. They will not be able to access and share any data once they leave the OP.

Copy data between a SP and CP/SIP: Users can copy data from SPs of their home domains to a CP and SIP. Users may be scoped to multiple projects in their home domains, but only data from SPs are allowed to be copied to a CP/SIP. Admin users can export data from CPs and SIPs to SPs of their home domains.

4.4 Access Control in AWS Cloud IaaS

In this section, we investigate a model for the AWS public cloud and demonstrate its flexibility by extending the access-control model to include information and resource sharing. The content of this section has been published in (Zhang et al. 2015b). As we did for OpenStack, for simplicity, we assume that each organization from the cloud community has only one tenant that is an AWS account.

4.4.1 AWS Access-Control Model

As a public CSP, AWS provides web services to its customers through AWS accounts. Customers that own an account have access to cloud resources. They can create users and grant them access to cloud resources in the account. A user belongs to a unique account. Users can also access resources in other accounts with federated permissions. We discuss the AWS access control (AWS-AC) model from two perspectives: within a single account and across accounts. AWS offers a form of policy-based access control, wherein permissions are defined over cloud resources in a policy file and policies are attached to entities such as users, groups, roles, and resources. Figure 4.4 depicts this model within a single account. In this and other figures in this chapter, dotted lines denote virtual relations between entities, whereas solid lines denote explicit relations. Cross-account access will be discussed later in the context of Figure 4.5.

The AWS-AC model has seven components: accounts (A), users (U), groups (G), roles (R), services (S), object types (OT), and operations (OP). We also introduce other entities such as policies and credentials, which are implicitly included in the model:

- **Accounts**—In AWS, *accounts* are basic resource containers that allow customers to own specific amounts of (virtual) cloud resources. Accounts are the units of usages of cloud resources and billing. Customers get public cloud services through an AWS account.
- **Users** and **groups**—*Users* are individuals who can be authenticated by AWS and authorized to access cloud resources through an account. A *group* is simply a set of users. Users and groups belong to an account. The existence of groups is for the convenience of managing multiple users as a single unit. Each policy attached to a group

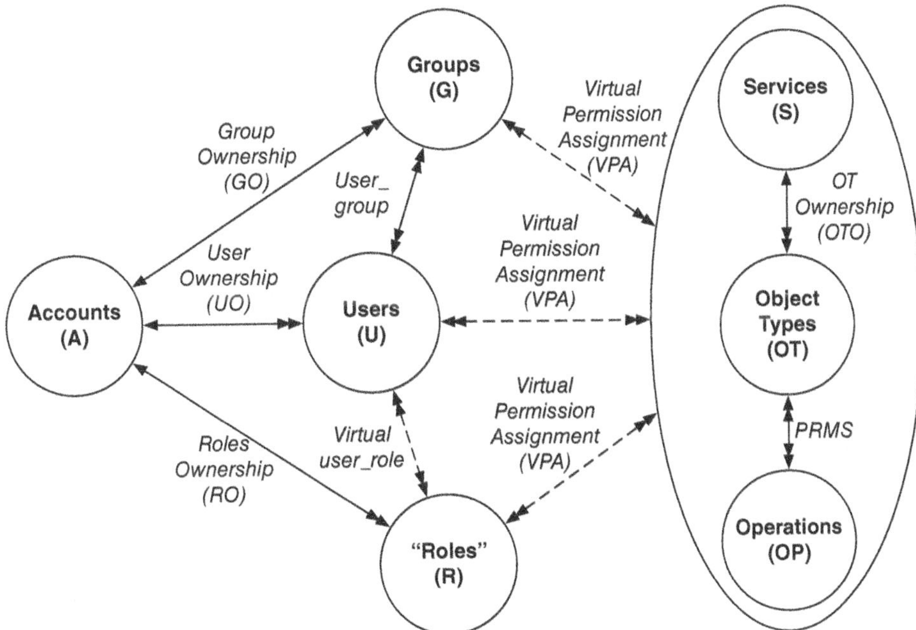

Figure 4.4 AWS access control within a single account.

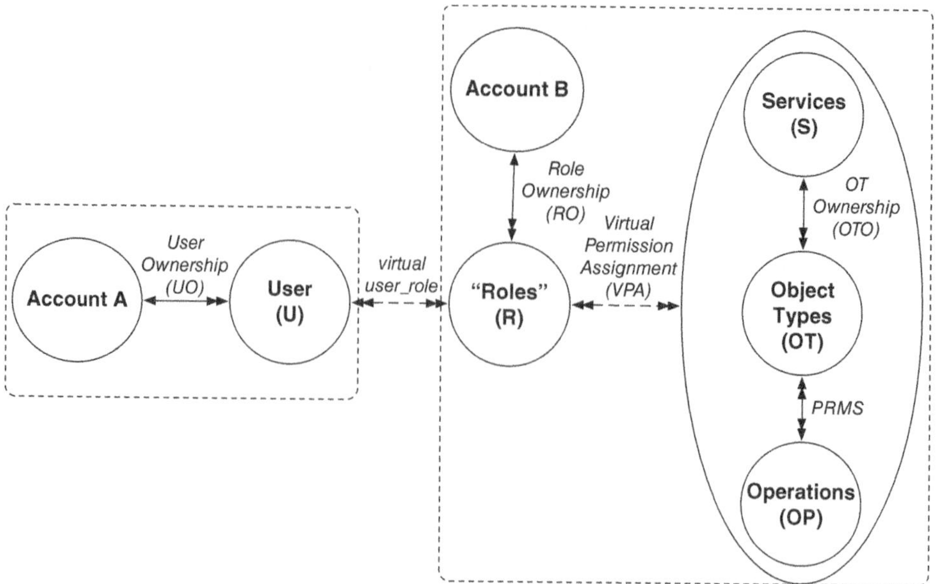

Figure 4.5 AWS access control across accounts (users in account A access services and resources in account B).

applies to all group members. For simplicity, we use the term *users* to represents both users and groups in the rest of this discussion.

- **Virtual permission assignment**—In AWS, users' permissions over services and resources are defined in *policy files*. Policy files can be attached to a user, a group, a role, or a specific cloud resource. By attaching a policy to a user, a group, or a role, users gain permissions to corresponding cloud resources. The policy defines the actions the user will perform and cloud resources on which the actions will function. Multiple permissions can be defined in one policy file. Multiple policy files can be attached to one entity. AWS achieves permission assignment in a virtual manner via the policies attached to various relevant entities.
- **Roles**—*Roles* in AWS are mainly used for cross-account permission purposes. However, roles can also be used for internal users in an account. Policy files can be attached to a role. Roles also define the trust relation between principals, which can be either AWS accounts or users. Users use roles through the *AssumeRole* action to access corresponding resources. To emphasize the difference between the usual concept of roles in role-based access control (RBAC) and roles in AWS, we use quotation marks around "Roles" in the figures.
- **Services**—*Services* refer to cloud services AWS provides to its customers. A CSP leases cloud resources to its customers in terms of services. AWS provides customers with services such as compute, storage, networking, administration, and database.
- **Object types and operations**—An *object type* represents a specific type of object. From the CSP's viewpoint, objects are more like services. We define object types as particular service types the Cloud provides. For instance, with the compute service EC2, the object type is a VM; with the storage service S3, the object type is a bucket, etc.

- **Credentials**—AWS *credentials* are used for both authentication and authorization. Account owners can create IAM users with their own security credentials to allow these users to access AWS services and resources. Account owners can also grant external federated users from other accounts temporary security credentials to allow them to access the account's AWS services and resources.
- **Cross-account access**—Users in one AWS account can access services and resources in another AWS account through the action *AssumeRole* with temporary security credentials, as shown in Figure 4.5. In this and other figures, a thick arrow represents an action taken by a user to assume a role. Users from account A access services and resources in account B through roles created in account B, by being attached with policies of the action *AssumeRole* and a defined target resource.

With these concepts described above, we can formalize the AWS-AC model as follows.

Definition 4.3 AWS-AC Model Components

- A, U, G, R, S, OT, and OP are finite sets of existing accounts, users, groups, roles, services, object types, and operations, respectively, in an AWS public cloud system.
- User Ownership (UO) is a function UO: U → A, mapping a user to its owning account. Equivalently viewed as a many-to-one relation UO ⊆ U × A.
- Group Ownership (GO) is a function GO: G → A, mapping a group to its owning account. Equivalently viewed as a many-to-one relation GO ⊆ G × A.
- Roles Ownership (RO) is a function RO: R → A, mapping a role to its owning account. Equivalently viewed as a many-to-one relation GO ⊆ R × A.
- Object Type Owner (OTO) is a function OTO: OT → S, mapping an object type to its owning service. Equivalently viewed as a many-to-one relation OTO ⊆ OT × S.
- PERMS = OT × OP is the set of permissions.
- Virtual Permission Assignment (VPA) is a many-to-many virtual relation VPA ⊆ (U ∪ G ∪ R) × PERMS, resulting from policies attached to users, groups, roles, and resources.
- user_group ⊆ U × G is a many-to-many relation assigning users to groups, where the user and group must be owned by the same account.
- virtual_user_role (VUR) is a virtual relation VUR ⊆ U × R, resulting from policies attached to various entities. *AssumeRole* is an action allowing users to activate a role authorized in the VUR.

4.4.2 Secure Information and Resource-Sharing Model in AWS

In this section, we present an access-control model for AWS with the SID extension (AWS-AC-SID). We build the AWS-AC-SID model on top of the AWS-AC model to include SID functionality (Zhang et al. 2014). We present the AWSAC-SID model so as to cover only the additional components added to the AWS-AC model. Figure 4.6 shows the AWS-AC-SID model.

The additional components included in AWSAC-SID model are SID, SIP, EU, CP, and OP. These are described next:

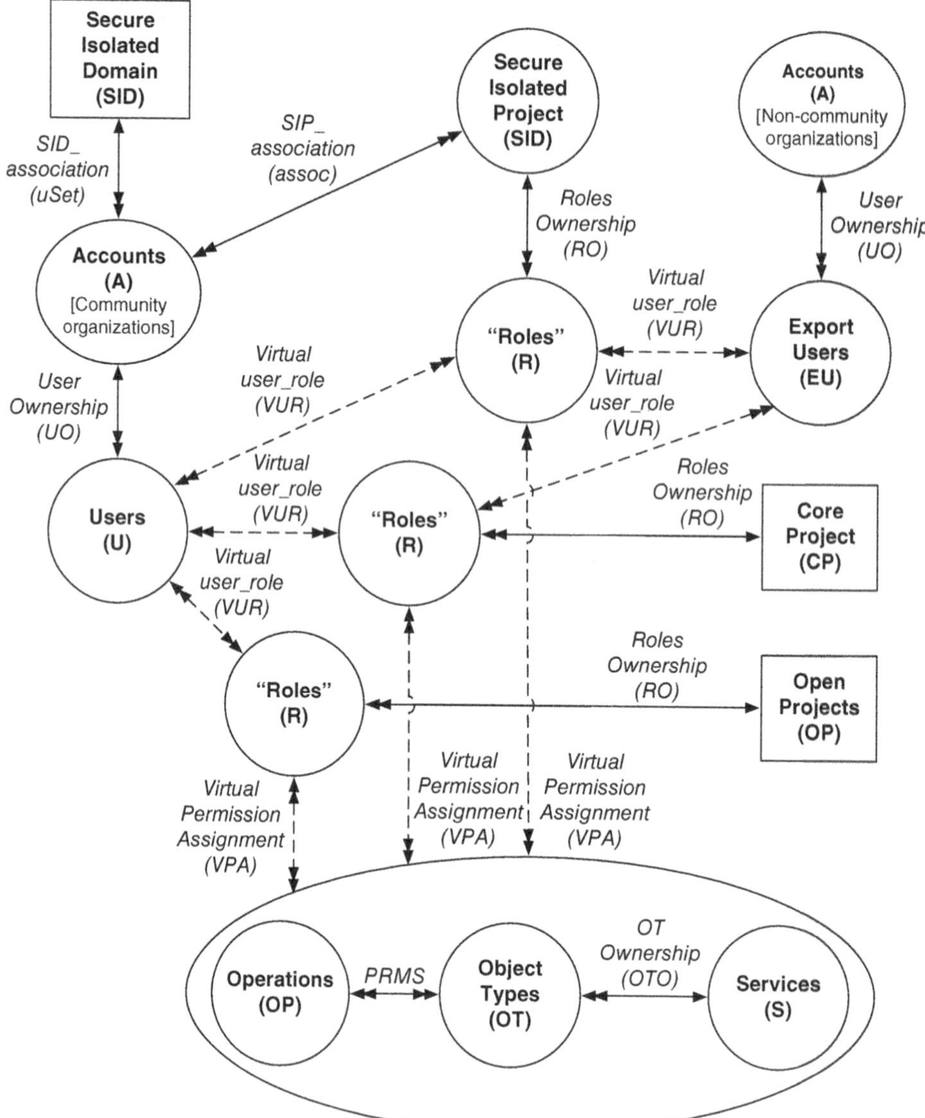

Figure 4.6 Amazon Web Services (AWS) Access Control model with SID extension (AWSAC-SID) (ignoring the groups entity).

- **Secure Isolated Domain (SID)**—A SID (Zhang et al. 2014) is a special domain holding security information and resources for cross-organizational security collaborations. The SID provides an administrative boundary for cybersecurity information and resource collection and analysis, and a secure isolated environment for cybersecurity collaborations in a community of organizations. The SID holds all SIPs designed for cyber-incident response and security collaboration within this community of organizations. SID also holds a CP and an OP, as shown in Figure 4.7.

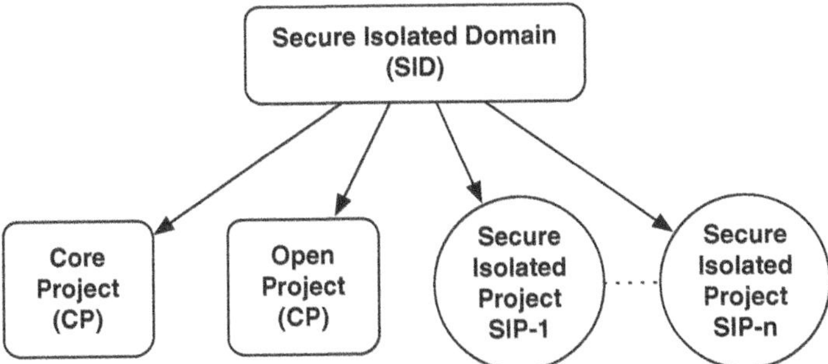

Figure 4.7 SID composition.

- **Secure Isolated Project (SIP)**—A SIP (Zhang et al. 2014) is a special project with constraints over its user membership. It is used to collect, store, and analyze cybersecurity information for specific security reasons. A SIP provides a controlled environment for a group of organizations within the community to collaborate and coordinate on cyber incidents and other security issues.
- **Core Project (CP)**—A CP is a shared project holding the cybersecurity committee (Sandhu et al. 2011) for the community of organizations. Each organization in the community has at least one representative security user in the committee.
- **Open Project (OP)**—An OP is an open shared project where users from the community of organizations share common cybersecurity information and resources (Sandhu et al. 2011). It is a common forum for all community users to share general security information. Information published in the OP is public to every user in the project.
- **Expert Users (EU)**—To involve outside professionals, EUs (Sandhu et al. 2011) are introduced to the SID. EU don't belong to the community of organizations. They are from other professional security organizations in the same public cloud. These experts bring different cybersecurity skills. For instance, they may come from an IT consultant company that focuses on specific cyber attacks. They may be cybersecurity law-enforcement officers specializing in cybercrime. The involvement of EUs helps organizations handle cyber collaborations more effectively. The SID maintains an EU list that is available for collaboration inside the SID.

The following formalizes these concepts as well as the relationships among them.

Definition 4.4 AWS-AC-SID Model Components in Addition to the AWS-AC Model

- SIP, EU, and O are finite sets of SIPs, EUs, and objects.
- SID is a unique SID serving a community of organizations. The SID owns a CP, an OP, and a number of SIPs. The SID also maintains EU resources.
- SIP association (assoc) is a function assoc: SIP → 2A, mapping a SIP to all its member accounts/organizations.
- Object Ownership (OO) is a function OO: O → A, mapping an object to its owning account. Equivalently viewed as a many-to-one relation OO ⊆ O × A. O is a resource that belongs to an account. We didn't include Object (O) and Object Ownership (OO) in Figure 4.6, since it mainly shows the administrative perspective of the model.

4.4.2.1 Administrative AWS-AC-SID Model

For proprietary products such as AWS, we cannot modify the cloud platform. SID functionality can be provided as a security service to all organizations in the SID community by a third party in AWS. The CP and OP are created with the SID. Each organization can join several SIDs with different communities of organizations. Each of these SIDs is isolated from the others.

The roles can be two types, administrative and member, which denote the permission of being able to manage users and permissions only for resources, respectively. The roles *CPadmin* and *SIPadmin* represent limited administrative power in the CP or a SIP, respectively, which gives the CP or SIP admin users permission to add and remove other users from their home account to the CP or a SIP. The roles *CPmember*, *OPmember*, and *SIPmember* represent operative permissions that can be given to normal users to access the CP, the OP, or a SIP. Since roles in AWS are local, *SIPadmin* and *SIPmember* are two sets of roles, separately representing the set of admin roles and the set of member roles in all SIPs; while *CPadmin*, *CPmember*, and *OPmember* are single roles in an account.

The administrative aspects of the AWS-AC-SID model are discussed informally below. A formal specification is given in Table 4.2.

Initially set up the SID: In the case of one SID serving one community of organizations, we can initially set up the SID with one CP and one OP. The member organizations of the SID are fixed. Let *uSet* denote a fixed group of security admin users from all organizations of the community, with one admin user for one organization. Each organization in the community has equal limited administrative power in the SID, which is carried through *uSet*. The SID maintains *uSet* as a core group of admin users in the SID. Only users from *uSet* later can dynamically create SIPs in the SID.

With the setting up of the SID, users in *uSet* automatically get limited administrative permission in the CP, represented by the role *CPadmin*. With this role, CP admin users can add and remove other users from their home account to the CP. The OP is open for all users from the community of organizations. No admin users are needed for the OP. All users can add themselves to the OP with the role *OPmember* as a normal member user.

Create a SIP—A SIP is created whenever there is a need for cyber collaboration among a subset of the community organizations. It might be because of a cyber incident, a collaborative security program, or a secure information-sharing program. A subset of the community of organizations' representative security admin users *subuSet* together creates a SIP. The creation of a SIP succeeds based on agreement among the subset of the community of organizations. Each organization in the SIP has equal limited administrative power, represented by a role in *SIPadmin*. The role gives SIP admin users permission to add and remove other users from their home account to the SIP. Organizations set up a SIP by sending the SIP-creation request to the SID manager account.

Delete a SIP—After the collaboration is finished, a SIP needs to be securely deleted. The delete command is issued by the same set of the security admin users (*subuSet*) who issue the SIP-creation request. All information and resources are securely deleted in the SIP. All users assigned to the SIP are removed from it.

Table 4.2 AWS-AC-SID administrative model.

Operation	Authorization Requirement	Update
SipCreate(subuSet, sip) /* *A subset of organization security admin users together create a sip* */	∀ u ∈ subuSet.(u ∈ *uSet*) ∧ sip ∉ SIP	assoc(sip) = $\cup_{u \in subuSet}$ UO(u) SIP′ = SIP ∪ {sip}
SipDelete(subuSet, sip) /* *The same subset of security admin users together delete a sip* */	∀ u ∈ subuSet.(u ∈ *uSet*) ∧ sip ∈ SIP ∧ assoc(sip) = $\cup_{u \in subuSet}$UO(u)	assoc(sip) = NULL SIP′ = SIP − {sip}
CpUserAdd(adminu, u) /* *CP admin adds a user from their home account to CP* */	adminu ∈ *uSet* ∧ u ∈ U ∧ UO(u) = UO(adminu)	VUR′ = VUR ∪ {(u, *CPmember*)}
CpUserRemove(adminu, u) /* *CP admin removes a user from CP* */	adminu ∈ *uSet* ∧ u ∈ U ∧ UO(u) = UO(adminu) ∧ (u, *CPmember*) ∈ VUR	VIR′ = VIR − {(u, *CPmember*)}
SIPUserAdd(adminu, u, r, sip) /* *Sip admin adds a user from their home account to SIP* */	adminu ∈ *uSet* ∧ UO(adminu) ∈ assoc.(sip) ∧ u ∈ U ∧ r ∈ *SIPmember* ∧ RO(r) = sip ∧ sip ∈ SIP ∧ UO(u) = UO(adminu)	VUR′ = VUR ∪ {(u, r)}
SIPUserRemove(adminu, u, r, sip) /* *Sip admin removes a user from SIP* */	adminu ∈ *uSet* ∧ UO(adminu) ∈ assoc.(sip) ∧ u ∈ U ∧ r ∈ *SIPmember* ∧ RO(r) = sip ∧ (u, r) ∈ VUR ∧ sip ∈ SIP ∧ UO(u) = UO(adminu)	VUR′ = VUR − {(u, r)}
OpenUserAdd(u) /* *Users add themselves to OP* */	u ∈ U ∧ UO(u) ∈ UO(*uSet*)	VUR′ = VUR ∪ {(u, *OPmember*)}
OpenUserRemove(u) /* *Users remove themselves from OP* */	u ∈ U ∧ UO(u) ∈ UO(*uSet*) ∧ (u, *OPmember*) ∈ VUR	VUR′ = VUR − {(u, *OPmember*)}
CpEUserAdd(adminu, eu) /* *CP admin adds an expert user to CP* */	adminu ∈ *uSet* ∧ eu ∈ EU	VUR′ = VUR ∪ {(eu, *CPmember*)}
CpEUserRemove(adminu, eu) /* *CP admin removes an expert user from CP* */	adminu ∈ *uSet* ∧ eu ∈ EU ∧ (eu, *CPmember*) ∈ VUR	VUR′ = VUR − {(eu, *CPmember*)}
SipEUserAdd(adminu, eu, r, sip) /* *SIP admin adds an expert user to SIP* */	adminu ∈ *uSet* ∧ UO(adminu) ∈ assoc(sip) ∧ eu ∈ EU ∧ r ∈ *SIPmember* ∧ RO(r) = sip ∧ sip ∈ SIP	VUR′ = VUR ∪ {(eu, r)}
SipEUserRemove(adminu, eu, r, sip) /* *SIP admin removes an expert user from SIP* */	adminu ∈ *uSet* ∧ UO(adminu) ∈ assoc(sip) ∧ eu ∈ EU ∧ r ∈ *SIPmember* ∧ RO(r) = sip ∧ (eu, r) ∈ VUR ∧ sip ∈ SIP	VUR′ = VUR − {(eu, r)}
CpCopyObject(u, o1, o2) /* *Users copy objects from organization accounts to CP* */	o1 ∈ O ∧ 02 ∉ O ∧ UO(u) = 00(o1) ∧ u ∈ U ∧ (u, *CPmember*) ∈ VUR	O′ = O ∪ {o2} OO(o2) = CP
CpExportObject(adminu, o1, o2) /* *Admin users export objects from CP to organizations accounts* */	adminu ∈ *uSet* ∧ o1 ∈ O ∧ OO(o1) = CP ∧ o2 ∉ O	O′ = O ∪ {o2} OO(o2) = UO(adminu)

(*Continued*)

Table 4.2 (Continued)

Operation	Authorization Requirement	Update
SipCopyObject(u, r, o1, o2, sip) /* *Users copy objects from organization accounts to a SIP* */	o1 ∈ O ∧ o2 ∉ O ∧ UO(u) = OO(o1) ∧ u ∈ U ∧ r ∈ *SIPmember* ∧ RO(r) = sip ∧ (u, r) ∈ VUR ∧ sip ∈ SIP	O′ = O ∪ {o2} OO(o2) = sip
SipExportObject(adminu, o1, o2, sip) /* *Admin users export objects from SIP to organization accounts* */	adminu ∈ *uSet* ∧ UO(adminu) ∈ assoc(sip) ∧ o1 ∈ O ∧ OO(o1) = sip ∧ o2 ∉ O	O′ = O ∪ {o2} OO(o2) = UO(adminu)

Add/remove a user to/from a CP—CP admin users are the set of security administrative users (*uSet*) from the community of organizations. These limited administrative users can add/remove users of their organizations to/from the CP. All users added to the CP are existing users from an organization's account. The limited administrative users don't have permission to create new users. They can only add existing users to the CP. When users are removed from the CP, they lose access to corresponding information and resources in the CP, regardless of the ownership of the piece of information in the past.

Add/remove a user to/from a SIP—Users from *subuSet* who are assigned the role *SIPadmin* have limited administrative power in the SIP. They can add/remove users of their home accounts to/from the corresponding SIP due to a need for collaboration. Users lose access to information and resources after they are removed from the SIP. Administrative users in a SIP can see all users added from the community of organizations, as well as information and resources they bring in, which means there are no hidden users, information, or resources in a SIP.

Add/remove a user to an OP—Every user in the collaborative community of organizations is allowed to join the OP. Users in the OP have equal but limited permissions. They can share cyber data but have no control over other users. We use the role *OPmember* to represent this limited permission. Users add/remove themselves from their organizations to/from OP. Users cannot access and share any data once they leave the OP.

Add/remove an EU to/from a SIP—EUs are required when external cyber expertise needs to be involved. For instance, a cyber incident requires experts from security consultant companies, government cyber experts, cyber police, etc. SID services maintain a relationship with external expertise. EUs can be added/remove to/from CPs and SIPs as members. Users from *uSet* can request to add/remove EUs to/from the CP, while users from *subuSet* can request to add/remove EUs to/from a SIP. There are situations in which an existing EU in a SIP needs to be removed. For instance, the contract with a cyber-consultant company ends, or a cybersecurity agent finishes their task as part of cyber collaboration. In such cases, securely deleting an EU is necessary. After the EU is deleted, the user loses all access to information and resource in the SIP.

Copy data between organization accounts and a CP/SIP—Users can copy data from their home accounts to the CP or a SIP. Administrative users from *uSet* or *subuSet* can export data from the CP or a SIP to their home accounts.

4.5 Access Control in Azure Cloud IaaS

In this section, we introduce a model for the Microsoft Azure cloud and demonstrate its flexibility by extending the access-control model to include information and resource sharing. As we did for AWS, we assume that each organization from the cloud community has only one tenant that is an Azure account.

4.5.1 Azure Access-Control Model

In Azure, any user has the ability to create an Azure account. The user who creates an Azure account will be the owner and super-administrative user of that account. Local users created in an Azure Active Directory (AAD) can create their own Azure accounts that are isolated from the parent account. Azure has two main components to manage users' access to resources in the Cloud: AAD and Subscriptions (Sub). To use resources in Azure, a user has to be assigned to a subscription. AAD helps to manage users, including both local AAD users and other valid Microsoft users. Azure offers a form of RBAC wherein permissions are defined over cloud resources within roles in resource groups. Roles can then be assigned to users. Roles are predefined in Azure.

The Azure Access Control (Azure-AC) model has 14 entities: Accounts (A), Azure Active Directory (AAD), Subscription (Sub), Azure Active Directory Role (AADR), Azure Active Directory User (AADU), Non-Azure Active Directory User (NAADU), Group (G), Resource Group (RG), Role (R), Subscription Role (SubR), Resource (RS), Service (S), Object Type (OT), and Operation (OP), as shown in Figure 4.8:

- **Account (A)**—To have its own public cloud resources, an organization needs to open an Azure *account*. An Azure account allows an organization to own specific (virtual) cloud resources that can be accessed through Azure cloud services.
- **Azure Active Directory (AAD)**—AAD is Microsoft's multitenant cloud-based directory and identity-management service. It provides a full suite of identity-management capabilities including multifactor authentication, device registration, self-service password management, privileged account management, RBAC, security monitoring, and so on. AAD also provides single sign-on (SSO) access to cloud SaaS applications. In addition, it can integrate with other identity-management solutions used in industry.
- **Subscription (Sub)**—Users have access to cloud resources via *subscriptions*. Subscriptions are the units of usage and billing for cloud resources. In order to have access to cloud resources, users must be assigned to at least one subscription.
- **Azure Active Directory Role (AADR)**—AADRs allow users to manage the directory and identity-related features. AAD has a set of administrative roles, including billing, global, password, service, and user administrator. Each of these administrative roles is designed for a different specific administrative purpose. It also has a normal user role, which has no administrative power.
- **Subscription Role (SubR)**—SubRs are a separate role set from AADRs. SubRs are administrative roles that give users permissions to manage cloud resources via a subscription. SubRs include service administrator and co-administrators, both of which can give users access to cloud services. The services administrator and co-administrators can be either Microsoft accounts or AAD users. A service administrator cannot be a local AAD user from the same AAD assigned to that subscription.

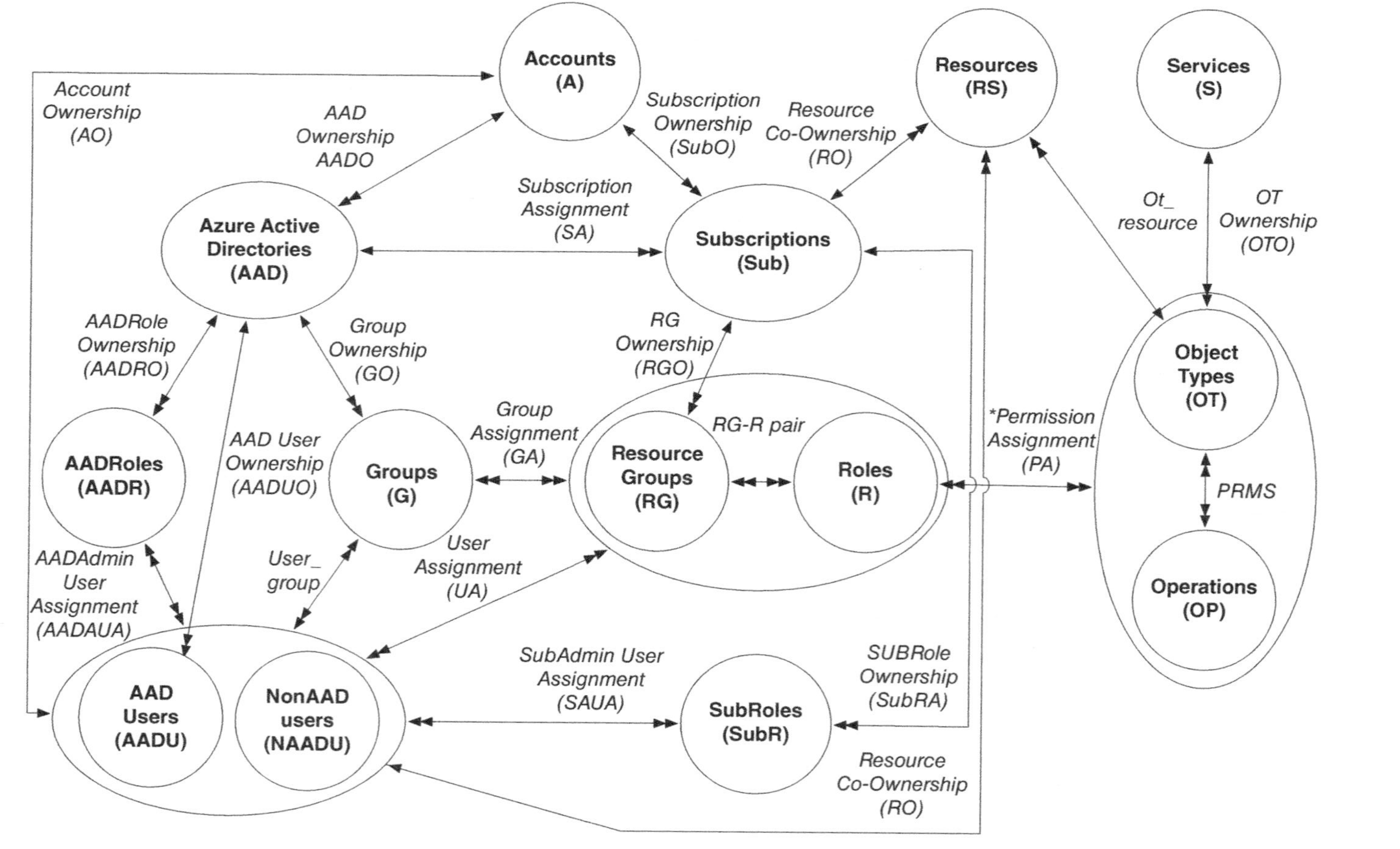

Figure 4.8 Azure Access Control (Azure-AC) model.

- **Azure Active Directory User (AADU)** and **Non-Azure Active Directory User (NAADU)**—These are individuals who can be authenticated by Azure and authorized to access cloud resources through an Azure account. Users from both Microsoft accounts and partner organization accounts are allowed to access to cloud resources in Azure. AADUs are users created in AAD. They can be administrative users of the directory or normal users. NAADUs are users not from the local AAD, but from partner organizations and other Microsoft users.
- **Group (G)**—A *group* is simply a set of users; it can include both AADUs and NAADUs. Groups belong to an AAD account. The existence of groups serves to allow the convenient management of multiple users as a single unit. Each policy attached to a group applies to all group members.
- **Resource Group (RG)**—RGs are logical resource containers that allow customers to add various cloud resources like databases, VMs, etc. RGs provides a way to monitor and control users' access to collections of cloud resources.
- **Role (R)**—Users are assigned to a RG with *roles* to get permissions to access cloud resources. Roles allow users to have permissions to access cloud resources: for instance, VMs, storage, networking, etc. Roles can be different collections of meta-permissions like read and write toward a specific resource. Roles can only be assigned to users inside a RG.
- **Resource (RS)**—*Resources* refer to cloud assets that can be owned by users. Cloud assets are cloud resources such as VMs, databases, storage, etc. Since the only way for users to access resources is through subscriptions, we also define that the subscription has ownership over the resources.
- **Service (S)**—*Services* refer to cloud services Azure provides to its customers. A CSP leases cloud resources to its customers in terms of services. Azure provides customers with services such as compute, storage, networking, administration, and databases.
- **Object Type (OT)** and **Operation (OP)**—An OT represents a specific type of object. From the CSP's viewpoint, objects are more like services. We define OTs as particular service types the Cloud provides. For instance, with the compute service, the OT is a VM; with the storage service, the OT is a storage container; etc.

With these concepts described, we can formalize the Azure-AC model as follows.

Definition 4.5 Azure-AC Model Components

- A, AAD, Sub, RG, R, AADR, SubR, AADU, NAADU, G, RS, S, OT, and OP are finite sets of existing accounts, Azure Active Directories, subscriptions, resource groups, roles, Azure AD roles, subscription roles, AAD users, non-Azure AD users, groups, resources, services, object types, and operations, respectively, in an Azure cloud system.
- Account Ownership (AO) is a function AO: $A \rightarrow U$, mapping an account to its owning user.
- AAD Ownership (AADO) is a function AADO: $AAD \rightarrow A$, mapping an AAD to its owning account. Equivalently viewed as a many-to-one relation $AADO \subseteq AAD \times A$.
- Subscription Ownership (SubO) is a function SubO: $Sub \rightarrow A$, mapping a subscription to its owning account. Equivalently viewed as a many-to-one relation $SubO \subseteq Sub \times A$.

- Resource Group Ownership (RGO) is a function RGO: U → Sub, mapping a RG to its owning subscription. Equivalently viewed as a many-to-one relation GRO ⊆ RG × Sub.
- AAD User Ownership (AADUO) is a function AADUO: AADU → AAD, mapping a user to its owning AAD. Equivalently viewed as a many-to-one relation AADUO ⊆ AADU × AAD.
- Group Ownership (GO) is a function GO: G → AAD, mapping a group to its owning AAD. Equivalently viewed as a many-to-one relation GO ⊆ G × AAD.
- Azure AD Roles Ownership (AADRO) is a function AADRO: AADR → AAD, mapping a Azure AD role to its owning AAD. Equivalently viewed as a many-to-one relation AADRO ⊆ U × A.
- Resource Co-Ownership (RSO) is a function RSO: RS → Sub ∨ RS → (AADU ∪ NAAUD), mapping a piece of a resource to its owning subscription and user. Equivalently viewed as a many-to-one relation RSO ⊆ RS × Sub ∪ RS × (AADU ∪ NAAUD).
- Object Type Owner (OTO) is a function OTO: OT → S, mapping an OT to its owning service. Equivalently viewed as a many-to-one relation OTO ⊆ OT × S.
- Resource Group Role (RG-R) pair ⊆ GR × R is a many-to-many relation mapping RGs to roles.
- Subscription Assignment (SubA) is a many-to-one relation SubA ⊆ Sub × AAD.
- Subscription Roles Assignment (SubRA) is a many-to- many relation SubRA ⊆ Sub × SubR.
- AADAdmin User Assignment (AADAUA) is a many-to-many relation AADAUA ⊆ (AADU ∪ NonAADU) × AADR, mapping a user to a AAD.
- SubAdmin User Assignment (SAUA) is a many-to-many relation SAUA ⊆ (AADU ∪ NonAADU) × SubR. There is one exception to the SAUA relation in assigning a service admin to a subscription. Every subscription has only one service admin user assigned to it, while it can have up to 200 co-admin users assigned to it.
- User Assignment (UA) is a many-to-many relation UA ⊆ (AADU ∪ NonAADU) × RG-R, mapping a user to a RG role pair.
- Group Assignment (GA) is a many-to-many relation GA ⊆ G × RG.
- Permission Assignment (PA) is a many-to-many relation PA ⊆ (RG × R) × PREM, assigning RG role pairs to permissions. One thing we need to mention is that Azure has fixed sets of collections of permissions that users can choose from, instead of giving users the capability to define their own permission sets.
- user_group ⊆ U × G is a many-to-many relation assigning users to groups, where the user and group must be owned by the same account.
- ot_resource ⊆ OT × RS is a one-to-many relation mapping resources to OTs.
- PRMS = OT × OP is the set of permissions.

4.5.2 Secure Information and Resource-Sharing Model in Azure

In this section, we present an access-control model for Azure with the SID extension (Azure-AC-SID). We extend the Azure-AC model to include SID functionality (Zhang et al. 2014). We present the Azure-AC-SID model so as to cover only the additional components added to the Azure-AC model. Figure 4.9 shows the Azure-AC-SID model.

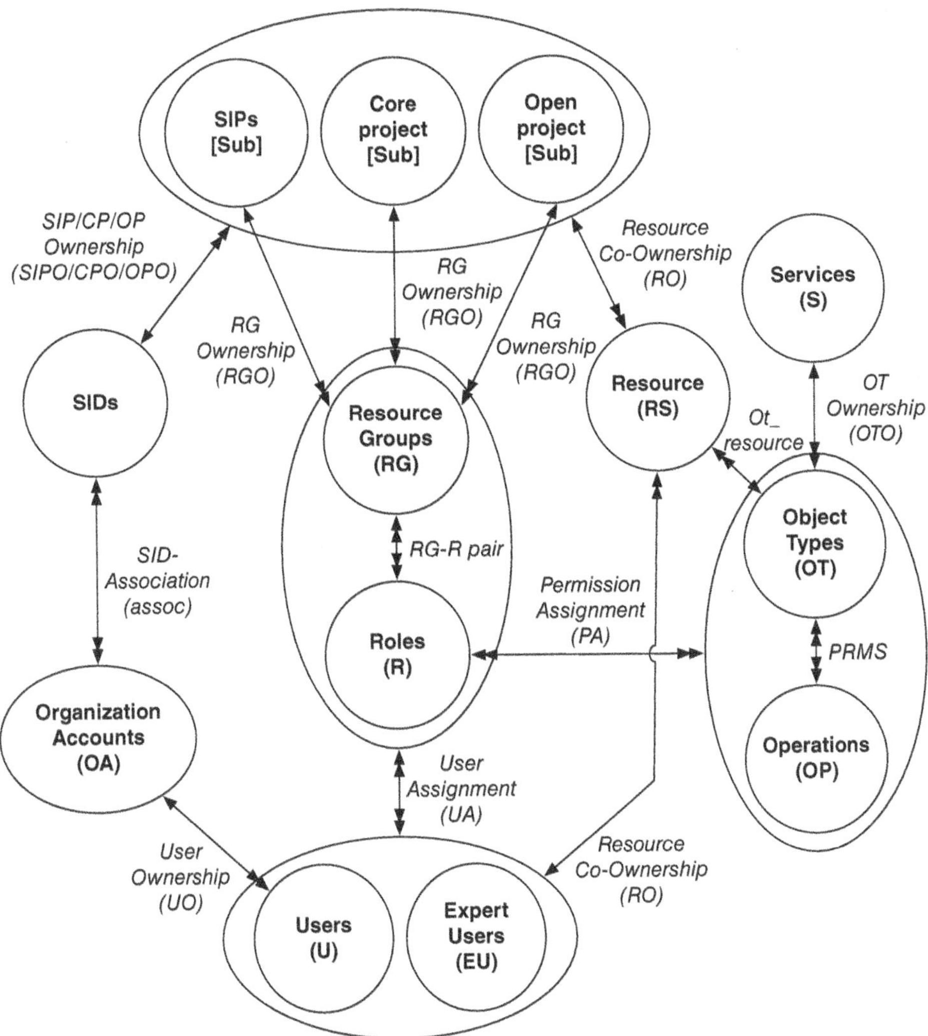

Figure 4.9 Azure Access Control model with SID extension (Azure-AC-SID) (ignoring the groups entity).

The following introduces the Azure-AC-SID model. The additional components included are Secure Isolated Domain (SID), Secure Isolated Project (SIP), Expert User (EU), User (U), Core Project (CP), and Open Project (OP):

- **Secure Isolated Domain (SID)**—The SID (Zhang et al. 2014) is a special domain, holding security information and resources for cross-organizational security collaboration. The SID provides an administrative boundary and a secure isolated environment for cybersecurity collaborations in a community of organizations. Each SID holds several SIPs designed for cyber-incident response and security collaboration among a group of organizations, a CP, and an OP for general secure information and resource sharing.

- **Secure Isolated Project (SIP)**—The SIP (Zhang et al. 2014) is a special project with limited user membership. It is used to collect, store, and analyze cybersecurity information for specific cyber incidents. A SIP provides an isolated, controlled environment for a group of organizations within the community to collaborate and coordinate on cyber incidents and other security issues. Subscriptions provide isolated resource containers for different projects to use. Thus, we design projects using subscriptions.
- **Core Project (CP)**—The CP is a shared project holding the cybersecurity committee (Sandhu et al. 2011) for the community of organizations. Each organization in the community has representative security users in the committee. CPs handle routine security tasks for the community.
- **Open Project (OP)**—The OP is an open shared project where users from the community of organizations share common cybersecurity information and resources (Sandhu et al. 2011). It is a common forum for all organizational users in the community to share general security information. Information published in the OP is public to every user associated with the subscription.
- **Expert User (EU)**—EUs (Sandhu et al. 2011) are external non-organizational professionals. They don't belong to the group of organizations. They are from other professional security organizations that bring different cybersecurity skills. They could be from IT consultant companies or from government cybersecurity law-enforcement departments. A SID maintains an EU list that is available to any project inside the SID.
- **User (U)**—Users include both AADUs and NAADUs, which refer to either Microsoft users or partner organization users. We use one User entity to represents all users that are allowed to access cloud resources, since from the standpoint of SID functionality, as long as the user is associated with the organization's AAD, it does not care where the user comes from.
- **Organization accounts**—Organization accounts represent organizations in the community. They can be either AAD accounts or organizations enterprise accounts that are identified by AAD. Organization accounts allow organizations to own a specific amount of (virtual) cloud resources.

The following formalizes these concepts, as well as the relationships among them.

Definition 4.6 Azure-AC-SID Model Components in Addition to the Azure-AC Model

- SID, SIP, CP, OP, EU, U, and O are finite sets of SIDs, SIPs, CPs, OPs, EU, users, and objects. The SID serves communities of organizations. A SID owns a CP, an OP, and a number of SIPs. A SID also maintains EU resources.
- CP/OP/SIP ownership (CPO/OPO/SIPO) is a function CPO/OPO/SIPO: CP/OP/SIPO $\rightarrow$ SID, mapping a single CP/OP/SIP to its owning SID, which equals mapping a specific subscription to a SID.
- SID association (assoc) is a function assoc: SID $\rightarrow 2^A$, mapping a SID to all its member organization accounts.
- User Ownership (UO) is a function UO: $U \rightarrow OA$, mapping a user to its owning organization account. Equivalently viewed as a many-to-one relation $UO \subseteq U \times OA$.
- Object Ownership (OO) is a function OO: $O \rightarrow OA$, mapping an object to its owning organization account. Equivalently viewed as a many-to-one relation $OO \subseteq O \times OA$.

4.5.2.1 Administrative Azure-AC-SID Model

Similar to the AWS-AC-SID model, each SID has a CP and an OP as a security service provided to all organizations in the SID community. The CP and OP are created with the SID. Each organization can join different SIDs with different communities of organizations. Each of these SIDs is isolated from the others. We only discuss the model in which the SIDs are manually set up, serving different communities of organizations in the Azure public cloud.

We design a SID manager as an automated agent that serves cloud communities of organizations and manages SIDs and their constituent components throughout their life cycle. The SID manager processes SID requests from communities of organizations and maintains a separate SID for each community. Within each SID, it facilitates the creation and deletion of SIPs. Each time a cyber-collaboration request is sent to the SID manager, it creates a new subscription, assigning the subscription to the group of organizations that made the request. After the collaboration is done, the SIP is deleted.

Considering that Azure already has dedicated roles for managing subscriptions and AAD, we will use those existing AAD administrative roles and subscription roles to manage SIPs, the CP, and the OP in a SID. Azure provides five AAD admin roles and two subscription admin roles. For simplicity, we will constrain the administrative roles to include only the AAD global admin role and subscription co-admin role. Azure also provides a set of operative roles in RGs, which allows users to have permission to access cloud resources.

To make role assignment simple and clear, we constrain roles to be two types, administrative roles and member roles, which denote the permission of being able to manage users and permissions only for accessing cloud resources. We use the admin role *SIDAdmin* to represent all admin permissions a user can get from AAD and subscriptions. We use the member role *SIDmember* to represent all normal roles a user can have in a RG. Admin users have the capability to add and remove other users from their home organizations to a CP subscription or a SIP subscription. Member users can be added/removed from/to a project subscription inside a SID. Member users are those who have access to real cloud services and resources, like creating or deleting a VM.

The administrative aspects of the Azure-AC-SID model are discussed informally next. A formal specification is given in Table 4.3.

Initially set up the SID: For every community of organizations that will have cyber collaboration, we offer one SID associated with the community. The number of organizations associated with the SID is fixed. Let *uSet* denotes the fixed group of security admin users, each of which represents one and only one organization in the community. Each organization in the community has equal limited administrative power in the SID, which is carried through *uSet*. The SID maintains *uSet* as a core group (Sandhu et al. 2011) of SID admin users. Only users from *uSet* later can dynamically create SIPs in the SID.

Inside the SID, organizations can request multiple SIPs for the convenience of different cyber collaborations. The number of SIPs depends on how much collaboration is initialized by the group of organizations. A SID is initially set up with a CP and an OP, and organizations can then automatically request to create and delete SIPs, as well as add or remove users to/from SIPs. With the initialization of a SID, admin users from *uSet* automatically get limited administrative permission in a CP in a SID, which is represented by role *SIDadmin*. Normal users from the community automatically get permissions to be able to add them to the OP with role the *SIDmember*.

Table 4.3 Azure-AC-SID administrative model.

Operation	Authorization Requirement	Update
SipCreate(uSet, sip, sid) /* *A set of organization security admin users together create a sip* */	∀ u ∈ uSet.(u ∈ *uSet*) ∧ sip ∉ SIP	assoc(sid) = $\cup_{u \in uSet}$UO(u) SIPO(sip) = sid SIP′ = SIP ∪ {sip}
SipDelete(subuSct, sip, sid) /* *The same subset of security admin users together delete a sip* */	∀ u ∈ subuSet.(u ∈ *uSet*) ∧ sip ∈ SIP ∧ assoc(sid) = $\cup_{u \in subuSet}$UO(u) ∧ SIPO(sip) = sid	assoc(sid) = NULL SIPO(sip) = NULL SIP′ = SIP – {sip}
UserAdd(adminu, u, p, sid) /* *Admin users add a user from their home account to a Cp/Sip* */	adminu ∈ *uSet* ∧ u ∈ U ∧ UO(u) = UO(adminu) ∧ p ∈ (CP ∪ SIP) ∧ (CPO(p) = sid ∪ SIP(p) = sid)	UA′ = ∃ rg ∈ p.(UA ∪ {(u, [rg, *SIDmember*])})
UserRemove(adminu, u, p, sid) /* *Admin users remove a user from a Cp/Sip* */	adminu ∈ *uSet* ∧ u ∈ U ∧ UO(u) = UO(adminu) ∧ p ∈ (CP ∪ SIP) ∧ (CPO(p) = sid ∪ SIP(p) = sid) ∧ ∃ rg ∈ p.(UA ∪ {(u, [rg, *SIDmember*])})	UA′ = UA – {(u, [rg, *SIDmember*])}
OpenUserAdd(u, op, sid) /* *Users add themselves to a Op* */	u ∈ U ∧ UO(u) ∈ UO(*uSet*) ∧ op ∈ OP ∧ OPO(op) = sid	UA′ = ∃ rg ∈ op.(UA ∪ {(u, [rg, *SIDmember*])})
OpenUserRemove(u, op sid) /* *Users remove themselves from a Op* */	u ∈ U ∧ UO(u) ∈ UO(*uSet*) ∧ op ∈ OP ∧ OPO(op) = sid ∧ ∃ rg ∈ op.(UA ∪ {(u, [rg, *SIDmember*])})	UA′ = UA – {(u, [rg, *SIDmember*])}
ExpertUserAdd(adminu, eu, p, sid) /* *Admin users add an expert user to a Cp/Sip* */	adminu ∈ *uSet* ∧ eu ∈ EU ∧ p ∈ (CP ∪ SIP) ∧ (CPO(p) = sid ∪ SIPO(p) = sid)	UA′ = ∃ rg ∈ p.(UA ∪ {(eu, [rg, *SIDmember*])})
ExpertUserRemove(adminu, eu, p, sid) /* *Admin users remove an expert user from a Cp/Sip* */	adminu ∈ *uSet* ∧ eu ∈ EU ∧ p ∈ (CP ∪ SIP) ∧ (CPO(p) = sid ∪ SIPO(p) = sid) ∧ ∃ rg ∈ p.(UA ∪ {(eu, [rg, *SIDmember*])})	UA′ = UA – {(eu, [rg, *SIDmember*])}
CopyObject(u, o1, o2, p) /* *Users copy objects from organization accounts to a Cp/Sip* */	o1 ∈ O ∧ o2 ∉ O ∧ UO(u) = OO(o1) ∧ u ∈ U ∧ p ∈ (CP ∪ SIP) ∧ 3 rg.((u, [rg, *SIDmember*]) ∈ UA)	O′ = O ∪ {o2} OO(o2) = p
ExportObject(adminu, o1, o2, p) /* *Admin users export objects from a Cp/Sip to organization accounts* */	adminu ∈ *uSet* ∧ o1 ∈ O ∧ o2 ∉ O ∧ OO(o1) = p ∧ p ∈ (CP ∪ SIP) ∧ ∃ rg.((adminu, [rg, *SIDadmin*]) ∈ UA)	O′ = O ∪ {o2} OO(o2) = UO(adminu)

Create a SIP: A set of security admin users *uSet* together creates a SIP for cyber collaboration among the community of organizations. The creation of a SIP succeeds based on agreement among the community of organizations. Each organization in the SIP has equally limited administrative power, which is represented by the role *SIDadmin*.

Delete a SIP: After the collaboration is finished, a SIP needs to be securely deleted. The delete command is issued by the same subset of the security admin users (*uSet*) who created the SIP. All information, data, and resources are securely deleted from the SIP. All users assigned to the SIP are removed from it.

Add/remove a user to/from a CP or SIPs: CP and SIPs admin users are the set of security administrative users (*uSet*) from the community of organizations. These limited administrative users can add/remove users of their organizations to/from the CP and SIPs. All the users added to the CP or SIPs are existing users from an organization's account. The limited administrative users don't have permission to create new users or delete an existing user. They can only add existing users to the CP or SIPs. When users are removed from the CP or a SIP, they lose access to corresponding information and resources in the CP or the SIP, regardless of the ownership of the piece of information in the past. Admin users in the CP or a SIP can see all users added from the community of organizations, as well as information and resources they bring in, which means there are no hidden users, information, or resources in a CP or a SIP.

Add/remove a user to/from an OP: Every user in the collaborative community of organizations is allowed to join the OP. Users in the OP have equal but limited permissions. They can share cyber data but have no control over other users. We use the role *SIDmember* to represent this limited permission. Users add/remove themselves from their organizations to/from the OP. Users cannot access and share any data once they leave the OP.

Add/remove an EU to/from a CP or SIPs: EUs are required when external cyber expertise needs to be involved. For instance, a cyber incident needs experts from security consultant companies, government cyber experts, cyber police, etc. SID services maintain a relationship with external experts. EUs can be added/removed to/from a CP and SIPs as members. Users from *uSet* can request to add/remove EUs to/from the CP or a SIP. An existing EU in the CP or a SIP can also be removed. For instance, at the end of a cyber collaboration, an unneeded EU is securely deleted. After the EU is deleted, the user loses all access to any information and resources in the CP or a SIP.

Copy data between organization accounts and a CP or SIPs: Users can copy data from their home accounts to the CP or a SIP. The administrative users from *uSet* can export data from the CP or a SIP to their home accounts.

4.6 Conclusions

In this chapter, we introduced access-control models for OpenStack, AWS, and Microsoft Azure cloud IaaS platforms. We identified fundamental elements of access control in cloud IaaS. We also explored models for information and resource sharing in cybersecurity to show the flexibility of those cloud access-control models. We designed these models mainly based on the concept and architecture of the cloud platforms. We gave formal descriptions of administrative models, which provide a clear specification of how the users and resources are managed and controlled in the model.

References

E. Cohen, R. K. Thomas, W. Winsborough, and D. Shands. (2002). Models for coalition-based access control (CBAC). In: Proceedings of the Seventh ACM Symposium on Access Control Models and Technologies, 97–106. New York: ACM.

Hassan, Q. (2011). Demystifying cloud computing. *The Journal of Defense Software Engineering (CrossTalk)* 24 (1): 16–21.

R. Krishnan, R. Sandhu, J. Niu, and W. Winsborough. (2009). Towards a framework for group-centric secure collaboration. In: 5th International Conference on Collaborative Computing, Networking, Applications and Worksharing, 1–10. Piscataway, NJ: IEEE.

P. Mell and T. Grance. (2011). The NIST definition of cloud computing. NIST Sp. Pub. 800-145.

L. Pearlman, V. Welch, I. Foster, C. Kesselman, and S. Tuecke. (2002). A community authorization service for group collaboration. In: 3rd IEEE International Workshop on Policies for Distributed Systems and Networks, 50–59. IEEE.

R. Sandhu, K. Z. Bijon, X. Jin, and R. Krishnan. (2011). RT-based administrative models for community cyber security information sharing. In: 7th International Conference on Collaborative Computing: Networking, Applications and Worksharing, 473–478. IEEE.

Shands, D., Yee, R., Jacobs, J., and Sebes, E.J. (2000). Secure virtual enclaves: Supporting coalition use of distributed application technologies. In: *IEEE DARPA Information Survivability Conference and Exposition*, 335–350. IEEE.

B. Tang and R. Sandhu. (2014). Extending OpenStack access control with domain trust. In: 8th International Conference on Network and System Security (NSS), 54–69.

Y. Zhang, R. Krishnan, and R. Sandhu. (2014). Secure information and resource sharing in cloud infrastructure as a service. In: Proceedings of the 2014 ACM Workshop on Information Sharing & Collaborative Security, 81–90. New York: ACM.

Y. Zhang, F. Patwa, R. Sandhu, and B. Tang. (2015). Hierarchical secure information and resource sharing in openstack community cloud. In: IEEE Conference on Information Reuse and Integration (IRI), 419–426. IEEE.

Y. Zhang, F. Patwa, and R. Sandhu. (2015). Community-based secure information and resource sharing in AWS public cloud. In: IEEE Conference on Collaboration and Internet Computing (CIC), 46–53, IEEE.

5

Cloud Security and Privacy Management

Patrick Kamongi

University of North Texas, Denton, TX, USA

5.1 Introduction and Background

Cloud computing technologies support delivery and consumption of computing resources and products as on-demand services. At the core of a cloud ecosystem, we observe five key actors (cloud consumer, cloud provider, cloud carrier, cloud auditor, and cloud broker), as defined in the National Institute of Standards and Technology (NIST) "Cloud Computing Reference Architecture" (http://www.nist.gov/customcf/get_pdf.cfm?pub_id=909505) and shown in Figure 5.1.

From the view of cloud system actors, there is a one-to-many interaction between them, as illustrated in Figure 5.2. At the service layer (shown in Figure 5.1), we can think of various abstracted interactions between the cloud provider via the cloud carrier to the cloud consumer, and vice versa. These interactions may use different service models, notably Infrastructure-as-a-Service (IaaS), Platform-as-a-Service (PaaS), and Software-as-a-Service (SaaS). When architecting and consuming on-demand cloud services, it is important to keep in mind the potential for software failures that could compromise data confidentiality, integrity, or availability.

In this chapter, our focus is on security and privacy of the SaaS cloud model architecture, deployment, and usage from the cloud provider, carrier, and consumer point of view. SaaS is defined as capabilities given to the consumer to facilitate the use of the provider applications running on a cloud infrastructure (these are not limited to the IaaS but can also rely on some aspects of the previously mentioned key actors). In the next section, we highlight some of the top SaaS security and privacy challenges and how they affect both cloud providers and consumers.

The idea of a cloud SaaS consumer accessing a service (i.e. application) on demand without worrying about how it is hosted or maintained is appealing. This idea drives the adoption of cloud-hosted SaaS. On the other hand, the SaaS provider has a large pool of available cloud infrastructure resources to meet all the needs of its consumers in terms of some key characteristics that a true SaaS service should exhibit. For instance:

Security, Privacy, and Digital Forensics in the Cloud, First Edition. Edited by Lei Chen, Hassan Takabi, and Nhien-An Le-Khac.

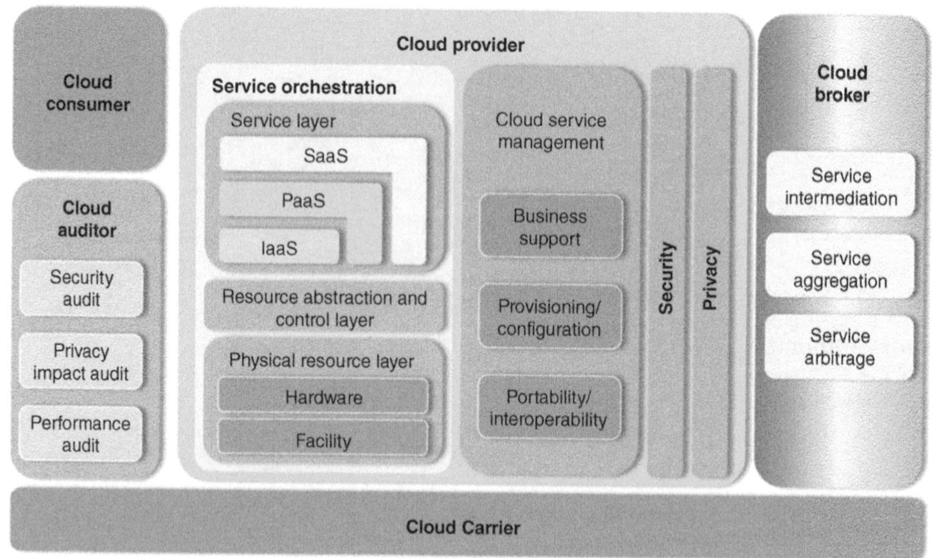

Figure 5.1 The conceptual reference model.

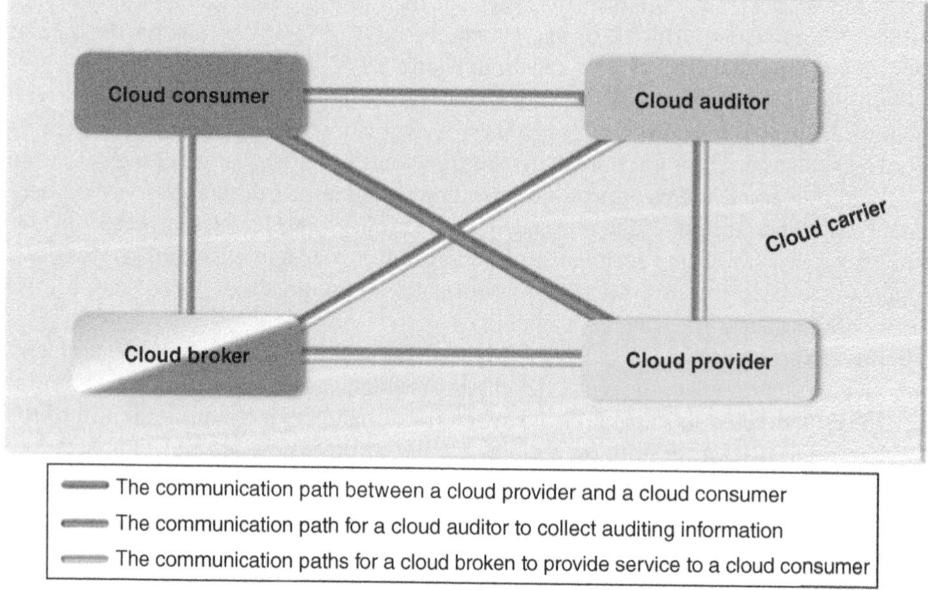

Figure 5.2 Interactions between the Actors in cloud computing.

- The ability to tailor the application to meet consumer requirements and needs
- Quick and timely pushing of software updates with negligible impact to application availability
- The delivery of a service that can be leveraged by other systems via cloud carrier-supported protocols
- Support for collaboration and sharing of data among consumers

In a perfect world, the functionalities of a SaaS application should meet consumer service-level needs. However, in reality, there is a need to ensure the security and privacy of the service for both the consumer and provider to meet applicable compliance requirements.

For a given SaaS application, we should question the extent to which the following important security issues (Patel and B.S. 2014), among many others, are being addressed:

- Authentication and authorization
- Availability
- Information security
- Data access
- Network security
- Data breaches
- Identity management and sign-on process

These issues must be addressed to meet the security and privacy requirements of the consumer subscribing to the SaaS application. NIST has published a draft document, "Cloud Computing Security Reference Architecture" (http://collaborate.nist.gov/twiki-cloud-computing/pub/CloudComputing/CloudSecurity/NIST_Security_Reference_Architecture_2013.05.15_v1.0.pdf), that provides technical guidance on how to model, securely architect, and deploy the Cloud from the ground up while addressing the needs of all key cloud actors (i.e. consumer, provider, broker, auditor, and carrier), service orchestration models (IaaS, PaaS, and SaaS) and deployment modes. We recommend this NIST draft and forthcoming cloud security publications as foundational reference documents for architecting and deploying any cloud service.

In the next sections, we present formal and practical solutions for performing and enforcing security and privacy analysis of cloud SaaS applications.

5.2 Security and Privacy Analysis

From the SaaS application-provider's view, security is part of the process of designing, developing, deploying, and maintaining the application; whereas from the consumer's view, the security aspect of the application is leveraged after the application has been deployed.

5.2.1 Vulnerability Assessment

At any point in time, the consumer or provider can determine the key components (inventory) that make up the offered SaaS application and then use them as a baseline set of configurations for analyzing the security of the application. Vulnerability assessment (Heck 1999) is one security aspect of interest. The process involves identification, quantification, and ranking of the vulnerabilities facing a system (or, in our case, a cloud application).

For instance, we can use an automated framework for assessing a cloud system's vulnerabilities, such as VULCAN (Kamongi et al. 2013) shown in Figure 5.3. A typical VULCAN assessment proceeds as follows:

- A user provides two primary inputs to the system with the first being, for example, "SaaS application configurations" (this data is provided to the System Classifications module of the VULCAN framework). The second input is a natural-language query

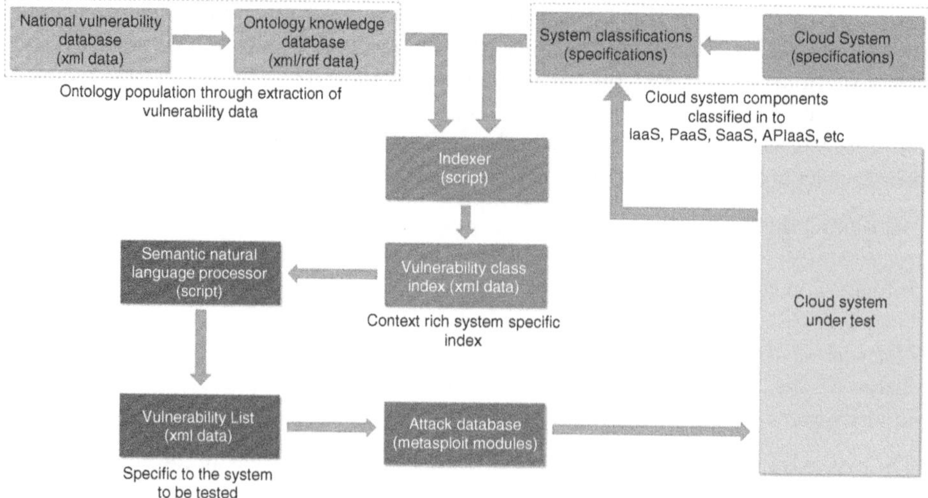

Figure 5.3 VULCAN: vulnerability assessment framework for cloud computing.

such as, "Assess for weaknesses that could allow an unauthorized access to my application." This query is processed within the VULCAN Semantic Natural Language Processor (SNLP).

- The System Classifications module generates possible SaaS application-based solutions and feeds them to the Indexer module. The Indexer then creates relevant vulnerability indexes, which are used to produce vulnerability groups from the Vulnerability Class Index module.
- The SNLP component performs reasoning tasks on the user query using the created vulnerabilities group data. Relevant results are returned to the user (SaaS application consumer or provider) via a dialogue agent interface. The results may include IT products that have vulnerabilities and other information relevant to the user's query.
- Using VULCAN's middleware application, we can also perform live penetration testing (assuming the user has the required permissions).
- VULCAN then reports the vulnerability status of the given SaaS application.

An example use of the VULCAN framework is presented in Section 5.4. We illustrate how a prototype web application of the VULCAN framework (shown in Figure 5.4) can assess the vulnerability of a sample of applications in a Microsoft Office 365 (https://products.office.com/en-us/home) subscription, shown in Table 5.1.

An alternative way to assess vulnerability, beyond using an open source framework like VULCAN, is to use any suitable commercial vulnerability-scanner solution, like those listed at https://www.owasp.org/index.php/Category:Vulnerability_Scanning_Tools.

Upon identifying the SaaS application's vulnerabilities, it is important to develop and implement strategies to reduce their potential impact and mitigate risk exposure.

5.2.2 Risk Exposure Assessment and Management

To estimate the real or perceived risk of any SaaS application, we can use a threat-centered approach. After first performing rigorous threat modeling of a given

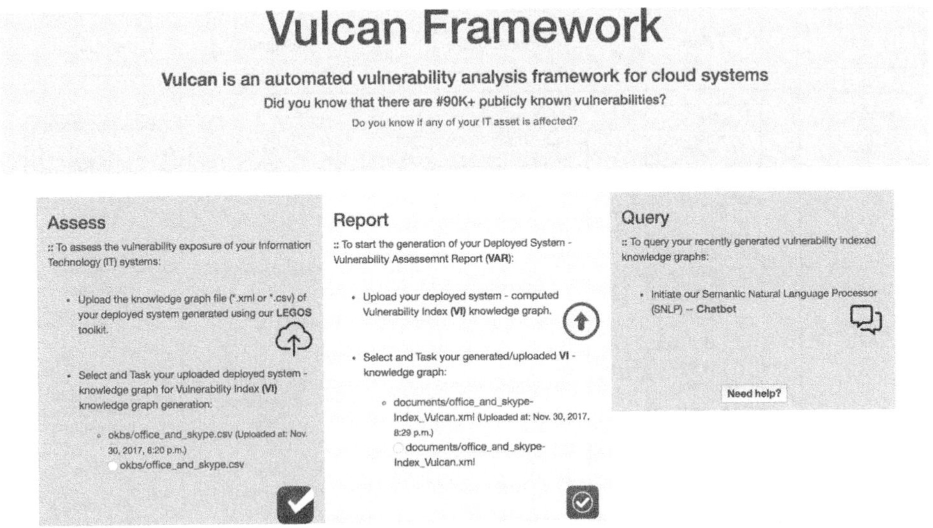

Figure 5.4 VULCAN framework: on-demand web application.

Table 5.1 A couple of applications within an Office 365 subscription.

Products (in CPE Format)
• cpe:/a:microsoft:office:2016
• cpe:/a:microsoft:skype_for_business:2016

application, we can estimate the risk of each of the modeled threats. Depending on the SaaS application domain, a proper threat classification can be defined. For example, the classification can be based on threat actors, assets, etc.

"Risk management is the process of identifying risk, assessing risk, and taking steps to reduce risk to an acceptable level" (https://msdn.microsoft.com/en-us/library/ee823878(v=cs.20).aspx).

For example, we can leverage an open source solution like Nemesis, which is an automated architecture for threat modeling and risk assessment of cloud computing assets (Kamongi et al. 2014). The Nemesis architecture is illustrated in Figure 5.5.

For a given cloud SaaS application, Nemesis requires the user to input details about the configuration of the application's components. The unified Nemesis framework then processes this information as follows:

- Measurements are collected about what type of known vulnerabilities exist for the given cloud's assets.
- For each applicable vulnerability found, Nemesis explores how the vulnerability can be exploited and looks for ways it can be mitigated.
- The previous details are used to generate a set of customized outputs such as these:
  - An estimated value of aggregated risk.
  - Metrics for exploitable vulnerabilities.

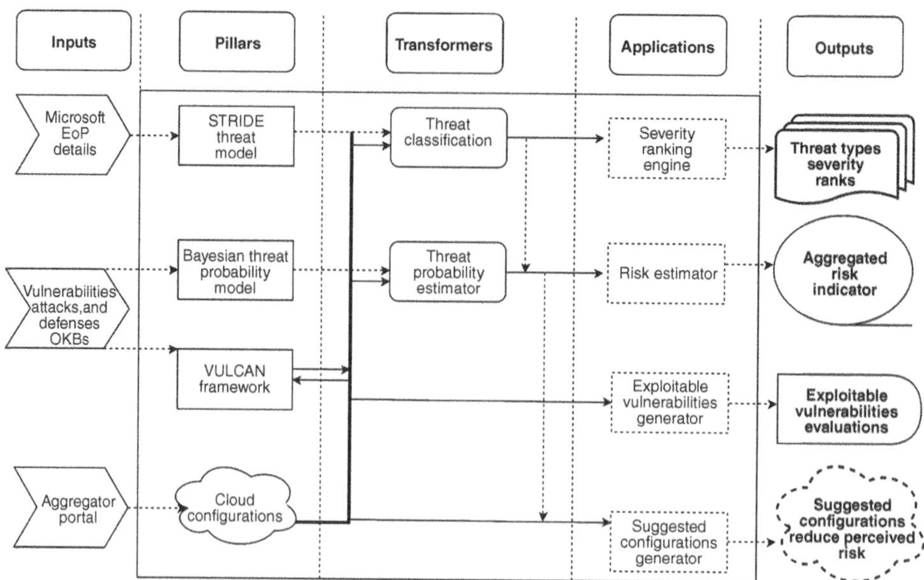

Figure 5.5 Nemesis: automated Architecture for threat modeling and risk assessment for cloud computing.

- Ranking of threat types by severity.
- New recommended cloud configurations with a lower risk, along with a detailed summary of relevant Nemesis evaluation data.

These simplified and highly abstracted automated solutions provide a rigorous threat model and risk assessment of the analyzed SaaS application. Consumers can benefit from Nemesis' capabilities even though they have limited access to the backend application configurations – they can use client-side configuration details facing the SaaS application being used. On the other hand, the SaaS application provider can use Nemesis' features in a similar fashion, with full assessment coverage, by providing a complete inventory of the IT products used to develop the offered SaaS application. In addition, the provider will be in a unique position to take into consideration the new recommended cloud configurations to reduce risk and improve their SaaS application security posture in their next release update.

A prototype web application that uses the Nemesis architecture is illustrated in Figure 5.6. It can be used to perform threat modeling and risk assessment for any cloud application (e.g. those in Table 5.1).

The SaaS application provider can incorporate risk management early in the application design and development processes to ensure delivery that is secure and that meets consumer security and privacy needs. During the architecture-planning phase, we can refer to the NIST Cloud Computing Security Reference Architecture (http://collaborate.nist.gov/twiki-cloud-computing/pub/CloudComputing/CloudSecurity/NIST_Security_Reference_Architecture_2013.05.15_v1.0.pdf), which suggests these steps (abstracted here):

1) Categorize the information system.
2) Identify security requirements, and perform a risk assessment to identify security components (confidentiality, integrity, availability [CIA] analysis), and select security controls.

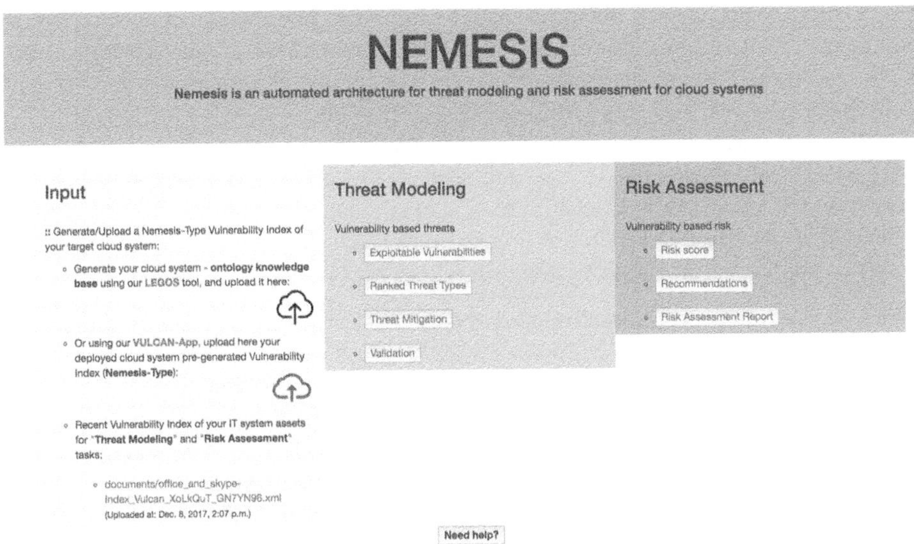

Figure 5.6 Nemesis Architecture: On-demand web application.

3) Select the best-fitting architecture (from the cloud infrastructure provider).
4) Assess service provider(s).
5) Approve use of service.
6) Monitor the service provider (to ensure a reliable platform has been configured on which to build their SaaS offerings).

Note that these steps can be applied to a cloud SaaS application consumer as well, as in the case where a consumer is running an application locally and wants to migrate to a cloud-based SaaS offering.

Moving toward a more checklist-oriented approach to ensure that the needed security and privacy controls are in place for the delivered cloud SaaS application, we can use the Cloud Security Alliance (CSA) cloud controls matrix (CCM) framework (https://cloudsecurityalliance.org/download/cloud-controls-matrix-v3-0-1). The framework is described as follows:

- Provides fundamental security principles to guide cloud vendors and to assist cloud customers in assessing the overall security risk of a cloud provider.
- Strengthens information security control environments by delineating control guidance by service provider and consumer, and by differentiating according to cloud model type and environment.
- Provides a controls framework in 16 domains that are cross-referenced to other industry-accepted security standards, regulations, and control frameworks to reduce audit complexity.
- Seeks to normalize security expectations, cloud taxonomy and terminology, and security measures implemented in the Cloud.

Within this framework, for every mentioned control domain, there is a control specification and a mapping to how it is applicable to the cloud service delivery model (i.e. IaaS, PaaS, and SaaS) via a checklist model approach.

The VULCAN framework, Nemesis architecture, and other supporting tools have been integrated into a holistic suite of tools called *Cockatoo*. These tools are integrated to form an automated solution for security risk assessment and mitigation for any cloud system that powers various cloud offerings (e.g. Office 365).

The Cockatoo toolchain (http://csrl.unt.edu/content/cockatoo-toolchain) offers a helping hand to address the need for a cloud-security and privacy-management solution. An example workflow of the Cockatoo toolchain is illustrated in Figure 5.7. Cockatoo can be used via a managed web interface to assess a given cloud application's configuration. When applicable, an authenticated user (cloud consumer/provider) can perform:

- A manual or automated guided/unguided collection of telemetry data for any given IT system/application.
- An on-demand vulnerability assessment task for the IT system/application.
- An on-demand threat modeling and risk assessment of the IT system/application.
- An automated large-dataset generation for machine learning experiments to predict the number of unknown vulnerabilities in a given software product.
- An on-the-fly prediction of the number of unknown vulnerabilities in a specific software product release/version.

A look at a cloud SaaS application's privacy assessment from the consumer and provider perspectives is presented in the next section.

5.2.3 Privacy Assessment Aspect

A privacy assessment starts with the SaaS provider and consumer data privacy policy negotiation which is documented in a Security Service Level Agreement (SSLA). Once

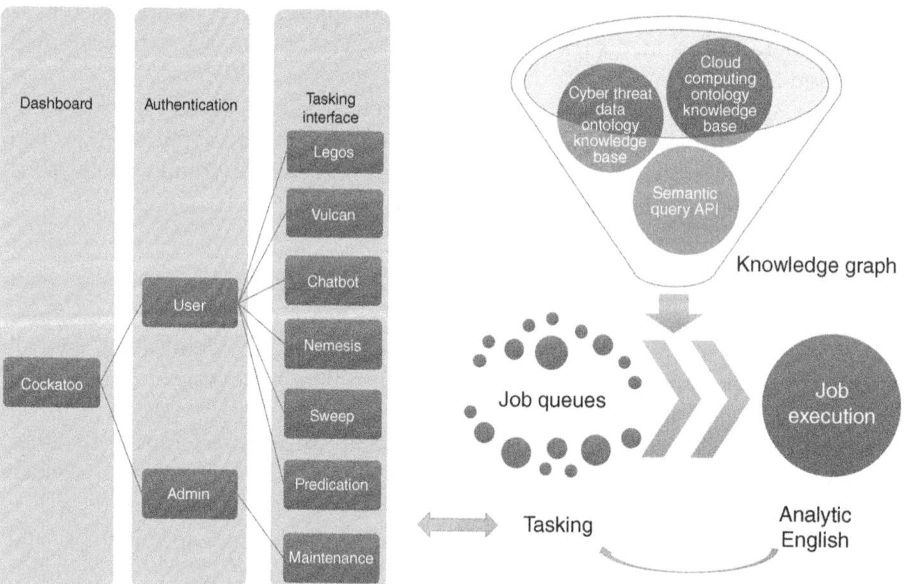

Figure 5.7 Cockatoo workflow – high level view.

the desired privacy policy is finalized, the task remains to identify and mitigate any threat that could violate the agreement.

An approach to identifying and resolving privacy threats has been presented in the work by (Smolen 2010), which provides a context for when privacy threats occur (i.e. when data is leaked in a transaction that violates the desired privacy policy). The following set of questions should be used to determine the potential severity of any such transaction:

- Are there existing technologies that have similar transactions?
- Is this transaction occurring with the actor's knowledge?
- Did the user consent to this transaction?
- Can the user prevent this transaction from occurring?
- Is this transaction something that most users would find acceptable?
- How could a vindictive or malicious actor abuse this transaction?

Once a privacy threat has been identified on either the consumer or provider side of the SaaS application, it should be logged. Then, a review process should address the threat accordingly using a relevant mitigation technique that considers how the data is processed.

(Deng et al. 2011) proposed a systematic approach for privacy threat modeling (called LINDDUN) to elicit the privacy requirements of software-intensive systems (which may be applicable to cloud SaaS applications as well) and select privacy-enhancing technologies accordingly. In this framework, the privacy threat types (**L**inkability, **I**dentifiability, **N**on-repudiation, **D**etectability, **D**isclosure of information, Content **U**nawareness, Policy, and consent **N**oncompliance) are obtained by negating privacy properties (Unlinkability, Anonymity, Pseudonymity, Plausible deniability, Undetectability, Unobservability, Confidentiality, Content awareness, Policy, and consent compliance).

The LINDDUN framework enables an analyst to identify privacy threats of a software-based system or an SaaS application (which is our interest here), by modeling the application using a data flow diagram (DFD) and then mapping it to relevant privacy threats. Note that these privacy threats can be elaborated via threat-tree patterns and reinforced by leveraging misuse cases as described in (Deng et al. 2011). Privacy-enhancing solutions are added accordingly.

5.3 Best Security Practices and Recommendation

In this section, we cover some important aspects of securing any given cloud SaaS application while preserving privacy from the consumer and provider perspectives.

At any point in time, the cloud SaaS provider should be able to receive security and privacy requirements from a potential consumer and negotiate a favorable course of action. Likewise, the cloud SaaS application provider can impose new requirements on the host cloud infrastructure vendor (provider). This approach extends the initial contract (SSLA) negotiation between the vendor/provider and consumer. The SSLA helps to assess the security and privacy of any cloud provider offerings before the initial subscription or during a renegotiation process. Ontologies for SSLAs (Lee et al. 2015) have been proposed to aid understanding and comparison of SSLAs from different providers and facilitate their adoption.

Using a SSLA, a consumer can negotiate with their SaaS application provider regarding the security and privacy requirements imposed by their specific use cases and how the provider will demonstrate compliance with those requirements. Areas to explore for suggested best practices to incorporate into the SSLA, from the consumer point of view, can be found in the NIST Cloud Computing Synopsis and Recommendations, (http://csrc.nist.gov/publications/nistpubs/800-146/sp800-146.pdf):

- Consumer-side vulnerabilities
- Encryption
- Authentication
- Identity and access management
- Visibility
- Data protection and privacy
- Client device/application protection
- Secure data deletion

Also, the SaaS provider should negotiate a SSLA with their cloud infrastructure provider to exhibit these attributes in a more concise way:

- Provider assessment
- Supplementary backup
- Physical isolation (if it is critical to the offered SaaS application)
- Logical isolation (highly recommended)
- Encryption (of the data at rest and secured channel of communication)
- Infrastructure automation (ensure that it is done in a secure way)
- Virtualization implications (specific to the security of the virtual environment)
- Guest hardening (tailored to the offered SaaS application)

This list of recommended best practices can only serve as a starting point due to the variety of SaaS applications available. Best practices applicable to each application should be tailored uniquely to ensure that specific security and privacy needs are properly addressed.

5.4 Use Case Example: Microsoft Office 365, SaaS Version

The Microsoft Office 365 cloud subscription offers a variety of high-end productivity solutions geared for personal and business use, including Microsoft Office (offline/online versions), cloud storage, Skype, e-mail, social networking services, and so on.

An article by the Microsoft Office 365 team (https://docs.microsoft.com/en-us/office365/securitycompliance/protect-against-threats) pinpoints some of the most prevalent threats (notably spoofing, malware, spam, phishing attempts, and unauthorized access to data) facing the adopters of Office 365. The article also provides best practices that an organization (that uses Office 365) can use to protect against a variety of threats.

Referring back to our earlier discussion on security and privacy analysis, a product like Office 365 should receive assessment considerations from both the consumer's and provider's point of view, on a real-time basis, to ensure that:

- A proper vulnerability assessment on all Office 365 products (along with their hosting infrastructure and delivery platforms) is done to ensure that any known or discovered vulnerability is quickly patched and mitigated.

- A security risk assessment is performed (taking into account the offered and consumed products, services, and users' interactions) to stay ahead of any threats and drive informed decisions to mitigate them.
- The privacy policy is not violated and is maintained to reflect user needs.
- The SSLA should offer some guarantees to the adopters of Office 365 and ensure that data security and privacy requirements for subscribed products are being met (i.e. comply with the SSLA).

An example workflow of a vulnerability assessment of Office 365 applications using the VULCAN framework (web application shown in Figure 5.4) would proceed as follows:

- Via the **Assess** window, a cloud provider/consumer can use the LEGOS tool to add the Office 365 application's configuration (e.g. shown in Table 5.1) information to assess vulnerabilities. A vulnerability index ontology knowledge base (OKB) is then generated for the supplied configurations (illustrated in Figures 5.8–5.10). Figure 5.8 illustrates over 2000 semantic facts captured by the information found about known vulnerabilities, exploits, and patches that impact the indexed Office 365 products. Figure 5.9 provides insight into the generated vulnerability index; we can see how the found vulnerabilities affect not only the original tasked products (shown in Table 5.1), but also other related products.
- Via the **Report** window, the user can then initiate the generation of a Vulnerability Assessment Report by selecting the generated vulnerability index OKB. The vulnerability report is rendered on-the-fly as shown in Figure 5.11. For example, the generated report informs the user about the overall vulnerability status of the assessed Office 365 products via the Executive Summary section, and the Vulnerability View section provides a thorough account of all found vulnerabilities that affect the assessed Office 365 products, etc.
- Via the **Query** window, the user can invoke the VULCAN/Chatbot service to get answers to any questions they may have about the generated Vulnerability Assessment Report or any publicly known vulnerability.

Using the Nemesis architecture, some example outputs of a security risk assessment for our selected Office 365 applications (shown in Table 5.1) are as follows:

- Figure 5.10 visualizes the found vulnerabilities that have publicly known exploits. Each of these assertions can also be rendered via the Nemesis web application **Threat Modeling** window, Exploitable Vulnerabilities Tab (shown in Figure 5.6). A Nemesis rendered exploitable vulnerabilities example is shown in Figure 5.12.
- Figure 5.13 shows the percentage of classified STRIDE (https://msdn.microsoft.com/en-us/library/ee823878(v=cs.20).aspx) based threat-type instances that could be exploited due to the presence of any of the found vulnerabilities.
- Figure 5.14 shows the severity rank of classified STRIDE-based threat type instances inferred from the severity of the found vulnerabilities.
- A risk score can be computed (using Nemesis' implementation of an ontology and Bayesian-based threat-probability model (Fenz 2011; Kamongi et al. 2014) and rendered via the "Risk score" shown in Figure 5.6 (Risk Assessment window).

A key takeaway from the security and privacy assessment of a SaaS product like Office 365 is that we must thoroughly analyze any security or privacy threat facing the consumer and provider. This requires thinking about the interactions between shared

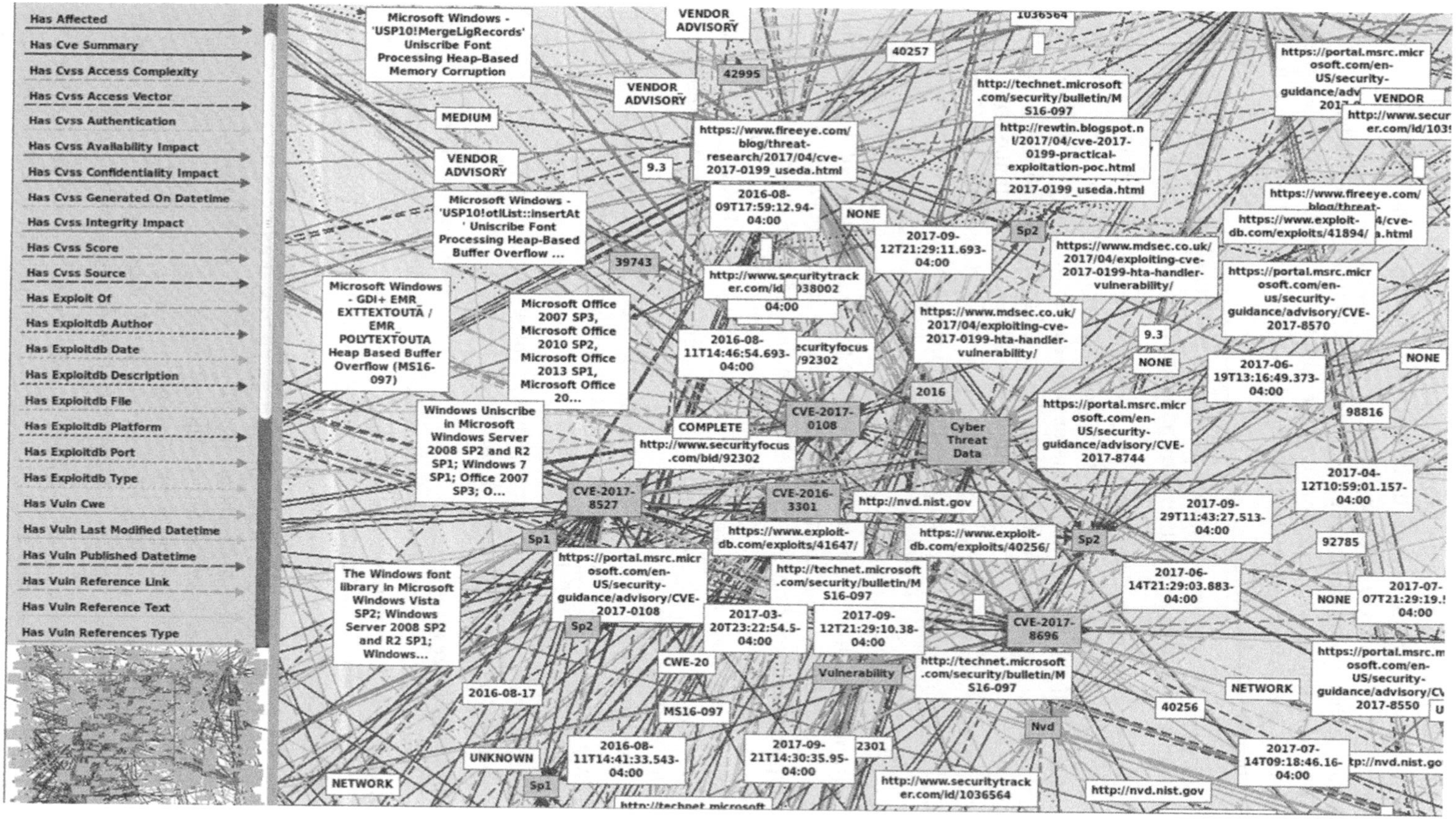

Figure 5.8 Office and Skype vulnerability index – OKB sample.

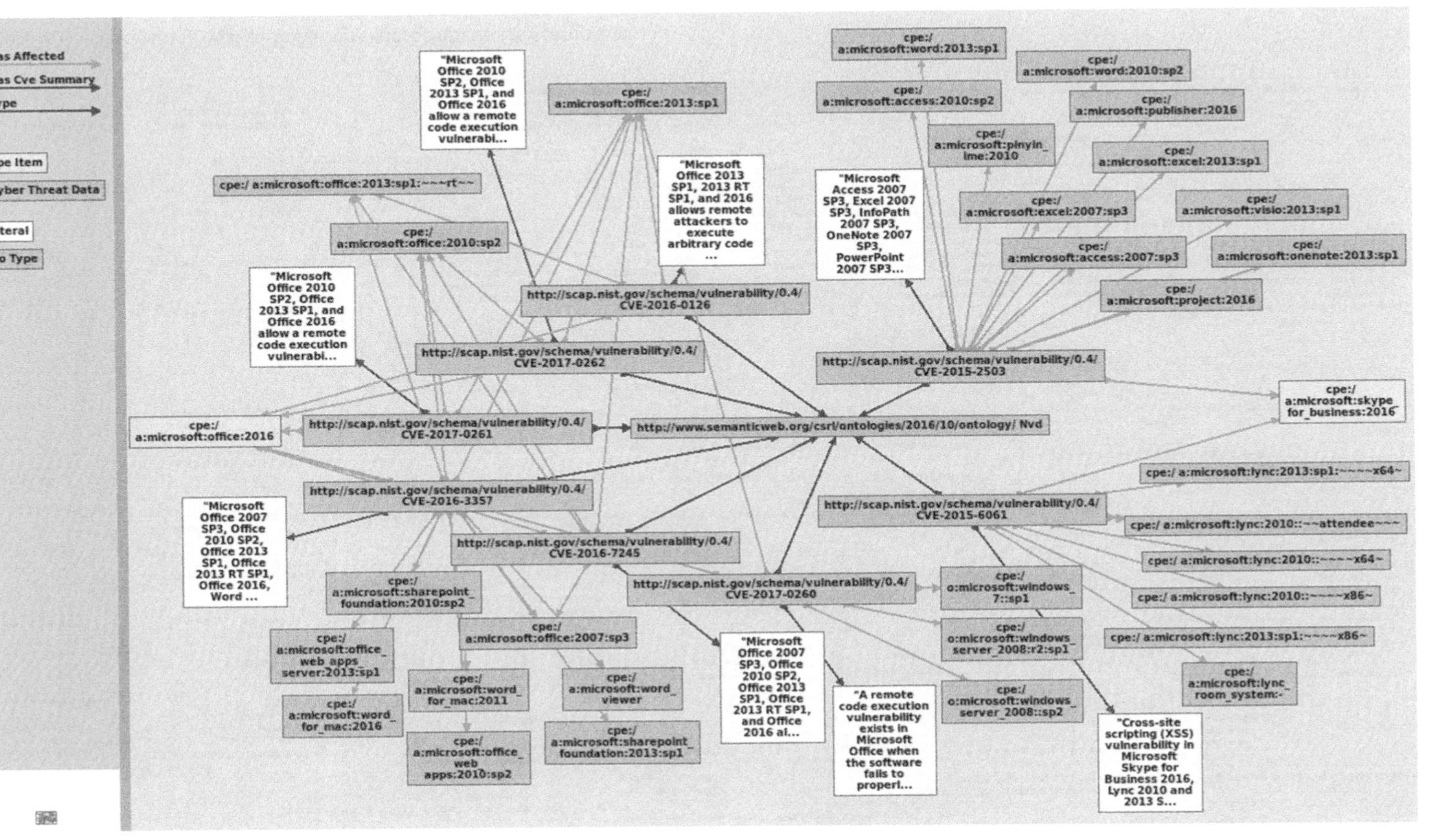

Figure 5.9 Office and Skype vulnerability index – OKB sample exploration.

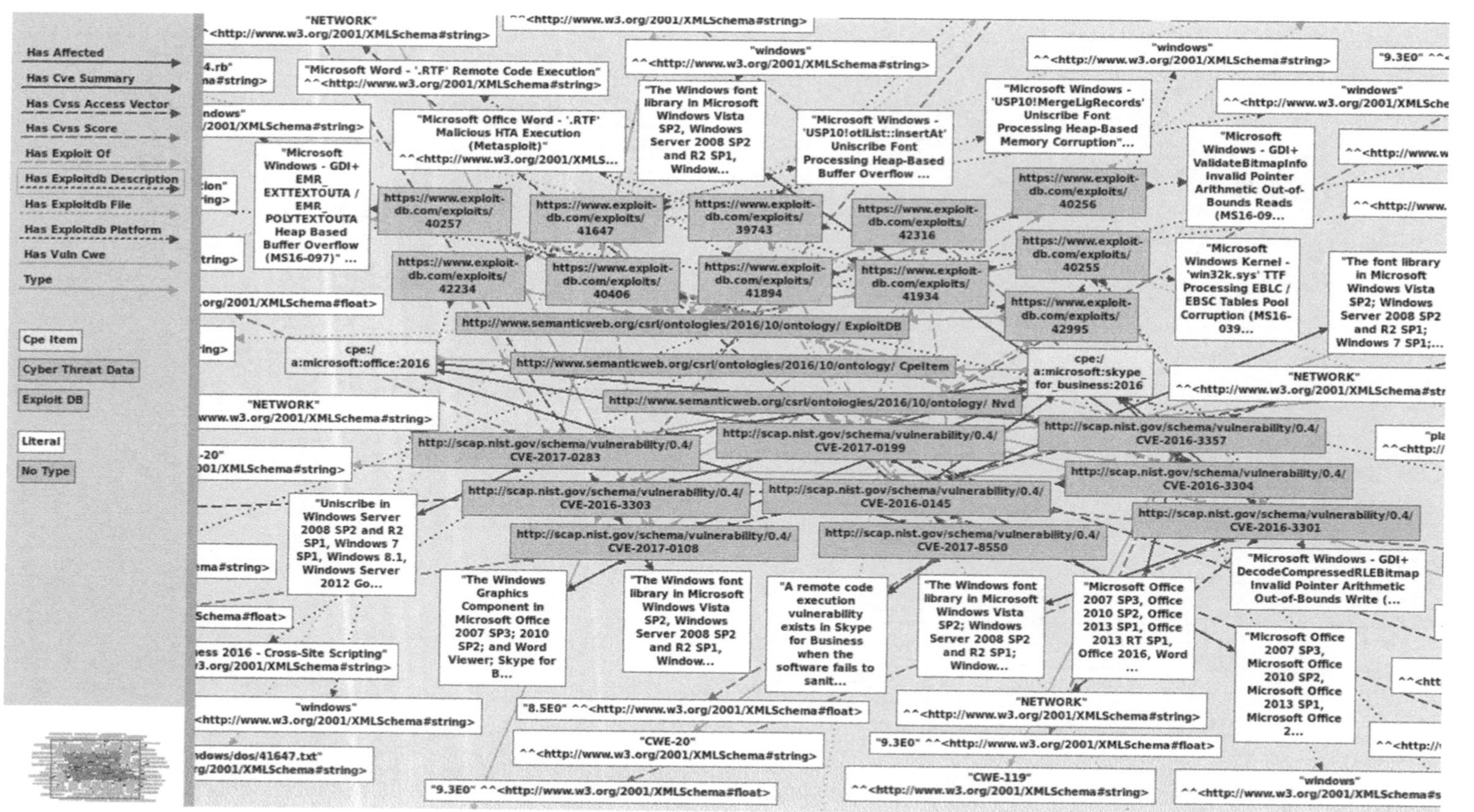

Figure 5.10 Office and Skype exploitable vulnerabilities – OKB sample.

Vulcan Framework

Vulcan is an automated vulnerability analysis framework for cloud systems

Do you know if any of your IT asset is affected by one of the known vulnerabilities?

VULCAN - Vulnerability Assessment Report (VAR) for **office_and_skype-Index_Vulcan.xml** - Input

Table of Contents

1. Executive Summary
2. Asset View
3. Vulnerability View
4. Exploit view
5. Mitigation View
6. Visualization View
7. Next Steps

Figure 5.11 VULCAN framework – vulnerability assessment report template.

NEMESIS

Nemesis is an automated architecture for threat modeling and risk assessment for cloud systems

Exploitable Vulnerabilities - Evaluation

Vulnerability	Description
CVE-2017-0108	"The Windows Graphics Component in Microsoft Office 2007 SP3; 2010 SP2; and Word Viewer; Skype for Business 2016; Lync 2013 SP1; Lync 2010; Live Meeting 2007; Silverlight 5; Windows Vista SP2; Windows Server 2008 SP2 and R2 SP1; and Windows 7 SP1 allows remote attackers to execute arbitrary code via a crafted web site, aka 'Graphics Component Remote Code Execution Vulnerability.' This vulnerability is different from that described in CVE-2017-0014."
CVE-2016-3301	"The Windows font library in Microsoft Windows Vista SP2; Windows Server 2008 SP2 and R2 SP1; Windows 7 SP1; Windows 8.1; Windows Server 2012 Gold and R2; Windows RT 8.1; Windows 10 Gold, 1511, and 1607; Office 2007 SP3; Office 2010 SP2; Word Viewer; Skype for Business 2016; Lync 2013 SP1; Lync 2010; Lync 2010 Attendee; and Live Meeting 2007 Console allows remote attackers to execute arbitrary code via a crafted embedded font, aka "Windows Graphics Component RCE Vulnerability.""
CVE-2016-3303	"The Windows font library in Microsoft Windows Vista SP2, Windows Server 2008 SP2 and R2 SP1, Windows 7 SP1, Office 2007 SP3, Office 2010 SP2, Word Viewer, Skype for Business 2016, Lync 2013 SP1, Lync 2010, Lync 2010 Attendee, and Live Meeting 2007 Console allows remote attackers to execute arbitrary code via a crafted embedded font, aka "Windows Graphics Component RCE Vulnerability," a different vulnerability than CVE-2016-3304."
CVE-2016-3304	"The Windows font library in Microsoft Windows Vista SP2, Windows Server 2008 SP2 and R2 SP1, Windows 7 SP1, Office 2007 SP3, Office 2010 SP2, Word Viewer, Skype for Business 2016, Lync 2013 SP1, Lync 2010, Lync 2010 Attendee, and Live Meeting 2007 Console allows remote attackers to execute arbitrary code via a crafted embedded font, aka "Windows Graphics Component RCE Vulnerability," a different vulnerability than CVE-2016-3303."
CVE-2017-8550	"A remote code execution vulnerability exists in Skype for Business when the software fails to sanitize specially crafted content, aka "Skype for Business Remote Code Execution Vulnerability"."
CVE-2016-0145	"The font library in Microsoft Windows Vista SP2; Windows Server 2008 SP2 and R2 SP1; Windows 7 SP1; Windows 8.1; Windows Server 2012 Gold and R2; Windows RT 8.1; Windows 10 Gold and 1511; Office 2007 SP3 and 2010 SP2; Word Viewer; .NET Framework 3.0 SP2, 3.5, and 3.5.1; Skype for Business 2016; Lync 2010; Lync 2010 Attendee; Lync 2013 SP1; and Live Meeting 2007 Console allows remote attackers to execute arbitrary code via a crafted embedded font, aka "Graphics Memory Corruption Vulnerability.""
CVE-2017-0283	"Uniscribe in Windows Server 2008 SP2 and R2 SP1, Windows 7 SP1, Windows 8.1, Windows Server 2012 Gold and R2, Windows RT 8.1, Windows 10 Gold, 1511, 1607, Windows Server 2016, Microsoft Office 2007 SP3, Microsoft Office 2010 SP2, Microsoft Office Word Viewer, Microsoft Lync 2013 SP1, Skype for Business 2016, Microsoft Silverlight 5 Developer Runtime when installed on Microsoft Windows, and Microsoft Silverlight 5 when installed on Microsoft Windows allows a remote code execution vulnerability due to the way it handles objects in memory, aka "Windows Uniscribe Remote Code Execution Vulnerability". This CVE ID is unique from CVE-2017-8528."
CVE-2016-3357	"Microsoft Office 2007 SP3, Office 2010 SP2, Office 2013 SP1, Office 2013 RT SP1, Office 2016, Word for Mac 2011, Word 2016 for Mac, Word Viewer, Word Automation Services on SharePoint Server 2010 SP2, SharePoint Server 2013 SP1, Excel Automation Services on SharePoint Server 2013 SP1, Word Automation Services on SharePoint Server 2013 SP1, Office Web Apps 2010 SP2, and Office Web Apps Server 2013 SP1 allow remote attackers to execute arbitrary code via a crafted document, aka "Microsoft Office Memory Corruption Vulnerability.""
CVE-2017-0199	"Microsoft Office 2007 SP3, Microsoft Office 2010 SP2, Microsoft Office 2013 SP1, Microsoft Office 2016, Microsoft Windows Vista SP2, Windows Server 2008 SP2, Windows 7 SP1, Windows 8.1 allow remote attackers to execute arbitrary code via a crafted document, aka "Microsoft Office/WordPad Remote Code Execution Vulnerability w/Windows API.""

Figure 5.12 Office and Skype – exploitable vulnerabilities.

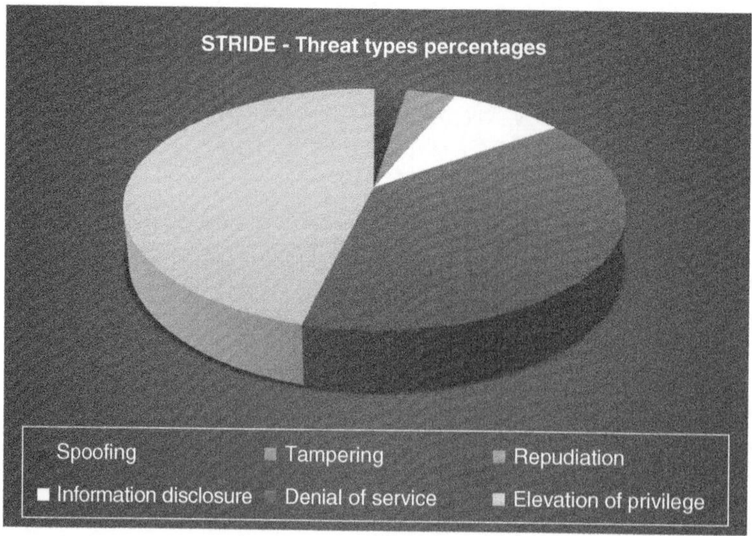

Figure 5.13 Office and Skype – STRIDE threat types' instances percentages.

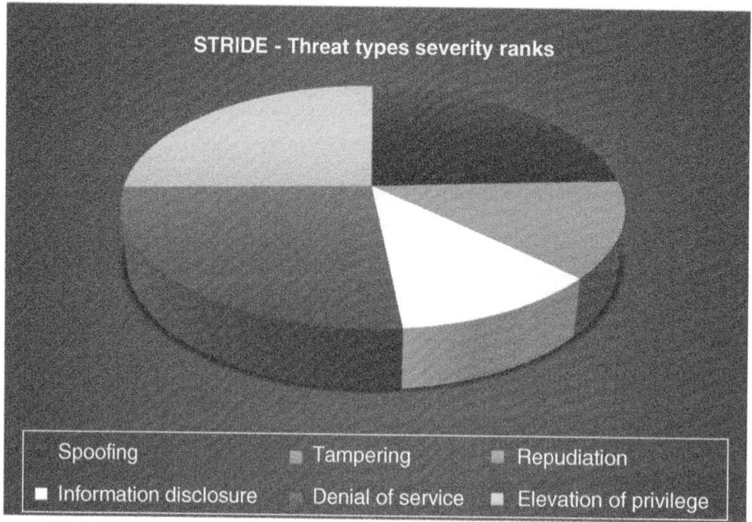

Figure 5.14 Office and Skype – STRIDE threat types' instances severity ranks.

technologies (and their compositions) and possible user interactions over the provided cloud SaaS while leveraging automated solutions wherever possible. In addition, we should realize that security is a shared responsibility, where a given cloud service provider does its share of securing the product, and consumers apply recommended security solutions either from the provider or from a third party (e.g. cloud access security brokers, threat intelligence providers, specialized solutions for one or more part(s) of the cloud SaaS application, and so on).

5.5 Current Trends and Future Direction

Although many cloud SaaS application vulnerabilities can be identified and mitigated effectively from both the consumer and provider points of view, new threats continue to emerge. This reality is reaffirmed almost daily by revelations of major data breaches and cyber attacks; but several risk-mitigation approaches are available, including the following:

- A continued push for exploring and adopting various vulnerability-management solutions.
- Using a secure hosting solution or privately developing a security team to actively monitor events at the host and network levels, then evaluating and mitigating any detected incident.
- Adoption of third-party or private solutions that seek to provide additional layers of security (i.e. defense in depth). Leveraging threat intelligence provides early warnings of impending threats and also exposes contextual and actionable details for any indicator of compromise (IOC).
- Using various security and privacy compliance standards tailored to specific industries (i.e. health, financial, etc.).

A holistic solution to this SaaS challenge should be agile in terms of using a security and privacy framework during the design, development, deployment, and maintenance stages. A futurist approach should implement a holistic solution using automated systems capable of defending against cyber attacks and privacy violations in real time.

5.6 Related Works

Recommended reading for more information on major security issues in cloud environments is available in (Sen 2013), which discusses the following:

- Threats against information assets residing in cloud computing environments.
- Types of attackers and their capability of attacking the Cloud.
- Security risks associated with the Cloud, including common attacks and countermeasures.
- Emerging cloud security risks.
- Some example cloud security incidents.

A security white paper by Hightail (www.hightail.com) provides a useful guide for assessing a cloud SaaS provider from the consumer's point of view. The guide explores multiple security layers for cloud-based sharing services with a focus on:

- What to look for in an information security program.
- The importance of application architecture for a secure environment.
- How to think about data security.
- Correctly assessing systems and network security.
- Key areas to focus on when determining data-center security.

For each of these topics, the white paper presents details on some best practices for assessing cloud SaaS provider offerings.

(Rashmi et al. 2013) present a collection of current solutions available for securing SaaS based on the following areas:

- Authentication and authorization
- Availability, data confidentiality, and VM security
- Information and network security
- Cloud standards and data access
- Web application security, data breaches, and backups
- Identity management and sign-on process

A good recommended work on privacy in the cloud environment is an ITU-T Technology Watch report (Guilloteau and Mauree 2012). This report provides a detailed discussion of various challenges posed by cloud computing and the standardization work being done by various standards development organizations (SDOs) to mitigate privacy risks in the Cloud, including the role of privacy-enhancing technologies (PETs).

5.7 Conclusion

Any provider or consumer of a cloud SaaS application should maintain situational awareness of their security and privacy status by doing the following:

- Identify and document security and privacy requirements.
- Perform a real-time vulnerability assessment of cloud assets.
- Proactively assess and track any relevant security and privacy threats.
- Perform risk assessment based on the identified threats.
- Proactively leverage proven processes, methods, and tools to mitigate perceived risks.

In this chapter, we have presented some key research contributions to the state of the art using a holistic approach to assessing and managing cloud SaaS application security and privacy threats. We have also recommended preferred security and privacy solutions that any cloud provider/consumer should adopt.

Acknowledgments

- **Takabi, Hassan**, University of North Texas, USA
- **Kavi, Krishna**, University of North Texas, USA
- **Gomathisankaran, Mahadevan**, University of North Texas, USA
- **Struble, David G.**, University of North Texas, USA

References

Deng, M., Wuyts, K., Scandariato, R. et al. (2011). A privacy threat analysis framework: supporting the elicitation and fulfillment of privacy requirements. *Requirements Engineering* 16 (1): 3–32.

Fenz, S. (2011). An ontology-and Bayesian-based approach for determining threat probabilities. In: Proceedings of the 6th ACM Symposium on Information, Computer and Communications Security. ACM.

Guilloteau, S. and Mauree, V. (2012). Privacy in cloud computing. ITU-T Technology Watch Report.

Nathan Heck. (1999). Best practices for vulnerability assessments. Presentation. https://slideplayer.com/slide/5683363.

Patrick Kamongi, Mahadevan Gomathisankaran, and Krishna Kavi. (2014). Nemesis: automated architecture for threat modeling and risk assessment for cloud computing. Paper presented at the Sixth ASE International Conference on Privacy, Security, Risk and Trust (PASSAT) in Cambridge, MA (December 13–16, 2014).

Patrick Kamongi, Srujan Kotikela, Krishna Kavi et al. (2013). VULCAN: vulnerability assessment framework for cloud computing. In: Proceedings of The Seventh International Conference on Software Security and Reliability. SERE (SSIRI) 2013. IEEE, 218–226).

Lee, Chen-Yu, Kavi, Krishna M., Paul, Raymond et al. (2015). Ontology of secure service level agreement. In: Proceedings of the 2015 IEEE 16th International Symposium on High Assurance Systems Engineering (HASE). IEEE, 166–172.

Patel, N.S. and Rekha, B.S. (2014). Software as a Service (SaaS): security issues and solutions. *International Journal of Computational Engineering Research* 2250–3005.

Rashmi, G. Sahoo, and S. Mehfuz. (2013). Securing software as a service model of cloud computing: issues and solutions. arXiv preprint arXiv:1309.2426.

Sen, J. (2013). Security and privacy issues in cloud computing. In: *Architectures and Protocols for Secure Information Technology Infrastructures*, 1–45. IGI Global.

Alex Smolen. (2010). Privacy design analysis: a framework for identifying and resolving privacy threats. Paper presented at CHI 2010, Atlanta, Georgia (April 10–15, 2010).

6

Hacking and Countermeasures in the Cloud

Farzaneh Abazari[1], Hassan Takabi[2], and Morteza Analoui[1]

[1]*School of Computer Engineering, Iran University of Science and Technology, Tehran, Iran*
[2]*Department of Computer Science and Engineering, University of North Texas, Denton, TX, USA*

6.1 Introduction

In recent years, there has been increasing interest in cloud computing. However, cloud providers and their customers have several security concerns about their assets. Security reports show that risks in the Cloud have increased dramatically, and the Cloud has become a major target for criminals. Recent evidence confirms the possibility of attacks such as data breaches, distributed denial of service (DDoS), man in the middle, and malware injection in the cloud environment. In addition, abuse of cloud resources by attackers is one of the top threats to the cloud environment.

Virtualization is a key technology in cloud computing that enables dynamic allocation of resources to cloud users. However, this technology introduces new threats to the cloud infrastructure. In addition to the virtualization threat, general features of cloud computing, such as multitenancy and using shared resources, enable attackers to penetrate the cloud infrastructure. Because users are managing their business, computation, and storage in the Cloud, they are concerned with the level of security the cloud infrastructure can provide. The purpose of this chapter is to provide perspective on current threats to the cloud environment and proposed countermeasures.

Based on (Stallings and Brawn 2008), we define a *countermeasure* as "An action, device, procedure, or technique that reduces a threat, a vulnerability, or an attack by eliminating or preventing it, by minimizing the harm it can cause, or by discovering and reporting it so that corrective action can be taken." Traditional countermeasures can disable part of an attack, while other parts of the attack require specific countermeasures. Although physical security is important in the overall security of the Cloud, we don't discuss it in this chapter. We assume that physical security is maintained by experienced experts.

The chapter is organized as follows. Background on cloud security issues is discussed in Section 6.2. We explore cloud security risks and threats in Section 6.3, and Section 6.4 discusses countermeasures. Section 6.5 presents real attacks in the Cloud, Section 6.6 predicts the future of the Cloud, and finally Section 6.7 concludes the chapter.

Security, Privacy, and Digital Forensics in the Cloud, First Edition. Edited by Lei Chen, Hassan Takabi, and Nhien-An Le-Khac.

6.2 Background

The *Cloud* is an Internet-based environment consists of computing, storage, and networking resources that provide servers, platforms, and applications that can be accessed by any individual or business with Internet connectivity. Customers get a piece of the Cloud that contains what they need to run their business, and they pay based on their usage. The National Institute of Standards and Technology (NIST) divides cloud services into three categories: Software-as-a-Service (SaaS), Platform-as-a-Service (PaaS), and Infrastructure-as-a-Service (IaaS).

Both cloud providers and consumers are responsible for establishing security in the Cloud. They must defend against advanced attacks, since the Cloud is a bigger target for hackers than any single machine and the rewards are higher for the attackers. Their responsibilities are different based on the type of cloud service. In IaaS, the cloud provider is responsible for security in the hypervisor and everything in the cloud backend; however, customers are responsible for hardening operating systems (OSs), applications, and data. In PaaS, the cloud provider should isolate the customers' applications and data from each other and establish security in the OS and hypervisor. On the other hand, customers are responsible for the security of their developed applications. In the SaaS service model, the cloud provider must provide security in the applications, data, and virtualized infrastructure. In all of the cloud service models, the cloud provider is in charge of physical security, which is maintained by experienced experts. Physical attacks will not happen often, but when they do occur, they can be very damaging (Szefer et al. 2014).

Increase in the acceptance of cloud computing in enterprise IT will force cloud providers to establish a greater level of security than traditional data centers. To meet this requirement, cloud providers must recognize the threats targeting cloud environments and study security solutions that can prevent attacks effectively. A superior understanding of the threats will guide further reactions at the operational level, including updating policies and making organizational changes (Juliadotter and Choo 2015).

(Ardagna et al. 2015) classified vulnerabilities, threats, and attacks based on attack surfaces and classified security threats in three groups: application level, tenant on tenant, and provider on tenant/tenant on provider. The first group mainly applies to the SaaS service model and threatens interactions between users and services. In other words, they focus on services and data at the highest level of a cloud stack. The second group consists of scenarios where a malicious tenant tries to attack other tenants in the same physical machine by exploiting misconfiguration or vulnerabilities on the virtualization infrastructure. The last group contains two types of attack: a malicious cloud provider that attacks its tenants, or compromised tenants attacking the cloud infrastructure by organizing a botnet.

6.3 Cloud Security Threats

According to a Gartner report (Columbus 2013), cloud computing is evolving rapidly as part of the economy. The report estimated that public cloud services would grow to $210 billion by 2016. However, this is leading to increased sharing of resources among more businesses and, at the same time, attracting more cybercriminals. Many factors make cloud computing less secure; in this section, we list the top seven.

6.3.1 Resource Exhaustion Attacks (DoS Attacks)

A denial of service (DoS) attack aims to overwhelm cloud resources such as computation resources with CPU-intensive requests and overload the network's infrastructure with bandwidth-consuming traffic. In order to deny service to other virtual machines (VMs) in a physical machine, attackers consume host resources unfairly. In addition to exhausting resources, this attack puts load balancers, network monitors, and firewalls out of service. Misconfiguration may also potentially lead to unintended resource exhaustion, such as boot storms and antivirus (AV) storms. For example, when most of the VMs in a physical machine try to boot at the same time, a boot storm happens and creates spikes of I/O calls and CPU consumption. Multiple AV scans at the same time have the same effect on resources (http://www.vmware.com/files/pdf/partners/trendmicro/vmware-trendmicro-anti-virus-virtual-datacenter-sb-en.pdf).

6.3.2 Attacks on the Cloud Interface

Cloud providers publish a set of software interfaces that enable users to interact with cloud services and manage them. Security and availability of the Cloud depends on the security of these application programming interfaces (APIs) (Modi et al. 2013). According to Alert Logic (https://info.cogecopeer1.com/hubfs/Alert%20Logic%20Cloud%20Security%20Report.pdf), brute-force attacks on cloud environments increased from 44–56% of customers in 2015. Brute-force attacks involve a large number of attempts to find a correct credential to log in as an authentic user and access cloud services. Suspicious activity in the Cloud has also increased, from 50–68%. In addition, attackers can launch browser-based attacks, such as Secure Sockets Layer (SSL) certificate spoofing, attacks on browser caches, key logging, and phishing attacks.

(Kim and Vouk 2014) surveyed common security vulnerabilities and corresponding countermeasures for SaaS as the most prevalent service-delivery mode. Since many SaaS services are accessed through the Web, vulnerabilities identified with Extensible Markup Language (XML), which is widely used to support web services (e.g. Simple Object Access Protocol [SOAP], Representational State Transfer [REST], and Web Services Description Language [WSDL]) have a real impact on SaaS security. SOAP, which is based on XML, is used to exchange services related structured information. SOAP data is vulnerable to a variety of man-in-the-middle attacks, such as interception, manipulation, and transmission.

6.3.3 Attacks on Cloud Infrastructure

OpenStack is an open source platform for cloud computing that is mostly deployed for IaaS. Several vulnerabilities in OpenStack components such as Keystone, Compute, Neutron, and Horizon can lead to serious attacks such as man-in-the-middle, DoS, session hijacking, and information disclosure. Nova has the most security issues; Keystone has the second most, but they are more important than Nova's (Murphy 2014).

6.3.4 Malware Propagation

Any malware, such as worms, with access to network components will propagate to wherever their addressing or routing allows; hence the communication of VMs and their access to the network leads to malware propagation in the cloud infrastructure. Containment of fast-spreading worms in the Cloud is an ongoing problem. Attackers attempts to inject malicious services or code, which appear to be valid instances of services running in the Cloud. Disk images in storage can be compromised through attacks such as malware installation and unauthorized access to cloud storage.

Previous studies in data-center security have indicated that malware botnet attacks were the most common attacks on data centers. Several approaches have been proposed to detect malware in cloud infrastructure (Marnerides et al. 2013; Watson et al. 2014). However, malware creators try to make their attacks undetectable by using polymorphic techniques to avoid detection. Cloud providers should minimize the time that malware actively scans the network for vulnerable machines to infect, and also limit malware propagation in their cloud networks (Shahin 2014).

6.3.5 Malicious Insiders

Malicious insiders are aware of vulnerabilities in an organizations. In addition, using a higher level of privilege can enable an employee to gain access to confidential data and services. Since insider network traffic often bypasses firewalls and intrusion detection systems, malicious activities in the Cloud remain undetected.

6.3.6 Data Breaches and Losses

Data privacy, integrity, and availability are always important concerns for users who migrate to the Cloud. Due to the dynamic and shared nature of the Cloud, user data may be compromised in many ways (Ali et al. 2015).

Data breaches and losses can be caused by both intentional and unintentional events. Losing the key for encrypted data and a disk drive crashing without a backup are good illustrations of unintentional data loss. An example of an intentional situation is the case of VMs on the same physical host, allocated to several organizations. If there is competition between the organizations, data leakage is unacceptable. So, establishing robust VM isolation is crucial. If a malicious cloud user gets access to the hypervisor, e.g. by exploiting a zero-day vulnerability, they can compromise isolation and deliberately modify or even delete competitors' files.

6.3.7 Abuse of Cloud Resources

A Cloud Security Alliance (CSA) survey shows that of all security issues, abuse of cloud resources is considered the top security threat (Cloud Security Alliance 2010). Malware is the first stage of larger security threats such as DDoS attacks. If malware propagates over most of a cloud's VMs, a botnet will emerge. An internal botnet in the cloud infrastructure can source a DDoS attack to an external target (Latanicki et al. 2010). Since the Cloud provides reliable infrastructure services at a relatively cheap price, a botmaster (attacker) can use the Cloud to organize a botnet. The command and control (C&C)

server is placed in a typical network environment outside the Cloud. Cloud instances (VMs) are commanded and controlled by the C&C entity to initiate a cyber attack while the C&C server runs a collection of VMs remotely (Mark and Wei 2015). Containment of fast-spreading worms in the Cloud is an open problem and important research issue (Biedermann and Katzenbeisser 2012).

6.3.8 Attacks on Virtualization

Virtualization is used in the Cloud to achieve multitenancy. However, some attacks on cloud infrastructure are caused by virtualization vulnerabilities (Shoaib and Olivia 2014). Attackers may incorporate several virtualization vulnerabilities in combination to achieve the intended effects. Shared resources in a virtualized environment are the dominant reason for vulnerabilities in the Cloud. (Ezhilchelvan and Mitrani 2015) described the security issues in isolation among VMs that allow a malicious VM to access a victim VM. Several factors attract attackers to compromise multiple VMs and deploy further large-scale attacks (Chung et al. 2013):

- The similar configuration of VMs in the Cloud, such as virtualization techniques, which causes them to have the same vulnerabilities.
- Cloud users installing vulnerable applications on VMs.
- VM migration, which provides quick deployment but leads to security problems, such as the quick spread of vulnerable configurations, allowing attackers to expose the security of a new host.
- Communication among VMs through a virtual network.
- Underlying components of the cloud infrastructure (e.g. CPU, CPU caches, GPUs, etc.) that were not designed to offer strong isolation properties for a multitenant architecture.

Although gaining control over multiple VMs is not easy, these factors make it simpler for attackers. A malicious user can misuse its VM to access host resources and then access other VMs. (Tsai et al. 2011) discussed several virtualization-related security issues in a cloud environment. The key threats to virtualization are as follows:

- **VM escape attack**—An attacker exploits vulnerabilities in an application, OS, or hypervisor and allows malware to escape from a VM to the host or hypervisor on which the victim VM is running. In another variation of this attack, malware escapes from a VM to another co-resident VM managed by a same hypervisor. This threat enables VMs to interfere with each other.
- **Cross-VM side-channel attack**—(Ristenpart et al. 2009) introduced cross-VM side-channel attacks in the cloud environment. They explored how VM placement can be misused to mount attacks to extract information from a victim VM on the same machine. In this attack, an attacker needs to gain access to a VM running within the cloud system.
- **Sharing of VM images**—(Jansen 2011) pointed out another serious threat in the cloud environment: sharing VM images in image repositories. If a malicious user can access this repository, they can investigate the image code for a potential vulnerability. Research conducted by (Balduzzi et al. 2012) confirmed that 98% of Windows images and 58% of Linux images in Amazon EC2 contained applications with critical

vulnerabilities, based on analyzing 5303 Amazon VM images. In addition, a malicious user can upload an image that contains malware. The VM instantiated through the infected image becomes the source of malware in the cloud computing environment.
- **Communication threat**—(Ali et al. 2015) listed two types of communication in the cloud infrastructure: internal and external. The first type of communication occurs inside the cloud infrastructure, and the second type is between users and the Cloud. Internal communication takes place in a virtualized environment. External, like other communication over the Internet, faces security challenges such as man-in-the-middle attacks, eavesdropping, spoofing, and DoS. A virtual network that is built over a physical network is responsible for managing communication among VMs (Wu et al. 2010). Software-based network components include bridges, routers, and switches, provide networking of VMs over the same host. Since security mechanisms over the physical network are not able to monitor traffic over the virtualized network, malicious traffic can pass through the network without being detected. This problem is mentioned in a security report released by Symantec (Wueest 2014).

(Juliadotter and Choo 2015) presented risk-assessment measures to evaluate the security of the Cloud based on the overall threat to user assets. Their measures include the attack source, vector, vulnerability type, target, defense type, and impact.

6.4 Cloud Security Countermeasures

Cloud providers are responsible for preventing attacks in the cloud infrastructure. (Okubo et al. 2014) divided security functions for which cloud providers are responsible as follows:

- Protection of internal servers
- Ruggedization of servers for disclosure
- User authentication
- Log acquisition
- Role-based access control (RBAC)
- Account lockouts
- Multifactor authentication
- Port scans

However, these countermeasures are not enough to defend against all threat types in the Cloud. In this section, we explain different countermeasures in detail.

(Datta and Goyal 2014) used annotated attack graphs to show security vulnerabilities in the cloud environment. They proposed a framework to share information about vulnerabilities with tenants so they can adopt their own security protection policies according to their business needs. An attack-mitigation framework for the Cloud that could facilitate the collection and utilization of security intelligence gathered from the cloud environment could secure tenants' resources from potential attacks.

Szefer et al. (2014) proposed a real-time cloud intrusion-prevention model. Their goal was protecting VMs from insider attacks in the network. Based on the time an initial sign of a potential attack is detected in the network, two kinds of mechanisms are employed: prevention and detection. Implementing each mechanism has its own cost and execution overhead, so the model suggested the best response mechanism that was effective and rapid in the cloud context.

Attackers exploit known and unknown vulnerabilities to initiate sophisticated attacks. The dynamic nature of the attacks allows attackers to stay stealthy and avoid intrusion detection systems (IDSs) and makes mitigation a challenging task. A fast-reacting adaptive system is presented in (Emami-Taba et al. 2014): it is capable of detecting and mitigating threats by engineering self-protecting software (SPS) that incorporates an attacker's possible strategies when selecting countermeasures. They utilized game theory to model the competition between the adaptation manager in the SPS and the attacker.

In addition to these countermeasures for attacks in the Cloud, each attack can be prevented by a specific mechanism. In the following section, we present specific countermeasures for each attack type.

The best approach to prevent a resource exhaustion or DoS attack is to limit resource allocation by using the proper configuration of the hypervisor. Performance isolation also avoids this type of attack; however, it reduces cloud efficiency.

Attacks on the cloud interface affect the IaaS, PaaS, and SaaS cloud service models and can be avoided by establishing strong authentication and access-control mechanisms in the cloud provider's interface. Moreover, all transmitted data must be encrypted securely. Cloud APIs should support all key agreement protocols specified in the WS-Security standards, since the resulting keys must be stored in the user's browser. WS-Security uses XML Signature and XML Encryption to protect against man-in-the-middle attacks, such as interception, manipulation, and transmission (Kim and Vouk 2014).

An important security issue in the Cloud is malware propagation. By checking the integrity of cloud services and VM images in the hypervisor, any changes can be detected by the cloud provider. Infrastructure, hypervisor, and storage attacks in the Cloud may threaten the security of VM images. Therefore, VM images must be secured in cloud storage to protect sensitive user data, maintaining the integrity of disk images and ensuring confidentiality of images through encryption (Muhammad et al. 2013). Allocation of malicious VMs to the physical host has an effect on the speed of malware propagation in the Cloud (Abazari and Analoui 2014).

Malicious insiders can affect SaaS, PaaS, and IaaS cloud service models. To avoid this threat, cloud providers should offer more transparency in security and management processes, including compliance reporting and breach notification. (Khorshed et al. 2012) investigated and compared performances of several machine learning techniques to monitor insider activities in the Cloud. They detected malicious activity by monitoring VM performance.

Using authentication, authorization, audit control, and identity and access management (IAM) helps prevent malicious and intrusive actions by attackers. Applying strong encryption algorithms, disaster recovery, using reliable data centers, and effective data-backup strategies can reduce data breaches and the threat of loss. Deploying IAM solutions across cloud-based applications and monitoring user activities can manage multiple user login under a single AWS account without interference. Amazon S3 supports IAM policies that let an organization manage multiple users. In SaaS, access-control components are responsible for resource access.

(Tangwongsan and Itthisombat 2014) proposed a working model for preserving file privacy in cloud storage. The model first encrypts the file and then executes the following steps: (i) assign a privacy map that shows what group names have access to each file, and (ii) notify privilege members by email. The model also preserves privacy in retrieving data.

Several approaches have been proposed to detect malware in cloud infrastructure (Marnerides et al. 2013; Watson et al. 2014) and prevent abuse of cloud resources. However, malware creators try to make it undetectable by using polymorphic techniques. Cloud providers should work to minimize malware active time and also limit malware propagation in their cloud networks (Shahin 2014). The best approach to prevent DDoS attacks is to limit resource allocation using proper configuration.

To minimize the threat of a VM escape attack, communication channels between the hypervisor and VMs such as clipboard sharing, memory management, device management, and specific vendor channels should be minimized (Ros 2012). Patching vulnerabilities, using strong authentication, and access-control mechanisms are some of the solutions to address this issue.

Cross-VM side-channel attacks make it clear that the Cloud should support hypervisor security mechanisms to ensure process isolation (avoid VM escape), mediated information sharing, and secure communication. (Han et al. 2015) presented a method that applied VM allocation policies to defend against co-resident attacks in cloud computing. We also present a method to respond to co-resident threats (Abazari et al. 2017).

Patching VM vulnerabilities periodically prevents malicious port scanning in the cloud network. Additionally, using security mechanisms such as IDS and firewalls can mitigate attacks.

Self-defended VMs that are capable of monitoring outbound and inbound traffic to detect malicious traffic can mitigate VM communication threats (Abazari et al. 2016). Isolating customer networks from each other and from management networks is another solution. Cloud providers can employ virtual appliances such as firewalls, IDSs, and intrusion prevention systems (IPSs) can provide powerful security between networks. Providers must ensure that no traffic is routed between networks.

The following section discusses the most serious attacks against the cloud environment.

6.5 Hacking the Cloud: Reality Check

Hackers are increasingly taking aim at cloud resources when they launch attacks. They also attack cloud tenants and access their secure information. Consider the following examples of recent cloud attacks:

- **Man-in-the-cloud attack (2015)**—Attackers used SaaS service synchronization to steal users' enterprise data. Once attackers gained control of the user token, they were free to perform manipulations that resulted in data loss or outright breaches. Attackers could take control of a victim's cloud synchronization key and use this information to exploit the organization (Imperva 2015).
- **DoS attack by Sony (2014)**—Sony misused AWS cloud servers to launch DoS attacks against websites that contained leaked company information (Butler 2014).
- **VM escape in VirtualBox (2014)**—Attackers escaped a guest VM and gained access to the host server. CVE-2014-0983 is an example of a guest-to-host breakout

vulnerability for the VirtualBox hypervisor. The attacker can execute arbitrary code on the host OS (MITRE 2014a).
- **VM escape in many virtualization platforms (2015)**—CVE-2015-3456 (VENOM) is a vulnerability in the virtual floppy drive code used by many hypervisors. This vulnerability allows an attacker to escape from the guest VM and potentially obtain code-execution access to the host. This VM escape leads to access to the host and all other VMs running on that host (MITRE 2015).
- **Remote access to data (2014)**—CVE-2014-9047 consists of multiple unspecified vulnerabilities in the preview system in Cloud 6.x before 6.0.6 and 7.x before 7.0.3 that allows remote attackers to read arbitrary files via unknown vectors (MITRE 2014b).
- **DDoS attack on the Rackspace DNS (December 2014)**—This attack affected Rackspace's domain name system (DNS) setup and caused problems accessing Rackspace cloud services for 11 hours (O'Connor 2014).
- **Attack on Amazon EC2 server (late-2014)**—Attackers hijacked cloud servers for Bitcoin-mining purposes. In that case, a GitHub user discovered a bot scanning for Amazon API keys. The hacker used the keys to grab Amazon cloud-based computing resources (Leopold 2017).
- **DDoS attack on Microsoft's Hyper-V (2011)**—Microsoft reported that malicious code run by an authenticated user in a VM caused a DDoS attacks (SecureAuth Labs 2011).
- **DoS attack against Amazon (2009)**—A code-hosting site caused an outage of over 19 hours of downtime during an apparent DoS attack on the Amazon cloud infrastructure (Metz 2009).
- **Cloudburst VM escape attack (2009)**—Attackers exploit a flaw in VMware Workstation and enabled a VM to attack its host (MITRE 2009).
- **Data loss in Amazon EC2 (2011)**—Small amounts of data were lost for some AWS customers when its EC2 cloud suffered a "remirroring storm" due to human operator error on Easter weekend in 2011 (Jennings 2011).

These examples support the facts that cloud computing is already at risk. Table 6.1 shows the mapping between the types of threats and real attacks that have been reported.

Some of the threats haven't been reported yet as real attacks. In the future, we will see more reported attacks on the cloud infrastructure.

6.6 Future of Cloud Security

The following cloud security issues need to be addressed in order to provide more secure cloud services in the future. Attackers continue to enhance their strategies, and at the same time security professionals predict and prepare for these attacks. The future of cloud security falls under four headings (Mogull 2014):

- Cloud providers should consider incident response in the cloud-distributed enterprise.
- Cloud providers should ensure security via auditing and penetration testing.

Table 6.1 Mapping between attacks and threat in the cloud.

Attack Type	Reality Check
Resource exhaustion attacks / DoS attack	The DDoS attack to the RackSpace (2014) DoS attack by Sony (2014) A Dos attack against Amazon (2009) DDoS attack on Microsoft's Hyper-V (2011)
Attack to the cloud interface	VM escape in many virtualization platforms(2014)
Malware Propagation	—
Attack to cloud infrastructure	
Malicious insider	—
Data breach and loss	Man in the Cloud Attack (2015) Data loss in Amazon EC2 (2011) CVE-2014-9047(2014)
Abuse of cloud resources	Attack on Amazon EC2 server (2014)
Attacks on virtualization	Cloudburst VM escape attack (2009) VM escape in VirtualBox (2014): CVE-2015-3456

- Secure programming leads to automated security across cloud, mobile, and internal security tools.
- Security architects should measure and implement security controls internally for applications and across cloud providers.

(Kumari and Nath 2015) noted that migration of data from one cloud to another introduced new threats. They also mentioned that research on the mobile platform with respect to cloud computing is another open research issue.

Recently, (Ardagna et al. 2015) surveyed the interface between cloud security and cloud security assurance. Cloud security assurance refers to a way to gain justifiable confidence that infrastructure will consistently exhibit one or more security properties and operate as expected despite failures and attacks. Assurance is a much wider notion than security, because it includes methodologies for collecting and validating evidence supporting security properties. They recommended the design of next-generation cloud security and assurance solutions.

6.6.1 Cloud Security for the IoT

Traditional security solutions are not able to provide security for billions of devices interconnected over the Internet. Many of these devices have limited processing power. In addition, running sophisticated security mechanisms at the device level is impossible and prohibitively expensive in terms of performance and cost. Hence, using cloud resources to provide security for the Internet of Things (IoT) improves total security for IoT participants. Securing IoT devices through the secure cloud network enables policies to be automatically applied and ensures that communications, devices, and services are not compromised.

6.7 Conclusions

The cloud environment consists of virtualized data centers. VMs in these data centers, similar to physical machines, are under security risks. Some features of cloud service models can inhibit certain virtualization vulnerabilities. Due to abuse and nefarious use of cloud resources, cloud providers must enhance the security of the Cloud to prevent attackers from penetrating.

In this chapter, we have discussed cloud security issues and possible countermeasures. We studied a number of cyber-defense strategies that can be activated when an attack is detected, some of which can even take effect before the actual attack occurs. We hope this study can help cloud providers and cloud users to understand cloud-specific security issues and design appropriate countermeasures.

References

Abazari, F. and Analoui, M. (2014). Exploring the effects of virtual machine placement on the transmission of infections in cloud. In: *Proceedings of the 7th International Symposium on Telecommunications (IST)*, 278–282. IEEE.

Abazari, F., Analoui, M., and Takabi, H. (2016). Effect of anti-malware software on infectious nodes in cloud environment. *Computers & Security* 58: 139–148.

Abazari, F., Analoui, M., and Takabi, H. (2017). Multi-objective response to co-resident attacks in cloud environment. *International Journal of Information & Communication Technology Research* 9: 25–36.

Ali, M., Khan, S.U., and Vasilakos, A.V. (2015). Security in cloud computing: opportunities and challenges. *Information Sciences* 305: 357–383.

Ardagna, A., Claudio, R.A., Damiani, E., and Quang Hieu, V. (2015). From security to assurance in the Cloud: a survey. *ACM Computing Surveys* 48: 2.

Biedermann, S. and Katzenbeisser, S. (2012). Detecting computer worms in the cloud. In: *Open Problems in Network Security*, 43–54. Springer.

Brandon Butler. (2014). Sony may have used Amazon's cloud to launch a counter DoS attack. https://www.networkworld.com/article/2858874/cloud-computing/sony-may-have-used-amazon-s-cloud-to-launch-a-counter-dos-attack-after-its-breach.html (accessed 24 October 2018).

Balduzzi, M., Zaddach, J., Balzarotti, D. et al. (2012). A security analysis of Amazon's elastic compute cloud service. In: *Proceedings of the 27th Annual ACM Symposium on Applied Computing*, 1427–1434. ACM.

Chung, C.-J., Khatkar, P., Xing, T. et al. (2013). NICE: network intrusion detection and countermeasure selection in virtual network systems. *IEEE Transactions on Dependable and Secure Computing* 10 (4): 198–211.

Cloud Security Alliance. (2010). Top threats to cloud computing v1.0. http://cloudsecurityalliance.org/topthreats/csathreats.v1.0.pdf.

Columbus, Louis. (2013). Gartner predicts infrastructure services will accelerate cloud computing growth. http://www.forbes.com/sites/louiscolumbus/2013/02/19/gartner-predicts-infrastructure-services-will-accelerate-cloud-computing-growth.

Datta, E. and Goyal, N. (2014). Security attack mitigation framework for the cloud. In: Proceedings of the 2014 Annual Reliability and Maintainability Symposium (RAMS), 1–6. IEEE.

Emami-Taba, M., Amoui, M., and Tahvildari, L. (2014). Mitigating dynamic attacks using multi-agent game-theoretic techniques. In: *Proceedings of 24th Annual International Conference on Computer Science and Software Engineering*, 375–378. ACM.

Ezhilchelvan, P. and Mitrani, I. (2015). Evaluating the probability of malicious co-residency in public clouds. *IEEE Transactions on Cloud Computing.*

Han, Y., Chan, J., Alpcan, T., and Leckie, C. (2015). Using virtual machine allocation policies to defend against co-resident attacks in cloud computing. *IEEE Transactions on Dependable and Secure Computing.*

Imperva. (2015). Man in the cloud (MITC) attacks. https://www.imperva.com/docs/HII_Man_In_The_Cloud_Attacks.pdf (accessed 24 October 2018).

Jansen, Wayne. (2011). Cloud hooks: security and privacy issues in cloud computing. 44th Hawaii International Conference on System Sciences (HICSS).

Jennings, Richi. 2011. Amazon Web Services EC2 cloud lost data. https://www.computerworld.com/article/2471227/network-software/oops--amazon-web-services-ec2-cloud-lost-data.html ((accessed 24 October 2018).

Juliadotter, N.V. and Choo, K.-K.R. (2015). Cloud attack and risk assessment taxonomy. *IEEE Cloud Computing* 2 (1): 14–20.

Khorshed, M.T., Shawkat, A.A.B.M., and Wasimi, S.A. (2012). A survey on gaps, threat remediation challenges and some thoughts for proactive attack detection in cloud computing. *Future Generation Computer Systems* 28 (6): 833–851.

Kim, D. and Vouk, M.A. (2014). A survey of common security vulnerabilities and corresponding countermeasures for SaaS. In: *Globecom Workshops (GC Wkshps)*, 59–63. IEEE.

Kumari, M. and Nath, R. (2015). Security concerns and countermeasures in cloud computing paradigm. In: *2015 Fifth International Conference on Advanced Computing Communication Technologies (ACCT)*, 534–540. IEEE.

Latanicki, Joseph, Massonet, Philippe, Naqvi, Syed et al. (2010). Scalable cloud defenses for detection, analysis and mitigation of DDoS attacks. In: Proceeds of Future Internet Assembly, 127–137.

Leopold, George. (2017). AWS cloud hacked by bitcoin miners. https://www.enterprisetech.com/2017/10/09/aws-cloud-hacked-bitcoin-miners (accessed 24 October 2018).

Marnerides, A.K., Watson, M.R., Shirazi, N. et al. (2013). Malware analysis in cloud computing: network and system characteristics. In: *Globecom Workshops (GC Wkshps)*, 482–487. IEEE.

Metz, Cade. (2009). DDoS attack rains down on Amazon cloud. https://www.theregister.co.uk/2009/10/05/amazon_bitbucket_outage (accessed 24 October 2018).

Miller, Mark, and Wei, Lu. (2015). Detecting botnets in the cloud. ASEE Northeast Section Conference.

MITRE. (2009). CVE-2009-1244. https://cve.mitre.org/cgi-bin/cvename.cgi?name=cve-2009-1244 (accessed 24 October 2018).

MITRE. (2014a). CVE-2014-0983. https://cve.mitre.org/cgi-bin/cvename.cgi?name=cve-2014-0983 (accessed 24 October 2018).

MITRE. (2014b). CVE-2014-9047. https://cve.mitre.org/cgi-bin/cvename.cgi?name=2014-9047 (accessed 24 October 2018).

MITRE. (2015). CVE-2015-3456. https://cve.mitre.org/cgi-bin/cvename.cgi?name=cve-2015-3456 (accessed 24 October 2018).

Modi, C., Patel, D., Borisaniya, B. et al. (2013). A survey on security issues and solutions at different layers of cloud computing. *The Journal of Supercomputing* 63: 561–592.

Mogull, Rich. (2014). The future of security. Securosis.

Muhammad, Kazim, Rahat, Masood, and Awais, Shibli Muhammad. (2013). Securing the virtual machine images in cloud computing. 6th International Conference on Security of Information and Networks (SIN 2013). Aksaray-Turkey: ACM-SIGSAC.

Murphy, Grant. (2014). OpenStack security. Red Hat product security. https://www.youtube.com/watch?v=VrXup6wr7EQ.

O'Connor, Fred. (2014). Rackspace DNS recovers after DDoS brings system down. https://www.computerworld.com/article/2862982/rackspace-dns-recovers-after-ddos-brings-system-down.html (accessed 24 October 2018).

Okubo, T., Wataguchi, Y., and Kanaya, N. (2014). Threat and countermeasure patterns for cloud computing. In: *Proceedings of 2014 IEEE 4th International Workshop on Requirements Patterns (RePa)*, 43–46. IEEE.

Ristenpart, Thomas, Tromer, Eran, Shacham, Hovav et al. (2009). Hey, you, get off of my cloud: exploring information leakage in third-party compute clouds. In: Proceedings of the 16th ACM Conference on Computer and Communications Security, 199–212. ACM.

Ros, J. (2012). *Security in the Cloud: The Threat of Coexist with an Unknown Tenant on a Public Environment.* Royal Holloway University of London.

SecureAuth Labs. (2011). MS HyperV persistent DoS vulnerability. https://www.secureauth.com/labs/advisories/hyperv-vmbus-persistent-dos-vulnerability (accessed 24 October 2018).

Shahin, A.A. (2014). Polymorphic worms collection in cloud computing. *International Journal of Computer Science and Mobile Computing* 3 (8): 645–652.

Shoaib, Yasir and Olivia, Das. (2014). Pouring cloud virtualization security inside out. arXiv preprint arXiv:1411.3771.

Stallings, W. and Brawn, L. (2008). *Computer Security: Principles and Practice.* Pearson Education.

Szefer, Jakub, Jamkhedkar, Pramod, Perez-Botero, Diego et al. (2014). Cyber defenses for physical attacks and insider threats in cloud computing. In: Proceedings of the 9th ACM Symposium on Information, Computer and Communications Security, 519–524. ACM.

Tangwongsan, S. and Itthisombat, V. (2014). A highly effective security model for privacy preserving on cloud storage. In: Proceedings of the 2014 IEEE 3rd International Conference on Cloud Computing and Intelligence Systems (CCIS), 505–509. IEEE.

Tsai, H.-Y., Siebenhaar, M., Miede, A. et al. (2011). Threat as a service?: virtualization's impact on cloud security. *IT Professional* 14: 32–37.

Watson, M.R., Marnerides, A.K., Mauthe, A. et al. (2014). Towards a distributed, self-organising approach to malware detection in cloud computing. In: *Self-Organizing Systems* (ed. M. Hirsch, T. Dunkelberger and C. Snyder), 182–185. Springer.

Wu, Hanqian, Ding, Yi, Winer, Chucket al. (2010). Network security for virtual machine in cloud computing. In: Proceedings of the 5th International Conference on Computer Sciences and Convergence Information Technology (ICCIT), 18–21. IEEE.

Wueest, Candid. (2014). Threats to virtual environments. Symantec.

7

Risk Management and Disaster Recovery in the Cloud

Saman Zonouz

Rutgers University, New Brunswick, NJ, USA

7.1 Introduction

Keeping cloud infrastructures, systems, and networks secure is a continual race against attackers. The growing number of security incidents indicates that current approaches to building systems do not sufficiently address the increasing variety and sophistication of threats and do not block attacks before systems are compromised. Organizations must resort to trying to detect malicious activity that occurs, so efficient intrusion detection systems (IDSs) are deployed to monitor systems and identify misbehavior. However, IDSs alone are not sufficient to allow operators to understand the security state of their organization, because monitoring sensors usually report all potentially malicious traffic without regard to the actual network configuration, vulnerabilities, and mission impact. Moreover, given large volumes of network traffic, IDSs with even small error rates can overwhelm operators with false alarms. Even when true intrusions are detected, the actual mission threat is often unclear, and operators are unsure what actions they should take. Security administrators need to obtain updated estimate summaries regarding the security status of their mission-critical assets precisely and continuously, based on alerts that occur, in order to respond effectively to system compromises and prioritize their response and recovery actions. This requirement is even stronger in the context of smart energy infrastructure where incorrect decision-making related to the security of process controls can have dramatic consequences.

7.2 Background

Extensive research has been conducted over the past decade on the topics of system situational awareness and security metrics. Security metrics and evaluation techniques fall into two categories. First, with static solutions, an IDS alert scoring value is hard-coded on each detection rule; the (alert, score) mappings are stored in a lookup table to be used later to prioritize alerts. The advantages of static techniques are their simplicity and their rapidity. However, they suffer from a lack of flexibility, mainly because they

Security, Privacy, and Digital Forensics in the Cloud, First Edition. Edited by Lei Chen, Hassan Takabi, and Nhien-An Le-Khac.

completely ignore system configuration and scalability, since it is infeasible to predict all the alert combinations from IDSs in a large-scale network.

Second, there are dynamic methods, which are mostly based on attack-graph analysis. The main idea is to capture potential system vulnerabilities and then extract all possible attack paths. The generated graph can be used to compute security metrics and assess the security strength of a network. These techniques can also be used predictively to rank IDS alerts. In particular, Topological Vulnerability Analysis (TVA) matches the network configuration with an attack simulation in order to optimize IDS sensor placement and to prioritize IDS alerts. The primary issue with attack-graph-based techniques is that they require important assumptions about attacker capabilities and vulnerabilities. While these approaches are important in planning for future attack scenarios, we take a different perspective by relying on past consequences, actual security requirements, and low-level system characteristics, such as file and process dependencies, instead of hypothetical attack paths. As a result, our method is defense-centric rather than attack-centric and does not suffer from the issues of unknown vulnerabilities and incomplete attack coverage.

Defense-centric approaches, on the other hand, use manually filled knowledge bases of alert applicability, system configuration, or target importance to associate a context with each alert and to provide situational awareness accordingly. Damage-assessment capabilities have previously been explored via file-tainting analysis for malware detection, for offline forensic analysis using backtracking or forward-tracking techniques, and for online damage situational awareness.

The current techniques for the security-state estimation problem generally fall short in two major respects. First, existing solutions rely heavily on human knowledge and involvement. The system administrator should observe the triggered IDS alerts (possibly in a visual manner) and manually evaluate their criticality, which can depend on the alerts' accuracy, the underlying system configuration, and high-level security requirements. As the size of cloud infrastructures and their networks increases, the manual inspection of alerts usually becomes very tedious, if not impossible, in practice. Requiring extensive human knowledge, the current model-based approaches try to compute security metrics based on a manually designed model and a strong set of assumptions about attackers' behaviors and the vulnerabilities within the system.

Second, previous techniques for IDS alert correlation and system security state[1] estimation usually focus only on the attack paths and subsequent privilege escalations, without considering dependencies between system assets. In doing so, they define the security metric of a given system state to be the least required number of vulnerability exploitations (i.e. privilege escalations) needed to get from that state to the goal state in which the attacker gains the privileges necessary to cause the final malicious consequence (e.g. a sensitive file modification). We call these *attack-centric metrics*. Therefore, regardless of the transitions, this type of metric is not defined for a non-goal state. Equivalently, attack-metric definitions are created with the assumption that all attackers will pursue exploitations until they get to the goal state, which is insecure by definition. However, in practice, there are often unsuccessful attacks that cause partial damage to

1 A *security state* in the attack graph literature is usually defined to be the set of the attacker's privileges in that state, and the state transitions represent vulnerability exploitations leading to privilege escalations.

systems, such as a web server crash as the result of an unsuccessful buffer-overflow exploitation. Hence, it is important to consider not only future vulnerability exploitations, but also the damage already caused by the attacker.

7.3 Consequence-Centric Security Assessment

To address various limitations of past solutions, we introduce an information flow-based system security metric called Seclius. Seclius works by evaluating IDS alerts received in real time to assess how much attackers affect the system and network asset security. This online evaluation is performed using two components: (i) a dependency graph and (ii) a consequence tree. These two components are designed to identify the context required around each IDS alert to accurately assess the security state of the different assets in the organization.

Specifically, the dependency graph is a Bayesian network automatically learned during a training phase when the system was behaving normally. The dependency graph captures the low-level dependencies among all the files and processes used in the organization. The consequence tree is a simple tree structure defined manually by administrators to formally describe at a high level the most critical assets in the organization. When a new IDS alert is received, a belief propagation algorithm, the Monte Carlo Gibbs sampling, combines the dependency graph and the consequence tree to calculate online the probability that the critical assets in the organization have not been affected and are still secure. Consequently, Seclius assesses organizational security using a bottom-up logical propagation of the probabilities that assets are or are not compromised.

Seclius minimizes reliance on human expertise by clearly separating high-level security requirements from the low-level system characteristics of an IT infrastructure. We developed an algorithm and a set of instruments to automatically learn the dependency graph, which represents the system characteristics by capturing information flows between files and processes, within virtual machines (VMs) of the cloud infrastructure and across the network. As a result, administrators are not required to define such low-level input, so they can focus on identifying high-level organizational security requirements using the consequence tree. These requirements are most often subjective and cannot be automatically discovered. In practice, even in large organizations, the consequence tree contains very few assets, e.g. a web server and a database, and does not require detailed system-level expertise. In addition, as a defense-centric metric, Seclius assesses system security by focusing solely on past consequences, and hence it assumes nothing about system vulnerabilities and attackers' future behaviors, e.g. possible attack paths.

It is worth emphasizing that we do not provide an intrusion-detection capability per se; instead, Seclius assesses organizational security based on the set of alerts triggered by underlying IDSs. Therefore, Seclius would not update the security measure if an attack were not detected by an IDS. Furthermore, it is not an intrusion-response system and does not, as in our experiments, explicitly respond to attacks, but instead helps administrators or response systems react by providing situational awareness capabilities.

7.3.1 High-Level Overview of Cloud Risk Assessment and Disaster Recovery

We first describe how attack-centric and defense-centric security metric are distinguished. In past related work on attack-centric security metrics, e.g. attack graph-based techniques, where there is one (or more) goal states, the security measure of a non-goal state in the attack graph is not independently calculated, i.e. it is calculated as a function of "how close" the non-goal state is to the goal state (from an attack-centric viewpoint, how much is left to reach the destination). Therefore, from an attack-centric viewpoint, if the attack stops in a non-goal state, the attacker gains nothing (according to the model); however, from a defense-centric viewpoint, the system may have already been affected through past exploitations on the attacker's way to get to the current non-goal state. For instance, let us assume that the attacker's end goal is to read a sensitive file residing in a back-end database server; on the attacker's way in the current non-goal state, a buffer-overflow vulnerability in a web server system is exploited, resulting in a server process crash (unavailable web server). According to the attacker's objective, the attacker has not gained anything yet; however, the defense-centric system security has been affected because a network functionality is lost (web server crash). Consequently, the defense-centric security measure of a non-goal state, independent of the goal state and regardless of whether the attack will succeed, may not be the highest value (1 in this case).

Seclius's high-level goal (Figure 7.1) is to assess the security of each possible system state with minimal human involvement. In particular, we define the security of a system state as a binary vector in which each bit indicates whether a specific malicious event has occurred in the system. We consider two types of malicious events. First there are vulnerability exploitations, which are carried out by an attacker to obtain specific privileges and improve the attacker's control over the system. Therefore, the first set of bits in a state denotes the attacker's privileges in that state, e.g. root access on the web server VM. Those bits are used to determine what further malicious damage the attacker can cause in that state. Second, there are attack consequences, which are caused by the attacker after they obtain new privileges. Specifically, we defined consequences as the violations of the CIA criteria (confidentiality, integrity, and availability) applied to

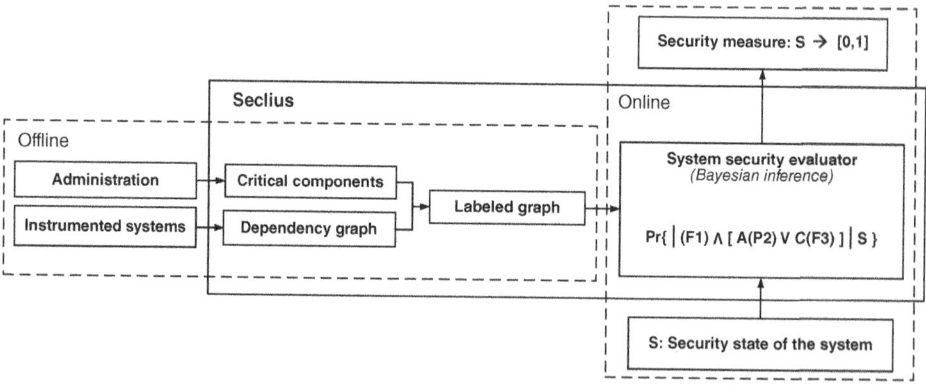

Figure 7.1 High-level architecture for security risk assessment and disaster recovery.

critical assets in the organization, such as specific files and processes. For example, the integrity of a file F2, denoted by I(F2), is compromised if F2 is either directly or indirectly modified by the attacker.

The security of any given system is characterized by a set of its identifiable attributes, such as security criteria of the critical assets, e.g. integrity of a database file; the notion of a security metric is defined as a quantitative measure of how much of that attribute the system possesses. Our goal is to provide administrators with a framework to compute such measures in an online manner. We believe that there are two major barriers to achieving this goal. First, while critical assets are system-specific and should be defined by administrators, a framework that requires too much human involvement is prone to errors and has limited usability. As a result, a formalism is needed so that administrators can define assets simply and unambiguously. Second, low-level IDS alerts usually report on local consequences with respect to a specific domain. Consequently, we need a method that provides understanding of what the low-level consequences represent in a larger context and quantifies how many of the security attributes the whole system currently possesses, given the set of triggered alerts.

The Seclius framework addresses those two challenges. Seclius works based on two inputs: a manually defined consequence tree and an automatically learned dependency graph. The hierarchical, formal structure of the consequence tree enables administrators to define critical assets easily and unambiguously with respect to the subjective mission of the organization. The dependency graph captures the dependencies between these assets and all the files and processes in the system during a training period. In production mode, Seclius receives low-level alerts from intrusion-detection sensors and uses a taint-propagation analysis method to evaluate online the probabilities that the security attributes of the critical assets are affected.

Regarding how large a consequence tree can become in a real-world setting, we highlight that the consequence tree needs to include only the primary critical assets. For instance, in a banking environment, the credit card database would be labeled as critical. However, the consequence tree does not have to include *indirectly critical assets*, which are defined as assets that become critical because of their (possible) interaction with other critical assets. For instance, a web server that interacts with a credit card database would also be partially considered as critical but would not need to be labeled as such. We emphasize that the number of primary critical assets is usually very low even for large target infrastructures. All inter-asset dependencies and system-level details are captured by the dependency graph that is generated and analyzed automatically. The small size of the manually constructed consequence tree and the automated generation of the dependency graph improves the scalability of Seclius remarkably, as shown in the experiments.

To further clarify the conceptual meaning of the system security measure in Seclius, here we describe in more detail what it represents mathematically. The security measure value that Seclius calculates represents the probability that the system is "insecure" according to the consequence tree designed by the administrator. For instance, if the consequence tree includes a single node "credit-card-numbers.db confidentiality," the ultimate system security measure value will denote the probability that the confidentiality of "credit-card-numbers.db" has been compromised at any given state. Consequently, the calculated measures range continuously between 0 and 1, inclusive. In our implementations, we used discretization from [0,1] to the set {low, medium, high} to indicate when the system's security is high or when it needs to be taken care of. Seclius combines these two components to measure the security of the system as the probability that the critical assets become directly or indirectly affected by intruders. The critical assets, encoding the security requirements, are defined by system administrators. The probability value is evaluated using cross dependencies among the system assets. The dependencies are captured during an offline learning phase, but the probability evaluation works online and is triggered by security alerts received from sensors and IDSs.

To illustrate how Seclius works in practice, consider a scenario in which the IT infrastructure of a cloud provider is instrumented to enable comprehensive security monitoring of systems and networks. To use Seclius on top of the deployed IDSs, administrators would first define critical assets and organizational security requirements through the consequence tree. We emphasize that this task does not require deep-knowledge expertise about the IT infrastructure. In our example, the critical assets would include end-user VMs and a database server. In particular, the security requirements would consist of the availability of the VMs and the integrity and confidentiality of the database files.

The second step would be to run a training phase with no ongoing attack in order to collect data on intra- and inter-VM dependencies between files and processes. After a few hours, the results of this training phase would be automatically stored in the dependency graph, and the instruments used to track the dependencies would be turned off.

The third and final step would be to run Seclius in production mode. Seclius starts processing alerts from IDSs by using the generated dependency graph and probabilistically determines whether the critical assets are compromised. After a training phase of a few hours with no ongoing attacks, where the Seclius instruments have collected intra- and inter-VM dependencies between files and processes, the instruments would be turned off. The framework would be ready to process alerts from IDSs and probabilistically determine if the critical assets are compromised. If a vulnerability exploitation in the customer web server was detected by an IDS, Seclius would update not only the security measure of the corresponding web server, but also that of the set of systems that depend on the web server (e.g. the back-end database), according to the learned dependency graph. By observing the real-time IDS alerts and the learned inter-asset dependencies, Seclius can precisely measure (i) the privileges gained by the attacker and which security domains the attacker was able to reach; and (ii) how the integrity, confidentiality, or availability of the assets were affected by the exploit directly or indirectly. In the next sections, we further describe the mathematical tools and formalism used by the various components of Seclius to provide that information.

7.3.2 Cloud Security Consequence Tree

In this section, we discuss the first manual input required by Seclius: the consequence tree (CT). The goal of the CT is to capture critical IT assets and organizational security requirements. The criticality level of individual assets within an organization is indeed an environment-specific issue. In other words, the criticality levels heavily depend on organizational missions and/or business-level objectives. For instance, consider a security-critical cloud infrastructure network, whose mission is to provide millions of end users with crucial data-storage and computational services. In such an environment, provision of high-availability guarantees for a server VM sample, which happens to be a critical cyber asset of the enterprise, is often much more critical than for a logging database, which is used to store historical system incidents for later analyses. Hence, Seclius requires system administrators to manually provide the list of organizational critical assets.

The critical assets could be provided using any function: a simple list (meaning that all items are equally important), a weighted list, or a more complex combination of assets. In this chapter, we use a logical tree structure. We believe that it offers a good trade-off between simplicity and expressiveness, and the fact that it can be represented visually makes it a particularly helpful resource for administrators. The formalism of the CT follows the traditional fault-tree model; however, unlike fault trees, the leaf nodes of the CTs in Seclius address security requirements (confidentiality, integrity, and availability) of critical assets, rather than dependability criteria.

The CT formalism consists of two major types of logical nodes: AND and OR gates. To design an organizational CT, the administrator starts with the tree's root node, which identifies the primary high-level security concern/requirement, e.g. "Organization is not secure." The rest of the tree recursively defines how different combinations of the more concrete and lower-level consequences can lead to the undesired status described by the tree's root node. The recursive decomposition procedure stops once a node explicitly refers to a consequence regarding a security criterion of a system asset, e.g. "availability of the Apache server is compromised." These nodes are in fact the CT's leaf consequence nodes, each of which takes on a binary value indicating whether its corresponding consequence has happened (1) or not (0). Throughout the chapter, we use the C, I, and A function notations to refer to the CIA criteria of the assets. For instance, C(F2) and I(P6) denote the confidentiality of file F2 and integrity of process P6, respectively. The leaves' values can be updated by IDSs, e.g. Samhain. The CT is derived as a Boolean expression, and the root node's value is consequently updated to indicate whether organizational security is still being maintained.

A CT indeed formulates subjective aspects of the system. Its leaf nodes list security criteria of the organization's critical assets. Additionally, the CT implicitly encodes how critical each asset is, using the depth of its corresponding node in the tree; that is, the deeper the node, the less critical the asset is in the fulfillment of organizational security requirements. Furthermore, the CT formulates redundant assets using AND gates. Seclius requires administrators to explicitly mention redundancies because it is often infeasible to discover redundancies automatically over a short learning phase.

Although the CT formulation can be considered as a particular kind of the general attack-tree formalism, its application in Seclius is different from how attack trees have been used typically in the past: CTs formulate how past consequences contribute to the overall security requirements, whereas attack trees usually address attackers' potential intents against the organization. In other words, at each instant, given the consequences already caused by the attackers in the system, Seclius employs the CT to estimate the current system security, whereas the system's attack tree is often used to probabilistically estimate how an attacker could or would penetrate the system in the future. Therefore, the consequence tree formalism mainly considers adversarial consequences against assets, such as a web server process, needed for the organization to fulfill its mission objectives, and may not address vulnerability exploitations that cause privilege escalations for the attackers without affecting the system's current performance.

7.3.3 Cloud-Based Dependency Graph

As mentioned in the previous section, the CT captures only subjective security requirements and does not require deep-knowledge expertise about the IT infrastructure, thanks to the dependency graph (DG). The goal of the DG is to free the administrator from providing low-level details about the organization. Those details are automatically captured by Seclius through a learning phase, during which the interactions between files and processes are tracked in order to probabilistically identify direct or indirect dependencies among all the system assets. For instance, in a database server, the administrator only needs to list the sensitive database files, and Seclius later marks the process "mysqld" as critical because it is in charge of reading and modifying the databases. Such a design greatly reduces the resources and time spent by administrators in deploying Seclius.

Each vertex in the DG (Figure 7.2) represents an object—a file, a process, or a socket—and the direct dependency between two objects is established by any type of information flow between them. For instance, if data flows from object o_i to o_j, then object o_j becomes dependent on o_i; the dependency is represented by a directed edge in the DG, i.e. from o_i to o_j. To capture that information, Seclius intercepts system calls (syscalls) and logs them during the learning phase. In particular, we are interested in the syscalls that cause data dependencies among OS-level objects. A dependency relationship is stored by three elements: a source object, a sink object, and their security contexts.

The security context can be object privileges, or, if SE-Linux is deployed, a security type. We classify dependency-causing events based on the source and sink objects for the dependency they induce: process-process, process-file, and process-filename. The first category of events includes those for which one process directly affects the execution of another process. One process can affect another directly by creating it, sharing memory with it, or sending a signal to it. The second category of events includes those for which a process affects or is affected by data or attributes associated with a file. Syscalls like write and writev cause a process-to-file dependency, whereas syscalls like read and readv cause a file-to-process dependency. The third category of events is for processes affecting or being affected by a filename object. Any syscall that includes a filename argument, e.g. open, causes a filename-to-process dependency, as the return value of the syscall depends on the existence of that filename in the file system directory tree. When the learning phase is over, syscall logs are automatically parsed and analyzed line by line to generate the DG. Each dependence edge is tagged with a frequency label indicating how many times the corresponding syscalls were called during the execution.

We make use of the Bayesian network formalism to store probabilistic dependencies in the DG; a conditional probability table (CPT) is generated and associated with each vertex. This CPT encodes how the information flows through that vertex from its parents (sources of incoming edges) to its children. For example, if some of the parent vertices of a vertex become tainted directly or indirectly by attacker data, the CPT in the vertex saves the probability that the vertex (specifically, the OS-level object represented by the vertex) also is tainted. More specifically, each DG vertex is modeled as a binary random variable (representing a single information flow), equal to either 1 (true) or 0 (false) depending on whether the vertex has been tainted; the CPT in a vertex v stores the probability that the corresponding random variable will take the true value (v = 1), given the binary vector of values of the parent vertices P(v).

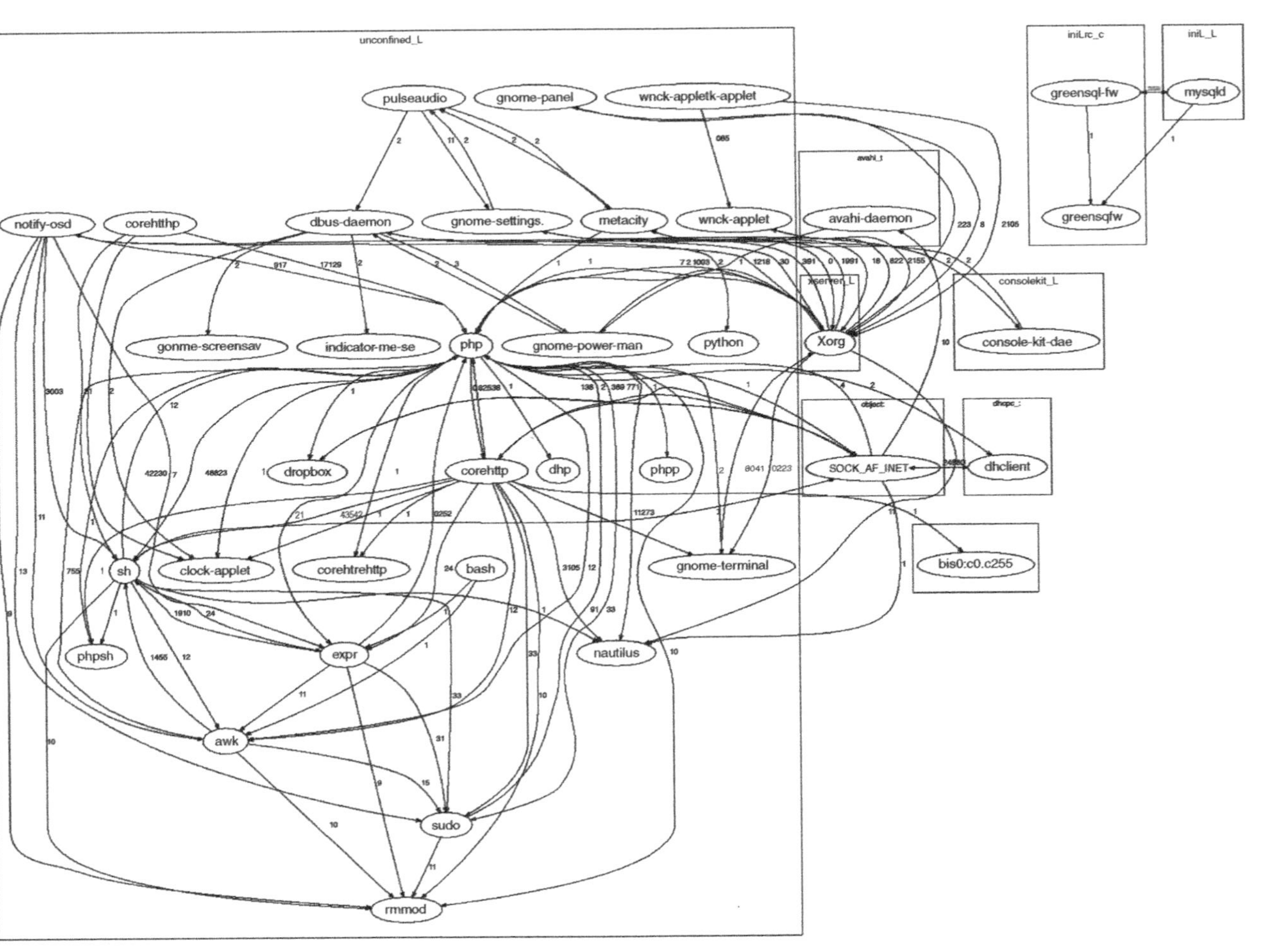

Figure 7.2 Generated dependency graph through system-call interception.

Figure 7.3 illustrates how a CPT for a single flow (with 1-bit random variables) is produced for a sample vertex, i.e. the file F4. The probabilities on the edges represent probability values. For instance, process P1 writes data to files F4 and F7 with probabilities 0.3 and 0.7, respectively. As shown in the figure, the file F4 cannot become tainted if none of its parents are tainted, i.e. Pr(F4 |! P1,! P9) = 0. If only process P1 is tainted, F4 can become tainted only when information flows from P1, i.e. Pr(F4 | P1,! P9) = 0.3. If both of the parents are already tainted, then F4 would be tainted when information flows from either of its parent vertices. In that case, the probability of F4 being tainted would be the complement probability of the case when information flows from none of its parents. Therefore, Pr(F4 | P1, P9) = 1−(1−0.3)*(1−0.8) = 0.86.

Each CT leaf node that represents a CIA criterion of a critical asset is modeled by Seclius as an information flow between the privilege domains controlled by the attacker (according to the current system state) and those that are not yet compromised. Confidentiality of an object is compromised if information flows from the object to any of the compromised domains. Integrity of an object is similarly defined, but the flow is in the reverse direction. Availability is not considered an information flow by itself; however, an object's unavailability causes a flow originating at the object, because once an object becomes unavailable, it no longer receives or sends out data as it would if it was not compromised. For instance, if a process frequently writes to a file, then once the process crashes, the file is not modified by the process, possibly causing inconsistent data integrity; this is modeled as a propagation of tainted data from the process to the file. We consider all the leaf nodes that concern the integrity criterion of critical assets as a single information flow, because they conceptually address the same flow from any of the compromised domains to the assets. However, confidentiality flows cannot be grouped, as they originate individually at separate sources.

If each information flow is represented as a bit, then to completely address "n" concurrent information flows, we define the random variable in each vertex as an "n"-bit binary vector in which each bit value indicates whether the vertex is already tainted by the bit's corresponding flow. In other words, to consider all the security criteria mentioned in a CT with "n" leaves, every vertex represents an "n"-bit random variable (assuming integrity bits are not grouped), where each bit addresses a single flow (i.e. a leaf node). The CPTs are generated accordingly; a vertex CPT stores the probability of

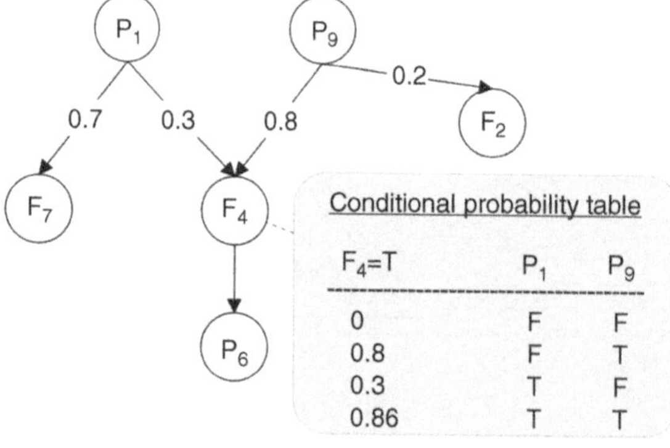

F_4=T	P_1	P_9
0	F	F
0.8	F	T
0.3	T	F
0.86	T	T

Figure 7.3 Conditional probability table construction.

the vertex's value given the value of its parents, each of which, instead of true or false, can take on any "n"-bit value.

7.3.4 Cloud Security Evaluation

Given the DG generated during the learning phase, the operator turns off the syscall interception instruments and puts the system in production mode. The learned DG is then used in an online manner to evaluate the security of any system security state. The goal of this section is to explain how this online evaluation works in detail. We first assume that the IDSs report the exact system state with no uncertainty. We discuss later how Seclius deals with IDS inaccuracies.

At each instant, to evaluate the security of the system's current state "s," DG vertices are first updated according to "s," which indicates the attacker's privileges and past consequences (CT's leaf nodes). For each consequence in "s," the corresponding flow's origin bit in DG is tainted. For instance, if file F4 is modified by the attacker (integrity compromise), the corresponding source bit in DG is set to 1 (evidence bit).

The security measure for a given state "s" is defined to be the probability that the CT's root value is still 0 (Pr(!root(CT) | s)), which means organizational security has not yet been compromised. More specifically, if the CT is considered as a Boolean expression, e.g. CT = (C(F10) AND A(P6)) OR I(F2), Seclius calculates the corresponding marginal joint distribution, e.g. Pr[(C(F10) AND A(P6)) OR I(F2)], conditioned on the current system state (tainted evidence vertices).

Seclius estimates the security of the state "s" by calling a belief propagation procedure—the Gibbs sampler—on the DG to probabilistically estimate how the tainted data (evidence bits) are propagated through the system while it is in state "s."

Generally, the Gibbs sampler algorithm is a Monte Carlo simulation technique that generates a sequence of samples from a joint probability distribution of two or more random variables X1, X2, ..., Xn. The purpose of such a sequence in Seclius is to approximate the joint distribution numerically using large number of samples. In particular, to calculate a joint distribution Pr(X1, X2, ..., Xn | e1, ..., em), where ei represents an evidence, the Gibbs sampler runs a Markov chain on X = (X1, X2, ..., Xn) by (i) initializing X to one of its possible values x = (x_1, x_2, ..., x_n); (ii) picking a uniformly random index i (1 <= i <= n); (iii) sampling x_i from Pr(Xi | x, e) (represented by the conditional probability tables in the generated Bayesian network); (iv) updating the "x" vector; and (v) going back to step 2. It has been proven that the stationary distribution of the Markov chain is just the sought-after joint distribution. Thus, drawing samples from the Markov chain at long enough intervals, i.e. allowing enough time for the chain to reach the stationary distribution, gives independent samples from the distribution P(X1, ..., Xn|e).

We make use of the Gibbs sampler algorithm in Seclius for two main reasons. First, the DG model's joint distribution is not explicitly known initially; and second, analytical calculation of it can be tedious, if it is even possible, especially for large DG graphs. The Gibbs sampler uses the DG's CPT to generate a large number of samples from the Pr[CT| s] distribution without directly calculating the density function. Similarly, the security measure is estimated individually for each system state. Therefore, if the attacker modified any other object and/or got more privileges, the system would switch to a new state, whose security measure would be separately evaluated.

It is worth emphasizing that Seclius does not use the DG model to estimate how the attacker contacts other objects from a compromised object, such as a tainted process, to exploit a vulnerability and/or escalate their privileges. Seclius uses the DG only to estimate how the tainted data would propagate through other non-compromised system assets, which would behave normally as they did during the learning phase. For every asset already compromised, Seclius assumes a pessimistic behavior model, i.e. the asset deterministically contacts all other assets in its privilege domain.

Seclius estimates the security measure of each system state in the state space and stores the values in a table in an offline manner. Thus, given the system state, it looks up the table and instantly retrieves the corresponding value. If the state space is too large to be preprocessed, Seclius dynamically runs the belief propagation given a system state and estimates the security measure in an online manner.

The state notion also encodes the privilege domains controlled by the attacker in each state. When estimating the security of each state, Seclius assumes that OS objects in the privilege domains that have not yet been compromised behave normally, i.e. they respect the system's dependency graph generated during the learning phase without any attack. However, Seclius pessimistically assumes that the objects in the compromised privilege domains contact (i.e. propagate the tainted data to) all the possible objects in that domain.[2]

That approach can evaluate the security of each system state. However, the exact current security state of the system usually is not completely observable, due to IDS inaccuracies, i.e. false positive and negative rates. We define the notion of the information state of the system, which formally is a probability distribution over all states in the state space of the system S. Once the information state of the system has been estimated, Seclius computes the expected security measure of the information state.

7.4 Future Directions

In this section, we discuss current limitations of Seclius and potential solutions to address each of them.

First, as in any learning algorithm, it is not guaranteed that the learned DG actually captures every dependency. One trivial solution would be to make sure that the learning phase is long enough to capture all the dependencies. Alternatively, an active learning algorithm could be used. For instance, the configuration files could be parsed to extract potential dependencies, or a mechanism could make sure all the program paths are traversed. Replacing passive learning with an active algorithm would require application-specific knowledge; however, it would help to accelerate the learning phase.

Second, the evaluated security value will be affected by the accuracy of the underlying intrusion-detection solutions, i.e. if the intrusion detectors miss some malicious events. Our main contribution in this paper is in showing how to make use of the system dependency graph and the security requirements to evaluate the security of any given

2 Alternatively, Seclius could optimistically assume that objects in the compromised domains also behave as they do when there is no attack. Since the attackers could make use of the optimistic assumption while attacking/damaging the system, we chose to consider the pessimistic assumption by modifying and making the objects behave as they want while keeping the security metric high.

state; in other words, we do not claim to have come up with a new intrusion-detection technique. However, our tool, which makes use of Seclius to evaluate system security, takes under consideration intrusion-detection inaccuracies, i.e. false positive and negative rates, if provided. Additionally, security evaluation by Seclius is done based on past consequences, which are easier to detect than exploitations. As a case in point, detecting that a web server is unavailable is usually simpler than determining the exploit that caused the server crash.

Additionally, because Seclius is an information flow-based metric, when the system has not yet been attacked, Seclius usually evaluates the system security to be close to absolute, but not 100% secure. This is because even during the system's normal operational mode, information is often flowing from external end points, where attackers potentially reside, to critical assets. A possible solution to this problem would be to normalize the evaluated security measure based on the measure of the non-compromised system.

7.5 Conclusions

We discussed the major challenges provisioning scalable and efficient risk-assessment and disaster-recovery techniques within large-scale cloud infrastructures. Additionally, we proposed Seclius, an online security-evaluation framework that uses dependencies between OS-level objects to measure the probability that critical assets have been directly or indirectly compromised. The different components of our framework address three important limitations faced by traditional security-evaluation techniques. First, a consequence tree captures the subjective security requirements and minimizes administrator input. Second, Seclius processes IDS alerts online to measure actual attack consequences and does not rely on assumptions about attacker behaviors or system vulnerabilities. Third, a dependency graph is combined with a taint-tracking method to probabilistically evaluate the system-wide impact of locally detected intrusions as well as attacker privileges and security domains, without making assumptions about attack paths.

8

Cloud Auditing and Compliance[1]

Paolina Centonze

Iona College, New Rochelle, NY, USA

8.1 Introduction

The global cloud computing market is expected to exceed $1 trillion by 2024. This is based on the latest research report covering cloud computing products, technologies, and services for the global market by Market Research Media (https://www.marketresearchmedia.com/?p=839).

Companies, industries, and agencies, such as financial services organizations, health organizations, and government agencies, are looking into new cloud-based auditing research and methodologies to alleviate security, privacy, trust, and forensics challenges.

The rest of this chapter is organized as follows. Section 8.2 discusses the major cloud security problems and explains how auditing can alleviate these issues. Section 8.3 presents the state of the art of cloud auditing and discusses modifications and extensions needed in order to minimize cloud security challenges. Section 8.4 focuses on cloud compliance challenges and describes how national and international organizations are extending and modifying these compliance regulations in order to make them standardized. Section 8.5 discusses future research directions for cloud audits and compliance. Finally, Section 8.6 summarizes the main points and concludes this chapter.

8.2 Background

There is no doubt that cloud computing offerings are completely transforming ways of delivering and investing for IT services, which enable companies, industries, agencies, and academia to make deep changes in IT solutions and adapt their business solutions and processes. Figure 8.1 shows a survey, based on data reported by Gartner, Inc. (https://www.gartner.com/newsroom/id/2352816) (NYSE: IT), one of the world's leading IT research and advisory companies, on how the cloud global market's spending has

1 This chapter was written in 2014–2015, and some content may have evolved since then.

Security, Privacy, and Digital Forensics in the Cloud, First Edition. Edited by Lei Chen, Hassan Takabi, and Nhien-An Le-Khac.

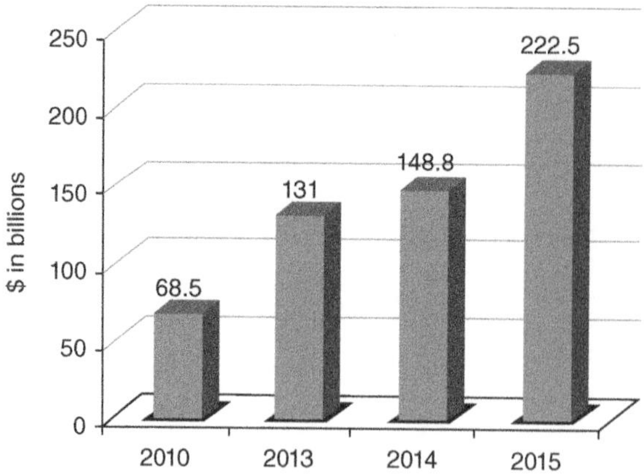

Figure 8.1 Worldwide cloud market forecast (Garner Survey, 2014).

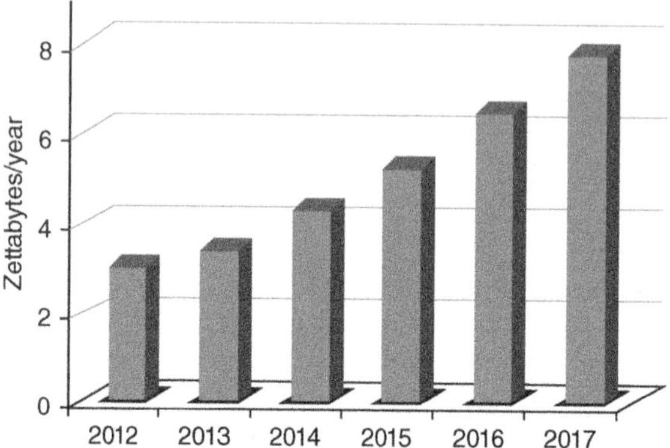

Figure 8.2 Global data center IP traffic growth (Cisco global index survey, 2014).

changed over the past few years, with global spending of $222.5 billion by 2015. Figure 8.2 shows a global index survey based on data reported by Cisco Systems, Inc. (https://www.cisco.com/c/en/us/solutions/collateral/service-provider/global-cloud-index-gci/white-paper-c11-738085.html), an American IT multinational corporation, with an overall data center Internet Protocol (IP) traffic compound annual growth rate (CAGR) of 25% from 2012 to 2017. While cloud services can bring many advantages to business solutions, such as cost reduction, on-demand provisioning mechanisms, and enablement of a pay-per-use business model, today security and privacy are still among the top concerns that discourage cloud-service consumers from adopting cloud solutions to the fullest, as shown in Figure 8.3. One dominant characteristic of cloud computing is that parts of an IT infrastructure's trust boundary move to third-party providers. Therefore, lack of direct control over cloud consumers' data or computation requires new techniques for the service provider to guarantee transparency and accountability.

According to the Cloud Security Alliance (CSA), a cloud service model comprises seven layers: facility, network, hardware, operating system, middleware, application, and user (https://cloudsecurityalliance.org/topthreats.html). Table 8.1 shows whether

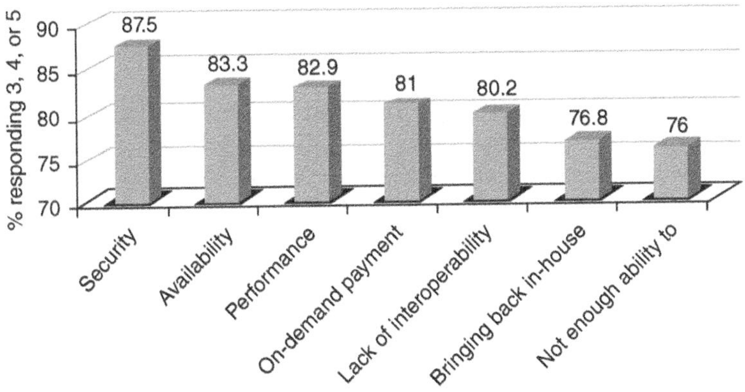

Figure 8.3 Cloud consumers' issues (Gartner survey, 2014).

Table 8.1 CSA: layers a cloud provider controls (2010).

	Cloud service model		
Layer	**SaaS**	**PaaS**	**IaaS**
Facility	Provider	Provider	Provider
Network	Provider	Provider	Provider
Hardware	Provider	Provider	Provider
Operating system	Provider	Provider	Provider or customer
Middleware	Provider	Provider or customer	Customer
Application	Provider	Customer	Customer
User	Customer	Customer	Customer

the cloud provider or the cloud customer is in control of each layer for every specific deployment model: Software-as-a-Service (SaaS), Platform-as-a-Service (PaaS), and Infrastructure-as-a-Service (IaaS). Choosing the proper cloud deployment model is crucial, since once a model is selected to deliver business solutions, responsibilities are agreed upon and accepted by the party hosting the cloud solution and the subscribers to the services.

When a cloud consumer subscribes to a particular service-delivery model, that consumer agrees to a certain level of access control over the resources managed by the CSP. Therefore, when assessing a cloud system, cloud customers must recognize, and be concerned with, the limitations of each service-delivery model. If a specific capability, such as security, trust, traceability, or accountability is needed but not yet completely provided within a given delivery model, a subscriber has to either negotiate with the service provider for that capability to be fully implemented and deployed, and specify this request clearly in the service-level agreement (SLA), or request a different delivery model that has the desired functionality. Incomplete understanding of the separation of responsibilities may result in false expectations of what a CSP can offer. Security, trust, integrity, and forensics are challenges for classic IT environments, but they are even more complex in cloud environments due to the Cloud's inherent characteristics, such as seamless scalability, ability to share resources, multitenancy, ubiquitous access, on-demand availability, and third-party hosting. Another complication is the fact that the underlying infrastructure is not standard; every CSP implements the underlying infrastructure using different hardware and software systems. Therefore, security-enforcement mechanisms must be adapted to each cloud system. SLA requirements are essential in order to meet the security expectations of cloud services and resources.

Cloud auditing and fast response processes are essential in order to properly and efficiently describe the levels of availability, performance, security, serviceability, and other characteristics of a cloud service. However, this requirement may be hard to meet because the amounts of cloud-auditing data stored on the Cloud itself, consisting of client and server logs, network logs, database logs, etc. may be extremely large.

For example, Apprenda, a PaaS software-layer cloud-provider company based in the United States, defines *cloud federation* as "the unionization of software, infrastructure and platform services from disparate networks that can be accessed by a client via the Internet." A federation of cloud resources uses network gateways that connect public or external clouds, private or internal clouds, and/or community clouds by creating a hybrid cloud-computing environment. Since cloud computing may deploy services in federated cloud environments, audit data is collected and stored in distributed environments. It is necessary to properly capture, store, and analyze such data in order to identify and quantify threats, and prevents security attacks.

Capturing security-relevant information and auditing results to determine the existence of security threats in the cloud are still challenging problems. Following are some examples that illustrate the need for cloud audits:

- A cryptographic attack that hijacked Windows Update went mainstream on the Amazon cloud. A collision attack against the widely used MD5 algorithm took 10 hours, for a cost of only 65 cents (Goodin 2014a).
- A distributed denial of service (DDoS) attack, performed through the Amazon EC2 control panel, resulted in hosting provider Code Spaces shutting down its business (Goodin 2014b).
- An attack against Apple's iCloud allowed attackers to steal users' login credentials (Weise 2014)

In 2010, the Cloud Security Alliance released a research document entitled *Top Threats to Cloud Computing v1.0* (https://cloudsecurityalliance.org/topthreats.html) in order to assist organizations in making educated risk-management decisions regarding their cloud adoption strategies. Here is the list of the top cloud computing threats according to that report:

1) Abuse and nefarious use of cloud computing
2) Insecure interfaces and APIs
3) Malicious insiders
4) Shared technology issues
5) Data loss or leakage
6) Account or service hijacking
7) Unknown risk profile

The Cloud Security Alliance encourages organizations to also use—along with the research document just mentioned—*Security Guidance for Critical Areas in Cloud Computing V3.0,* which was last updated in 2011 (https://cloudsecurityalliance.org/guidance/csaguide.v3.0.pdf). In this document, the CSA includes a collection of facts and ideas gathered from over 70 industry experts worldwide.

Understanding how to manage cloud opportunities and security challenges is crucial to business development. Security audits and penetration testing are used in classic IT infrastructures to document a data center's compliance to security best practices and laws. One of the most serious downsides of traditional security auditing is that it only provides a snapshot of an environment's security state at the time of the audit. This may be sufficient for classic IT infrastructures since they do not change very frequently. However, auditing a cloud environment is a much more complex task, for which traditional security auditing is not adequate. This is because a cloud system has inherent characteristics that make the auditing process more complicated. Such characteristics include on-demand self service, broad network access, resource pooling, rapid elasticity, multitenancy, and lack of hardware governance.

When performing cloud auditing, it is necessary to consider the point in time when changes in the underlying infrastructure occur, and the ability to decide if any such changes give rise to a security gap or an infrastructure misuse. It is also important to have knowledge of the underlying business processes: for example, to automatically infer whether an immediate increase in a high-pick cloud-service request is being made for true business needs or is rather caused by a hacker misusing the system to perform a denial of service (DoS) attack. In 2012, to increase cloud transparency, the Cloud Research Lab at Furtwangen University, Germany, developed the Security Audit as a Service (SAaaS) architecture for IaaS cloud environments. The SAaaS architecture ensures that a desired security level is reached and maintained within any cloud infrastructure where changes occur very frequently. The work required of research institutions, government agencies, and academic organizations in order to provide secure cloud computing is still immense, and demands the collaboration and participation of a broad community of stakeholders on a global basis. However, this initiative is very encouraging and promising, since it is the right step in the right direction; new cloud-security solutions are regularly appearing, enterprises are using CSA's guidance to engage with CSPs, and a vigorous public dialogue over compliance and trust issues has begun around the world. The most important outcome in the field of cloud computing that has been achieved is that security professionals are now eagerly engaged in securing the future, instead of only focusing on protecting the present. In fact, there is a growing demand for cloud-computing standards. These standards may be very complex to integrate with existing infrastructures in order to provide reliable cloud services in cloud-computing environments. However, the creation and adoption of standards is an important step forward since it minimizes the differences between cloud implementations and simplifies the enforcement of security and auditing. As shown in Table 8.2, standard organizations and working groups worldwide are producing documentation, guidelines and specifications to create the foundation of cloud-computing standardizations. Details of these cloud-security standardization and compliance efforts are covered in Section 8.4 of this chapter, which also discusses the Federal Risk and Authorization Management Program (FedRAMP), a US government-wide program that provides a standardized approach to security assessment, authorization, and continuous monitoring for cloud products and services (Table 8.3).

Table 8.2 Standards organizations and their nationalities (2014).

Cloud-related standards organizations	Nationality
National Institute of Standards and Technology (NIST)	United States
Distributed Management Task Force (DMTF)	International
IEEE Standards Association (IEEE-SA)	International
International Telecommunications Union (ITC)	International
European Telecommunications Standards Institute (ETSI)	European
Organization for the Advancement of Structured Information Standards (OASIS)	International
System Administration Networking and Security	United States
International Organization for Standardization (ISO)/IEC	International
Federal Risk and Authorization Management Program (FedRAMP)	United States

Table 8.3 Cloud security and auditing publications (2014).

Cloud security and auditing publications (publication title)	Organization
Challenging Security Requirements for US Government Cloud Computing Adoption	NIST
Cloud Computing Security Reference Architecture	NIST
Guide to Security for Full Virtualization Technologies	NIST
Security Guidance for Critical Areas of Cloud Computing	CSA
Trusted Cloud Initiative (TCI) Reference Guidelines	CSA
Cloud Auditing Data Federation (CADF) Data Format and Interface Definition Spec	DMTF
Quick Guide to the FedRAMP Readiness Process	FedRAMP
Cloud Security and Compliance: A Primer	SANS
A Guide to Virtualization Hardening Guides	SANS
Focus Group on Cloud Computing Technical Report	CSC
Saving Money Through Cloud Computing	OACIS

8.3 Cloud Auditing

This section describes the importance of auditing in solving specific cloud security issues. It highlights the most crucial security issues that need to be considered when deploying a service to a cloud infrastructure. In particular, it explains how auditing methodologies can help in alleviating identified security issues. Furthermore, it discusses how classic auditing need to change and be extended in order to include complex cloud-computing environment characteristics. Different challenges complicating cloud auditing are discussed, and important questions that a cloud audit must answer are raised. Moreover, this section describes the importance of diagnosing vulnerability patterns in cloud audit logs, especially for web service compositions for cloud service architectures. In fact, in these systems auditable events are not always well defined and processed. This section also gives an overview of the latest state of the art of cloud auditing for addressing security- and privacy-related issues.

Security-related challenges are the main reason enterprises are hesitant to adopt cloud computing. Therefore, these challenges have become a significant area of research and the object of important economic studies. A precise understanding of the security implications behind a given cloud infrastructure has not always been completely achieved since cloud architectures are often based on proprietary hardware and software, which complicates the study and detection of security vulnerabilities. Furthermore, very often, essential and well-defined security terms, such as *threat*, *vulnerability*, and *risk*, are not used and understood properly. These security terms are crucial when performing risk analysis for creating and deploying a service on a cloud environment. In cloud computing, contrary to classic IT outsourcing, a customer may also rent a certain infrastructure and end up sharing infrastructure resources with other customers. This architecture is known as the ***multitenant model***. Between 2009 and 2010, researchers (Sotto et al. 2010; Chen et al. 2010) and the European Network and Information Security Agency (https://www.enisa.europa.eu/activities/risk-management/files/deliverables/cloud-computing-risk-assessment) identified numerous cloud security and privacy problems, which all have in common the following two categories of problems:

- *Amplified cloud security problems:* Problems already known from traditional, distributed IT environments but amplified through cloud computing attributes
- *Cloud-specific security problems:* Security problems that arise only due to the special characteristics of cloud computing

8.3.1 Amplified Cloud Security Problems

Amplified cloud security problems are those deriving from the underlying technologies upon which cloud computing is heavily built, such as virtualization, web application servers, and multitenant software architectures. This category of problems includes those originating from failing to adhere to well-known and commonly established security best practices, which are hard or infeasible to implement in a cloud computing environment.

The most common amplified cloud security problems are the following:

- Misuse of administrator rights and/or activities of malicious insiders: In cloud computing, virtual machines (VMs) are used for managed servers. A CSP is responsible for the underlying host system and always has access to the VMs running on the host through the hypervisor. As of today, it is still hard to detect misuse of administrator rights or the presence of malicious insiders due to a general lack of transparency into the CSP's processes and procedures. This problem may violate core security principles, such as confidentiality, authenticity, authorization, integrity, data protection, accountability, and nonrepudiation.
- Missing transparency of applied security measures: In traditional IT outsourcing, service providers can prove their security compliance to their customers by showing the usage of the baseline security measures through, for example, International Organization for Standardization (ISO) 27001 or Payment Card Industry (PCI) Data Security Standard (DSS) certificates. In cloud computing, not every CSP follows these baseline rules, although today global government agencies and laws are changing in order to require CSPs to follow these regulations. This problem may cause a violation of one or more of the following core security principles: integrity, availability, and data protection. A notable exception is Amazon Web Services (AWS)—one of the

first CSPs that has started to follow global security compliance very seriously. More about cloud compliance and regulations will be described in Section 8.4 of this chapter.

- Missing transparency with security incidents: In traditional IT outsourcing, responsibility for security-incident response is transferred to the service provider, which uses experienced personnel (for example, a computer emergency response team (CERT). When it comes to cloud computing, things are more complicated. In this case, a customer and the CSP have to work together to collect all users' data information generated before and during a security incident. Any concern about the cloud hardware and software infrastructure must be associated with the different cloud resources available to the customer and involved during the incident. Today, a standardized procedure is still missing. In fact, cloud offers available on the market do not offer a transparent process for customers on how security incidents are detected. This problem may affect the following core security principles: data protection, integrity, availability, and nonrepudiation. Section 8.4 of this chapter also explains what the SysAdmin, Audit, Network, Security (SANS) organization is doing to correct this problem, especially when it comes to public cloud services. Section 8.4 also explains how the SAaaS can be used for cloud incident detection and as a possible enabler to perform cloud audits while respecting cloud-specific characteristics.
- Shared-technology issues: In the multitenant cloud-computing model, virtual resources are shared with multiple customers. Furthermore, there may be misconfigured VMs that endanger other resources due to lack of proper isolation. Exploits have already been demonstrated by (Kortchorski and Rutkowska 2009). The increasing code complexity in hypervisor software amplifies this threat. Memory-cache isolation is another issue since some of the underlying components that make up the cloud infrastructure do not lend themselves to offering proper isolation. For example, graphics processing unit (GPU) and central processing unit (CPU) caches were not designed to offer strong isolation properties in a multitenant architecture. As of today, no CSP discloses information on how shared resources are securely wiped before being reassigned to a different customer. Furthermore, cloud consumers get a default source access point to a VM in the current IaaS. It has been proven that using this default source access point, attackers have an easier way to break through the isolation of shared resources. The Federal Office for Information Security suggested that using certified Common Criteria (CC) compliant hypervisor software (minimum EAL 4) might alleviate this threat (https://www.bsi.bund.de/EN/Topics/Certification/certification_node.html). This problem may affect the following core security principles: integrity, availability, data protection, confidentiality, authentication, and nonrepudiation.
- Data life cycle in case of a provider switch or termination: In cloud computing, due to shared usage of resources, this threat is particularly serious. The CSA states that, in the absence of satisfactory rules defined by the CSP, every cloud consumer needs to impose specific rules for when the contract with the CSP ends. Such rules must clearly regulate how customers' data is exported from the Cloud and how the CSP will securely erase that data at the end of the contract. This problem may affect the data protection and confidentiality core security principles.
- Monitoring service-level agreements (SLAs): In cloud computing, several multitenant applications running in a virtualized environment need a special technology for

monitoring SLAs. New technologies for the hypervisor, virtualized networking, monitoring, etc. must be used. (Patel et al. 2009) proposed a mechanism for managing SLAs in a cloud-computing environment using the web service-level agreement (WSLA) framework, developed for SLA monitoring and SLA enforcement in a service-oriented architecture (SOA). In June 2014, the European Commission (EC) published the *Cloud Service Level Agreement Standardization Guidelines* (https://ec.europa.eu/digital-single-market/en/cloud-select-industry-group-service-level-agreements). More about this standardization is described in Section 8.4 of this chapter. This problem may affect the availability and integrity core security principles.

8.3.2 Cloud-Specific Security Problems

Cloud-specific security problems are those that are inherent to the Cloud itself and its characteristics, and not necessarily inherited from the technologies used in the underlying infrastructure. The most common cloud-specific security problems are the following:

- Unclear data location: Today, many cloud customers do not know in which country their data is saved or processed. Perhaps the only exception is AWS, which exposes to consumers the approximate cloud data center's continental location in which their data is stored (for example, the AWS data center in Northern Ireland). As of today, there is no way to know whether a customer's data has been outsourced by a cloud provider. (Tiwana et al. 2010) proposed a solution to expose the network location of data to applications. There are only a few specific acts and laws related to protecting users' data. Among these is Germany's Data Protection Act, §11 (Mell and Grance 2009; German Parliament 2009). Section 8.4 talks more about different global data-location compliance rules. The uncertainty related to the geographical location in which a consumer's data is stored may affect the following core security principles: data protection, confidentiality, and availability.
- Abuse and nefarious use of cloud resources: Cloud computing offers many attractive characteristics. Among these is easy, fast access to many virtual supercomputing machines. Unfortunately, these great characteristics also attract malicious users, who find the high-performance computing infrastructure of a modern cloud system the right platform for attacking other systems. For example, in 2011, malicious users took advantage of AWS and used it to host malware, the Zeus botnet, a phishing Trojan horse that steals banking information within AWS. Cloud hackers can also easily aggregate as many VMs as they need to perform DDoS attacks on a single CSP, which can also affect the cloud consumer. This problem may affect the availability and confidentiality core security principles.
- Missing monitoring: If cloud consumers' data, especially personal data, is at risk of fraud or loss of integrity, it is essential that a CSP be able to detect these risks and eliminate them. As of today, it is not trivial for a CSP to use an information-policy system that automatically detects security issues and informs customers. When designing a risk analysis that runs a service on a cloud, it is important to include data-protection measures to secure the cloud environment, such as antivirus software and intrusion detection systems (IDSs), as well as measures for DoS detection and prevention. For large IT environments, the best practice to monitor against these

types of attach is to run IDSs with distributed sensors as input feeds. However, this solution is not sufficient and flexible enough for cloud-computing environments due to their inherent complexity and the dynamic changes driven by users. (Meng et al. 2012) published a work on reliable state monitoring in cloud data centers for better monitoring such complex and dynamic environments. (Doelitzscher et al. 2012) introduced SAaaS as a cloud incident-detection system built upon intelligent autonomous agents that are aware of underlying business-driven intercommunicating cloud services. This problem may affect the following core security principles: nonrepudiation, availability, data protection, and confidentiality.

- Unsecure APIs: A CSP offers application programming interfaces (APIs) to cloud consumers in order for them to deploy, control, and manage their cloud resources. Therefore, it is crucial for these APIs to provide access control, encryption, and activity monitoring in order to protect against both malicious and unintentional attempts to bypass a security policy. For instance, a load-balancing service is a complex architectural layer that can be inserted into a system to improve the performance of a service and increase its availability. When such a complex component is used, it is necessary to carefully examine the overall system in order to make sure that no security holes are made available to attackers. To prevent attacks from being mounted against the system through the use of unsecure APIs, standardized protocols and measurements for secure software development are available. These include Microsoft Secure Development Lifecycle (SDL) and the Open Web Application Security Project (OWASP) Software Assurance Maturity Model (SAMM). The inadvertent use of unsecure APIs is a problem that may violate the following core security principles: confidentiality, integrity, availability, nonrepudiation, data protection, and accountability.
- Missing monitoring of cloud scalability: Scalability is one of the most attractive characteristics of cloud computing. For this reason, it is essential to be able to deal with service usage peaks: for instance, if there is a new update of a popular software program, and a huge number of downloads is expected. Usually, peaks are predictable and confined to specific time frames. Therefore, cloud-application engineers design their solutions to initiate new instances if a certain threshold is reached to provide service availability. However, this raises two new challenges for cloud security:
  a) Scaling driven up by IaaS business: Since a cloud consumer's infrastructure can vary quickly (for example, by growing and shrinking as in the case of a peak scenario), a monitoring system must take care of all the peak events and the defined scalability thresholds.
  b) Scaling driven up by IaaS attacks: A cloud attacker can control the creation of new cloud instances to the maximum scalability threshold number of allowed requests, which could cause, for example, the distribution of malicious software.

  These issues may violate the availability and accountability core security principles.

- Missing interoperability of cloud providers: Today, CSPs are often incompatible with each other, particularly because each CSP uses customized VM formats and proprietary APIs. This may increase the risk of data lock-in, a phenomenon that prevents data portability across different CSPs. (Loutas et al. 2013) wrote a comprehensive and systematic survey of cloud-computing interoperability efforts by standardization groups, industrial organizations, and research communities. More details about this work are described in Section 8.4. There are some initial development projects working on this issue. These include the Open Cloud Computing Interface (OCCI), Open Virtualization Format (OVF), OpenStack cloud software Rackspace hosting, and the National Aeronautics and Space Administration (NASA). Moreover, a specific strategy must be agreed upon between provider and customer for regulating data formats, perpetuating logic relations, and total costs if a CSP change occurs. This issue may cause a violation of the availability core security principle.

8.3.3 Correlation of Cloud Security Issues and Research Efforts

In order to better emphasize the complexity and importance of auditing in cloud computing, this section correlates each of the cloud audit issues with the current state of the art in research. Since a cloud consumer is not exposed to the details of how a CSP governs the underlying cloud infrastructure, the only choice for the consumer is to give complete trust to the CSP and hope the CSP applies compliance regulations and data-protection laws for protecting confidential and sensitive data. Furthermore, unknown or unclear geographic location of data in the Cloud may cause unexpected issues since different jurisdictions enforce different legislation and compliance requirements when it comes to data governance. Following is a list of some of the current research work to alleviate this problem:

- (Ries et al. 2011) proposed a new geographic location approach based on network coordinate systems, and evaluated the accuracy of their solution on the three prevalent cloud deployment models: IaaS, PaaS, and SaaS. Even though a CSP may use additional measures, such as traffic relaying, to hide the location of the resources stored in the Cloud, a high probability of location disclosure is achieved by means of supervised classification algorithms.
- (Vaish et al. 2013) published a mechanism that uses remote-attestation technology of trusted platform modules. A remote-attestation technique is used to validate the current location of the data, and the generated result is passed to the user verifier. The fact that the trusted platform module is tamperproof provides the basis for the accuracy of the result.
- (Gondree and Peterson 2013) introduced and analyzed a general framework for authentically binding data to a location while providing strong assurance against CSPs that, either inadvertently or maliciously, attempt to relocate cloud data.
- (Paladi et al. 2014) proposed a mechanism allowing cloud users to control the geographical location of their data, stored or processed in plaintext on the premises of IaaS CSPs. They used trusted computing principles and remote attestation to establish platform state. They also enabled cloud users to constrain plaintext data exclusively to the jurisdictions they specify, by sealing the decryption keys used to obtain plaintext data to the combination of the cloud host's geographic location and platform state.
- Cloud storage permits moving remote data to the centralized data centers, where loss of data integrity can arise. (Sunagar et al. 2014) proposed a study of the problem of ensuring the integrity of data storage in the Cloud.

Cloud auditing can also be used to help detect abuse and nefarious use of cloud resources, although this is still a complex task. (Hamza and Omar 2013) explored and investigated the scope and magnitude of this problem, which is one of the most serious security threats in cloud computing. The authors also presented some of the specific attacks related to this threat, since it constitutes a major restriction for moving business to the Cloud. Following are some of the most common attacks that relate to this problem and the related research work that has been done in order to resolve them:

- *Host-hopping attacks:* These attacks can be easily mounted when a CSP has no mechanism to restrict shared access to cloud resources, such as data storage and VMs, and to enforce isolation of different customers or hosts. Failing to enforce customer-resource separation may facilitate hackers hopping on other hosts, endangering their resources, or interrupting their services, thereby damaging their reputation and impacting their revenue. These types of attacks are particularly common in a public PaaS deployment model, where multiple clients share the same physical machine.
- *Malicious insider and abuse of privileges:* Since cloud infrastructures are based on multitenancy and shared resources, there is the risk of unauthorized access to customers' confidential data. This may lead to the exposure, leak, or selling of sensitive customer information. This problem may lead to even graver risks if a CSP does not correctly enforce the foundation security rule known as the *principle of least privilege* (Bishop 2002). In such cases, malicious users may exploit rights that they were not intended to be granted to subvert the integrity of the system or steal confidential data.
- *Identity theft attacks:* Cloud hackers can easily create temporary accounts with CSPs, use cloud resources, and only pay for the usage of those resources. By doing this, they can try to get access to customer data and sell it, leading to identify theft. This type of attack also occurs when cyber criminals set up a fake cloud and attract users by hosting their sensitive information and providing them with cloud-based services such as email and web hosting. This is a great catch for stealing customers' identities and financial information.
- *Service-engine attacks:* An attractive characteristic of cloud computing is highly customizable platforms. For example, in the IaaS deployment model, attackers can rent a VM to hack the service engine from the inside, and use it to their advantage. In particular, they can try to escape VM isolation to reach other VMs, steal sensitive business information, and compromise data of other cloud customers.

To address the lack of transparent monitoring of a cloud infrastructure, the Cloud Research Lab at Furtwangen University, Germany, in 2012, started to develop SAaaS, a prototype for incident detection in the cloud. SAaaS is an audit solution where techniques of behavioral analysis and anomaly detection are used to distinguish between normal and nefarious use of cloud resources. SAaaS uses intelligent autonomous agents, which support cross-customer event monitoring within a cloud infrastructure. This work also evaluated which cloud-specific security problems are addressed by SAaaS. The results of this work shows that autonomous agents and behavioral analysis are sufficient to identify cloud-specific security problems and can create an efficient cloud-audit system.

(Meng et al. 2012) proposed state monitoring for detecting critical events and abnormalities of cloud-distributed systems. When it comes to cloud computing, as the scale of the underlying infrastructure grows and the amount of workload consolidation increases in cloud data centers, node failures and performance interferences (in particular, transient ones) become quite common. Therefore, distributed state-monitoring tasks are very often exposed to broken communication. This can bring about misleading results and cause problems for cloud consumers who heavily rely on state monitoring to perform automatic management tasks, such as autoscaling. This work introduced a new state-monitoring approach that addresses this challenge by exposing and handling communication dynamics, such as message delay and loss in cloud-monitoring environments. This methodology delivers two different characteristics. First, it quantitatively approximates the accuracy of monitoring results to capture uncertainties introduced by messaging dynamics. This feature helps users differentiate trustworthy monitoring results from ones that heavily deviate from the truth, yet significantly improves monitoring utilities compared to simple techniques that invalidate all monitoring results generated in the presence of messaging dynamics. Second, it adapts itself to nontransient messaging problems by reconfiguring distributed monitoring algorithms to minimize monitoring errors. This work demonstrates that, even under severe message loss and delay, this new approach consistently improves monitoring precision and, when applied to cloud application auto-scaling, outperforms existing state-monitoring techniques.

In distributed systems, the security of the host platform is critical. Platform administrators use security-automation methodologies, such as those provided by the Security Content Automation Protocol (SCAP) standards, to check that the outsourced platforms are set up correctly and follow security recommendations, e.g. those provided by governmental or industrial organizations. Nevertheless, users of remote platforms must still have confidence in the platform administrators. (Aslam et al. 2013) proposed a remote platform-evaluation mechanism that can be used by remote platform users or by auditors, to perform frequent platform-security audits. The authors analyzed the existing SCAP and Trusted Computing Group (TCG) standards for this solution. They also identified shortcomings and suggested ways to integrate these standards. This platform-security-evaluation framework uses the combined effort of SCAP and TCG to address the limitations of each technology when used independently.

Auditing systems are extremely important to make sure that customer data is properly hosted in the cloud. (Yu et al. 2014) investigated the possibility for active adversary attacks in three auditing mechanisms for shared data in the Cloud, including two identity-privacy-preserving auditing mechanisms named *Oruta* and *Knox*, and a distributed-storage integrity-auditing mechanism. The authors showed that these schemes start to become insecure when active adversaries are involved in the cloud storage. In particular, they proved that there are ways for an active adversary to change cloud information without being detected by the auditor. The authors claimed to have found a solution to this downside without sacrificing the benefits of these mechanisms.

CSPs have control over enforcing cloud security in order to ensure the integrity and confidentiality of their customers' data. Cloud-computing security infrastructure is an extremely important research area and the subject of a consistent body of work by both the academic and industrial research communities. In a cloud environment, resources are under the control of the CSP, and third-party auditors must ensure data integrity and confidentiality, particularly when data storage is outsourced. (Sathiskumar and Retnaraj 2014) proposed data-encryption and proxy-encryption algorithms for CSPs to enable privacy and integrity of outsourced data in cloud-computing infrastructures.

A service cloud infrastructure that offers web-service composition improves the accessibility and flexibility of web services hosted on the cloud. Nevertheless, security challenges exist, which include both vulnerabilities due to classic web-service communication and new, specific issues carried by intercloud communication. Cloud auditing is a complex task, due to the enormous scale of the system, the noncentralized architecture of the Cloud, and the wide range of security issues that need to be taken into account. Of course, there exist security standards, protocols, and auditing methodologies that provide audit logs, which can be subsequently analyzed, but these logs are not always suitable to reveal the type, location, and impact of the security threats that might have occurred. Assuming a cloud infrastructure that explicitly declares the scope of its audit logs, defines the expected auditable events in the cloud, and provides evidence of potential threats, in 2013, researchers introduced the concept of vulnerability diagnostic trees (VDTs) to formally demonstrate vulnerability patterns across many audit trails created within the cloud service. They accounted for attack scenarios based on the allocation of services to a web-service composition that provides end-to-end client-request round-trip messaging.

In spite of the large body of research in the area of cloud security and auditing, performed by both the academic and industrial research communities, a collaborative cloud architecture for security and auditing that does not require a third-party auditor (TPA) has not yet been fully explored. In their cloud-security research survey, (Waqas et al. 2013) suggested a collaborative cloud architecture that can securely share resources when needed and audit itself without the involvement of a TPA.

8.4 Cloud Compliance

Cloud compliance has been the subject of intense research among industry, academia, and government. Nowadays, cloud security compliance is more important than ever since defining and enforcing security standardization and compliance regulations in clouds with complex architectures—especially those that support cross-domain services on federated multilevel servers—is not an easy task. In order to properly secure cloud services and resources, as we observed in Section 8.3, cloud auditing is a crucial component that must be in place to meet SLAs and guarantee CSP compliance. This section discusses cloud-compliance requirements, regulations, acts, laws, and guidelines, and describes the joint effort by IT standards organizations and industries worldwide to meet security-compliance requirements for cloud computing.

Industry demand for cloud technology and the promising revenues of new information communication technology (ICT) investments have created excellent market encouragement for cloud computing. Businesses and organizations are moving their solutions and data toward cloud computing for scalability and cost efficiency. Moreover, there is an enormous need for cloud compliance and standardization: research institutions, academic organizations, business industries, and government agencies are now aware of the underlying problems caused by lack of compliance and more knowledgeable about the security impacts and serious consequences deriving from CSPs not meeting the right security regulations and compliance requirements. As shown in Table 8.2, standards organizations and working groups are making guidelines and specifications publically available, with the goal of achieving cloud-computing standardization. (Han et al. 2014), in the book *High Performance Cloud Auditing and Applications*, include a summary about organizations and documents for standardization. And the

NIST, CSA, and DMTF CADF Working Group have released important cloud-computing-related publications:

- The NIST cloud-computing publication includes a comprehensive view of cloud computing, with a particular focus on security and auditing guidelines (Mell and Grance, 2009).
- NIST has worked on cloud computing to design and advance standards with United States Government (USG) agencies, federal Chief Information Officers (CIOs), private experts, and international bodies, in order to find consensus on cloud-computing technology and standardization priorities.
- NIST also published the two-volume *USG Cloud Computing Technology Roadmap* document (NIST Special Publication 500-293) to help in effectively securing cloud computing, with the intent of reducing costs and developing federated cloud-computing services (Badger et al. 2011). This publication focuses on NIST strategic requirements related to cloud computing. NIST has also established public working groups to meet those requirements by using the expertise of the broad cloud-computing stakeholder community. The NIST Cloud Computing Security Working Group (NCC-SWG) is working on some of these requirements, with the specific intent of simplifying secure acceptance of cloud services.
- The CSA released cloud security guidelines for secure cloud operations.
- The DMTF CADF cloud-auditing specifications include rules for standardizing cloud auditing.
- The aim of the Cloud Security Alliance Trusted Computing Initiative (TCI, https://cloudsecurityalliance.org/wp-content/uploads/2011/10/TCI_Whitepaper.pdf) is to promote cloud interoperability, compliance management configurations, and security best practices.
- The Cloud Security Alliance TCI Reference Architecture (TCI-RA, https://cloudsecurityalliance.org/media/press-releases/csa-launches-updated-tci-reference-architecture-research-website) has been designed to provide procedures and tools that enable security architects, enterprise engineers, and risk-management professionals to use a common set of solutions and follow the security requirements to implement a secure and trusted cloud.
- Subsequently, the NCC-SWG created the NIST Cloud Computing Security Reference Architecture (NCC-SRA), extending from the NIST Cloud Computing Reference Architecture and the TCI-RA, to identify the security components for a secure cloud (https://bigdatawg.nist.gov/_uploadfiles/M0007_v1_3376532289.pdf). These security components are carried on the three root domains:
  a) Business Operation Support Service (BOSS)
  b) Information Technology Operation Support (ITOS)
  c) Security and Risk Management (S&RM)
- The DMTF CADF Working Group suggested the open standards that would allow tenant consumers to manage and audit application security by themselves. It is crucial for CSPs to provide specific audit events, logs, and information reports for each cloud tenant and for each application. In fact, the DMTF CADF Working Group has published the CADF Data Format and Interface Definition Specification in order to allow data-information sharing and offer the federation of normative audit event data (Rutkowski 2013).

- In June 2014, an article entitled "FedRAMP to Monitor Cloud Service Providers" was published on the TechTank website (Schaub 2014). Since June 5, 2014, the federal government required that all CSPs have FedRAMP approval. As explained in Section 8.2, FedRAMP is a federal program initiative to help standardize the security of cloud services. One of its goals is to reduce the time and effort required for independent CSPs to ensure cloud security. According to a 2013 annual report by the General Service Administration (GSA), agencies that use FedRAMP could save 50% on the number of employees and an average of $200 000 in costs. FedRAMP operates under rules similar to those of the Federal Information Security Management Act-FISMA(https://searchsecurity.techtarget.com/definition/Federal-Information-Security-Management-Act) and helps maintain security of federal IT systems, applications, and databases. Both FISMA and FedRAMP provide enhanced protection and scrutiny for federal and independent agencies. The FedRAMP readiness process is used to determine a CSP's eligibility for the Joint Authorization Board (JAB) Process Provisional Authorization program. In 2014, FedRAMP published the article "Quick Guide to Readiness Process" with the intent of helping in determining a CSP's eligibility (https://www.fedramp.gov/new-fedramp-readiness-assessment-report-for-high-and-moderate-impact-systems). To be eligible, a CSP must meet the following requirements:
  - Have an understanding of the FISMA and FedRAMP requirements and process
  - Be able to commit the resources needed to complete a FedRAMP assessment
  - Have the ability to implement the FedRAMP control baseline
  - Meet the FedRAMP requirements in documenting the control implementation

Cloud federation, defined in Section 8.2, is just starting to be taken into consideration by the research community. Cloud federation may generate new security issues that need to be addressed. Cloud-computing-related specifications, standards, and implementation technologies are required to establish security, interoperability, and portability in order to support federated cloud computing. Standards organizations, as mentioned previously, have jointly worked together with many cloud-security and auditing working groups to design and create cloud-computing standards. Moreover, the United States Air Force Research Laboratory (AFRL) CyberBAT Cloud Security and Auditing Team, during the summer of 2011, started an effort to investigate the directions of future cloud auditing research (https://cps-vo.org/node/6062). Also in 2011, NIST defined the key characteristics for cloud services: on-demand self-service, broad network access, resource pooling, rapid elasticity or expansion, and measured service. Furthermore, clouds allow for virtual back ends, which make them cloud-computing dynamic. Data, applications, and users are moving between internal and external clouds for different uses. Therefore, dealing with all the security and compliance problems that can arise in a dynamic environment may be very challenging. In 2010, the SANS Institute released a white paper entitled "Cloud Security and Compliance: A Primer." The author, Dave Shackleford, stated that since cloud-security and compliance efforts are so complex to deal with, it is necessary to classify all the issues in three main problem areas that apply to all types of cloud-computing systems:

- Mobility and multitenancy
- Identity and access management
- Data protection

The SANS Institute released this white paper to help organizations that are starting cloud-computing programs and give them guidance to keep these problematic cloud-security compliance areas under control.

Cloud consumers need assurance. They want to see evidence that CSPs have audit mechanisms in place. However, most auditors do not have complete knowledge or the appropriate skills in virtualization or cloud computing, which makes things even harder. CSPs are starting to deliver Statement on Auditing Standards (SAS) 70 type II audit reports, providing evidence of the control measures adopted within their cloud environments, but many security and compliance professionals still think this step is inadequate. Even though SAS 70 type II audit reports have been used for nearly 20 years, the problem with the SAS 70 standard—according to the American Institute of Certified Public Accountants (AICPA)—is that these reports were not designed to be used by service institutions that offer colocation, managed servers, or cloud-hosting services in this way. In other words, the SAS 70 type II standard is not the right one for cloud computing because it was developed to take care of internal controls over financial reporting and not cloud systems. Specifically, a SAS 70 type II audit only checks that the controls and processes a data center operator has in place are followed. There are no specific minimum expectations that a data center operator must achieve, nor a benchmark to hold data center operators responsible to. A data center with excellent controls and processes can claim the same level of audit as a data-center operator with no good controls and systems. A major misinterpretation about SAS 70 type II audits is that, after completing an audit, a data center becomes "SAS 70 type II certified"; but in reality there is no such official certification. Many service providers that have outlasted a SAS 70 type II audit have established their own logo, indicating the need for such certification by outside auditors.

The Internal Organization for Standardization (ISO) 27001 and 27002 standards, which provide a more specific and well-structured framework of best practices, are much better models to adhere to. This is a good reason why, in 2010, the SANS Institute published a guide for virtualized infrastructures, entitled "A Guide to Virtualization Hardening Guides" (https://www.intralinks.com/sites/default/files/file_attach/wp-sas70ii.pdf). The CSA, along with other virtualization and cloud-computing security experts, has decided that CSPs should use the ISO 27001 and 27002 standards for auditing and reporting on the state of controls within their cloud infrastructure environments.

The CSA has founded Achieving Governance, Risk Management, and Compliance (GRC), an integrated suite comprising the following four Cloud Security Alliance initiatives (https://cloudsecurityalliance.org/media/news/csa-releases-new-ccm-caiq-v3-0-1): CloudAudit, Cloud Controls Matrix (CCM), Consensus Assessments Initiative Questionnaire (CAIQ), and Cloud Trust Protocol (CTP), which are described next.

The GRC's goals require appropriate assessment criteria, relevant control objectives, and timely access to necessary supporting data. Whether implementing private, or hybrid clouds, the shift to compute as a service presents new challenges across the spectrum of GRC requirements. The CSA GRC stack provides a set of tools for enterprises, CSPs, security-solution providers, IT auditors, and other key stakeholders to instrument and assess both private and public clouds against industry-established best practices, standards, and critical compliance requirements.

CloudAudit (cloudaudit.org) is a volunteer cross-industry cloud effort initiative gathering the best intellectuals and capacity in cloud, networking, security, audit, assurance, and architecture backgrounds. The CloudAudit Working Group officially started in January 2010 and has the participation of many of the largest CSPs, integrators, and professionals. In October 2010, CloudAudit officially came under the support of the Cloud Security Alliance (https://cloudsecurityalliance.org/guidance/csaguide.v3.0.pdf). The goal of CloudAudit is to provide a standard interface and namespace that helps CSPs in the areas of automated audit, assertion, assessment, and assurance (A6) for their IaaS, PaaS, and SaaS environments, and to permit authorized consumers of their services to do the same via an open, extensible, secure interface and methodology. CloudAudit offers the technical baseline to enable transparency and trust in private and public cloud systems.

In July 2014, the CSA revealed the release of the extremely important updates to two de facto industry standards: CCM V3.0.1 and CAIQ V3.0.1 (https://cloudsecurityalliance.org/media/press-releases/ccm-caiq-v3-0-1-soft-launch). Thanks to these two updates, the CSA accomplished a major milestone in the alignment between the Security Guidance for Critical Areas of Focus in Cloud Computing V3, CCM, and CAIQ. Jim Reavis, CEO of CSA, stated the following: "This will allow cloud providers to be more transparent in the baseline assessment process, helping accelerate the implementation process where cloud consumers will be able to make smart, efficient decisions." This also maps CAIQ questions to the latest compliance requirements found in CCM V3.0.1. Daniele Catteddu, managing director of CSA EMEA, said, "With the release of the new CCM and CAIQ, we are creating an incredibly efficient and effective process for cloud providers to better demonstrate transparency and improve trust in the cloud, which is the ultimate mission of the CSA." Specifically, the CSA CAIQ is the first empirical document between a cloud customer and a CSP. It provides a series of yes-or-no control assertion questions. The CSA CAIQ helps organizations build the necessary assessment processes when engaging with CSPs. It simplifies distillation of the issues, best practices, and control specifications from the CSA CCM, thereby allowing all the parties involved to quickly understand areas that require more specific discussion between consumer and CSP. The CSA CCM reinforces some of the well-established information-security control environments by reducing security threats and vulnerabilities in the Cloud. It also provides standardized security and operational risk management, and works to normalize security expectations, cloud taxonomy and terminology, and security procedures employed in the Cloud. The foundation of the CCM rests on its customized relationship to other industry standards, regulations, and control frameworks, such as ISO 27001:2013, COBIT 5.0, PCI DSS V3, and the AICPA 2014 Trust Service Principles and Criteria. Furthermore, it augments internal control directions for service-organization control-report attestations.

The CTP is the method by which cloud-service consumers inquire for, and receive information about, the essential elements of transparency as applied by CSPs. The main intention of the CTP is to produce evidence-based assurance that anything that is asserted as happening in the Cloud is guaranteed to happen as described. This is obtained as an application of digital trust, whose goal is to make cloud consumers more knowledgeable about the underlying infrastructure that constitutes the foundation of the cloud system. When consumers know more about the cloud infrastructure, they tend to feel more confident, which translates into more business and even larger payoffs for the CSP. With the CTP, a CSP gives an instrument to cloud consumers to understand important pieces of information related to the compliance, security, privacy, integrity, and operational-security history of the services being performed in the Cloud. These extremely important pieces of evidence are known as the *elements of transparency*, and they convey proof about vital security settings and operational attributes for systems deployed in the Cloud. These transparent pieces of information give cloud consumers the knowledge necessary to make educated decisions about what service processes and data are appropriate to add to the Cloud, and to decide which cloud best lends itself to satisfy the consumers' needs.

Cloud-compliance-regulation issues become even more challenging and serious as soon as a cloud consumer uses cloud-storage or backup infrastructures. For a CSP, it is essential not only to make sure customer data is well protected—especially sensitive and private data—but also to enforce the appropriate integrity and confidentiality mechanisms when customer data is saved or transferred to a third-party CSP. A CSP must obey relevant laws and industry-standards regulations. According to the CSA, "support for global data privacy standards and the consumer's bill of rights is definitely increasing." This statement is based on the Cloud Security Alliance's Data Protection Heat Index (DPHI) survey report (https://cloudsecurityalliance.org/download/data-protection-heat-index-survey-report), which Cisco Systems Inc. funded. In September 2014, this survey examined some of the top complications around data protection and privacy in the Cloud, including data residency, sovereignty, and lawful interception. The survey participants included 40 among "the most influential cloud security leaders" (as defined by the CSA) in the world, from Chief Information Security Officers (CISOs) to professional privacy and legal specialists. Specifically, the survey showed that there is a solid consensus for more global standards to guide the use and protection of private data. For example, the survey showed broad support for the Organisation for Economic Co-operation and Development (OECD) Privacy Principles, which establish rules for better data privacy standards and protection. For cloud computing, 62% of the participants said that industry implementation of the OECD's data-collection-limitation principle adds restrictions on the quantity of personal data that is collected but also on the content of the data itself. Moreover, the survey showed that 71% of the participating industrial organizations adhered to the OECD's security-safeguards principle, which requests "reasonable security safeguards" to counter unauthorized access, disclosure, modification and damage of personal and private data. Additionally, 73% of respondents indicated that there should be a global consumer's bill of rights for data privacy, while 65% said that the United Nations (UN) should be more involved and take more responsibility in defining and developing such bill. Nevertheless, Trevor Hughes, president and CEO of the International Association of Privacy Professionals (IAPP), warned that achieving this agreement could be very challenging. Specifically, Hughes said, "The concept of privacy varies greatly according to region, and there are cultural differences that manifest themselves into different international laws. I'm not confident that we'll be able to develop one universal framework that can take all of those concepts and cultural views, and distill that down into one simple framework." However, Hughes remained optimistic since he stated that, as challenging as this may sound, government agencies and research organizations should still work toward an agreement on data-privacy standards in cloud computing. Quoting his words, "When it comes to private data, I like to say that just because something is legal doesn't mean it's not stupid."

According to Hughes, it is necessary to have standards and frameworks in order to enforce data privacy since compliance and regulations are not enough.

One of the most pressing questions related to cloud computing is how data privacy is defined internationally. At the 2014 Privacy Academia conference, both the IAPP and CSA strongly emphasized that there is an even greater demand for privacy professionals in the enterprise and for a better cooperation with information-security professionals in order to help organizations better identify and protect sensitive data. This issue is even more complicated for the Cloud because data on the Cloud is not limited to one region or location. The survey just described showed that there is a separation among participants about how data residency and sovereignty should be enforced. The majority of the respondents agreed that personal identifiable information (PII) must stay within the geographic boundaries of the subject's country. However, during this survey, participants were asked to define their own country's concept of data residency or sovereignty compared to other regions; 37% responded that they are more open, 35% that they are more restricted, and 28% that they do not know. Finally, Hughes emphasized the importance of identifying a common language to better define the concepts of data privacy and protection across all countries.

Customers' uncertainty about data security is the number-one obstacle toward fully adopting cloud computing, followed by compliance, privacy, trust, and legal issues. Data security has always been a major issue in traditional IT infrastructure, but it becomes even more serious in the cloud-computing environment: data is dispersed across different machines and storage devices, including servers and mobile devices, potentially in different countries with different legislations. The major concerns for data in the Cloud are integrity, confidentiality, availability, and privacy, which are discussed in Sections 8.4.1 through 8.4.4.

8.4.1 Data Integrity

Data integrity is a security principle that establishes that users must not modify data unless they are authorized to do so. For all the cloud-computing deployment models—IaaS, PaaS, and SaaS—data integrity is the foundation for providing service. Clouds offer a large number of entry and access points. Therefore, enforcing a good authorization mechanism is crucial to maintain data integrity. It is also important to provide third-party supervision. In fact, analyzing data integrity is the prerequisite to deploying applications securely. (Bowers et al. 2009a) proposed a theoretical framework called Proofs of Retrievability (POR) for verifying remote data integrity by combining error-correction code and spot-checking. (Bowers et al. 2009b) also developed a high-availability and integrity layer (HAIL) by using POR checking the storage of data across many different clouds servers. HAIL can also detect duplication of data copies and understand data availability and integrity. (Schiffman et al. 2010) presented a Trusted Platform Module (TPM) to check data integrity remotely.

When it comes to cloud computing, it is important not only to protect cloud consumers' sensitive data via use of cryptographic routines, but also to protect consumers from malicious behaviors by validating the operations performing computations on the data. (Venkatesa and Poornima 2012) proposed a novel data-encoding scheme called *layered interleaving*, designed for time-sensitive packet recovery in the presence of sudden data loss. This is a high-speed data-recovery scheme with minimal loss probability, which uses a forward-error-correction scheme to handle data loss. This methodology is highly efficient in recovering data right after sudden losses. In 2013, research started to design a cloud computing security development life-cycle model to enforce data safety and minimize consumer data exposure risks. A data-integrity-verification algorithm eliminates the need for third-party auditing by protecting static and dynamic data from unauthorized observation, modification, and interference. (Saxena and Dey 2014) proposed work to achieve better data-integrity verification and help users utilize Data-as-a-Service (DaaS) in cloud computing. This framework is partitioned into three platforms: *platinum* for storing sensitive data, *gold* for a medium level of security, and *silver* for nonsensitive data. The authors have also designed different algorithms for implementing these three platforms. Their results showed that this framework is easy to implement and provides strong security without affecting performance in any significant way.

8.4.2 Data Confidentiality

Cloud computing, among many other offerings, provides high availability and elastic access to resources. Third-party cloud infrastructures, such as Amazon Elastic Compute Cloud (EC2), are completely transforming the way today's businesses operate. While we all take advantage of the benefits of cloud computing, businesses must realize that there can be serious risks to data security, particularly to data confidentiality, a security principle that establishes that private data cannot be exposed to unauthorized users. Very important factors, such as software bugs, operator errors, and external attacks, can interfere with the confidentiality of sensitive data stored on external clouds, thereby making that data vulnerable to unauthorized access by malicious parties. (Puttaswamy et al. 2011) studied how to improve the confidentiality of application data stored on third-party computing clouds. They identified all *functionally encryptable* data—sensitive data that can be encrypted without reducing the functionality of the application on the Cloud. This data will only be stored on the Cloud in encrypted form, accessible exclusively to users with the correct keys. This mechanism protects data confidentiality against unintentional errors and attacks. The authors also described *Silverline*, a set of tools that automatically (i) recognize all functionally encryptable data in a cloud application, (ii) assign encryption keys to specific data subsets to minimize key-management complexity while ensuring robustness against key compromise, and (iii) provide transparent data access at the user device while preventing key compromise even from malicious clouds. Via a thorough evaluation, the authors were able to report that numerous web applications heavily use storage and sharing components that do not require raw-data interpretation. Thus, Silverline can protect the vast majority of data manipulated by such applications, simplify key management, and protect against key compromise. These techniques provided an important first step toward simplifying the complex process of incorporating data confidentiality into cloud applications.

Cloud data storage mainly gives small and medium-sized enterprises (SMEs) the capability to reduce investments and maintenance of storage servers while still providing high data availability. The majority of SMEs now outsource their data to cloud storage services. User data sent to the Cloud must be stored in the public cloud environment. Data stored in the Cloud might intersperse with other user data, which leads to data-protection issues in cloud storage. Thus, if the confidentiality of cloud data is broken, serious losses may occur.

Data confidentiality is one of the most important requirements that a CSP must meet. The most used method for ensuring cloud-storage data protection is encryption. However, encryption by itself does not completely guarantee data protection. (Arockiam and Monikandan 2014) proposed a new way for achieving efficient cloud-storage confidentiality. The authors used encryption and obfuscation as two different techniques to protect the data stored in the Cloud. Depending on the type of data, encryption and obfuscation can be applied. Encryption can be applied to strings and symbols, while obfuscation can be more appropriate for numeric data types. Combining encryption and obfuscation provides stronger protection against unauthorized users. In addition, (Alomari and Monowar 2014) addressed the problem of portability and secure file sharing in cloud storage. Their work consists of four different components: (i) the encryption/decryption provider (EDP), which performs the cryptographic operations; (ii) a TPA, which traces the EDP operations and audits them; (iii) a key storage provider (KSP), for key management; and (iv) a data storage provider (DSP), which stores user files in an encrypted form. Based on the experimental results, the authors demonstrated that this new encryption ensures data confidentiality and maintains portability and secure sharing of files among users. (Djebaili et al. 2014) listed the latest trends in cloud data outsourcing and the many different threats that may undermine data integrity, availability, and confidentiality unless cloud data centers are properly secured. The authors observed that different schemes addressing data integrity, availability, and confidentiality, and complying with all the security requirements must be in place. These include high scheme efficiency, stateless verification, unbounded use of queries, and retrievability of data. However, very important questions remain, particularly how to use these schemes efficiently and how often data should be verified. Constantly checking data is a clear waste of resources, but checking only periodically increases risks. The authors attempt to resolve this tricky issue by defining the data-check problem as a noncooperative game, and by performing an in-depth analysis on the Nash Equilibrium and the underlying engineering implications. Based on the game's theoretical analysis, the sequence of reactions is to anticipate the CSP's behavior; this leads to the identification of the minimum resource verification requirement and the optimal strategy for the verifier.

8.4.3 Data Availability

It is essential that an organization is ready to respond in case a disaster occurs. A provider hosting a cloud data center must be prepared for such events and make sure that cloud data becomes available within seconds. It is crucial that organizations define strategies for protecting and restoring access to data appropriately according to operational needs. It is not possible to transfer terabytes (TB) or petabytes (PB) of data information through the network in a few seconds right after a disaster has occurred, and it is necessary for data to be saved in different locations in order to facilitate data access in the event of a failure in a given primary location. Different strategies are used by system architects for backing up data. (Cabot and Pizette 2014) concluded that replicated databases in cloud environments are a cost-effective alternative for ensuring the availability of data in cloud systems, although some other issues arise, such as data synchronization and privacy. Since the cloud-computing paradigm is based on the concept of shared infrastructure by multitenants, DDoS attacks on a specific target can quickly affect many or even all tenants. By guaranteeing that availability is given the necessary importance, organizations can enable stakeholders to properly assess the risks associated with a specific cloud-computing model and successfully mitigate those risks in order to obtain the advantages of cloud computing while ensuring continuity of functions. Intrusion protection systems (IPSs) and firewalls are a crucial defense from these attacks, but they miss an important capability: these solutions do not protect the availability of services. Moreover, these technologies can themselves become targets of DDoS attacks.

8.4.4 Data Privacy

Based on an article published at the end of 2014 on searchcloudsecurity.techtarget.com (Wright 2014), the CSA said that cloud data privacy and the issue of defining authority over data would be the top problems for enterprises in both the United States and abroad for the year 2015. In fact, during that time, a legal battle between the United States government and Microsoft over e-mails located in an offshore data center in Dublin, Ireland was going on. These issues were caused by different data-privacy regulations among countries. These include the USA Patriot Act (http://www.justice.gov/archive/ll/highlights.htm), which is an act of the U.S. Congress that was signed into law by President George W. Bush on October 26, 2001, and a U.S. search warrant. Ireland's Minister for Data Protection has it made clear that "when governments seek to obtain customer information in other countries, they need to comply with the local laws in those countries." The US Congress did not clearly express its intent to put a US business in the difficult position of violating the local laws of countries where customer data is saved in order to comply with a US search warrant. Instead of using a search warrant in the Microsoft case, the U.S. government should have followed the procedures of the Mutual Legal Assistance Treaty (MLAT) between the US and Ireland to ask to receive the necessary information from the Irish government in a way that is consistent with Ireland's laws. This episode may have negative impact on cloud investment and, ultimately, on the economy. This example is a perfect illustration of the types of conflicts that may arise in the near future.

Jim Reavis, co-founder and CEO of the CSA, said that cloud data sovereignty is "probably the number-one issue" for European enterprises using, or planning to use, cloud services. We must ensure that individuals and organizations can have confidence in the rules and processes that have been put in place to safeguard privacy." On April 3, 2014 the Cloud Service Alliance announced the launch of the second version of its Privacy Level Agreement (PLA) Working Group (https://cloudsecurityalliance.org/media/news/csa-announces-pla-v-2). In an effort to help CSPs and future cloud customers objectively evaluate privacy standards, PLA V2, being sponsored by CSA corporate member EMC, aims to provide a clearer and more effective way to communicate to customers regarding the layer of data protection offered by a CSP. The PLA Working Group was originally founded in 2012 with the goal of defining compliance baselines for data-protection legislation as well as establishing best practices for defining a standard for communicating the level of privacy measures (such as data protection and security) that a CSP agrees to follow while hosting third-party data. Moreover, the PLA Working Group is composed of independent privacy and data-protection subject matter experts, privacy officers, and representatives from data protection authorities (DPAs). The PLA

Working Group released three core documents over the course of a year (April 2014–April 2015), as follows:

- The first document is the PLA V2, with special emphasis on the European Union (EU) market. The first deliverable of the PLA WG was a transparency tool for the EU market. Based on those initial results, the PLA Working Group is creating a compliance tool that will satisfy the requirements expressed by the Article 29 Working Party and by the Code of Conduct currently development by the European Commission (EC).
- The second document is the Feasibility Study on Certification/Seal based on the PLA. The group will provide a document assessing the feasibility of a Privacy Certification Module (PCM) in the context of the Open Certification Framework (OCF), and establish a roadmap and guidance for its creation and implementation.
- The third document is the PLA Outline for the Global Market. The CSA will expand the scope of the PLA V1 by considering relevant privacy legislation outside the EU.

8.4.5 Dataflows

One of the most attractive, yet most dangerous characteristics of cloud computing is to promote flow and remote storage of data. Within the public cloud-computing deployment, new applications for data sharing are encouraging internet users to store their data on the Cloud with no mention of any geographical boundaries. The relevant CSPs may have their service centers anywhere in the world. In some jurisdictions, there are laws governing the use of personal data, for example by prohibiting the exportation of personal data to countries that have no enforceable data-protection law. Data transfers *from* all countries with national legislation are restricted. These include all the countries in the EU and the European Economic Area (EEA), Argentina, Australia, Canada, Hong Kong, and New Zealand. From EU and EEA countries, personal information can be transferred to countries that have "adequate protection," namely all other EU and EEA member states plus Switzerland, Canada, Argentina, and Israel. Germany's Data Protection Act, §11, introduced in Section 8.3.2, states that "where other bodies are commissioned to collect, process or use personal data, the responsibility for compliance within the provisions of this Act and with other data protection provisions shall rest with the principal." The implication of this Act is that users must know the exact location of their data and their cloud providers' court of jurisdiction, and export or movement of data is not possible without prior notification of the customer.

Transborder dataflow is the transfer of computerized data across national borders. Restricting it is a form of prevention necessary to protect the personal data of the citizens of a country, but this has indirectly limited cooperation between countries and affected economic development. (Manap and Rouhani 2014) reported the outcome of a study they conducted. They described the fundamental concepts of free dataflow and how it can help the growth of a country's economic power, and proved that unrestricted dataflow allows for more competition in business activities and, therefore, more growth. Internationally dealing with businesses such as research and development, design, protection, sales, and support services, companies gain profit from transborder dataflow because they can receive the best services from the best suppliers. Furthermore, transborder dataflow can promote not only the economic growth of a country, but also its political and social development.

Cyberspace technology, including cloud computing, has changed the way data flows. Through global communication, the distribution of information permits efficient management of businesses by allowing a better way of using resources and services. However, growing public concern about the misuse of personal data has led to the introduction of privacy laws in various countries, with the disadvantage that cross-border restrictions can negatively impact the choice and quality of products and services offered to the consumers around the world. In addition to the ban of transborder dataflow, another factor that can adversely affect a country's economy is the presence of different and incompatible standards and regulations of privacy protection from one country to another. Unstandardized data protection has created challenges in dealing with transfer of data worldwide. Moreover, complicated regulations on cross-border restrictions lead to lost business prospects, with dramatic effects particularly in developing countries. It is suggested that the protection of law is important to enforce the proper use of data and assure the rights and concern of individuals. In order to alleviate the challenges introduced by strict laws, the mixture of procedures and cross-border privacy protections can be minimized through the development of standard privacy regulations. These standard regulations should be adopted by corporate sectors in delivering business transactions over the internet. Adopting consistent corporate privacy rules would resolve several difficulties caused by the various personal-data laws enforced in different countries. In addition, such adoption would allow the administration of data in a more unified and consistent way throughout organizations, independent of where the data may be exported.

8.4.6 The Need for Compliance

Because of the many cloud challenges mentioned so far, cloud customers must understand the terms and conditions of a CSP and which of these terms have to be spelled out in SLAs to maintain cloud compliance. Unfortunately, not all CSPs are in favor of providing detailed security assurances to customers. As Donna Scott, a Gartner Vice President (VP), said during an interview in 2013, "Gartner customers have logged many complaints about weak SLAs lacking the necessary guarantees when it comes to security, confidentiality and transparency." It is essential, as John Morency, a Gartner Research VP, stated: "The devil is in the details," meaning that these contracts should be written very clearly, with no ambiguity, and should explicitly indicate which party is responsible for which security operation. Jay Heiser, another Gartner Research VP, said that enterprises very often struggle to explain, when asked, what security controls a CSP can provide to its cloud customers. Many CSPs answer with very vague responses or unclear documentation. Heiser said that it is necessary for industries to have to define common certifications, so enterprises can offer their services more easily: for example, by using the US government's FedRAMP initiative, which is one of the closest to a global standard. On June 26, 2014 the EC published the Cloud Service Level Agreement Standardization (Cloud SLAS) Guideline. This document is a crucial component of the contractual relationship between a cloud service customer and a CSP. Based on the global nature of the Cloud, SLAs usually cover many jurisdictions, often with varying applicable legal requirements, in particular with respect to the protection of personal data hosted in the cloud service. In addition, different cloud services and deployment models require different approaches to SLAs, which add to the complexity of the SLAs.

Moreover, SLA vocabulary, as of today, very often varies from one CSP to another, which makes it even more difficult for customers to compare cloud services. In fact, standardizing characteristics of SLAs improves clarity and increases the understanding of SLAs for cloud services in the market, in particular by highlighting and providing information on the concepts usually covered by SLAs. These are some of the reasons the Cloud Computing Strategy company is working on the development of standardization guidelines for cloud-computing SLAs for contracts between cloud service providers and cloud service customers.

In February 2013, the EC Directorate General for Communications Networks, Content, and Technology (DG Connect) set up the Cloud Select Industry Group, Subgroup on Service Level Agreement (C-SIG-SLA) to work on these issues. The C-SIG-SLA, an industry consortium assisted by DG Connect, has created the Cloud SLA Standardization Guidelines document to provide a set of SLA standardization guidelines for CSPs and professional cloud service customers, while still ensuring that the specific necessities of the European cloud market and industry are taken into account. This initial standardization effort has will have the highest impact if standardization of SLAs is done at an international level, rather than at a national or regional level. Taking this into consideration, the C-SIG-SLA set up a connection with the ISO Cloud Computing Working Group to provide concrete input and present the European position at the international level.

In 2013, PCI DSS was updated to the next major revision, PCI DSS V3.0 (https://www.pcisecuritystandards.org/minisite/en/pci-padss-supporting-docs-v31.php). In January 2015, the first set of requirement changes rolled out for PCI-DSS. While there are a number of areas where new requirements could affect the compliance plans of suppliers and service providers, both cloud-based and traditional ones, the part that may potentially have the greatest impact related to the Cloud is in situations where the cardholder data environment (CDE) deals with cloud technologies. Suppliers are aware that PCI DSS compliance in the Cloud is a challenging topic, and for this reason the PCI Security Standards Council published a document intentionally for those providers using the Cloud in a PCI context. Three new requirements in PCI DSS V3.0 are particularly relevant to the use of cloud technologies in a PCI-regulated infrastructure:

1) Requirement 2.4: "Maintain an inventory of system components that are in scope for PCI DSS."
2) Requirement 1.1.3: "[Maintain a] current diagram that shows all cardholder dataflows across systems and networks."
3) Requirement 12.8.5: "Maintain information about which PCI DSS requirements are managed by each service provider."

Today, enterprises have to deal with increasing challenges meeting the different compliance and regulatory requirements applicable to them. The challenge significantly increases if the enterprise offers services in various geographies or across different verticals. For instance, an e-commerce supplier with international customers needs to comply with data-privacy and -disclosure mandates such as the EU data-protection directive, California privacy laws, and PCI-DSS. In addition, as a response to the recent economic losses experienced by enterprises as a result of e-commerce hacking, more regulatory and compliance orders are expected as governments and regulatory organizations design requirements in an attempt to prevent future incidents.

Instead of handling each compliance requirement as an independent effort, an organization can obtain significant reductions in effort and cost by adopting standards such as ISO 27001 and 27002 (introduced earlier in Section 8.4) as their base security guidance. In addition, a governance, risk management, and compliance (GRC) framework allows an organization to avoid conflict, reduce overlap and gaps, and obtain better executive visibility to the risks faced. It also enables the organization to be proactive in addressing risk and compliance issues. There is no doubt that meeting compliance requirements by moving to a cloud-based solution offers significant benefits.

Cloud compliance, or rather the lack of it, is an obstacle to cloud adoption. A lack of compliance for services in the Cloud makes the elasticity of the Cloud difficult for operations that must meet compliance mandates. However, a cloud-based solution that includes compliance services opens up the general benefits of the Cloud to many more applications. Based on the type of business process (for example, handling credit-card transactions) or industry (such as healthcare), the majority of organizations are subject to different compliance and regulatory authorizations. For instance, openly traded financial services institutions situated in the US, running their own data centers where both customer and corporate data and applications are located, must comply with the following standards:

- Gramm-Leach-Bliley Act (GLBA) guidelines
- PCI
- SAS 70 type II
- Various state and federal privacy- and data-breach disclosure requirements

Companies depend heavily on reporting and auditing frameworks that include requests to detail controls and policies that have been implemented in order to ensure compliance. In general, a cloud solution must prove that it possesses identical types of safeguards and controls that are otherwise implemented privately. A CSP must also be able to provide evidence of compliance by showing regulation-specific reports and audits, such as SAS 70 type II audit reports. In 2014, Citrix Systems Inc. published a document entitled *Citrix Cloud Solution for Compliance* describing the Citrix-specific solutions and products that Citrix offers in helping cloud services comply with various regulations (https://www.citrix.com/content/dam/citrix/en_us/documents/products-solutions/citrix-cloud-solution-for-compliance.pdf). The IEEE Cloud Computing group, which is part of the IEEE organization, is also working on standards for cloud computing (https://cloudcomputing.ieee.org/standards).

8.5 Future Research Directions for Cloud Auditing and Compliance

A large body of research and effort has been conducted by organizations worldwide, with the purpose of addressing cloud auditing and improve security, privacy, and trust for cloud consumers. However, a lot still needs to be done in order to make cloud infrastructures more secure and trusted, attract investments from industrial enterprise and government agencies, and give companies the confidence to move their businesses to the Cloud and also store their customers' sensitive and privacy data in cloud storage. Moreover, there is great demand from organizations to globally design and enforce cloud compliance regulations, which are necessary for cloud service providers to prove trust and reliability to their consumers. Following is a list of open problems that future research should address:

- *Misuse of administrator rights and/or malicious insiders:* In cloud computing, VMs are the basis for the cloud infrastructure. More work needs to be done to effectively monitor and detect VM misuse by malicious insiders.
- *Lack of transparency of applied security measures:* In cloud computing, not every CSP follows baseline standards, although today global government agencies and laws are working together to define cloud baseline standards and compliance regulations for CSPs. As a result, the particular security measures implemented by a CSP often are not completely known.
- *Shared technology issues (multitenancy) and misconfigurations of VMs:* In cloud computing, poorly implemented multitenancy can allow a customer to endanger other customers' resources, either maliciously or unintentionally. This is caused by the use of virtualization without proper isolation. Exploits due to the increasing code complexity of hypervisor software have already been demonstrated. Memory-cache isolation is another issue. As of today, no CSP releases complete information on how shared resources are securely wiped before being reassigned to a different customer.
  - *Data life cycle in case of provider switch or termination.* In cloud computing, due to shared usage of resources, this threat is particularly serious. The CSA states that cloud consumers need to define specific rules for ending-of-contract scenarios regulating how customers' data is exported from the Cloud and how a provider promises to securely erase customer data. Both the consumer and the CSP must agree on these rules. Global standardizations and compliance regulations are still heavily needed in this area.
  - *Unclear data location:* Cloud customers often do not have any certainty about the country in which their data is saved or processed. As of today, there is no way to prove if customer data has or has not been outsourced by a CSP. Customer data-privacy laws are different in each country, which make it even more difficult to respect all the regulations when transferring and storing data across different geographic locations. More global compliance and standardization directives are needed to solve the issue of enforcing privacy when the location of the data is unknown or unclear.
- *Missing monitoring:* If cloud consumer data, especially personal data, is at risk of fraud or integrity, it is essential for a CSP to be able to detect these risks, warn customers, and eliminate the risks. As of today, it is a challenge for a cloud providers to use an information-policy system that automatically informs customers in the presence of security violations.
- *Missing interoperability of CSPs:* CSPs are not compatible with each other, since each service provider uses customized VM formats and proprietary APIs. As a consequence, more work is required to standardize cloud operations and achieve better interoperability between CSPs.

8.6 Conclusion

This chapter provided an overview of the latest cloud security problems and how cloud auditing can alleviate these issues. This chapter covered the state of the art in cloud auditing and discussed the modifications and extensions that need to be implement to enable effective cloud audits and minimize cloud security and privacy challenges. A significant body of research has been dedicated to improving cloud auditing, but many aspects of cloud auditing need more work, particularly in the area of standardization. In addition, this chapter described the complexity behind cloud compliance and explained how numerous organizations worldwide are eagerly collaborating to standardize compliance regulations. Once this goal is achieved, CSPs can finally prove compliance and gain the trust of cloud consumers, who are still hesitant to adopt cloud deployments for fear of compromising the integrity and confidentiality of their data—especially when CSPs transport and store data in other countries. The chapter also explained how data-protection laws in different countries have complicated transborder dataflow, to the point of reducing cloud adoptions and affecting the economic growth of developing countries.

References

Alomari, E.A. and Monowar, M.M. (2014). Towards data confidentiality and portability in cloud storage. Design, user experience, and usability. User experience design for diverse interaction platforms and environments. *Lecture Notes in Computer Science* 8518: 38–49.

Arockiam, L. and Monikandan, S. (2014). Efficient Cloud Storage Confidentiality to Ensure Data Security. 2014 International Conference on Computer Communication and Informatics (ICCCI), Coimbatore, India.

Aslam, M., Gehrmann, C., and Björkman, M. (2013). Continuous security evaluation and auditing of remote platforms by combining trusted computing and security automation techniques. The 6th International Conference on Security of Information and Networks, Aksaray, Turkey.

Badger, L., Bernstein, D., Bohn, R., et al. (2011). National Institute of Standards and Technology Special Publication 500–293 (Draft). US Government Cloud Computing Technology Roadmap Volume I Release 1.0 (Draft). http://www.nist.gov/itl/cloud/upload/SP_500_293_volumeI-2.pdf (accessed 16 December 2014).

Bishop, M. (2002). Design principles. *In: Computer Security: Art and Science.* Professional: Addison-Wesley.

Bowers, K.D., Juels, A., and Oprea, A. (2009a). Proofs of retrievability: theory and implementation. In: *Proceedings of the 2009 ACM Workshop on Cloud Computing Security*, 43–54. ACM.

Bowers, K.D., Juels, A., and Oprea, A. (2009b). HAIL: a high-availability and integrity layer for cloud storage. In: *Proceedings of the 16th ACM Conference on Computer and Communications Security*, 187–198. ACM.

Cabot, T. and Pizette, L. (2014). Leveraging public clouds to ensure data availability. White paper. http://www.mitre.org/sites/default/files/pdf/12_0230.pdf (accessed 10 January 2015).

Chen, Y., Paxon, V., and Katz, R.H. (2010). What's new about cloud computing security? EECS Department, University of California, Berkeley. Technical report UCB/EECS-2010-5

Djebaili, B., Kiennert, C., Leneutre, J. et al. (2014). Data integrity and availability verification game in untrusted cloud storage. Decision and game theory for security. *Lecture Notes in Computer Science* 8840: 287–306.

Doelitzscher, F., Reich, C., Knah, M. et al. (2012). An agent based business aware incident detection system for cloud environments. *Journal of Cloud Computing: Advances, Systems and Applications* 1: 9.

German Parliament (2009). Federal Data Protection Act. Federal Law Gazette I p. 66, as most recently amended by Article 1 of the Act of 14 August 2009 (Federal Law Gazette I p. 2814). http://www.gesetze-im-internet.de/englisch_bdsg/englisch_bdsg.html (accessed 13 December 2014).

Gondree, M. and Peterson, Z.N.J. (2013). Geolocation of data in the cloud. In: Proceedings of the Third ACM Conference on Data and Application Security and Privacy, 24–36. ACM.

Goodin, Dan. (2014a). Crypto attack that hijacked Windows Update goes mainstream in Amazon Cloud. http://arstechnica.com/security/2014/11/crypto-attack-that-hijacked-windows-update-goes-mainstream-in-amazon-cloud (accessed 12 December).

Goodin, Dan. (2014b). AWS console breach leads to demise of service with "proven" backup plan. http://arstechnica.com/security/2014/06/aws-console-breach-leads-to-demise-of-service-with-proven-backup-plan (accessed 20 December 2014).

Hamza, Y.A. and Omar, M.D. (2013). Cloud computing security: abuse and nefarious use of cloud computing. *International Journal of Computational Engineering Research* 3 (6): 22–27.

Han, K.J., Choi, B.Y., and Song, S. (2014). *High Performance Cloud Auditing and Applications*, 6–7. Heidelberg, Dordrecht, London: Springer New York.

Kortchorski, B. and Rutkowska, S. (2009). Cloudburst. Technical paper. http://www.blackhat.com/presentations/bh-usa-09/KORTCHINSKY/BHUSA09-Kortchinsky-Cloudburst-PAPER.pdf (accessed 15 December 2014).

Loutas, N., Kamateri, E., and Tarabanis, K. (2013). Cloud computing interoperability: the state of play. Centre for Research and Technology Hellas, Thessaloniki, Greece; Information Systems Lab, University of Macedonia, Thessaloniki, Greece.

Manap, N.A. and Rouhani, A. (2014). Issue of transborder data flows in cloud computing the impact on economic growth. *International Business Management* 8: 113–117.

Meng, S., Iyengar, A.K., Rouvellou, I.M. et al. (2012). Reliable state monitoring in cloud datacenter. Proceedings of the IEEE Fifth International Conference on Cloud Computing, 951–958. IEEE.

Mell, P. and Grance, T. (2009). The NIST definition of cloud computing. http://csrc.nist.gov/publications/nistpubs/800-145/SP800-145.pdf (accessed 28 January 2014).

Paladi, N., Aslam, M., and Gehrmann, C. (2014). Trusted geolocation-aware data placement in infrastructure. The 13th IEEE International Conference on Trust, Security and Privacy in Computing and Communications IEEE (TrustCom), Beijing, China.

Patel, P., Ranabah, A., and Sheth, A. (2009). *Service Level Agreement in Cloud Computing*. Fairborn, Ohio: Wright State University CORE Scholar.

Puttaswamy, K.P.N., Kruegel, C., and Zhao, B.Y. (2011). Silverline: toward data confidentiality in storage-intensive cloud applications. In: Proceedings of the 2nd ACM Symposium on Cloud Computing, article 10. ACM.

Ries, T., Fusenig, V., Vilbois, C. et al. (2011). Verification of data location in cloud networking. In: Proceedings of the Fourth IEEE International Conference on Utility and Cloud Computing (UCC), 439–444. IEEE.

Rutkowski, M. (2013). An Introduction to DMTF cloud auditing using the CADF event model and taxonomies. https://wiki.openstack.org/w/images/e/e1/Introduction_to_Cloud_

Auditing_using_CADF_Event_Model_and_Taxonomy_2013-10-22.pdf (accessed 27 December 2014).
Sathiskumar, R. and Retnaraj, J. (2014). Secure privacy preserving public auditing for cloud storage. International Conference on Engineering Technology and Science (ICETS'14), Tamilnadu, India.
Saxena, R. and Dey, S. (2014). Collaborative approach for data integrity. Verification in cloud computing. Recent Trends in Computer Networks and Distributed Systems Security. *Communications in Computer and Information Science* 420: 1–15.
Schaub, Hillary. (2014). FedRAMP to monitor cloud service providers. https://www.brookings.edu/blog/techtank/2014/06/05/fedramp-to-monitor-cloud-service-providers (accessed 22 January 2015).
Schiffman, J., Moyer, T., Vijayakumar, H. et al. (2010). Seeding clouds with trust anchors. In: Proceedings of the ACM Workshop on Cloud Computing Security, 43–46. ACM.
Sotto, L.J., Treacy, B.C., and McLellan, M.L. (2010). Privacy and data security risks and cloud computing. Electron. Comm. Law Rep.
Sunagar, S., Patil, U., and Sheshgiri (2014). Dynamic auditing protocol for data storage and authentication forwarding in cloud computing. *IJRIT International Journal of Research in Information Technology* 2 (4): 429–436.
Tiwana, B., Balakrishnan, M., Aguilera, M. et al. (2010). Location, location, location!: modeling data proximity. In: Proceedings of Hotnets, the 9th ACM Workshop on Hot Topics. ACM.
Vaish, A., Kushwaha, A., Das, R. et al. (2013). Data location verification in cloud computing. *International Journal of Computer Applications* 68 (12): (0975–8887).
Venkatesa, K.V. and Poornima, G. (2012). Ensuring data integrity in cloud computing. *Journal of Computer Applications* 5 (EICA2012-4): ISSN: 0974–1925.
Waqas, A., Yusof, Z.M., and Shah, A. (2013). A security-based survey and classification of cloud architectures, state of art and future directions. In: Proceedings of the Advanced Computer Science Applications and Technologies (ACSAT), International Conference, 284–289.
Weise, E. (2014). Apple's iCloud network under attack. http://www.usatoday.com/story/tech/2014/10/21/apple-icloud--attack-network/17669603 (accessed 21 December 2014).
Wright, Rob. (2014). CSA to closely monitor enterprise cloud data privacy issues in 2015. http://searchcloudsecurity.techtarget.com/news/2240237429/CSA-to-closely-monitor-enterprise-cloud-data-privacy-issues-in-2015 (accessed 11 January 2015).
Yu, Y., Niu, L., Yang, G. et al. (2014). On the security of auditing mechanisms for secure cloud storage. University of Wollongong Research Online, Faculty of Engineering and Information Sciences. University of Wollongong, New South Wales, Australia and University of Electronic Science and Technology of China.

Further Reading

Arockiam, L. and Monikandan, S. (2013). Data security and privacy in cloud storage using hybrid symmetric encryption algorithm. *International Journal of Advanced Research in Computer and Communication Engineering* 2 (8): 3064–3070.
Arora, R. and Parashar, A. (2013). Secure user data in cloud computing using encryption algorithms. *International Journal of Engineering Research and Applications* 3 (4): 1922–1926.

Bugiel, S., Nurnberger, S., Poppelmann, T. et al. (2011). Amazonia: when elasticity snaps back. In: Proceedings of the 18th ACM Conference on Computer and Communications Security, 389–400. ACM.

Doelitzscher, F., Reich, C., Knahl, M. et al. (2012). An agent based business aware incident detection system for cloud environments. *Journal of Cloud Computing: Advances, Systems and Applications* 1 (1): 9.

Kamara, S. and Lauter, K. (2010). Cryptographic Cloud Storage. In: *Financial Cryptography and Data Security (FC 2010) Workshops, RLCPS, WECSR, and WLC 2010, Revised Selected Papers*, 136–149. Springer-Verlag.

Karbe, T. (2013). Design and development of an audit policy language for cloud computing environments. Cloud Research Lab; University of Applied Sciences Furtwangen, technical report. http://wolke.hs-furtwangen.de/publications/theses (accessed 10 January 2015).

Khorshed, M.T., Ali, A.B.M., and Wasimi, S.A. (2012). A survey on gaps, threat remediation challenges and some thoughts for proactive attack detection in cloud computing. *Future Generation Computer Systems* 28 (6): 833–851.

Krutz, R.L. and Vines, R.D. (2010). *Cloud Security A Comprehensive Guide to Secure Cloud Computing*. Wiley Publishing, Inc.

Mather, T., Kumaraswamy, S., and Latif, S. (2009). *Cloud Security and Privacy: An Enterprise Perspective on Risks and Compliance*. O' Reilly Media.

Morsy, A. and Faheem, H. (2009). A new standard security policy language. *IEEE Potentials* 28 (2): 19–26.

Ristenpart, T., Tromer, E., Shacham, H. et al. (2009). Hey, you, get off of my cloud: exploring information leakage in third-party compute clouds. In: Proceedings of the 16th ACM Conference on Computer and Communication Security (CCS'09), 199–212. ACM.

Vieira, K., Schulter, A., and Westphall, C.B. (2010). Intrusion detection techniques for grid and cloud computing environment. *IT Professional, IEEE Computer Society* 12 (4): 38–43.

Wang, B., Li, B., and Li, H. (2012). Oruta: privacy preserving public auditing for shared data in the Cloud. In: *Proceedings of the IEEE International Conference on Cloud Computing*, 293–302. IEEE.

Wang, C., Wang, Q., Ren, K. et al. (2010). Privacy preserving public auditing for data storage security in cloud computing. In: *Proceedings of INFOCOM*, 525–533. IEEE.

Xiao, Z. and Xiao, Y. (2013). Security and privacy in cloud computing. *IEEE Communications Surveys & Tutorials* 15 (2): 843–859.

Yang, K. and Jia, X. (2012). Data storage auditing service in cloud computing: challenges, methods and opportunities. *World Wide Web* 15 (4): 409–428.

Zhang, L.J. and Zhou, Q. (2009). CCOA: cloud computing open architecture. In: *IEEE International Conference on Web Services*, 607–616. IEEE.

Zhang, X., Wuwong, N., Li, H. et al. (2010). Information security risk management framework for the cloud computing environments. In: Proceedings of 10th IEEE International Conference on Computer and Information Technology, 1328–1334. IEEE.

Zhu, Y., Hu, H., Ahn, G. et al. (2012). Cooperative provable data possession for integrity verification in multi-cloud storage. *IEEE Transactions on Parallel and Distributed Systems* 23 (12): 2231–2244.

9

Security-as-a-Service (SECaaS) in the Cloud

Saman Taghavi Zargar[1], Hassan Takabi[2], and Jay Iyer[1]

[1]*Office of CTO Security Business Group, Cisco Systems, San Jose, CA, USA*
[2]*Department of Computer Science and Engineering, University of North Texas, Denton, TX, USA*

9.1 Introduction

Cloud computing has gained extensive interest within both academic and industry communities. It tries to consolidate the economic utility model with the evolutionary development of many existing approaches and computing technologies including distributed services, applications, and information infrastructures consisting of pools of computers, networks, and storage resources (Cloud Security Alliance 2009). Confusion exists in information technology (IT) communities about how the Cloud is different from existing models and how these differences might affect its adoption. Some see the Cloud as a novel technical revolution while others consider it a natural evolution of technology, economy, and culture (Cloud Security Alliance 2009). Nevertheless, cloud computing is a very important paradigm that provides tremendous potential for significant cost reduction through optimization and the increased operating and economic efficiencies in computing (Cloud Security Alliance 2009; Mell and Grance 2009). Furthermore, cloud computing has the potential to significantly enhance collaboration, agility, and scale, thus enabling a truly global computing model over the internet infrastructure.

While several researchers have tried to define *cloud computing*, there is no single agreed-upon definition. Its definitions, issues, underlying technologies, risks, and values need to be refined. These definitions, attributes, and characteristics have been evolving and will change over time. The U.S. National Institute of Standards and Technology (NIST) defines cloud computing as follows: "Cloud computing is a model for enabling convenient, on-demand network access to a shared pool of configurable computing resources (e.g., networks, servers, storage, applications, and services) that can be rapidly provisioned and released with minimal management effort or service provider interaction. This cloud model promotes availability and is composed of five essential characteristics, three delivery models, and four deployment models" (Mell and Grance 2009). In order to understand the importance of cloud computing and its adoption, we need to understand its principal characteristics, its delivery and deployment

Security, Privacy, and Digital Forensics in the Cloud, First Edition. Edited by Lei Chen, Hassan Takabi, and Nhien-An Le-Khac.

models, how customers use these services, and how these services need to be safeguarded. The five key characteristics of cloud computing are *on-demand self service, ubiquitous network access, location-independent resource pooling, rapid elasticity,* and *measured service,* which are geared toward allowing the seamless and transparent use of clouds. Rapid elasticity allows resources provisioned to be quickly scaled up (or down). Measured services are primarily derived from properties of the business model and indicate that the cloud service provider controls and optimizes the use of computing resources through automated resource allocation, load balancing, and metering tools (Takabi et al. 2010a).

The cloud computing paradigm ignited the rapid growth of novel virtualization methods (i.e. containers vs. hypervisors (Soltesz et al. 2007)), the emergence of the Internet of Everything (IoE), and the rapid adoption of smartphones that led to the evolution of business applications and systems worldwide. At the same time, there is an increasing trend of security threats against these assets by malicious entities. Applications running on or being developed for cloud computing platforms pose various security and privacy challenges depending on the underlying delivery and deployment models. Three key cloud delivery models are Software-as-a-Service (SaaS), Platform-as-a-Service (PaaS), and Infrastructure-as-a-Service (IaaS). In IaaS, the cloud provider provides a set of virtualized infrastructural components such as virtual machines and storage on which the customers can build and run applications. The most basic components are a virtual machine (VM) and the virtual operating system (OS) where the application will eventually reside. Issues such as trusting the VM image, hardening hosts, and securing inter-host communication are critical areas in IaaS. PaaS enables the programming environments to access and utilize the additional application building blocks. Such programming environments have a visible impact on the application architecture. One such impact would be that of the constraints on what services the application can request from an OS. For example, a PaaS environment may limit access to well-defined parts of the file system, thus requiring a fine-grained authorization service. In SaaS, cloud providers enable and provide application software enabled as on-demand-services. As clients acquire and use software components from different providers, securely composing them and ensuring that information handled by these composed services is well protected become crucial issues.

The cloud deployment models include public clouds, private clouds, community clouds, and hybrid clouds. A *public cloud* refers to an external or publicly available cloud environment that is accessible to multiple tenants, while a *private cloud* is typically a tailored environment with dedicated virtualized resources for a particular organization. Similarly, a *community cloud* is tailored for a particular group of customers.

Cloud computing's flexible and scalable economic solutions can be both a friend and an enemy from a security perspective, as the large resources and data gathered in datacenters makes them more attractive targets for attackers. Despite the enormous opportunities and values that the Cloud presents for organizations, without appropriate security and privacy solutions designed for clouds this potentially revolutionizing computing paradigm could become a huge failure. Several surveys of potential cloud adopters indicate that security and privacy are the primary concerns delaying its adoption (Catteddu and Hogben 2009). For example, on March 30, 2010, Yale University placed a migration to Google Apps for its email services on hold over privacy and security concerns (Tidmarsh 2010). However, cloud computing appears to be an unstoppable force because of its potential benefits. Hence, understanding the security and privacy risks in cloud computing and developing effective solutions are critical to the success of this new computing paradigm.

When we move our information into the Cloud, we may lose control of it. The Cloud gives us access to the data, but the challenge is to ensure that only authorized entities have. For instance, on June 19, 2011, Dropbox users reported that they were allowed into their Dropbox accounts after entering the wrong password (Peppetta 2011). It is crucial to understand how we can protect our data and resources from a security breach in a Cloud that provides shared platforms and services. It is critical to have appropriate mechanisms to prevent cloud providers from using customers' data in a way that has not been agreed upon in the past. In collaborative web applications that are built for groups, like Google Apps or any web-based project management software, the security concerns spread across everyone involved. The security of the entire system is only as strong as the weakest user's setup. Once one person's weak password is brute-forced or guessed, everyone's documents and information are at risk.

The architectural features of the Cloud allow users to achieve better operating costs and be very agile by facilitating fast acquisition of services and infrastructural resources as and when needed. However, these unique features also give rise to various security concerns. Table 9.1 summarizes these unique features with corresponding security implications (Takabi et al. 2010a).

In order to address the critical security requirements of enterprises, in the past couple of years, there has been a tremendous effort toward proposing security services that could be delivered as cloud-based services (a.k.a. Security-as-a-Service [SECaaS]).

Table 9.1 Security implications of cloud features.

Feature	Security Implications
Outsourcing	Users may lose control of their data. Appropriate mechanisms are needed to prevent cloud providers from using customers' data in a way that has not been agreed upon.
Extensibility and shared responsibility	In general, there is a trade-off between extensibility and security responsibility for customers within different delivery models; the sharing level differs for different delivery models, which in turn affects cloud extensibility for customers.
Virtualization	There need to be mechanisms to ensure strong isolation, mediated sharing, and communication between VMs. This could be done using an access-control system to enforce access policies that govern the control and sharing capabilities of VMs within a cloud host.
Multitenancy	Issues like access policies, application deployment, and data access and protection should be taken into account to provide a secure multitenant environment.
Service-level agreement	The main goal is to build a new layer to create a negotiation mechanism for the contract between providers and consumers of services as well as the monitoring of its fulfillment at runtime.
Heterogeneity	Different cloud providers may have different approaches to provide security and privacy mechanisms, thus creating integration challenges.

Some of the services provided by SECaaS providers are intrusion detection systems and intrusion prevention systems (IDS/IPS), antivirus programs and antimalware, email and web applications security, identity and access management, traffic scrubbing, Secure Sockets Layer (SSL) certificates, encryption, integrity monitoring, security information and event management (SIEM), tokenization (payment card industry data security standard), etc. These security services have had and will continue to have an intense impact on securing enterprises of any size in the near future, a benefit that was not otherwise affordable especially for small enterprises. SECaaS enables security controls and functions to be delivered in new ways and by new types of service providers. It also enables enterprises to use security technologies and techniques that are not otherwise cost effective. Enterprises that use cloud-based security services to reduce the cost of security controls and to address the new security challenges that cloud-based computing brings are most likely to prosper. However, the main challenge for all enterprises that employ SECaaS is to implement robust, scalable, cost-effective security services by performing a comprehensive risk analysis, because with rewards comes risk. More importantly, there are always trade-offs and pros and cons for various SECaaS services that could be employed by enterprises. Therefore, a comprehensive risk-analysis framework customized to a specific enterprise's goal for employing SECaaS, considering the enterprise's unique architecture, is necessary and tremendously helpful. Such a framework will lead to a smooth transition to the Cloud by any enterprise, and will let them benefit from SECaaS services provided by SECaaS providers. In this chapter, we propose SECaaS, a framework that aims to facilitate adoption of security services offered in the Cloud by assisting security managers to assess and choose from many security and privacy services provided by different cloud service providers and also for cloud providers to provide their security services more efficiently.

The remainder of this chapter is organized as follows: Section 9.2 discusses the related work. Section 9.3 presents the Security-as-a-Service framework, describes its components, and provides its life cycle. Finally, Section 9.4 concludes the chapter.

9.2 Related Work

The Cloud Security Alliance (CSA) released its initial report in 2009, "Security Guidance for Critical Areas of Focus in Cloud Computing" (Cloud Security Alliance 2009). The CSA is an effort to facilitate the mission to create and apply best practices to secure cloud computing. Its initial report outlined areas of concern and guidance for organizations adopting cloud computing. The intention was to provide security practitioners with a comprehensive roadmap for being proactive in developing positive and secure relationships with cloud providers. NIST cloud efforts intend to promote the effective and secure use of the technology within government and industry by providing technical guidance and promoting standards. NIST released an early definition of cloud computing and also documented how to effectively and securely use the cloud computing paradigm (Mell and Grance 2009). (Trusted Computing Group 2010) discusses fundamental technologies on which the cloud security approaches are based. These technologies include Trusted Platform Module (TPM), Trusted Network Communications (TNC) architecture, and Trusted Storage. It selected six specific areas of the cloud computing environment from the CSA's security guide where equipment and software implementing Trusted Computing Group's (TCG) specifications can provide substantial security improvements, and explained how to apply these technologies in the Cloud.

(Takabi et al. 2010a) discuss security and privacy challenges in a cloud computing environment. They present unique issues of cloud computing that exacerbate security and privacy challenges in clouds, and discuss these challenges along with possible approaches and research directions to address them. They also proposed SecureCloud, a comprehensive security framework for cloud computing environments (Takabi et al. 2010b). The framework consists of different modules to handle security, and trust issues of key components of cloud computing environments. These modules deal with issues such as identity management, access control, policy integration among multiple clouds, trust management between different clouds and between a cloud and its users, secure service composition and integration, and semantic heterogeneity among policies from different clouds. (Jaeger and Schiffman 2010) discuss security challenges in the Cloud, the foundation of future systems' security, and key areas for cloud system improvement. (Jung and Chung 2010) propose an adaptive access algorithm that uses contextual information of the environments such as time, location, and security information to decide the access control to the resources. They also present an adaptive security management model using an improved role-based access control (RBAC) model to solve more complex and difficult problems in cloud computing environments.

(Kandukuri et al. 2009) present security issues that must be included in a service-level agreement (SLA) in a cloud computing environment. (Jensen et al. 2009) provide an overview of technical security issues of the Cloud. They start with real-world examples of attacks performed on the Amazon EC2 service and then give an overview of existing and future threats to the Cloud. They also briefly discuss appropriate countermeasures to these threats, and further issues to be considered in future research. (Chen et al. 2010) try to frame the full space of cloud security issues by examining contemporary and historical perspectives from industry, academia, government, and the black-hat community. They argue that most cloud computing security issues are not fundamentally new or fundamentally intractable. However, they suggest that two issues—the complexities of multiparty trust and mutual auditability—are to some degree new to the Cloud and propose future research directions for these issues.

The information security management system (ISMS) family of standards (the ISO/IEC 27000-series) includes information security standards published jointly by the International Organization for Standardization (ISO) and the International Electrotechnical Commission (IEC) (International Organization for Standardization 2009). The objectives of the ISO/IEC 27000-series are to provide definitions and an introduction to the ISMS family of standards. It provides best-practice recommendations on information security management, risks, and controls within the context of an overall ISMS. The plan, do, check, act (PDCA) model is an accepted life cycle for information security management that seeks to address changes in the threats, vulnerabilities, and impacts of information security incidents. The *plan* phase is responsible for setting policies, a strategy for implementing controls to achieve security objectives, and specific roadmaps to achieve control implementations within systems. In the *do* phase, controls are executed; and in the *check* phase, tests are performed to ensure that controls are operating as intended and meet objectives. In the *act* phase, gaps are remediated. Then the cycle repeats. This standard series is broad in scope and covers more than just privacy, confidentiality, and technical security issues; it is applicable to organizations of all shapes and sizes. The NIST Risk Management Framework defines a more detailed security life cycle that focuses on the implementation of controls in a specific IT system rather than at the overall ISMS level (Stoneburner et al. 2002). It provides "a foundation for the development of an effective risk management program, containing both the definitions and the practical guidance necessary for assessing and mitigating risks identified within IT systems" (Stoneburner et al. 2002). (Alberts and Dorofee 2005) have proposed the Mission Assurance Analysis Protocol (MAAP) to define an advanced, systematic approach for analyzing operational risk and gauging mission assurance in complex work processes.

9.3 Security-as-a-Service Framework

In this section, we present a framework to assess and efficiently deliver cloud-based security services to enterprises. First, we describe the framework by explaining its components in detail. Then, we explain how security administrators can use this framework to evaluate and adopt security services offered by various cloud service providers.

We propose the SECaaS framework as a new paradigm in cloud environment. We define SECaaS as the capabilities provided to the consumer to use providers' security products running on a cloud infrastructure and accessible through an interface. The consumer does not manage or control the underlying cloud infrastructure, network, servers, operating systems, storage, or even individual application capabilities. The goal is to develop a framework that facilitates provisioning of cloud-based security applications and defines how to compose different security applications from different providers and come up with desirable solutions. It is critical to understand how architectures, technologies, processes, and human requirements change or remain the same when deploying cloud computing services (Cloud Security Alliance 2009). In order to understand how the cloud architecture impacts the security architecture, cloud services and architecture should be analyzed and mapped to a model of technical security, management and operational controls, risk assessment, and management frameworks. This is essentially an analysis to determine the general security posture of cloud services and how they relate to the protection requirements of an organization's assets. Once this analysis is complete, it becomes easier to decide what needs to be done in order to feed back into a risk-assessment framework to determine how the risk should be addressed.

For SECaaS to be considered a practical cloud service, it must provide customers with the ability to establish their own security policies and risk-management framework. Customers must be able to characterize, assess, measure, and prioritize their system risks. Cloud providers must offer security services independent of any platform and adaptable to constantly changing cloud environments and also ensure that their security measures are not too complex for efficient resource application. Prior to using a cloud service, customers must determine what security measures it provides and what extra security services are needed to deal with any potential vulnerability. Customers can identify from these analyses the common security services they can entrust to service providers. Figure 9.1, borrowed from (Cloud Security Alliance 2009), shows an example of various types of security controls needed when migrating to the Cloud. Depending on the cloud delivery model, the cloud service can be compared to a set of security controls to determine which controls already exist, provided by either the

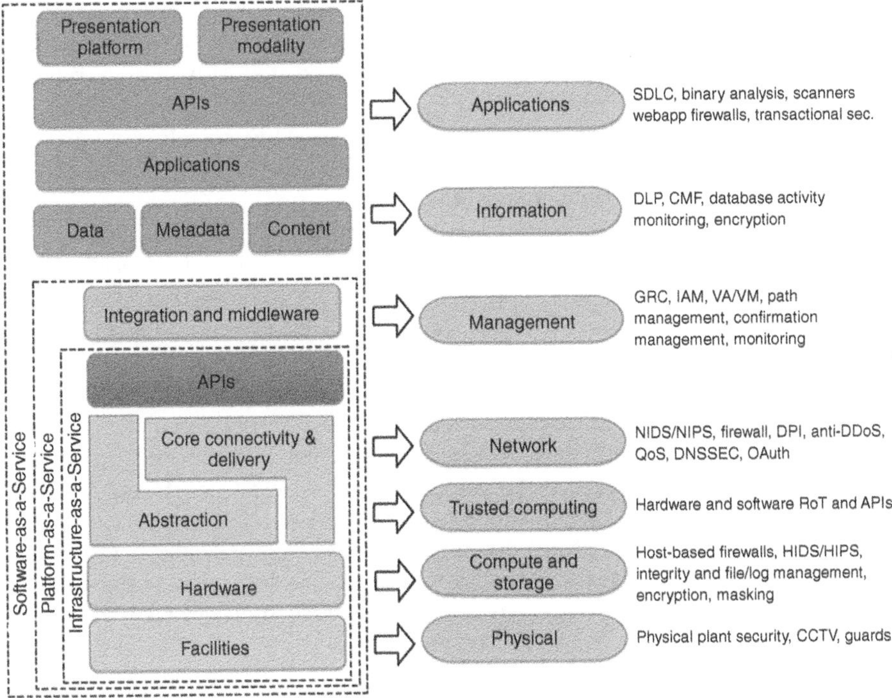

Figure 9.1 Security controls mapped to cloud delivery models.

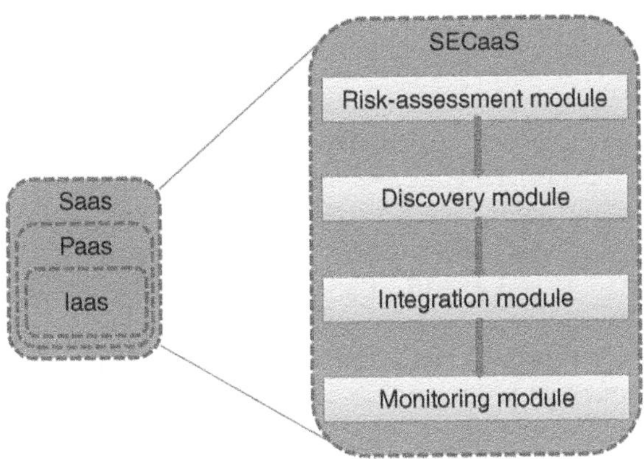

Figure 9.2 Security-as-a-Service framework.

consumer or the cloud service provider, and which controls need to be solicited from other cloud providers.

As shown in Figure 9.2, the proposed framework includes four main components: the *risk-assessment module*, the *discovery module*, the *integration module*, and the *monitoring module*. The security risk-assessment module is responsible for identifying and evaluating risks and risk impacts, and recommending security controls to deal with these risks. *Risk* is defined as "a function of the likelihood of a given threat-source's exercising a particular potential vulnerability, and the resulting impact of that adverse event on the organization" (Stoneburner et al. 2002). Customers use risk assessment to determine the extent of potential threats and the risk associated with an organization. Through a comprehensive risk analysis, the customer identifies what security controls and applications are needed to secure the organization. Then, the customer determines what security application will run on premises and what security applications should be adopted from cloud service providers. According to NIST's risk management guide, this module includes system characterization, threat identification, vulnerability identification, control analysis, likelihood determination, impact analysis, risk determination, and control recommendations (Stoneburner et al. 2002). The recommended security controls give security administrators basic building blocks to make their particular solution secure. We suggest that during the risk-assessment process, mission assurance should also be taken into account. *Mission assurance* is defined as "establishing a reasonable degree of confidence in mission success" (Alberts and Dorofee 2005). It is a continuous attribute, and the degree of mission assurance in a process is inversely related to the amount of operational risk affecting that process (Alberts and Dorofee 2005). In order to do this, the MAAP can be used. The MAAP is a heuristic to determine the degree of mission assurance in complex processes; it provides a structured approach for analyzing operational risk (Alberts and Dorofee 2005). It uses the mission to frame a risk analysis and is designed to sort through complex distributed environments. Ultimately, it produces an accurate operational risk profile. The outcome of this module is a combination of technical, management, and operational security applications that aim to eliminate or reduce identified risks. Its technical security recommendations are input to the discovery module, during which the recommended procedural and technical security applications are chosen from existing cloud service providers.

The discovery module is designed to find service providers that provide required security services identified by the security risk-assessment module. This can be done using a public repository that stores a list of services and their features, which can be accessed by customers. While looking for appropriate services, three factors should be taken into account: least cost, most appropriate, and minimal adverse impact. NIST's risk management guide suggests that customers "address the greatest risks and strive for sufficient risk mitigation at the lowest cost, with minimal impact on other mission capabilities" (Stoneburner et al. 2002). Customers use the public repository to find services that match best the identified requirements; service providers are ranked based on these factors, and finally the most appropriate ones are chosen. This module enables customers to compare services that different cloud providers offer and obtain assurance from selected cloud providers. The output of this module is a set of security services, possibly from different cloud service providers, that will be fed as input into the integration module.

Next, the integration module tailors the chosen security services from the discovery module to finalize the security building blocks the solution security administrators are developing for the organization. The output of this module is the system's security architecture, which includes an orchestrated security solution consisting of multiple security building blocks to address various security requirements. At this stage, the security architecture is embedded into the wider solution architecture that is being developed. During the integration process, confidentiality and privacy for services and data should be maintained.

The monitoring module is responsible for monitoring security services on a continuous basis. It is a real-time security-monitoring service that continuously tracks changes to system requirements that may affect security controls and reassesses control effectiveness. It monitors SLA commitments and context changes, among many other things that may affect the enterprise, and manages the migration, configuration, and contextualization of service components as a function of changes in context and/or SLA. It is also responsible for business-continuity management and incident-handling processes. In order to provide continuity, problems like recovery priorities (the customer's priorities regarding what is to be restored in case of an incident) and dependencies relevant to the restoration process should be considered. Incident management and response are part of business-continuity management. This process aims to limit the impact of unexpected and potentially disruptive events to an acceptable level for an organization. It evaluates the capacity of an organization to minimize the probability of occurrence or reduce the negative impact of an information security incident.

The framework also offers a standardized, open interface for managing security services, to create a more open and readily available market for security services.

As shown in Figure 9.3, the life cycle of the SECaaS framework is as follows:

- *Assess security risks and define security requirements:* Identify and evaluate risks and their impacts, and then recommend security controls.
- *Discover security services:* Find providers that offer required services, and choose appropriate providers.
- *Integrate security services:* Tailor the discovered security services, and finalize the security architecture.
- *Monitor security services:* Track changes to the requirements that may affect security controls.

The framework can be integrated into the enterprise's life cycle and effectively manages the different steps of the security service management life cycle.

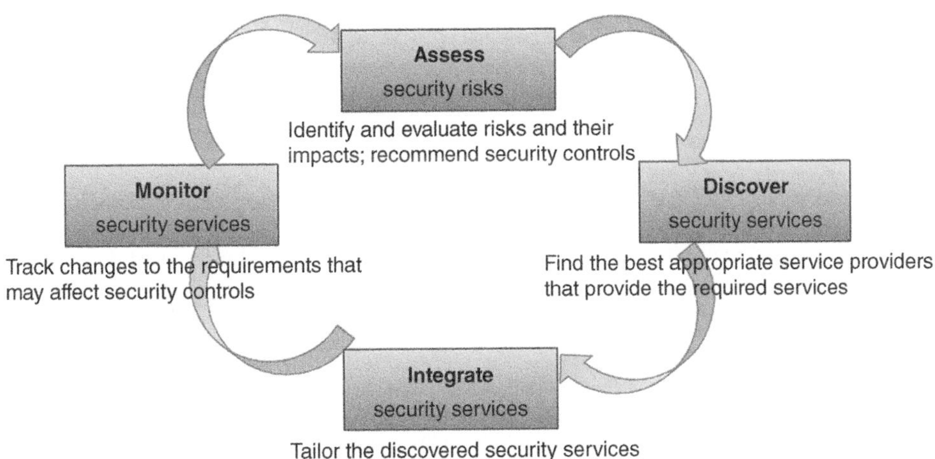

Figure 9.3 Security-as-a-Service flowchart.

An enterprise can employ our proposed framework to perform a risk analysis on various services it needs and weigh their pros and cons in order to wisely decide which assets can be secured through cloud-based SECaaS and which are too risky and costly to be based on SECaaS. For instance, an enterprise could employ the SECaaS assessment framework and decide to only consider SECaaS for its information as an asset (e.g. database activity monitoring) and its network as an asset (e.g. IPS and firewall-as-a-service [Zargar et al. 2011]), with the rest of its assets to be secured through existing or to-be-employed non-cloud-based services.

After deciding which categories of assets an enterprise would like to shop for that are available from SECaaS vendors, the next phase is to employ our risk-analysis framework again for each of the categories to evaluate various SECaaS providers available in the market. For instance, various vendors provide IPS and firewall-as-a-service, and each has pros and cons that the enterprise should evaluate before making a final decision. In order to employ our risk-assessment framework, customized, specific enterprise metrics based on the need of the enterprise should be defined to evaluate which assets to secure through SECaaS. Then, for each chosen category of assets, different customized, specific enterprise metrics should be defined to evaluate the available SECaaS services in the market. The two phases that our framework employed in this example are shown in Figure 9.4.

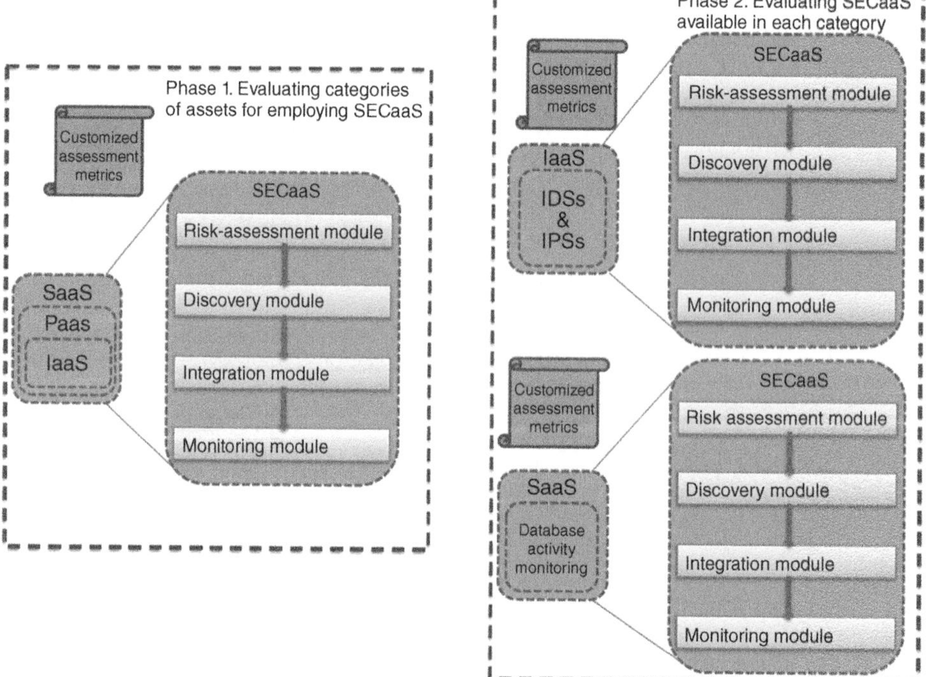

Figure 9.4 Two phases of the proposed framework that an enterprise should employ to choose SECaaS suitable for its security goals.

9.4 Conclusions

In this chapter, we have discussed the critical security requirements of enterprises. While security and privacy services in the Cloud can be fine-tuned and managed by experienced experts and hence have the potential to provide more efficient security-management and threat-assessment services, a framework is needed to assist security managers in choosing from many security and privacy services provided by different cloud service providers, and also to assist cloud providers in providing their security services more efficiently.

We have proposed an SECaaS framework that aims to facilitate adoption of security services offered in the Cloud. We introduced the framework, described its components, and explained how security managers can use it to efficiently solicit security applications required for enterprises from different cloud providers.

References

Alberts, C.J., and Dorofee, A.J. (2005). Mission Assurance Analysis Protocol (MAAP): assessing risk in complex environments. Technical Note CMU/SEI-2005-TN-032. https://resources.sei.cmu.edu/asset_files/TechnicalNote/2005_004_001_14537.pdf (accessed 6 January 2015).

Catteddu, D. and Hogben, G. (2009). Cloud computing: benefits, risks and recommendations for information security. European Network and Information Security Agency (ENISA) Report. http://www.enisa.europa.eu/act/rm/files/deliverables/cloud-computing-risk-assessment/at_download/fullReport (accessed 6 January 2015).

Chen, Y., Paxson, V., and Katz, R.H. (2010). What's new about cloud computing security? Technical Report No. UCB/EECS-2010-5, EECS Department, University of California at Berkeley. http://www.eecs.berkeley.edu/Pubs/TechRpts/2010/EECS-2010-5.html (accessed 6 January 2015).

Cloud Security Alliance (2009). Security Guidance for Critical Areas of Focus in Cloud Computing V2.1. http://cloudsecurityalliance.org/csaguide.pdf (accessed 6 January 2015).

International Organization for Standardization. (2009). Information Security Management System (ISMS) family of standards: ISO/IEC 27000:2009. http://www.iso.org/iso/catalogue_detail?csnumber=41933 (accessed 6 January 2015).

Jaeger, T. and Schiffman, J. (2010). Outlook: cloudy with a chance of security challenges and improvements. *IEEE Security and Privacy* 8 (1): 77–80.

Jensen, M., Schwenk, J., Gruschka, N. et al. (2009). On technical security issues in cloud computing. In: *Proceedings of the IEEE International Conference on Cloud Computing*, 109–116. IEEE.

Jung, Y. and Chung, M. (2010). Adaptive security management model in the cloud computing environment. In: Proceedings of the 12th International Conference on Advanced Communication Technology (ICACT), 1664–1669).

Kandukuri, B.R., Paturi, R. and Rakshit, A. (2009). Cloud security issues. In: Proceedings of the 2009 IEEE International Conference on Services Computing, 517–520).

Mell, P. and Grance, T. (2009). NIST definition of cloud computing v15. https://nvlpubs.nist.gov/nistpubs/legacy/sp/nistspecialpublication800-145.pdf (accessed 6 January 2015).

Peppetta, M. (2011). Dropbox, leading cloud computing service, suffers security failure. http://memeburn.com/2011/06/dropbox-leading-cloud-computing-service-suffers-security-failure.

Soltesz, S., Pötzl, H., Fiuczynski, M.E. et al. (2007). Container-based operating system virtualization: a scalable, high-performance alternative to hypervisors. *SIGOPS Operating Systems Review* 41 (3): 275–287.

Stoneburner, G., Goguen, A., and Feringa, A. (2002). Risk management guide for information technology systems. http://csrc.nist.gov/publications/nistpubs/800-30/sp800-30.pdf (accessed 6 January 2015).

Takabi, H., Joshi, J.B.D., and Ahn, G.J. (2010a). Security and privacy challenges in cloud computing environments. *IEEE Security and Privacy* 8 (6): 24–31.

Takabi, H., Joshi, J.B.D., and Ahn, G.J. (2010b). SecureCloud: Towards a comprehensive security framework for cloud computing environments. In: *34th Annual IEEE Computer Software and Applications Conference Workshops (COMPSACW 2010)* (ed. S.I. Ahamed, D.H. Bae, S. Cha, et al.), 393–398. IEEE Press.

Tidmarsh, D. (2010). ITS delays switch to Gmail. http://www.yaledailynews.com/news/university-news/2010/03/30/its-delays-switch-gmail-community-input (accessed August 2010).

Trusted Computing Group. (2010). Cloud computing and security – a natural match. www.trustedcomputinggroup.org (accessed 6 January 2015).

Zargar, S.T., Takabi, H., and Joshi, J.B.D. (2011). DCDIDP: A distributed, collaborative, and data-driven intrusion detection and prevention framework for cloud computing environments. Proceedings of CollaborateCom'11, 332–341).

Part II

Cloud Forensics

10

Cloud Forensics

Model, Challenges, and Approaches

Lei Chen[1], Nhien-An Le-Khac[2], Sebastian Schlepphorst[2], and Lanchuan Xu[3]

[1]*Georgia Southern University, Statesboro, GA, USA*
[2]*University College Dublin, Dublin, Ireland*
[3]*Chengdu Railway Public Security Bureau, Chengdu, China*

10.1 Introduction

As cloud technologies have emerged in recent years, cloud storage and computing have greatly enhanced everyone's work productivity and life quality in many ways. These technologies allow reliable, scalable, flexible, and cost-effective data storage and data processing through using networked systems and databases, virtual environments, and a set of cloud management and operational methods. Nonetheless, the ubiquitous applications of the Cloud provide potential opportunities for cybercriminals to hack into organizational and personal cloud environments and acquire sensitive and private data. The ever-increasing number and scale of such cyber and cloud attacks has drawn the attention of digital forensic investigators.

Traditional digital forensic investigation approaches and processes focus on the acquisition of potential digital evidence from traditional data storage devices, such as hard drives, solid state drives (SSDs), computer memory, and external storage, such as Universal Serial Bus (USB) memory keys and Secure Digital (SD) cards. Due to the distributed nature of data storage and processing in cloud computing, some of these traditional acquisition techniques have proven to be no longer valid, effective, or efficient. In a similar way, traditional digital evidence analysis is typically conducted against a digital image of a storage device, commonly loading a single file system with relatively limited total data volume to process. In the cloud environment, however, analyses occur locally and remotely, often in virtual environments.

Cloud forensics has emerged as an important area of research and practice in recent years due to the ever-growing number of cloud applications and cyberattacks. Many research findings have been presented in this field, including but are not limited to cloud acquisition, analysis, and presentation methods and tools; improved efficiency and effectiveness of these methods and tools in the cloud forensic process; and the challenges faced during forensic investigations in the cloud environment. A critical issue that demands discussion is how digital forensics, as a key component and integral part

Security, Privacy, and Digital Forensics in the Cloud, First Edition. Edited by Lei Chen, Hassan Takabi, and Nhien-An Le-Khac.

just like security, can fit into the cloud service models: i.e. Infrastructure-as-a-Service (IaaS), Platform-as-a-Service (PaaS), and Software-as-a-Service (SaaS).

In this chapter, we aim to address and discuss this important issue by first reviewing and understanding the current cloud computing model and digital forensics defined by the National Institute of Standards and Technology (NIST). Then we analyze how each digital forensic process may affect and be integrated in the cloud environment. Finally, we present our proposed model of digital forensics in the Cloud for facilitating present and future digital investigations in law enforcement.

10.2 Background

10.2.1 Cloud Computing

Cloud computing is a completely new paradigm in information technology (IT), allowing the sharing, exchange, and processing of data via a massive infrastructure and a network of properly connected and configured systems and networks. By using cloud computing and storage, there is no need for most individuals and organizations to purchase hardware and software that is not fully utilized, as was the case in the past. Instead, users and organizations may subscribe to cloud services from vendors and providers; they only need terminal systems for the purpose of human interaction and decision-making while pushing most computing and storage to the Cloud.

Cloud computing greatly extends the current IT capabilities of organizations and individuals by providing subscription-based or pay-per-use services. The study "Quantitative Estimates of the Demand for Cloud Computing in Europe and the Likely Barriers to Up-take" by the International Data Corporation (IDC) illustrated that the adoption of cloud computing is on the rise (Bradshaw et al. 2012). In fact, 32.7% of the 1,056 surveyed organizations had fully adopted cloud computing in more than one business area and 13.4% had full adoption in a single business area (Bradshaw et al. 2012).

NIST has defined cloud computing and included this definition in its released official document: "cloud computing is a model for enabling ubiquitous, convenient, on-demand network access to a shared pool of configurable computing resources (e.g. networks, servers, storage, applications, and services) that can be rapidly provisioned and released with minimal management effort or service provider interaction. This cloud model is composed of five essential characteristics, three service models, and four deployment models" (Mell and Grance 2011, p. 2). These characteristics, service models, and deployment models are discussed in detail in the next few paragraphs.

According to NIST, the five characteristics of cloud computing are on-demand self service, broad network access, resource pooling, rapid elasticity, and measured service (Kent et al. 2006). These characteristics of cloud computing indicate dramatic departures from traditional computing in many ways, e.g. user applications and interaction; data storage, transportation, and processing; individual and organizational communication; etc. (Kent et al. 2006). Consequently, the tools, methods, approaches, and procedures of digital investigation must adapt to this new paradigm to remain effective and efficient.

NIST has categorized cloud computing's service models into three types: IaaS, PaaS), and SaaS) (Mell and Grance 2011). The goal of IaaS is to provide processing, storage, networks, and other fundamental computing resources to consumers so that they can deploy and use operating systems (OSs) and applications that run on top of the OS. In IaaS, typically customers or end users have control of the OS, storage, and applications, and in certain scenarios they may also have limited control over network components and configurations, such as the host firewalls and intrusion detection systems (IDSs) (Mell and Grance 2011). In the PaaS service model, customers are typically allowed to deploy applications and software generated on their own or acquired from a third party. Such a service model requires cloud service providers to facilitate customers and provide platform-relevant components, including hardware, programming languages, libraries, services, and tools (Mell and Grance 2011). Given that in PaaS, customers' interests mainly involve application development, they may not need or may not have much control over the underlying cloud infrastructure; this saves developers the cost and time of purchasing and configuring their own hardware, network, and OS environment (Mell and Grance 2011). SaaS aims to provide applications and software tools to customers either by subscription or by a pay-per-use model, instead of paying for an up-front perpetual software license. In this service model, typically, customers do not manage or control the cloud infrastructure, although they may have access to user-specific application configuration settings and applications or user data, which are typically stored in the cloud environment and may impose some cost (Mell and Grance 2011).

In each of these cloud service models, end users have different levels of access to the cloud infrastructure, OSs, application software, and data; and levels of access should be clearly defined for security, privacy, and management purposes. Table 10.1 illustrates access control for customers in the three cloud service models (Edington and Kishore 2016). The SaaS model give customers the least amount of access because they only need to run the software applications, while PaaS provides application access because software developers need to modify the application code for development purposes. IaaS provides the most access to customers: essentially, customers have virtual machines running in the cloud environment, facilitated by cloud service providers.

Four cloud computing deployment models are defined by NIST: public cloud, private cloud, hybrid cloud, and community cloud (Mell and Grance 2011). In a public cloud, service providers typically provide resources like virtual machines (VMs), application

Table 10.1 Customer access control in three different cloud service models.

Level of access / Service model	IaaS	PaaS	SaaS
Basic access	✓	✓	✓
Applications	✓	✓	✗
Data	✓	✗	✗
Runtime	✓	✗	✗
Middleware	✓	✗	✗
Operating systems	✓	✗	✗
Virtualization	✗	✗	✗
Servers	✗	✗	✗
Storage	✗	✗	✗
Networking	✗	✗	✗

software, and storage to general public end customers. In contrast, a private cloud provides services to specified clients or customers; therefore, the underlying cloud infrastructure, OSs, software applications, and user and environment configurations and settings can be highly customized for security and many other reasons. A community cloud commonly has shared resources and applications among multiple entities or organizations, with an agreed-on policy for the deployment and use of the Cloud. A hybrid cloud is a mixture of two or more cloud deployment types (Mell and Grance 2011).

10.2.2 Digital Forensics

While the increased adoption of cloud computing greatly helps organizations improve their work productivity and efficiency, it may create opportunities for cybercriminals to expand their illegal activities through or in the Cloud. Commonly found cybercrimes and illegal cyber activities include, but are not limited to, identity and data theft, internet fraud, business espionage, child pornography, and cyberterrorism, among others (Chen et al. 2015). Law-enforcement personnel and agencies from around the world are increasingly faced with companies and individuals engaged in illegal cyber activities. Some of the digital forensic investigation leaders, in terms of technologies, implementation, and enforcement, are the United States, Mainland China, the United Kingdom, Ireland, Canada, Australia, and Hong Kong (Chen et al. 2015).

NIST defines *digital forensics* as "the application of science to the identification, collection, examination, and analysis of data while preserving the integrity of the information and maintaining a strict chain of custody for the data" (Kent et al. 2006, p. 9). Given that the storage, processing, and transmission of data has changed in the cloud environment compared to the traditional environment, it is obvious that some of the conventional approaches and tools use by digital investigators may no longer be valid, effective, or efficient. In the literature, there is discussion and analysis of digital forensics in the IaaS cloud service model; however, no existing work or proposals in the context of digital forensics can be found for the PaaS or SaaS cloud service models.

Compared to the definition of digital forensics given by NIST, that given by Palmer at the Digital Forensic Research Workshop (DFRWS) was welcomed by researchers and practitioners: "the use of scientifically derived and proven methods toward the preservation, collection, validation, identification, analysis, interpretation and presentation of digital evidence derived from digital sources for the purpose of facilitating or furthering the reconstruction of events found to be criminal, or helping to anticipate unauthorized actions shown to be disruptive to planned operations" (Palmer 2001, p. 16). The proposed process of digital forensics can be compressed into four main phases: identification, collection, examination, and presentation of the digital data and evidence. These four phases are further discussed in the following paragraphs.

Identification is the phase where investigators identify the potential system, storage, and location where critical crime-related data may be found for solving a case (Palmer 2001). Traditionally, this would refer to hard drives, USB memory keys, CD-ROMs, computer memory, and network component buffers or cache, among others. In the cloud environment, however, it becomes a challenge to identify where potential digital evidence may reside, as this varies among cloud service models, along with how much access customers may have and what can be accessed by customers, as well as the underlying cloud infrastructure.

In the phase of collection, the investigator collects and seizes the hardware devices, along with the OSs, applications and data found in these hardware devices while preserving the chain of custody and integrity of hardware, software and data (Palmer 2001). Due to the same aforementioned reasons, this becomes extremely difficult.

In the *examination* phase, investigators analyze the identified and collected hardware, software, and data using appropriate digital forensic tools, which help locate, retrieve, and interpret digital evidence so that it can be used to support proof of illegal activities (Palmer 2001). Almost all the conventional digital forensics tools were developed for non-cloud devices and environments and therefore may not work or may need significant modifications in the cloud environment.

In the *presentation* phase, investigators prepare a final report stating the conclusion from the examination phase with the support of identified and analyzed digital evidence. This report will be presented to the judge and jury, who may not fully understand the cloud infrastructure or service models and may not be convinced by the presented linkage between the digital evidence and potential illegal activities (Palmer 2001).

For these and many other reasons, there is an increased demand for a well-considered model for digital forensics in cloud computing. Some existing works in the literature have prepared for this purpose by providing a definition of cloud forensics. For example, (Ruan et al. 2011) conducted a survey among digital forensic experts and practitioners on cloud forensics and critical criteria for cloud forensics capabilities. Based on the survey results and a continuing survey in 2013 (Ruan et al. 2013), they defined *cloud forensics* as "the application of digital forensic science in cloud computing environments. Technically, it consists of a hybrid forensic approach (e.g. remote, virtual, network, live, large-scale, thin-client, thick-client) towards the generation of digital evidence. Organizationally it involves interactions among cloud actors (i.e. cloud provider, cloud consumer, cloud broker, cloud carrier, and cloud auditor) for the purpose of facilitating both internal and external investigations. Legally it often implies multi- jurisdictional and multi-tenant situations" (Ruan et al. 2013). With the foundation laid out by this study, we further investigate the process and propose our cloud forensic model in the following section.

10.3 Process and Model of Cloud Forensics

In recent years, cloud computing and storage services have provided customers with massive amounts of data storage space and enormous computing capabilities. Service providers such as Amazon, Dropbox, and Google all have cloud service plans and packages available at reasonable costs to customers. The storage and organization of data, compared to the conventional computing environment, has changed from local or traditional networks to the Cloud. This indicates that data may not be stored on a single server at a single location; data storage and communications may span more than one jurisdictional region, and there exist significant challenges to digital investigations in such a new environment (Zargari and Smith 2013; Thethi and Keane 2014; Chen et al. 2015). As an example, a photo posted on a user's Facebook wall may be shared through a link to a directory in the same user's Microsoft OneDrive.

10.3.1 Forensics Moving into the Cloud

Data in the Cloud may be stored in different cloud servers and nodes, and there may be one or more synchronized or unsynchronized copies of data in the Cloud and connected personal or organizational computers. As an example, users of Google Drive File Stream have the option of having a synchronized copy of selected data on multiple computers and devices. A user may choose to have certain files and directories be synchronized on a certain device. Some devices may not always be connected to the Cloud or may not be synchronized to what is stored in the user's Google Drive. Therefore, there is a challenge as to what and from where potential digital evidence should be acquired. In addition, cloud data may be shared among multiple users or parties, and a user may not own certain files found in that user's cloud storage (Chen et al. 2015). The access control and privileges of shared files also vary and may cause difficulty and confusion in digital forensic investigations (Chen et al. 2015). Furthermore, it is not uncommon for files to be split into data blocks that may be stored over multiple cloud computer nodes and even in different jurisdiction regions (Wu et al. 2012).

Given the aforementioned situations and challenges, it is crucially important to conduct redundant data cleaning and data validation throughout the entire digital investigation process. The timing of data acquisition also plays an important role in the process due to the dynamic and sharing characteristics of cloud data (Chen et al. 2015). Consequently, traditional digital forensic processes and models may not be effective or efficient for cloud forensics, and a new process model that reflects the cloud environment and pertinent approaches is urgently needed.

10.3.2 Cloud Forensics Process

While the methods and approaches in each digital forensic phase are quite different, the overall forensic process in the Cloud resembles that in a traditional environment. The initial step is to determine the locations of data for acquisition purposes. In the traditional digital forensic process, this refers to identifying local or network user accounts, specific hard disks, partitions, volumes, USB memory keys, external memory storage, and memory segments, among others (Chen et al. 2015). In the cloud environment, this requires identifying the cloud storage service providers, cloud user accounts and pertinent cloud drives, shared data, users among whom the data is shared, etc. The next phase is to preserve data integrity, which is commonly implemented by running hash functions over acquired data images in traditional digital forensics. However, in the cloud environment, it becomes a challenge to determine what data to hash and where the hashing should be performed (Wu and Yang 2010).

Details of the collection, extraction, analysis, and fixation of digital evidence are further discussed in the rest of this section. These discussions and elaborations will help us visualize a dynamic cloud forensic model that is proposed in Section 10.3.3.

10.3.2.1 Digital Evidence Collection and Extraction

Digital evidence may reside in all kinds of data and information, including but not limited to network and system information, files and directories, file system information, user and group information, policies, and logs, among many others (Chen et al. 2015). In the cloud environment, such data and information are found in distributed storage and virtual environments, which increases data volatility and makes it difficult to track data (Li and Deng 2012). Therefore, it is critically important for the digital evidence acquirer to obtain the order and locations of data creation and processing (Li and Deng 2012). Four different aspects of the cloud environment must be examined by investigators (Chen et al. 2013) for these reasons, and they are further elaborated in the following paragraphs.

Regardless of the cloud service model (IaaS, PaaS, or SaaS), the foremost examination must be conducted directly in the Cloud (Zhang 2010). While the digital investigator may not be an expert in cloud technologies, they must understand the technical details of cloud services, including but not limited to commonly used cloud devices, platforms, software, configurations, and access control by providers (Zhang 2010). When possible, investigators may need to obtain saved data, user access, and system logs from providers. (Zhang 2010) suggested that four categories of information need to be collected: infrastructure and equipment information, virtual information, application and service information, and information regarding intrusion-alarm records and relevant access logs. In addition, we consider that, depending on the cloud service model, the quantity and level of information to collect should vary. Table 10.1, for example, indicates that information at the virtualization, server, storage, and networking levels should be examined regardless of the cloud model. For the IaaS model, however, since clients have the access to the OS and all levels above it, detailed information pertinent to user activities and control at these levels should be collected and examined.

Local computer systems should also be examined for any possible digital evidence (Zhang 2010). The reason is that, regardless of the cloud service model, data transfers occur between local computers and the Cloud, and therefore data fragments and caches may still reside locally. Possible valuable information includes partial, deleted, or damaged files; user activities and data-communication logs; remote computer and server information; security parameters; and digital certificates and public keys, among others (Zhang 2010). Traditional digital forensics tools and methods can be very useful in this process.

In addition to the cloud environment and local systems, network audit nodes should also be examined (Zhang 2010). Such nodes include but are not limited to proxy servers and servers or systems where cloud computing security audits run. Typically, these computer nodes understand data up to the application layer in the Open Systems Interconnection (OSI) or Transmission Control Protocol/Internet Protocol (TCP/IP) network model, and are likely equipped with traffic analyzers and IDSs; therefore, they may provide invaluable information.

If potential digital evidence may exist in the subclouds of a large-scale cloud, then these subclouds should also be examined (Zhang 2010). In fact, examination and data acquisition directly conducted in the subcloud environment typically cost less and are less time-consuming when compared to the parent large-scale cloud (Zhang 2010).

The extraction of data aims to restore deleted data and reconstruct hidden files. If the Cloud supports Forensics-as-a-Service (FaaS), this process can then be accomplished entirely on the cloud side; otherwise, cloud-oriented forensic tools and methods need to be employed to retrieve data from the Cloud to the local investigation lab. The details of this process are discussed in later sections of this chapter as well as in later chapters of this book.

10.3.2.2 Evidence Analysis and Fixation

Redundant data cleaning and deep data analysis are two main evidence-analysis aspects in cloud forensics (Chen et al. 2015). The sharing of cloud data may generate multiple complete or partial copies of data across the Cloud and on more than one local system. Such redundant data should be identified, and a track of changes should be recorded for files and directories. Deep data analysis is essential in correlating data from various locations and sources (Chen et al. 2015). One example would be finding the same file or different versions of the same file on cloud storage and local systems, synchronized among a group of clients who have shared the same document. Finding the correlation of the evidence among different sources can often assist in investigations. Software technology and data mining are suggested for solving the problems of incomplete and inadequate evidence (Huang et al. 2013). Ultimately, the purpose of deep data analysis is to ensure that acquired data is complete, accurate, and not redundant.

The purpose of evidence fixation is to guarantee the integrity and genuineness of the evidence throughout the investigation process following relevant regulations (Miao 2013). Similar to traditional digital forensics, it is equally important to ensure the credibility and validity of digital evidence; therefore, the operating environment should avoid any possible unnecessary changes. Necessary changes should be justified and proven without jeopardizing the integrity of the evidence. For such purposes, environmental variables should be recorded, and a track of changes should be documented (Chen et al. 2015).

10.3.3 Dynamic Cloud Forensics Model

This section further discusses the processes of cloud forensics. Based on these processes, we propose a cloud forensic model, shown in Figure 10.1, aiming at providing overall guidance for cloud investigations. More details of this model are addressed toward the end of this section.

Many researchers have proposed cloud-based forensic architecture and models. For example, (Lin 2013) proposed a cloud-based forensic architecture expected to enhance the efficiency of data acquisition and analysis. A cloud forensics model aiming to improve the efficiency and safety of digital evidence was proposed by (Gong et al. 2012). The cloud forensic model presented by (Zhang and Mai 2011) tackles the problem of efficiency by using dynamic parallel processing. An example of a model to solve cloud security problems is the computer cloud forensic system was presented by (Wu et al. 2012). (Chen et al. 2015) proposed a dynamic cloud forensic model considering both redundant data cleaning and deep data analysis for cloud data. Based on these cloud models, we propose a cloud forensic model that is simple and clear yet shows the important mandatory processes and components in cloud forensics.

Figure 10.1 shows our proposed model in a top-down architecture. The first step in cloud forensics is to determine what to collect and where to collect artifacts. Digital artifacts may be found in the cloud environment at service providers, in subclouds, end users' devices, and proxy and audit servers (refer to Section 10.3.2.1). The orange arrows in Figure 10.1 refer to data acquisition. The components and functionalities in the green box can be implemented at a cloud forensic service center, which may support more than one end digital forensic lab and its associated investigators. The center collects raw forensic data from various sources and completes three major tasks: redundant data

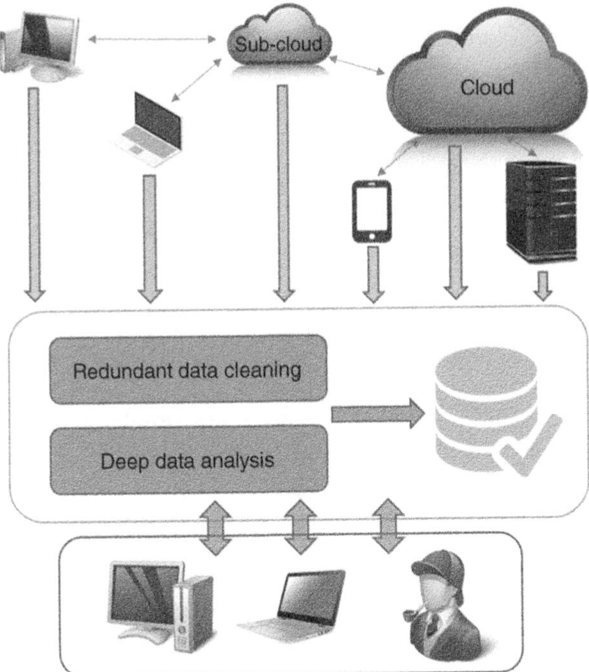

Figure 10.1 Proposed cloud forensic model.

cleaning, deep data analysis, and storing the processed data in a database, ready to be further processed by end forensic labs and investigators. We consider that this process should be separated from the end forensic lab and investigators for a few reasons. Many forensics labs and private investigators do not have the resources or time to cope with cloud service providers. They may not have the hardware, software, or direct access to cloud data needed for forensic investigations. Cloud forensic service centers, which may be funded by the government or authorized companies with sufficient funding and resources, can serve as agents in acquiring raw cloud data and preprocessing, analyzing, and preparing the data in the form preferred by end forensic labs and investigators. We estimate that this model helps reduce the complexity and overhead to the investigators and therefore leads to a more efficient, reliable, accurate cloud forensic process. The authors of Chapter 12 of this book review a number of existing cloud forensic models and propose their model, which may provide readers with more insight into cloud forensic modeling and processes.

10.4 Cloud Forensics Methods, Approaches, and Tools

10.4.1 Methods and Approaches

Forensic triage is essentially a quick investigative screening process that typically happens at the initial stage of the investigation (Roussev et al. 2013; Parsonage 2014; Thethi and Keane 2014). This is especially useful when dealing with enormous amounts of data in a cloud investigation case; particularly, it is suggested that forensic triage should be conducted outside the lab environment and before acquiring or analyzing any digital evidence (Parsonage 2014). In cloud forensic practice, investigators are typically facing the challenge of determining and retrieving the most pertinent information from an immense amount of raw data, within time constraints. In addition, compared to traditional forensics, there is a strong demand for standard forensics methods and tools. Given this situation, triage is considered necessary in cloud forensics and defined as "a partial forensic examination conducted under (significant) time and resource constraints" (Roussev et al. 2013).

High-performance computing systems and high-speed networks should be utilized for cloud data acquisition and analysis in the cloud environment (Roussev et al. 2013; Thethi and Keane 2014). The enormous amount of data transferred and processed in cloud forensics requires that the investigation process be treated as a formal software-engineering process (Roussev et al. 2013). In other words, there should be well-recognized, widely agreed-on principles and techniques to be applied to cloud forensics, and investigative activities should be traceable, measurable with regard to efficiency and effectiveness, repeatable, predictable, and subsequently optimizable (Roussev et al. 2013).

Compared to utilizing high-performance computing, FaaS gives users an advantage by allowing simple, basic forensic investigations on their end (Zargari and Smith 2013; Thethi and Keane 2014). Such investigations include accessing certain logs and configuration files and recovering deleted files, among others. FaaS further indicates that the Cloud can provide interfaces and functionalities supporting remote forensic investigations. As an example, XIRAF, a service-based digital forensic system and approach, was proposed in 2016 to process large volumes of acquired data (Alink et al. 2006). As early as 2010, the Netherlands Forensic Institute began to use XIRAF for more efficient digital forensic investigations. (Lee and Un 2012) described a type of FaaS using the term *forensic cloud*, where cloud servers allow remote indexing against terms and meaningful patterns for forensic keyword searches in Apache HBase. HBase, part of the Apache Hadoop project, is an open source, distributed, nonrelational database used by many cloud and social network services, including Facebook Messenger Platform (https://hbase.apache.org). More discussion of FaaS can be found in Chapter 16.

Users and organizations have a long list of choices in terms of cloud storage and service providers. Many of them, such as Amazon, Dropbox, Google, and Microsoft, provide similar services at comparable prices. (Chung et al. 2012) suggested that digital investigators should be familiar with file system locations, tools, and techniques for identifying and acquiring digital artifacts among various providers. For instance, for a behavior such as downloading and opening a file or accessing cloud storage using a web browser on a local computer, an investigator should know where and how to find and retrieve artifacts based on a combination of the type of file (Microsoft Office, Google Docs, etc.), cloud service provider (Amazon, Dropbox, Google Drive, etc.), web browser (Chrome, Internet Explorer, Firefox, etc.), and OS (Windows 10, Windows 7, Linux, macOS, iOS, Android, etc.) (Chung et al. 2012). As an example, this same user behavior using IE 8.0 in a Windows 7 environment might generate a file named s3.amazonaws.com.lnk in a local path while leaving little or no trace when using Firefox 9.0 in a Mac environment after the browser is closed (Chung et al. 2012).

Users' social network profiles, activities, and behaviors may provide valuable information to digital investigators. For example, a Facebook user may share photos stored on Google Drive via posted links. And interactions with work-related friends on Facebook may indicate a possible profile of the same user on LinkedIn and other social networks that utilize cloud storage and computing, possibly linking to potential artifacts. For different social networks, different forensic tools, programming APIs, and credentials are required to extract user profile and data. As an example, the Representational State Transfer (REST) API, JavaScript Object Notation (JSON), and Python programming language are needed to extract a Twitter user's profile and status (Howden et al. 2013).

10.4.2 Tools

Many traditional digital forensics tools have been updated with new features to support cloud forensics. For example, the industry-leading digital forensic tools EnCase (https://www.guidancesoftware.com/encase-forensic) and AccessData Forensic Toolkit (FTK) (https://www.accessdata.com/products-services/forensic-toolkit-ftk) can acquire data from a cloud environment from certain cloud providers. According to (Zawoad and Hasan 2014), data can be acquired from the Amazon Elastic Compute Cloud (EC2) cloud environment using an EnCase servlet or FTK Remote Agent. Magnet Forensics' Internet Evidence Finder (IEF) and other third-party software extensions and hardware dongles may help further expand the capability to cope with other providers' clouds and even social networks (https://www.magnetforensics.com/magnet-ief). F-Response, an example competitor tool, utilizes software extensions and hardware connectors to remotely mount cloud storage, such as Amazon S3, Windows Azure storage, and OpenStack Cloud Files, thus providing seamless, efficient cloud forensics (www.f-response.com).

Enormous amounts of data must be acquired in cloud forensics. It is common for acquiring just 1TB of cloud data to take a few days, which may not be acceptable in certain investigations. In order to test and evaluate the speed and efficiency of cloud data acquisition, (Thethi and Keane 2014) performed testing against Amazon EC2 with different tools. In their testing, the total time consisted of two parts: actual data acquisition time (AT) and data verification time (VT). The winner used a combination of Amazon AWS Snapshot (https://cloudranger.com/aws-snapshots) and the dd command in Linux (http://+www.forensicswiki.org/wiki/Dd) to acquire 30GB of cloud data; the process required 5.09 hours AT and 0.33 hours VT with a total acquisition time of 5.42 hours (Thethi and Keane 2014). As a comparison, FTK Imager Lite achieved 6.76 total AT, and FTK Remote Agent needed 9.23 hours to complete the same task (Thethi and Keane 2014). With FaaS, this process is expected to be much faster and more efficient.

10.5 Challenges in Cloud Forensics

This section discusses challenges in cloud forensics. The cloud forensics processes and model presented in Section 10.3 are meaningful in providing an essential framework to investigators. The methods, approaches, and tools for cloud forensics discussed in Section 10.4 can be practical and helpful for cloud forensic investigations in reality.

Nonetheless, challenges still exist in cloud forensics, and some of them are discussed in this section.

With cloud storage and computing widely used in many countries and regions, one of the main challenges is that data may reside on and transfer among computers and networks in different jurisdictional areas, where laws and regulations regarding data security and privacy may be very different (Chen et al. 2013). While technical issues can be solved by employing the same or similar tools and methods in data acquisition and analysis, these nontechnical issues should be addressed by following the laws and regulations of the country and local regions, which typically introduces overhead such as cost, time, and difficulties (Chen et al. 2015).

Cloud services and programs typically run continuously in a distributed environment maintained by service providers. Compared to mobile service carriers, cloud service providers store and process much larger volumes of customer data, and they may not be willing to pause or stop services and support data acquisition and restoration, or give access permissions to the cloud environment for investigation purpose (Chen et al. 2013). Given such situations, working with service providers may significantly delay the progress of digital investigations.

Much of the data from the Cloud is nontraditional or nonstandard, thus imposing significant challenges to data acquisition and fixation (Chen et al. 2013). It is also very difficult to preserve digital evidence over time due to the dynamic, heterogeneous nature of cloud data. In traditional digital forensics, system and network audits are very helpful in quickly identifying potential artifacts. However, in the cloud environment, audits become very difficult due to extremely dynamic networks and highly complex data organization and processing (Zheng 2012). This also indicates that due to short life cycles, artifacts may not be traceable or available at all time, and subsequently it can be very difficult to distinguish suspicious and regular activities (Zheng 2012).

10.6 Conclusions

This chapter is the opening for Part II of this book. We discussed models, processes, approaches, methods, tools, and challenges in cloud forensics. Some of these topics are further deliberated in the following chapters. In summary, the Cloud is a dynamic and complex environment in many ways: how and where data is stored and processed, user activities and accesses, service providers' roles and control over the Cloud, and jurisdictions on the legal side, among others. We hope that this chapter and this book provide readers and practitioners with information that can help improve the efficiency and enhance the accuracy of cloud forensic investigations.

References

Alink, W., Bhoedjang, R., Boncz, P.A., and De Vries, A.P. (2006). Xiraf-xml-based indexing and querying for digital forensics. *Digital Investigation* 3: 50–58.

Bradshaw, D., Folco, G., Cattaneo, G. et al. (2012). Quantitative estimates of the demand for cloud computing in Europe and the likely barriers to up-take. European Commission - DG Information Society.

Chen, G., Du, Y., Du, J., and Li, N. (2013). Research of digital forensics under cloud computing environment. *Netinfo Security* 2013 (8): 87–90.

Chen, L., Xu, L., Yuan, X. et al. (2015). Digital forensics in social networks and the cloud: process, approaches, methods, tools, and challenges. In: Proceedings of the 2015 IEEE International Conference on Computing, Networking and Communications (ICNC). IEEE.

Chung, H., Park, P., Lee, S. et al. (2012). Digital forensic investigation of cloud storage services. *Digital Investigation* 9 (2): 81–95.

Edington, M. and Kishore, R. (2016). Forensic model for cloud computing: an overview. In Proceedings of the 2016 International Conference on Wireless Communications, Signal Processing and Networking (WiSPNET), Chennai, India, March 23-25, 2016. IEEE.

Gong, W., Liu, P., and Chi, X. (2012). Construction and analysis of cloud forensics model. *Computer Engineer* 38 (11): 14–16.

Howden, C., Liu, L., Ding, Z. et al. (2013). Moments in time: a forensic view of Twitter. In: 2013 IEEE International Conference on Green Computing and Communications and IEEE Internet of Things and IEEE Cyber, Physical and Social Computing, 899–908. IEEE.

Huang, W., Pang, R., and Rong, Z. (2013). A new type of electronic evidence study based on cloud computing platform. *Chinese Criminal Science* 10 (10): 61–65.

Kent, K., Chevalier, S., Grance, T. et al. (2006). Guide to integrating forensic techniques into incident response. https://www.nist.gov/publications/guide-integrating-forensic-techniques-incident-response (accessed 24 March 2018).

Lin, Q. (2013). Research on cloud forensics based on the internet of things. *Netinfo Security* 2013 (7): 61–64.

Lee, J. and Un, S. (2012). Digital forensics as a service: a case study of forensic indexed search. In: 2012 International Conference on ICT Convergence, 499–503. IEEE.

Li, X. and Deng, Z. (2012). Study on electronic forensic in cloud computing environment. *China Information Security* 2012 (11): 52–54.

Miao, H. (2013). Forensics scheme in cloud computing environment. *Practical Electronics* 2013 (24): 88–89.

Mell, P. and Grance, T. (2011). The NIST definition of cloud computing: recommendations of the National Institute of Standards and Technology. https://nvlpubs.nist.gov/nistpubs/legacy/sp/nistspecialpublication800-145.pdf (accessed 24 March 2018).

Parsonage, H. (2014). Computer forensics case assessment and triage. http://computerforensics.parsonage.co.uk/triage.

Palmer, G. (ed.) (2001). A road map for digital forensic research. From the Proceedings of The Digital Forensic Research Conference. DFRWS.

Roussev, Y., Quates, C., and Martell, R. (2013). Real-time digital forensics and triage. *Digital Investigation* 10 (2): 158–167.

Ruan, K., Baggili, I.P., Carthy, J. et al. (2011). Survey on cloud forensics and critical criteria for cloud forensic capability: a preliminary analysis. In: Proceedings of the Conference on Digital Forensics, Security and Law, 16.

Ruan, K., Carthy, J., Kechadi, T., and Baggili, I. (2013). Cloud forensics definitions and critical criteria for cloud forensic capability: an overview of survey results. *Digital Investigation* 10 (1): 34–43.

Thethi, N. and Keane, A. (2014). Digital forensics investigations in the Cloud. In: Proceedings of the 2014 IEEE International Advance Computing Conference, 1475–1480. IEEE.

Wu, L., Wang, L., and Gu, W. (2012). Research on computer forensics system based on cloud computing. *Computer Science* 39 (5): 83–85.

Wu, T. and Yang, Y. (2010). Study on security analysis and forensics in cloud computing. *Telecommunications Science* 26 (12): 79–82.

Zargari, S.A. and Smith, A. (2013). Policing as a service in the Cloud. In: Proceedings of the 2013 Fourth International Conference on Emerging Intelligent Data and Web Technologies, 589–596. doi:10.1109/EIDWT.2013.106 (accessed 24 March 2018).

Zawoad, S. and Hasan, R. (2014). Cloud forensics: a meta-study of challenges, approaches, and open problems. http://arxiv.org/pdf/1302.6312.pdf.

Zhang, C. (2010). Under cloud calculative environment electronic data investigation and evidence collection. *Netinfo Security* 2010 (11): 52–54.

Zhang, J. and Mai, Y. (2011). Cloud computing environment simulation computer forensics. *Netinfo Security* 2011 (10): 87–90.

Zheng, Q. (2012). Computer forensic research base on cloud architecture. *Journal of Fujian Police Academy* 26 (2): 60–63.

11

Cyberterrorism in the Cloud

Through a Glass Darkly

Barry Cartwright[1], George R. S. Weir[2], and Richard Frank[1]

[1]Simon Fraser University, Burnaby, BC, Canada
[2]University of Strathclyde, Glasgow, UK

11.1 Introduction

A 2002 article in the *Washington Post* carried the headline: "Cyber-Attacks by Al Qaeda Feared; Terrorists at Threshold of Using Internet as Tool of Bloodshed, Experts Say" (Gellman 2002). In the same year, a Global Information Assurance Certification Paper appeared, bearing the title "Ghosts in the Machine: The Who, Why, and How of Attacks on Information Security" (Barker 2002). Indeed, from the late 1990s onward – shortly after the emergence of the World Wide Web – governments, law enforcement agencies, and nongovernmental observers alike were sounding early alarm bells regarding the prospects of information security breaches and terrorist attacks in cyberspace (Luiijf 2014). As Thomas (2003) observed in his article about Al Qaeda's love for the internet, "people are afraid of things that are invisible and things that they don't understand."

Much the same can be said for the oft-stated concerns about vulnerabilities in the Cloud. If you ask the average person on the street (or even the average first-year university student) to explain the origin of the term *cloud computing*, many will respond by pointing upward and saying that "it's in the Cloud," or by saying that it involves satellite technology (and therefore, that "it's in the clouds"), or by opining that it's called cloud computing because of Apple's iCloud. Few, if any, will know that it is called cloud computing because computer engineers have for decades drawn a picture of a cloud in the center of their flow charts and diagrams, with the cloud representing the internet, surrounded by the servers, databases, corporate local area networks (LANs), wireless networks, mobile devices, and other digital devices too numerous to mention, all of which are connected to the internet, or the Cloud (Weinberger 2015). But while users (or observers) of cloud services might feel that it is all very mysterious, and be worried about unknown vulnerabilities in the Cloud, it could be said that the Cloud has so far proven to be less vulnerable to attack than in-house information technology (IT) services, perhaps because it involves comparatively new and sophisticated technology (Beazer 2016). Moreover, because of the finances required to implement a cloud host, they tend to be well defended.

Security, Privacy, and Digital Forensics in the Cloud, First Edition. Edited by Lei Chen, Hassan Takabi, and Nhien-An Le-Khac.

The precise origins of the term *cloud computing* are a bit up in the air, with some claiming that it first appeared in a *New York Times* article in 2001, wherein the internet was described as a "cloud of computers"; others claiming that it originated at a 1996 meeting at Compaq in Houston; and still others pointing out that telecom engineers were putting a cloud in the center of their diagrams as far back as the 1970s and 1980s. However, the term *cloud computing* did not truly enter the common lexicon until a 2006 conference, at which Eric Schmidt of Google stated that Google's services belonged "in a cloud somewhere" (Fogarty 2012). Nowadays, despite not thinking about it or understanding exactly how cloud technology works, billions of people make daily use of cloud-based services such as YouTube, Facebook, and Flickr (Gayathri et al. 2012). That said, if cyberterrorism and cloud computing are mentioned in the same sentence, it is likely to evoke a fear-based response.

In this chapter, we will explore the degree to which cyberterrorism and cloud computing are interrelated (or not, as the case may be). To accomplish this, we will first consider whether there have been any meaningful incidents of cyberterrorism to date, and offer a definition against which future incidents purporting to be representative of cyberterrorism can be measured. We will then consider how terrorists make use of cyberspace, and ask whether there is anything that renders cloud-based services more vulnerable or more amenable to terrorist activities in cyberspace. We will also explore the nexus between cyberlaw and cyberterrorism, paying attention to jurisdictional issues and the problems that invariably crop up when dealing with politically charged, transnational events. Finally, we will consider future directions that cyberterrorism might take, and whether the Cloud might be a facilitator or a target of such attacks.

11.2 What Is Terrorism?

According to the *Oxford English Dictionary*, the term *terrorism* (*terrorisme*) first appeared in 1795, when it was used by Thomas Paine to describe the "reign of terror" carried out by the political leaders of France during the French Revolution. Since then, it has been applied to a vast range of seemingly unconnected scenarios, from being used by G. J. Adler in 1854 to describe the manner in which the "terrorism of a narrow-minded clique" of academics in New York contributed to the subjugation of university students, to the "social terrorism" committed by trade unions in the United Kingdom in 1863, to being used by an American newspaper in 1935 to describe the 28 "terrorism suspects" who were arrested in connection with a coal miners' strike in the United States (www.oed.com).

It is only since the late 1960s that the term *terrorism* has been widely used to describe politically motivated attacks by disenfranchised or disenchanted fringe groups, who deliberately set out to inflict maximal physical destruction and/or casualties on a civilian population, ostensibly for the purpose of creating terror in the general population, but with the underlying intention of sending a powerful message to their political leaders. The concept of terrorism as we know it today sprang into the public imagination as the world watched in July 1968, when "Palestinian terrorists" hijacked el Al flight 426 from Rome to Tel Aviv and diverted it to Rome with 10 crew members and 38 passengers on board (Jenkins and Johnson 1975), and again in September 1972, when eight "Arab terrorists" kidnapped the members of the Israeli team at the Olympics in Munich, leading to the death of 11 Israelis and four of the hostage-takers (Binder 1972). The 9/11 attack on the World Trade Center in New York, orchestrated by Al Qaeda, serves as a more recent example of this type of terrorism.

Sometimes, terrorist activities are orchestrated by political leaders, in an effort to instill terror in their own civilian population for the purpose of maintaining or restoring social order, and ultimately, to protect the power and privilege of the leaders. To illustrate, we need look no further than Bashar al-Assad and his bombings of and chemical attacks on the Syrian people. Al-Assad insists that the Syrian regime and its Russian allies are working together on the front lines, busily fighting ISIS "terrorists" (TASS 2017), and has even invited the US to join his "fight against terrorism" (Solomon 2017). At the same time, al-Assad has claimed that "the West, mainly the United States, is hand-in-glove with the terrorists" (Knox and Hodge 2017). On the other hand, British Foreign Secretary Boris Johnson has accused al-Assad of being an "arch terrorist" following the chemical attacks in the province of Idlib (Chaplain 2017), while a Spanish court is presently investigating "Syrian 'state terrorism' by the Assad regime" in connection with the kidnapping, torture, and death of a truck driver whose sister lives in Spain (Jones 2017).

Thus, we can say that terms such as *terrorism* and *terrorist* tend to be applied in a highly subjective fashion. Terrorists are typically portrayed as the very personification of evil, while those who designate others as terrorists are portrayed as the rightfully elected upholders of the law – as the defenders of life, liberty, and freedom. Wherever possible, leaders of the "civilized world" refer to insurgents as "unlawful combatants," thereby conferring legitimacy onto their own actions, while denying legitimacy to those who are fighting back against superior and in many cases overwhelming military force (van Baarda 2009). As Howard Becker (1963) pointed out in his renowned work on labelling theory, deviance is not so much the quality of the act itself, but rather, the consequence of rules and sanctions being applied to the offender by rule makers and rule enforcers. To extrapolate from this, the likelihood of an act being defined as terrorism – or a "freedom fighter" being labeled successfully as an "unlawful combatant" – depends very much on who commits the act, who believes that they are being harmed, and who has the power to impose (or to deflect) the label.

To look at it from a different angle, one person's terrorist might well be regarded as another person's freedom fighter. Consider for the moment that the United States and its allies are wont to characterize Al Qaeda and its various subsidiaries as terrorists. On the other hand, Al Qaeda and its various subsidiaries are as wont to characterize the United States and its allies as terrorists. Indeed, in a 1998 interview with ABC-TV, Osama Bin-Laden stated, "the worst terrorists are the Americans" (National Commission of Terrorist Attacks upon the United States 2004). To follow this line of thinking, the inhabitants of Afghanistan and Iraq might legitimately ask, "Who is invading whose territories by land, sea and air? Who is bombing and killing whose civilians in the greatest number?" These are uncomfortable questions, often glossed over or ignored in the discourse on terrorism (Jarvis et al. 2016).

Arguably, cyberterrorism – to the degree that it exists – is simply a contemporary manifestation of the sort of asymmetrical warfare employed and enjoyed by weaker forces throughout history when confronted with seemingly overwhelming military might. Often, insurgents or guerrillas are accused by the superior forces of not fighting fairly, or of not playing by the agreed-upon rules of military conflict (Svete 2009).

History is replete with examples of asymmetrical warfare, including hijackings, suicide bombings, and improvised explosive devices, not to mention guerrilla attacks that appear suddenly from the mountains, forests, or jungles, and then disappear just as suddenly when the superior forces get their boots on the ground (Sexton 2011). American forces learned about the effectiveness of this type of asymmetrical warfare during the Vietnam War, much to their chagrin. So did English forces when confronting William Wallace and his much smaller and more lightly armed group of Scottish rebels, back in the thirteenth century. While Wallace was much reviled by the English and, once captured, was put to a gruesome death by his English captors, he became a national hero of Scotland (Stevens 2013) and the subject of the internationally renowned film, *Braveheart*. Terrorism and asymmetrical warfare are not necessarily part and parcel of each other, but terrorism is often employed as a tactic by the weaker forces (Heickerö 2014).

This is not to suggest that the notion of terrorism should be dismissed out of hand or treated lightly. In truth, innocent civilians are maimed or killed all too frequently in terrorist attacks, usually while going about their routine daily activities, such as walking or commuting to and from work, attending sporting events, going out for dinner and drinks, or simply engaging in some leisurely sightseeing. Just as the general population has been impacted by technology, specifically the rise of computers, the internet, and telecommunications, so too have terrorists. They are able to take advantage of the anonymity, speed, and safety of the internet to carry out their activities. However, we should stop and ask ourselves how many cyberterrorist attacks have been perpetrated to date, who the perpetrators of the main attacks have been, and whether these attacks (if any) have resulted in the killing of innocent civilians or in significant damage to physical infrastructure.

11.3 Defining Cyberterrorism

The term *cyber terrorism* was first coined in 1982 by Barry Collin, a research fellow at the Institute for Security and Intelligence in the United States, who simply defined it at that time as "the convergence of cybernetics and terrorism" (Awan 2014; Luiijf 2014). So far, however, it could be said there has yet to be a universally agreed-upon definition of cyberterrorism (Archer 2014). When it comes down to it, there seems to be no agreement among the experts as to whether it should be called *cyber terrorism* (two words) *cyberterrorism* (one word) or *cyber-terrorism* (a hyphenated word).

One of the challenges in arriving at a precise definition of cyberterrorism is that incidents offered to elucidate the concept are often intertwined with elements of cyberwarfare and cyberespionage. The much-referenced case of the 2009 Stuxnet worm attack on Iran's nuclear enrichment facilities, for example, has sometimes been mistaken for (or misconstrued as) an incident of cyberterrorism, or if not, then presented as a dire warning about the direction in which cyberterrorism could be heading (cf. Awan 2014; Helms et al. 2012).

With Stuxnet, it could be argued that the three ingredients of cyberterrorism, cyberwarfare, and cyberespionage were all present to one degree or another. The Stuxnet attack was purportedly carried out by Israel, possibly with assistance from the United States, although neither country has ever acknowledged responsibility. If this attribution of responsibility is correct, however, then this would more accurately be classified as an act of cyberwarfare, committed by one or more countries against another country, aimed at reducing the targeted country's ability to wage war. The Stuxnet worm was imported into the air-gapped nuclear enrichment facility at Nantanz, on infected Universal Serial Bus (USB) jump drives carried by unsuspecting engineers. Stuxnet targeted the programmable logic controllers (PLCs) that ran the centrifuges at the facility, causing them to alter velocity, and in many cases destroying them (Kenney 2015; Wattanajantra 2012). This prelude to the Stuxnet attack would actually be more consistent with cyberespionage than cyberterrorism, in that it involved infiltration of the enemy's military infrastructure and the collection of enough secret, insider information to plan the attack (Rid 2011). Nevertheless, Stuxnet has often been mobilized as an example of cyberterrorism, despite lack of evidence that the political leaders, nuclear engineers, or Iranian populace experienced any significant degree of fear, panic, or terror as a consequence, or even suffered any casualties. Apart from that, it might be politically inexpedient to suggest that the governments of the United States and Israel would be willing to engage in terrorist activities (or unprovoked cyberwarfare) against other countries.

The absence of physical casualties invariably presents a challenge when it comes to defining cyberterrorism and enumerating the dangers that it supposedly presents. Those who warn against the dire consequences of cyberterrorism are hard pressed to come up with concrete examples of incidents where lives have been threatened or lost, or populations have truly been terrorized. The question also remains as to whether the computer has to be the deadly weapon, or if it is sufficient for the computer to be a "facilitator" (Awan 2012). That said, some of the examples discussed later in this chapter – e.g. the 2013 cyberattack on France's TV5Monde and the 2015 cyberattack on the Ukrainian power grid – do come considerably closer than Stuxnet to approximating what a future cyberterrorist attack might look like.

For the moment, we can say that for an act to qualify as cyberterrorism, it should be politically, religiously, or ideologically motivated; it should take place in cyberspace; it should involve the use of a computer, computer system, or computer network, either as a weapon used to commit the act or as a target of the act (ideally both); and it should involve civilian casualties or damage to critical infrastructure. At a minimum, to qualify as cyberterrorism, the act should cause genuine terror and large-scale, lasting damage, well beyond the sort of fright, inconvenience, or expense associated with the various quasi-cyberterrorist incidents reported to date (Ayres and Maglaras 2016; Cohen 2014).

11.4 Cyberterrorism vs. Terrorist Use of Cyberspace

When wielded by terrorists, the computer could be either a facilitator or a deadly weapon in a cyberterrorism event, but not all uses of the computer by terrorists are considered cyberterrorist events. A cyberterrorist event is one that delivers terror, either through cyberspace or other digital means toward members of the public, and is usually politically motivated. If it meets the definition of terrorism, then it is assumed that such an event is perpetrated by a terrorist. However, a terrorist can use cyberspace for many other purposes. Researchers from the Institute for Security Technology

Studies examined dozens of websites from terrorist/extremist organizations and found that terrorist uses of cyberspace fall into six categories (Conway 2005; McPherson 2004):

- Cyberspace allows terrorists to spread radical messages through websites that deliver their group's propaganda to anyone who will listen.
- Cyberspace allows for international communication with and recruitment of new members to the cause in a very passive and inexpensive fashion. A group puts up a website, and motivated visitors stumble across the site and, if so inclined, reach out to the terrorist group, after which communication is taken offline and the visitor is recruited to join the violent Jihad.
- Group members disseminate and seek further training material through instructional videos or websites, as well as propaganda magazines created by the terrorist groups (such as the ISIS-authored magazine *Dabiq*).
- Cyberspace allows for the group to solicit funds from supporters internationally, which is now facilitated by digital cryptocurrencies such as Bitcoin, which enable peer-to-peer transfers that disregard international borders and/or financial laws (Fanusie 2017).
- Cyberspace allows members of terrorist organizations to communicate within the group, to share resources, and to provide moral and financial support to each other.
- Cyberspace allows terrorist organizations to conduct targeting exercises, intelligence gathering, and online surveillance of potential targets, using open source intelligence tools that may be as simple as Google Maps.

In short, terrorist organizations make extensive use of the internet, just like non-terrorist users, because of the simplicity of information gathering and the ease of transferring financial resources.

While terrorists use cyberspace to support terrorism in the listed examples, none of these are pure cyberterrorism events. Some have argued that using computers for recruitment, propaganda, and dissemination of information subsequently used in terrorist attacks rises to the level of cyberterrorism, but others have insisted that to meet the definition, computer technology and cyberspace must actually be used to inflict civilian casualties or, at a minimum, cause significant damage to critical infrastructure (Bearse 2015). As noted earlier, the more widely accepted stance is that while there are cyber activities that evidently support terrorism and cyberterrorism, an actual cyberterrorism event must cause damage that is similar in effect to the damage that would be caused by a traditional terrorist act.

11.5 Cyberterrorism in the Cloud

11.5.1 The Cloud Context

Understanding the nature and operation of the Cloud is a critical element in appreciating its putative role in terrorist exploits. The Cloud facilitates a variety of different services, applications, and resources. A useful perspective on cloud characteristics is provided by the US National Institute of Standards and Technology (NIST) (Mell and Grance 2011). This account includes a description of typical service and deployment models, which are best understood in relation to the essential characteristics attributed to the Cloud. These characteristics are: (i) on-demand self-service access to services and facilities; (ii) network access supported from a range of heterogeneous clients; (iii) pooling of resources to service multiple clients without locational constraints; (iv) elasticity of provision to achieve quick changes in scale and service access according to demand; and (v) service usage being automatically measured to facilitate resource management, and to provide insight on provision and customer billing (Mell and Grance 2011).

The three common service models of the Cloud are outlined next. First, with Software-as-a-Service (SaaS), the end user purchases access to remote software services that are implemented on the cloud service provider's infrastructure. These services extend from access to data storage, through hosting of websites and database systems, to provision of web service components such as RESTful applications (Shaikh et al. 2008), containers (Richardson and Ruby 2007), and other microservices (Sill 2016). Second, with Platform-as-a-Service (PaaS), the cloud service provider's software infrastructure is used by customers to run their own programs, wherein the customers have remote access to a software computing platform. Finally, with Infrastructure-as-a-Service (IaaS), a greater degree of flexibility is afforded to the customer, whereby they purchase access to a virtual hardware platform on which they may install proprietary software, including their own choice of operating system and applications (Mell and Grance 2011, p. 3).

11.5.2 How Terrorists Might Use the Cloud

Given the many attractions of using cloud-based services, we may consider how terrorists could seek to gain advantage from such deployment. To simplify the context, we will focus on two varieties of cloud usage. In the first of these, the cloud service is employed solely as a data repository. This is our *repository scenario*. The second variety of cloud usage requires the service as a means of computation. This is our *application scenario*. In the following discussion, we consider the plausibility of these scenarios as a basis for terrorist activity in the Cloud.

The scope for significant terrorist advantage in the repository scenario may seem slight, but nevertheless it has some potential. Aside from the obvious appeal of the service provider's secure backup and the data resilience from offsite file storage, an organization may benefit through use of a remote file-exchange service. This only requires our repository scenario and at least one registered user account (to be shared across all operatives). Potentially, the cloud storage facility serves as a central distribution point for advice, forged documents, extremist propaganda, and information pertaining to planning and recruitment. Since the cloud service acts as a data drop, there is an additional advantage, since this requires no direct contact or communication between operatives.

Clearly, greater opportunity exists within the application scenario. In principle, the terrorist can seek to use the benefits of any available software, but aside from the general benefits from cloud usage, this offers little advantage over conventional networked computing facilities. Indeed, there are many examples of state-sponsored agencies deploying conventional network resources to further their objectives (cf. Al-Rawi 2014). Our application scenario seems more appealing as a launch point for exploits against targets that are opposed to the beliefs of the terrorists. We should consider what the nature of such terrorist exploits might be.

Although our focus is the potential for terrorist use of cloud facilities, the scope for cloud-based exploits seems to be limited to the distribution of propaganda and conventional hacking activities. The former may be achieved through web hosting, blogs, and e-mail distribution, with each of these employing cloud-based services as the distribution platform. Given the increasing focus in many quarters on obstructing terrorism, such applications are likely to be speedily detected and curtailed through intervention by the cloud service provider. This leaves hacking-type activities as a basis for terrorism-related cloud deployment.

The beliefs that motivate terrorists may differ radically between individual hackers, hacking groups, and state-sponsored agents, but the motivation makes no difference to the means available to further their goals. The technical activities that may be directed toward these goals, such as denial of service, social engineering, and network intrusion are usually accomplished through malware as a basis for the creation of botnets and distributed denial of service (DDOS) attacks; e-mail as a basis for spam, phishing, and social engineering attacks; web services as a basis for spoofed websites and social engineering; and remote network access as a basis for network intrusion through Trojan malware or software vulnerabilities. In turn, while some of these technical ingredients may be situated in the Cloud (such as e-mail or web services), others have nothing to gain from being cloud-based. Indeed, denial of service attacks and network intrusion often rely upon malware infection and hijacked systems as a launch point for their related exploits (cf. Alomari et al. 2012).

The main prospects for cloud-based activities with respect to the terrorist-related objectives (set out in Table 11.1) are the hosting of web and e-mail services. Such services can facilitate the distribution of propaganda, disinformation, and malware, as well as the hosting of spoofed websites, in support of social engineering exploits. From a protagonist perspective, the advantages of deploying such resources in the Cloud are no more than the standard cloud benefits of cost, reliability, resiliency, and extensibility (discussed later). Furthermore, such illicit use of cloud services would quickly be traced and disabled by the service provider, because the customer has breached the standard contract conditions of use.

As an extension to the idea of terrorist attacks on critical infrastructure, cloud installations may themselves become the target of network-based extremist action. There is some basis for considering the possibility of denial of service in the context of

Table 11.1 Exploit objectives and constituent technologies.

Objective	Likely exploit	Likely technical means
Data theft	Social engineering, malware	Phishing, malware, software vulnerabilities
Financial fraud	Social engineering, malware	Phishing, malware, software vulnerabilities
Service disruption	Social engineering, network attack	DDOS, malware, software vulnerabilities
Infrastructure damage	Social engineering, network attack	DDOS, phishing, software vulnerabilities
Propaganda	Spam, network attack	Spam, software vulnerabilities
Disinformation	Spam, network attack	Spam, software vulnerabilities

software-defined networks (SDNs), as found in some cloud configurations (cf. Yan and Yu 2015). Even here, the prospect of such attacks is mitigated by rapid recovery through the reinstancing that is a feature of cloud-based services. A related downside to this rapid-recovery mechanism is that cloud forensic readiness may be inadequate to capture evidence that could be used by investigators to pinpoint the culprit in the event of such malevolent action. Fortunately, there are mechanisms available to ensure that evidence of user activity is acquired and securely logged for post-event analysis (Nasreldin et al. 2017; Weir and Aßmuth 2017), and that data can be protected against such attacks (Weir et al. 2017). Nevertheless, we cannot discount the possibility that, as they extend to more critical functions, cloud services may themselves become the target of cyberterrorist activities.

11.6 The Benefits of the Cloud to Cyberterrorists

Many reasons for cloud adoption are common to all prospective users, whether their ambitions are commercial, academic, or more nefarious. As indicated in Weir and Aßmuth (2017), the principal benefits are:

- Cost
- Reliability
- Resilience
- Technical extensibility

Specifically, cloud services can prove to be cost effective, with the reduced requirement to purchase and maintain local facilities. The reliability of cloud provisioning may be guaranteed through service-level contracts. Resilience is addressed through fast reinstatement of any failed service, while the extensible nature of the cloud offering ensures that changes in the customer's demands are easily accommodated. Finally, cloud services are usually backed by large, stable organizations that have the financial capacity and human resources needed to defend their infrastructure against physical or virtual attacks.

Even with these resources at their disposal, cloud services can be attacked. These privately owned services present both a target and an opportunity. Since the infrastructure is used to support multiple organizations that live on that service, bringing down that infrastructure will take all of the organizations offline, making this a very tempting target. As a general rule, these services are superbly defended, both in terms of attacks against bandwidth (such as DDoS attacks) and against applications (using viruses or malware) – so much so that they are even being used by the US military. Given the massive financial and knowledge-based resources behind these online services, attacks against them have been rare, although they are increasing (Raywood 2017). One such attack method used a cross-site scripting (XSS) attack to crash an Azure cloud-hosted website and then attack its troubleshooting system to escape the sandbox, thus gaining access to the underlying cloud infrastructure and compromising everything that was running on that infrastructure (Dale 2016). Attacks have also used these services in other ways. For example, cloud services have been used to host botnet command-and-control servers, or software-infringement sites (such as The Pirate Bay, hosted on the Cloud), because the resilient cloud infrastructure allows them to operate on a very stable and relatively inexpensive platform. Provided that the monthly subscription fee is paid, these platforms are available for use by anyone. Thus, it is entirely conceivable that terrorists or malicious state actors have successfully co-opted existing cloud services and have made or are in the process of making preparations for cyberterrorist attacks.

Of course, there are further considerations that may attract terrorists to the Cloud. For instance, they may seek a software platform that permits them to obscure their identity and location. When using the Cloud, the cloud service provider is effectively an intermediary between the terrorist agency and any target. Prospective targets may trace the origin of any cloud-based exploit back to the cloud service provider, but not beyond (that it is to say, not without engaging directly with the cloud service provider and the corresponding jurisdiction). This reduces the likelihood that an individual agent behind a terrorist activity will be identified. Furthermore, the true location of the agent is concealed. This introduces scope for plausible deniability for the perpetrator.

This motivation for deploying terrorist activity via a cloud service is less plausible if the target of an exploit is a foreign government or major institution. In such cases, there is a real prospect that international security or law enforcement services will approach the cloud service provider to reveal the true source and recorded identity of the agency behind the exploit. While there may be no major impact upon the terrorist organization, the cloud service provision is likely to be terminated once the service provider is apprised of the customer's behavior. Since the registration and payment details for the customer may not have been genuine, termination of the cloud service may simply be a minor inconvenience until such time as a suitable replacement cloud service is identified and contracted.

A scenario of this type came to light recently, in which alleged Russian agents used servers rented from a UK company to launch several criminal exploits: phishing attacks on the German parliament, diverting traffic meant for a Nigerian government website, and targeting Apple devices. To conceal their identities, the culprits used "bogus identities, virtual private networks, and hard-to-trace payment systems" (Vallance 2017).

11.6.1 The Challenges of the Cloud for Cyberterrorists

The damage caused by traditional terrorism is usually obvious: physical damage to some (critical) infrastructure, death of civilians, or the downing of an airplane, for example. While the repercussions of these actions cannot be predicted, the target (or intended target) and the identity of the perpetrator are usually clear. However, the same cannot be said for cyberterrorism, as there are three significant challenges to taking terrorism online.

First, the damage inflicted by cyberterrorism often cannot be targeted so precisely, because cyberweapons cannot be controlled to the same degree as physical weapons (Heckman et al. 2015). With traditional terrorism, for example, a bomb placed at a specific location can reasonably be expected to detonate in that location, whereas a cyberweapon (such as a virus or worm) can cause friendly fire casualties by damaging unintended and untargeted friendly systems while missing the intended target. Stuxnet caused friendly fire victims when it escaped via the internet and roamed around the world in search of similar targets, eventually infecting over 100 000 machines (Lindsay 2013), including Chevron's corporate networks in the United States. Just as most software contains some sort of logic error (i.e. a bug), the same holds true for malware, even those of the caliber of Stuxnet, meaning that unintended consequences can and do occur. Any malware wielded by cyberterrorists would similarly be uncontrollable – a trait that might actually be desirable within the context of cyberterrorism, in view of its thirst for maximal collateral damage.

Second, cloud systems are being implemented privately by large organizations that are of sufficient size to support such an infrastructure. For example, the US Department of Defense is de-siloing its existing segregated data storages, along with their many associated business benefits (such as centralized security, cost efficiencies, standardized security assessment, authorization, and outsourced monitoring and support) (Verge 2015; ViON/Hitachi Data Systems Federal 2015). While these benefits are certainly attractive to businesses and governments, they at the same time pose an increasing challenge for cyberterrorists, in that the attack surface is significantly decreased. Instead of being able to take advantage of security holes in many disparate and possibly unpatched systems, they are increasingly faced with a single unified set of security standards that by design decrease the number of vulnerabilities they might attempt to exploit (Serbu 2017).

Third, outside of the more common cloud-like environments, such as Amazon Web Services (AWS) and Microsoft Azure, a malicious actor can coopt available unprotected computers from the public to build a custom cloud of computers (a *botnet*) that could be used in the same sense as an Amazon cloud platform. To accomplish this, the malicious user would need software tools capable of infecting vulnerable computers. This has posed a challenge in the past, but now such tools are commonly available for purchase or rent on the internet or the dark web (Dupont 2017). Some software of this nature is even available for free, provided the user splits any financial gain with the author of the malware (Dimov and Juzenaite 2017). This arrangement, called *malware-as-a-service*, allows any malicious user, including a would-be cyberterrorist, to assemble custom cloud-like computing facilities that are capable of carrying out cyber or cyberterrorist attacks. Such attacks could take other cloud platforms offline, in order to disable large organizations that are running on those platforms, or to overwhelm their internet connections, leading to a failure of critical infrastructure. Thus, using malware, aspiring cyberterrorists can cheaply and anonymously create the computing platforms needed to launch massive cyberterrorist attacks from abroad. With the proliferation of internet-enabled small devices (the Internet of Things [IoT]), which are usually designed and manufactured with cost as the priority and security as an afterthought, ever-more-capable platforms can now be assembled with even less effort. One recent example is the IoT botnet Mirai, which brought down large sections of the internet across the East coast of North America in October 2016 (The Economist 2016; Kolias et al. 2017). What made this attack special was both its severity and that it used insecure IoT devices to carry out the attack.

11.7 Cyberlaw and Cyberterrorism

Presently, there are no international laws or conventions that deal effectively with cyberterrorism (Fidler 2016). This is not entirely surprising, given that nation states have thus far been unable to come up with an agreed-on definition of what constitutes hate speech, let alone what constitutes cyberterrorism. Indeed, this lack of agreement was the primary reason that hate speech was not included in the 2001 European Convention on Cybercrime (Garland and Chakraborti 2012). The subsequent EU Council Framework Decision on Combating Terrorism of 2002/2008 attempted to address this deficiency by setting general ground rules for member states when interdicting the use of computers and computer systems for the purposes of disseminating racist and xenophobic materials, and/or for the making of racist and xenophobic threats (Seiber 2010). Also, Clean IT, a European internet policing research initiative, sought to shut down websites that disseminate terrorist information (Rediker 2015).

As observed at various junctures in this chapter, terrorist organizations do indeed make wide use of the internet, albeit for much the same purposes as other organizations, including those of mainstream political parties: for propaganda, information sharing, planning, coordination, recruitment, and fund-raising. In other words, they use the internet for getting their message out and trying to increase their number of followers (Argomaniz 2015). But when we start talking about which message or messages should be permitted in cyberspace, and which message or messages should be suppressed, it quickly boils down to an issue of freedom of speech, a cornerstone of most Western-style democracies. Where does censorship start, where does it end, and who gets to be the censor? Do Western-style democracies truly wish to move in the direction of the Great Firewall of China or the Supreme Council of Cyberspace in Iran (Spinello 2017), where the political elite get to determine what their citizens can and cannot be exposed to?

Before turning briefly to the subject of cyberfatwas, we should bear in mind that the majority of fatwas published in cyberspace concern religious rulings (or scholarly legal opinions on Islamic law), and simply provide legal and spiritual guidance on aspects of everyday life, such as social norms and acceptable behavior (Weimann 2011). On the other hand, an appreciable number of cyberfatwas, or calls to cyberjihad, could quite easily be regarded as hate speech or terrorist propaganda. In many cases, these jihadist cyberfatwas clearly state that it is acceptable to wage war on noncombatant civilians, the preferred target of terrorists, and in particular, to wage war on civilians of the Christian or Jewish faiths (Weimann 2011). With their unprecedented use of the internet in general, and social media in particular, Al Qaeda and ISIS have taken such cyber-facilitated tactics and strategies to new heights (Fidler 2016). Essentially, organizations like Al Qaeda and ISIS mobilize the internet (and cyberjihad) in an effort to inspire "lone wolf" terrorism, by tapping into the sense of disillusionment and resentment experienced by many Muslims throughout the world (Haykel 2016). It has been estimated that the UK government annually identifies and removes upwards of 15 000 items from the internet that are deemed to meet the government's definition of jihadist propaganda (Awan 2017).

Article 10 of the European Convention on Human Rights guarantees freedom of expression, which includes the right to hold opinions and to freely receive or impart such opinions without political interference (Rediker 2015). That said, Germany, France, and the United Kingdom tend to adopt comparatively hardline approaches toward hate speech, and extremist speech in particular, whereas many analogous forms of extremist or hate speech seem to enjoy greater latitude in other European countries (Garland and Chakraborti 2012). The differences become even more pronounced when comparing Europe with North America (Spinello 2017). To illustrate, Jayda Fransen of the far-right Britain First organization was criminally charged in the United Kingdom for using threatening and abusive speech, while Donald Trump, the President of the United

States, apparently felt quite comfortable when he retweeted some of Fransen's (allegedly illegal) anti-Islam videos to his many followers on Twitter (Weaver et al. 2017). On the Canadian front, when presented with an alleged case of criminal harassment on social media, a Toronto court judge ruled at considerable length that any number of distasteful or unpopular expressions are constitutionally protected in Canada, up to and including some forms of false news and hate propaganda (McDougall 2015). Whether we label it as terrorist speech, extremist speech, or hate speech, we should be reminded that such labels are often in the eye of the beholder and are most likely determined subjectively, on the basis of who is best positioned to affix the negative label and who is best positioned to deflect or resist that label.

The legal discourse pertaining to cyberterrorism involves issues other than the right to freedom of speech, and where that freedom might reasonably end, two of those being identifying the actual perpetrator (attribution) and the question of legal jurisdiction. A case in point might be the 2013 cyberattack on France's TV5Monde (the national broadcaster), wherein TV screens were switched to display jihadist messages and an image of The CyberCaliphate, ostensibly in retaliation for the French army's involvement in Syria and Iraq. In addition to taking over the TV screen, the hackers were able to block broadcasts and hack into the broadcaster's website and social media sites (Chrisafis and Gibbs 2015; Fidler 2016). This might arguably be construed as an incident of cyberterrorism, in that it was intended to instill terror in the French populace and, at the same time, deliver a political message to the French government. As is the case with almost all such purported incidents of cyberterrorism, however, there was no damage to the critical infrastructure, and there were no civilian casualties.

Initially, it was assumed by the French government that an ISIS-linked terrorist group had successfully targeted the TV station, because the caption included the name of ISIS and the picture was consistent with other ISIS propaganda on the internet (Chrisafis and Gibbs 2015). However, subsequent investigations revealed that the hacks appeared to originate from a Kremlin-linked group in Russia, perhaps with the objective of supporting Russia's Syrian ally, Bashar al-Assad. This group of Russian hackers, known variously as APT28 or Pawn Storm, had previously attempted to hack into NATO computers and into the computers of the White House, and was thought to have targeted pro-Ukrainian activists and Russian dissidents (Lichfield 2015). In this particular case, it seems highly unlikely that investigators will ever prove conclusively who orchestrated the attack on France's TV5Monde and, if the perpetrators were indeed Russian, even more unlikely that French or European authorities will ever succeed in persuading the Russian government to extradite them to face trial in France. Russia is the only European country so far that has refused to sign the European Convention on Cybercrime, insisting that certain sections of the Convention would violate Russian sovereignty and national security (Ruvic 2017).

There are, of course, international laws that deal with real-world terrorism, for example the UN Convention for the Suppression of Unlawful Seizure of Aircraft and the UN Protocol for the Suppression of Unlawful Acts of Violence at Airports Serving International Civil Aviation, which could be invoked in the event of a cyberterrorist attack on an aircraft's onboard computer or an air traffic control system. Another example is the UN Convention for the Suppression of Acts of Nuclear Terrorism, which could be invoked in the event of an attack on the computerized control system of a nuclear power plant (Seiber 2010). This latter convention on nuclear terrorism might well have been applied in the case of the Stuxnet attack on the Iranian nuclear facilities, except for the fact that nobody has been able to prove who orchestrated the attack. And if the Stuxnet attack was orchestrated by the United States and/or Israel, as has been widely speculated (cf. Kenney 2015), then it seems doubtful that either country would ever consent to extraditing one or more of its citizens to face trial in an Iranian court of law (or any court of law, for that matter).

As seen here, when it comes to cyberterrorism and jurisdictional issues, it can be difficult to determine in which state the act originated and, assuming that the state is inclined to investigate, difficult for the state to ascertain whether the act originated within its own borders. Even if the state is able to conclude that the act originated within its own borders (and thus within its legal jurisdiction), this does not necessarily prove that the act was committed by one of its own nationals (Tehrani and Manap 2013). Given the widespread proliferation of botnets and proxy servers, cyberattacks can originate from just about anywhere on the face of the earth, with the identity of the original perpetrators hidden from the view of all but the most skilled and determined of investigators. And as with the Stuxnet attack and the attack on TV5Monde, the act may not be against the law in the country in which it originated; it may be state-sponsored or, at a minimum, state-sanctioned (cf. Tehrani and Manap 2013).

11.8 Conclusion: Through a Glass Darkly

In his presentation to a 1996 cyberlaw conference at the University of Chicago, Frank Easterbrook – who was at that time a senior lecturer in the Law School at the University of Chicago and a circuit court judge for the US Court of Appeals – remarked that we were no more likely to see a law course on cyberlaw than we were to see a course on "the law of the horse." While we may have laws regulating the sale of horses and the licensing of race horses, not to mention laws against the theft of horses and the fixing of horse races, he felt it unlikely that these could or ever would be gathered into a unified law course. Judge Easterbrook further opined that the lawyers and politicians who drafted and promulgated laws knew little about computers and even less about the direction in which computer technology might be headed (Easterbrook 1996). This notion of the law of the horse was subsequently elaborated upon by Lawrence Lessig, a law professor at Stanford University. According to Lessig, social norms, market forces, the architecture of the internet, and protocol (or the power of code) would likely prove more effective in regulating cyberspace than any new, cyber-specific laws. As Lessig pointed out, we have an abundance of existing laws that regulate activity in the real world, any number of which could be used to regulate activity in cyberspace (Lessig 1999). To express it differently, theft is theft, and fraud is fraud, whether it takes place in the real world or in cyberspace. We already have laws against theft and fraud, so why not enforce them? And why should we think that such laws would be any more enforceable in cyberspace if we recast them as cybertheft and cyberfraud?

Clearly, one lesson to be taken from Judge Easterbrook's speech is that judges, law professors, and any like-minded crystal-ball readers should exercise considerable caution when it comes to predicting what the future might hold. Since Judge Easterbrook's 1996 speech at the cyberlaw conference, there have been any number of cyber-specific laws, such as the 2000 Children's Internet Protection Act in the United States and the

2014 Protecting Canadians from Online Crime Act in Canada (Cartwright 2017). We have also seen the introduction of the 2001 European Convention on Cybercrime, as well as the subsequent EU Council Framework Decision on Combating Terrorism (Seiber 2010). Moreover, many law schools around the world now offer courses on cyberlaw, including the Law School at the University of Chicago (where Judge Easterbrook was teaching), which offers courses on cybercrime and electronic commerce law; the Faculty of Law at the University of Ottawa, which offers courses on the regulation of internet communication and the regulation of cyber commerce; and the Faculties of Law at the University of Birmingham and the University of Leeds, both of which offer a course on technology and the law (i.e. cyberlaw).

Nevertheless, there is considerable merit to the notion set forth in the law of the horse that cyberspace and computer technology are changing so quickly that any new cyberlaw initiated today would be obsolete by the time it went through all the drafts and committees, circulated through the various legislative bodies for reading and amendment, and was finally promulgated and enforceable. With all that is going on in the fields of computer technology and cybercommunications, and the seemingly endless capacity of the computer generation to move rapidly from one innovation to the next, it is easy to lose sight of the fact that Facebook did not appear on the horizon until 2004, Twitter did not appear until 2006 (Fidler 2016), and the iPhone was not launched by Steve Jobs and Apple until 2007 (Price 2017). Nowadays, Facebook, Twitter, and iPhones have become integral parts of the terrorist toolkit in cyberspace (Awan 2017; Ayres and Maglaras 2016). But how could lawmakers (or law professors) back in the 1990s have even been aware of, let alone accurately predicted, such developments?

The European Convention on Cybercrime is a case in point. The Convention began taking shape in 1997 but was not open for signature until 2001 and did not become law until 2004 (Clough 2012). Although it was intended from the outset to apply internationally, only 55 countries had signed it as of 2017. The United States did not get around to ratifying the Convention until 2007, and Canada did not ratify it until 2015. It is noteworthy that Russia, China, Brazil, and India have never signed or ratified the Convention. These four countries are among the world leaders when it comes to malicious websites, the hosting of botnets, and phishing attacks (Kigerl 2012). Russia is of course thought to be behind the 2015 cyberattack on the Ukrainian power grid and the 2013 cyberattack on France's TV5Monde (Chrisafis and Gibbs 2015; Fidler 2016). China is widely believed to be the world's leader in cyberespionage, both against nation states and against commercial enterprises (Segal 2013; Wattanajantra 2012). If the main transgressors are unwilling to sign the Convention and enforce its provisions, then what force and effect can the Convention realistically be expected to have?

The same can be said for the UN-sponsored Comprehensive Convention on International Terrorism, which has been the subject of negotiation since 1996, a year earlier than negotiations commenced on the European Convention on Cybercrime. The provisions of the draft text of the Comprehensive Convention on International Terrorism are sufficiently broad as to cover cyberterrorism (Fidler 2016), but the process had mostly been drifting sideways, until it was recently revived at the instigation of India, following the deadly terrorist attack in Dhaka in July 2016 (Anam 2017; Haider 2016). But again, how likely is it that the nation states that are known to sponsor or at least sanction cyberterrorism are going to become signatories to the Convention, or enforce its provisions?

While we may not have witnessed any bona fide cyberterrorist attacks as of yet, this could simply be attributable to the fact that it has thus far proven difficult for terrorists to achieve the level of civilian casualties and damage to critical infrastructure in cyberspace that they can achieve by using more tried-and-true methods in the real world. To express it differently, terrorists want the biggest bang for their buck, just like everybody else. However, there is no question that terrorist organizations are keenly interested in cybertechnology and everything it has to offer. We should bear in mind that at any given moment, there are reportedly hundreds (if not thousands) of ISIS- and Al Qaeda-inspired computer science students around the world actively attempting to acquire the requisite knowledge to mount more sophisticated cyberterrorist attacks (Heickerö 2014). Thus it may be a question of *when* we will start to see cyberattacks that approximate the level of destruction associated with real-world terrorism, rather than *if* we will ever see such attacks (Archer 2014).

For now, however, terrorist organizations will continue to use cyberspace for the purposes outlined earlier in this chapter: recruitment, coordination, fund-raising, propaganda, and intelligence gathering. Where possible, they will continue to engage in disruptive activities such as DDoS attacks and network disruption, like the attack on France's TV5Monde (although this was thought in hindsight to be orchestrated by Russia, not by a terrorist organization). While cloud technology may be better equipped than conventional technology to deflect such attacks, due to its relative sophistication and enhanced protective measures, we cannot entirely discount the possibility of terrorist attacks on the Cloud and, in particular, on the cloud-connected components of the IoT, some of which are very poorly secured (Tzezana 2017).

On rare occasions, terrorists may succeed in mounting cyberattacks on critical infrastructure, along the lines of the attack on Iran's nuclear enrichment facilities and the more recent attack on the Ukrainian power grid (again thought to be orchestrated, respectively, by Israel and the United States, and by Russia, rather than by terrorist organizations). The malicious code for destructive attacks of this nature is certainly out there in cyberspace and is accessible to any terrorist organization that has the requisite knowledge and determination to mobilize the technology. And for the foreseeable future, it can be anticipated that governments and law enforcement agencies will continue to struggle with jurisdictional issues, the complexity of cyberspace itself, and the seemingly never-ending task of bringing noncompliant nations on side. In fact, terrorist organizations – which see themselves as engaged in asymmetrical warfare against much larger and more powerful entities – appear to revel in the jurisdictional issues, the complexities of cyberspace, and the seeming befuddlement of governments and law enforcement agencies around the world when it comes to dealing with cybercrime. One thing we can say for certain is that terrorist organizations will not play the game according to the rules and that, wherever possible, they will act in an unpredictable manner.

References

Alomari, E., Manickam, S., Gupta, B.B. et al. (2012). Botnet-based distributed denial of service (DDoS) attacks on web servers. *International Journal of Computer Applications* 49 (7): 24–32.

Al-Rawi, A.K. (2014). Cyber warriors in the Middle East: the case of the Syrian electronic Army. *Public Relations Review* 40 (3): 420–428. https://doi.org/10.1016/j.pubrev.2014.04.005.

Anam, Tahmima. (2017). Under the Shadow of Terrorism in Dhaka. *The New York Times*. https://www.nytimes.com/2017/08/09/opinion/under-the-shadow-of-terrorism-in-dhaka.html.

Archer, E.M. (2014). Crossing the Rubicon: understanding cyber terrorism in the European context. *The European Legacy: Toward New Paradigms* 19 (5): 606–621. https://doi.org/10.1080/10848770.2014.943495.

Argomaniz, J. (2015). European Union responses to terrorist use of the internet. *Cooperation and Conflict* 50 (2): 250–268. https://doi.org/10.1177/0010836714545690.

Awan, Imran. (2012). Cyber threats and cyber terrorism: The internet as a tool for extremism.

Awan, I. (2014). Debating the term cyber-terrorism: issues and problems. *Internet Journal of Criminology* https://doi.org/10.1007/978-1-4939-0962-9_6.

Awan, I. (2017). Cyber-extremism: Isis and the power of social media. *Social Science and Public Policy* 54 (2): 138–149. https://doi.org/10.1007/s12115-017-0114-0.

Ayres, N. and Maglaras, L.A. (2016). Cyberterrorism targeting the general public through social media. *Security and Communication Networks* 9: 2864–2875. https://doi.org/10.1002/sec.1568.

Barker, Cary. (2002). Ghosts in the machine: The who, why, and how of attacks on information security. GIAC Security Essentials Certification (GSEC), 1–38. SANS Institute Reading Room. https://www.sans.org/reading-room/whitepapers/awareness/ghosts-machine-who-why-attacks-information-security-914.

Bearse, R.S. (2015). Protecting critical information infrastructure for terrorist attacks and other threats: strategic challenges for NATO and its partner countries. In: *Terrorist Use of Cyberspace and Cyber Terrorism: New Challenges and Responses* (ed. M.N. Ogun), 29–44. Amsterdam: IOS Press.

Beazer, Daniel. (2016). Silver Linings While Clouds Gather. Scmagazine.com, 18–21.

Becker, H.S. (1963). *Outsiders; Studies in the Sociology of Deviance*. London: Free Press of Glencoe.

Binder, David. (1972). 9 Israelis on Olympic team killed with 4 Arab captors as police fight band that disrupted Munich games. The New York Times. http://www.nytimes.com/learning/general/onthisday/big/0905.html.

Cartwright, B. (2017). Cyberbullying and "the law of the horse": a Canadian viewpoint. *Journal of Internet Law* 20 (10): 14–26.

Chaplain, Chloe. (2017). Boris Johnson labels Syrian leader Bashar al-Assad a "terrorist" over chemical attack and warns US "could strike again." Evening Standard. www.standard.co.uk/news/world/boris-johnson-labels-syrian-leader-bashar-alassad-a-terrorist-over-chemical-attack-and-warns-us-a3515891.htm.

Chrisafis, Angelique and Gibbs, Samuel. (2015). French media groups to hold emergency meeting after Isis attack: Culture minister calls talks after television network TV5Monde is taken over by individuals claiming to belong to Islamic State. The Guardian. https://www.theguardian.com/world/2015/apr/09/french-tv-network-tv5monde-hijacked-by-pro-isis-hackers.

Clough, J. (2012). The Council of Europe Convention on cybercrime: defining "crime" in a digital world. *Criminal Law Forum* 23 (4): 363–391. https://doi.org/10.1007/s10609-012-9183-3.

Cohen, D. (2014). Cyber terrorism: case studies. In: *Cyber Crime and Cyber Terrorism Investigator's Handbook* (ed. B. Akhgar, A. Staniforth and F. Bosco), 165–175. Waltham, MA: Syngress.

Conway, Maura. (2005). Terrorist "use" of the Internet and fighting back. Presented at Cybersafety: Safety and Security in a Networked World: Balancing Cyber-Rights and Responsibilities, Oxford England. https://www.oii.ox.ac.uk/archive/downloads/research/cybersafety/papers/maura_conway.pdf.

Dale, Chris. (2016). Azure Oday cross-site scripting with sandbox escape. https://pen-testing.sans.org/blog/2016/08/19/azure-0day-cross-site-scripting-with-sandbox-escape (accessed 14 December 2017).

Dimov, Daniel and Juzenaite, Rasa. (2017). Malware-as-a-service. http://resources.infosecinstitute.com/malware-as-a-service (accessed 14 December 2017).

Dupont, B. (2017). Bots, cops and corporations: on the limits of enforcement and the promise of polycentric regulation as a way to control large-scale cybercrime. *Crime, Law and Social Change* 67 (1): 97–116. https://doi.org/10.1007/s10611-016-9649-z.

Easterbrook, F.H. (1996). Cyberspace and the law of the horse. *University of Chicago Legal Forum* 1996: 207–216.

Fanusie, Yaya. (2017). Will a new generation of terrorists turn to bitcoin? Thecipherbrief.Com(11June11).https://www.thecipherbrief.com/article/tech/will-a-new-generation-of-terrorists-turn-to-bitcoin.

Fidler, D.P. (2016). Cyberspace, terrorism and international law. *Journal of Conflict and Security Law* 21 (3): 475–493. https://doi.org/10.1093/jcsl/krw013.

Fogarty, Kevin. (2012). Where did "cloud" come from? Users love it, many in IT hate it; cloud changed the relationship between the two forever. IT World. https://www.itworld.com/article/2726701/cloud-computing/where-did--cloud--come-from-.html.

Garland, J. and Chakraborti, N. (2012). Divided by a common concept? Assessing the implications of different conceptualizations of hate crime in the European Union. *European Journal of Criminology* 9 (1): 38–51. https://doi.org/10.1177/1477370811421645.

Gayathri, K.S., Thomas, T., and Jayasudha, J. (2012). Security issues of media sharing in social cloud. *Procedia Engineering* 38: 3806–3815. https://doi.org/10.1016/j.proeng.2012.06.43.

Gellman, Barton. (2002). Cyber-attacks by Al Qaeda feared: Terrorists at threshold of using Internet as tool of bloodshed, experts warn. The Washington Post, A1.

Haider, Suhasini. (2016). Delhi hopes UN will push global terror convention. The Hindu. http://www.thehindu.com/news/national/Delhi-hopes-UN-will-push-global-terror-convention/article14467324.ece.

Haykel, B. (2016). ISIS and Al Qaeda – what are they thinking? Understanding the adversary. *Annals of the American Academy of Political and Social Science* 668 (1): 71–81. https://doi.org/10.1177/0002716216672649.

Heckman, K.E., Stech, F.J., Thomas, R.K. et al. (2015). *Cyber Denial, Deception and Counter Deception: A Framework for Supporting Active Cyber Defense*. New York, NY: Springer.

Heickerö, R. (2014). Cyber terrorism: electronic Jihad. *Strategic Analysis* 38 (4): 554–565. https://doi.org/10.1080/09700161.2014.918435.

Helms, R., Constanza, S.E., and Johnson, N. (2012). Crouching Tiger or phantom dragon? Examining the global discourse on cyber-terror. *Security Journal* 25 (1): 57–75. https://doi.org/10.1057/sj.2011.6.

Jarvis, L., Macdonald, S., and Whiting, A. (2016). Analogy and Authority in Cyberterrorism Discourse: an analysis of global news media coverage. *Global Society* 30 (4): 605–623. https://doi.org/10.1080/13600826.2016.1158699.

Jenkins, Brian M. and Johnson, Janera. (1975). International terrorism: a chronology, 1968–1974: a report prepared for Department of State and Defense Advanced Research Projects Agency (No. R-1597-DOS/ARPA). Santa Monica, CA: Rand Corporation. http://www.dtic.mil/docs/citations/ADA008354.

Jones, Sam. (2017). Spanish court to investigate Syrian "state terrorism" by Assad regime. Theguardian.Com. https://www.theguardian.com/world/2017/mar/27/spanish-court-syria-state-terrorism-assad-regime-mrs-ah.

Kenney, M. (2015). *Cyber-Terrorism in a Post-Stuxnet World*, 110–128. Philadelphia, PA: Foreign Policy Research Institute Retrieved from www.sciencedirect.com.proxy.lib.sfu.ca/science/article/pii/S0030438714000787.

Kigerl, A. (2012). Routine activity theory and the determinants of high cybercrime countries. *Social Science Computer Review* 30 (4): 470–486. https://doi.org/10.1177/0894439311422689.

Knox, Patrick and Hodge, Mark. (2017). Killer cocktail: What was the Syria chemical attack and what has Donald Trump said about Bashar al-Assad? Here's everything you need to know. The Sun. www.thesun.co.uk/news/3267810/syria-chemical-weapons-trump-assad-russia-iran-france.

Kolias, C., Kambourakis, G., Stavrous, A., and Voas, J. (2017). DDoS in the IoT: Mirai and other botnets. *Computer* 50 (7): 80–84. https://doi.org/10.1109/MC.2017.201.

Lessig, L. (1999). The law of the horse: what Cyberlaw might teach. *Harvard Law Review* 113 (2): 501–549.

Lichfield, John. (2015). TV5Monde hack: "Jihadist" cyber attack on French TV station could have Russian link. The Independent. www.independent.co.uk/news/world/europe/tv5monde-hack-jihadist-cyber-attack-on-french-tv-station-could-have-russian-link-10311213.html.

Lindsay, J.R. (2013). Stuxnet and the limits of cyber warfare. *Security Studies* 22 (3): 365–404. https://doi.org/10.1080/09636412.2013.816122.

Luiijf, E. (2014). Definitions of cyber terrorism. In: *Cyber Crime and Cyber Terrorism Investigator's Handbook*, 10–17. Syngress.

McDougall, G. G. (2015). Crouch v. Snell, 2015 NSSC 340 (Case/Court Decisions).

McPherson, Andrew. (2004). Examining the cyber capabilities of Islamic terrorist groups. Hanover, NH: Institute for Security, Technology and Society. http://www.ists.dartmouth.edu/library/164.pdf.

Mell, Peter M. and Grance, Timothy. (2011). The NIST Definition of Cloud Computing. Special Publication (NIST SP) No. 800–145). National Institute of Standards and Technology. http://nvlpubs.nist.gov/nistpubs/Legacy/SP/nistspecialpublication800-145.pdf.

Nasreldin, M., Aslan, H., Rasslan, M., et al. (2017). Evidence acquisition in cloud forensics. Presented at the IEEE International Conference on New Paradigms in Electronics & Information Technology (PEIT '17), Alexandria, Egypt.

National Commission of Terrorist Attacks upon the United States. (2004). The 9/11 Commission report: final report of the National Commission on Terrorist attacks upon the United States, 1–585. https://www.9-11commission.gov/report/911Report.pdf.

Price, Rob. (2017). The first iPhone went on sale 10 years ago today--here's how Steve Jobs announced it. Business Insider UK. http://uk.businessinsider.com/watch-steve-jobs-first-iphone-10-years-ago-legendary-keynote-macworld-sale-2017-6.

Raywood, Dan. (2017). Attacks on the cloud increase by 300%. Infosecurity Magazine. https://www.infosecurity-magazine.com/news/attacks-cloud-increase-300.

Rediker, E. (2015). The incitement of terrorism on the internet: legal standards, enforcement, and the role of the European Union. *Michigan Journal of International Law* 36 (2): 321–351.

Richardson, L. and Ruby, S. (2007). *RESTful Web Services*. Sebastopol, CA: O'Reilly Media Inc.

Rid, T. (2011). Cyber war will not take place. *Journal of Strategic Studies* 35 (1): 5–32. https://doi.org/10.1080/01402390.2011.608939.

Ruvic, Dado. (2017). Russia prepares new UN anti-cybercrime convention-report. Rt.Com. https://www.rt.com/politics/384728-russia-has-prepared-new-international.

Segal, A. (2013). The code not taken: China, the United States, and the future of cyber espionage. *Bulletin of the Atomic Scientists* 69 (5): 38–45. https://doi.org/10.1177/0096340213501344.

Seiber, U. (2010). Instruments of international law: against terrorist use of the internet. In: *A War on Terror? The European Stance on a New Threat, Changing Laws and Human Rights Implications* (ed. M. Wade and A. Maljevic), 171–220. New York, London: Springer Retrieved from https://link-springer-com.proxy.lib.sfu.ca/content/pdf/bfm%3A978-0-387-89291-7%2F1.pdf.

Serbu, Jared. (2017). DoD in discussions with vendors to simplify cloud security rules. Federal News Radio. https://federalnewsradio.com/cloud-computing/2017/10/dod-in-discussions-with-vendors-to-simplify-cloud-security-rules.

Sexton, E. (2011). Asymmetrical warfare. In: *The SAGE Encyclopedia of Terrorism* (ed. G. Martin), 71–72. Thousand Oaks, CA: SAGE Publications Retrieved from http://sk.sagepub.com.proxy.lib.sfu.ca/reference/download/terrorism2ed/n49.pdf.

Shaikh, S.A., Chivers, H., Nobles, P. et al. (2008). Network reconnaissance. *Network Security* 11: 12–16. https://doi.org/10.1016/S1353-4858(08)70129-6.

Sill, A. (2016). The design and architecture of microservices. *IEEE Cloud Computing* 3 (5): 76–80.

Solomon, Erika. (2017). Assad says US welcome to join "fight against terrorism." Financial Times. https://www.ft.com/content/6f06a3b4-efa5-11e6-ba01-119a44939bb6.

Spinello, R.A. (2017). *Cyberethics: Morality and Law in Cyberspace*, 6e. Burlington, MA: Jones & Bartlett Learning.

Stevens, D.A. (2013). William Wallace: the man behind the legend. *Saber and Scroll* 2 (2): 46–53.

Svete, U. (2009). Asymmetrical warfare and modern digital media: an old concept changed by new technology? In: *The Moral Dimension of Asymmetrical Warfare: Counter-Terrorism, Democratic Values and Military Ethics* (ed. T. van Baarda and D.E.M. Verweij), 381–398. Leiden, Boston: Martinus Nijhoff Publishers.

TASS. (2017). Assad praises Russia for succeeding in fighting terroists together. Russia Beyond. https://www.rbth.com/news/2017/03/13/assad-praises-russia-for-succeeding-in-fighting-terrorists-together_718898.

Tehrani, P.M. and Manap, N.A. (2013). A rational jurisdiction for cyber terrorism. *Computer Law & Security Review* 29 (6): 689–701. https://doi.org/10.1016/j.clsr.2013.07.009.

The Economist. (2016). The internet of stings: An electronic tsunami crashes down on a solitary journalist. https://www.economist.com/news/science-and-technology/21708220-electronic-tsunami-crashes-down-solitary-journalist-internet.

Thomas, T.L. (2003). Al Qaeda and the internet: the danger of "Cyberplanning." *Parameters* 23 (1): 112–123.

Tzezana, R. (2017). High-probability and wild-card scenarios for future crimes and terror attacks using the internet of things. *Foresight* 19 (1): 1–14. https://doi.org/10.1108/FS-11-2016-0056.

Vallance, Chris. (2017). Russian Fancy Bear hackers' UK link revealed. BBC Radio 4, PM. London: BBC. http://www.bbc.com/news/technology-42056555.

van Baarda, T. (2009). The moral dimension of asymmetrical warfare – an introduction. In: *The Moral Dimension of Asymmetrical Warfare: Counter-Terrorism, Democratic Values and Military Ethics* (ed. T. van Baarda and D.E.M. Verweij), 1–28. Leiden, Boston: Martinus Nijhoff Publishers.

Verge, Jason. (2015). Defense Department warming to commercial cloud servers: DOD getting more comfortable working with the big commercial cloud vendors. DataCenterKnowledge (5 February). http://www.datacenterknowledge.com/archives/2015/02/05/department-of-defense-works-with-commercial-cloud-providers.

ViON/Hitachi Data Systems Federal. (2015). DoD and cloud computing: where are we now? ViON/Hitachi Data Systems Federal. https://www.vion.com/assets/site_18/files/vion%20collateral/vion%20whitepaper-dod%20cloud%20trends%20(draft)%20 8_25_2025.pdf.

Wattanajantra, Asavin. (2012). The new Cold War. SC Media UK (November–December), 18–21.

Weaver, Matthew, Booth, Robert, and Jacobs, Ben. (2017). Theresa May condemns Trumps' retweets of UK far-right leader's anti-Muslim videos. The Guardian. https://www.theguardian.com/us-news/2017/nov/29/trump-account-retweets-anti-muslim-videos-of-british-far-right-leader.

Weimann, G. (2011). Cyber-fatwas and terrorism. *Studies in Conflict & Terrorism* 34 (10): 765–781. https://doi.org/10.1080/1057610X.2011.604831.

Weinberger, Matt. (2015). Why "cloud computing" is called "cloud computing." Business Insider (12 March). http://www.businessinsider.com/why-do-we-call-it-the-cloud-2015-3.

Weir, G.R.S. and Aßmuth, A. (2017). Strategies for intrusion monitoring in cloud services, cloud computing 2017. Presented at the Eighth International Conference on Cloud Computing, GRIDs, and Virtualization, IARIA, Athens, Greece.

Weir, George, Aßmuth, A., Whittington, M. et al. (2017). Cloud accounting systems, the audit trail, forensics and the EU GDPR: how hard can it be? Presented at the British Accountancy and Finance Association Conference, Aberdeen, Scotland.

Yan, Q. and Yu, F.R. (2015). Distributed denial of service attacks in software-defined networking with cloud computing. *IEEE Communications Magazine* 53 (4): 52–59.

12

Digital Forensic Process and Model in the Cloud

Nhien-An Le-Khac[1], *James Plunkett*[1], *M-Tahar Kechadi*[1], *and Lei Chen*[2]

[1] *University College Dublin, Dublin, Ireland*
[2] *Georgia Southern University, Statesboro, GA, USA*

12.1 Introduction

Cloud computing is a new approach to delivering information communications technology (ICT) to organizations. Cloud computing is built on the premise that organizations do not need to invest in buying hardware, software, and network infrastructures to support business-critical applications. Utilizing a cloud-based infrastructure, organizations can increase ICT capacity or add ICT capabilities without investing in new infrastructure, training new personnel, or licensing new software. Cloud computing encompasses any subscription-based or pay-per-use service that, in real time over the internet, extends organizations' existing ICT capabilities.

The advent of cloud computing is forcing a change from traditional software and hardware models to ICT being delivered over the internet or through private networks located in shared data centers (*public cloud*) or within private data centers (*private cloud*). As global markets change, organizations must also change to meet consumer demands. Organizations require flexible structures; and to complement this flexibility, they require the ability to provide new applications, hardware, and network infrastructures quickly, thus supporting changing market environments and enabling the organization to sustain a competitive advantage. A recent study by IDC, "Quantitative Estimates of the Demand for Cloud Computing in Europe and the Likely Barriers to Take-up 24," illustrates that the adoption of cloud computing is on the rise. *Information Week* has conducted a survey annually illustrating that organizations are increasingly implementing cloud-based solutions, and these adoption rates have risen from 16% in 2008 to 33% in 2012 (Emison 2013).

On the other hand, the increased adoption rates of cloud computing solutions are also an opportunity for criminals to store information within cloud-based environments. Criminals are aggressively expanding the use of digital technology for illegal activities. Crimes committed in cyberspace, such as data theft, internet fraud, business espionage, pornography, online child exploitation, and cyberterrorism are on the rise (Kolenbrander et al. 2016).

Security, Privacy, and Digital Forensics in the Cloud, First Edition. Edited by Lei Chen, Hassan Takabi, and Nhien-An Le-Khac.

Law enforcement agencies are increasingly faced with cloud computing solutions being used by companies and individuals who engage in illegal activities. Over the past 20 years, digital forensic techniques have become a vital tool employed by law enforcement agencies in combating criminal activity. The evolution of computer forensics has advanced at a rapid pace due to the rise in computer-related crime. *Computer forensics*, which is a branch of digital forensics, is the science of acquiring, retrieving, preserving, and presenting data that has been processed electronically and stored on computer media (Hayes 2014).

The rise of cloud computing not only exacerbates the problem of scale for digital forensic practitioners, but also creates a new forum for cybercrime, with associated challenges (Ruan et al. 2011). Law enforcement agencies can no longer rely on traditional digital forensics techniques during investigations that involve cloud computing platforms. The discovery and acquisition of digital evidence from remote, elastic, provider-controlled cloud platforms differs considerably from the discovery and acquisition of digital evidence from local suspect devices such as laptops, PCs and servers. Acquiring data from cloud-based environments requires different tools, techniques, and approaches. It is necessary to develop new processes and techniques to retrieve evidence from cloud-based environments (Lessing and Von Solms 2008; Faheem et al. 2015).

In this chapter, first we review and discuss digital forensic processes and models in the cloud computing platform. Next, we present a new digital forensics process within cloud-based environments. This approach will draw on various aspects of digital forensics, such as analysis and acquisition methods. To support this approach, a digital forensic framework model will be developed during live investigations. This new approach will focus on the identification and acquisition of data within cloud-based environments during the execution of search warrants by law enforcement agencies. The object of this approach is to meet the many challenges of conducting investigations in which evidential material is located within the Cloud. The rest of this chapter is organized as follows. We start in Section 12.2 by presenting digital forensics models and discussing the Digital Forensic Research Workshop (DFRWS) investigative model. We then focus on cloud forensics processes and models in Section 12.3. Finally, in Section 12.4, we discuss new and future cloud forensic models, taking into account what has been developed in this forensic area. We give a constructive analysis before concluding the chapter.

12.2 Digital Forensics Models

In this section, we describe and discuss different digital forensic models proposed in the literature, to see their impact on the current cloud forensic models.

12.2.1 Digital Forensic Framework Model Development

The digital forensic investigative model is vital to the outcome of any digital crime investigation. Overlooking one procedural step may lead to incomplete or inconclusive interpretations and conclusions; hence, incorrect procedures during digital forensic investigations may lead to evidence being inadmissible in court.

The need for a standard framework has been understood by many international law enforcement agencies, and many researchers have proposed frameworks and models to meet the changing requirements of digital forensic investigations. Throughout the rise of computer forensics, various digital forensic models have been developed and can be divided into three categories defined throughout the evolution of ICT:

- *The ad hoc phase:* The stage when law enforcement officers identified that there was a need for the development of a framework that could be applied to formal investigation processes when investigating computer-related crimes. However, there was a lack of structure, clear goals, adequate tools, and processes to develop such a framework. There were also many legal issues surrounding the gathering and handling of digital evidence that hindered the framework's development (Ryder and Le-Khac 2016).
- *The structured phase:* Characterized by the development of a more complex solution for computer forensics. This development included accepted procedures, frameworks, and tools that were developed specifically to solve computer forensic-related problems. This phase also led to the development of legislation to support the use of digital evidence during criminal and civil trials. The structured phase appeared the mid-1980s when the Computer Analysis Response Team (CART) and other entities were authorized to handle various types of computer-related criminal activity.
- *The enterprise phase:* The current state of computer forensics, and the most advanced phase. At this level, computer forensics is a mature science and involves the real-time collection of evidence, the development of effective tools and processes, and the use of structured protocols and procedures.

Various diverse digital forensic models and frameworks support digital forensic investigations. Since 1984, when a formalized digital forensic investigative model was introduced, a number of further models have been developed. For the purposes of this chapter, we have selected the principal models and documented them in chronological order to illustrate the history of their development, because they are a vital component when conducting digital forensic investigations.

(Pollitt 1995) proposed a methodology known as the Computer Forensic Investigative Process. This model was developed to support digital forensic investigations. The main objective of Pollitt's model was to ensure that all digital evidence could be scientifically relied upon and would be acceptable to the courts.

12.2.2 Digital Forensic Research Workshop (DFRWS) Investigative Model (2001)

DFRWS is a nonprofit organization dedicated to sharing knowledge and concepts regarding digital forensic research. During the first DFRWS workshop in 2001, researchers identified the need to develop a more comprehensive framework than Pollitt's. DFRWS developed a new digital forensic investigative model to support digital forensic investigations. This model was developed as a result of the complex and diverse nature of digital investigations and how these investigations were evolving with advancements in ICT. The framework introduces *digital investigation action classes*: these classes are defined by the framework, which categorizes the activities of a digital forensic investigation into groups.

The framework does not dictate what particular actions must be followed. Instead, it provides a list of candidate techniques, some of which are required. The specifics of the framework need to be redefined and tailored to meet the needs of each investigation and law enforcement agency.

12.2.3 Abstract Digital Forensic Model (ADFM) (2002)

(Reith et al. 2002) proposed a model inspired by the DFRWS investigative model. This model suggests a standardized digital forensics process with the addition of three extra phases, thus expanding the original DRFWS model to nine phases and strengthening it. For instance, in the preparation phase, particular significance is given to the preparation and testing of digital forensic tools, which is a vital component of the admissibility of evidence in court. The nine phases are as follows. The first phase, *identification*, is tasked with recognizing and determining the computer crime or incident. Once this is ascertained, the *preparation* phase identifies the tools and techniques required to conduct the investigation. The *approach* phase focuses on developing a strategy to maximize the collection of evidence. The *preservation* phase focuses on the isolation of suspect media, ensuring it is correctly secured and isolated. The *chain of custody* of evidence is an essential component of this phase. During the *collection* phase, digital evidential material is collected and duplicated. The identification of relevant evidence from the collection phase is conducted in the following *examination* phase. Determining significance and drawing conclusions based on the evidence found is carried out during the *analysis* phase. The *presentation* phase focuses on the presentation and reporting of the relevant evidence. The final stage, *return of evidence*, ensures that seized evidence is returned to the owner.

12.2.4 Integrated Digital Investigation Process (IDIP) (2003)

(Carrier and Spafford 2003) combined the available investigative framework models into one integrated model. The authors presented a new concept known as the *digital crime scene*. This refers to the virtual environment created by software and hardware, where digital evidence of a crime may exist. The model consists of five phases: *readiness, deployment, physical scene investigation, digital crime scene,* and *review*. The model uses the concept that a computer is itself a crime scene, and thus the investigation theory for a physical crime scene is applied to a digital investigation. The digital crime scene investigation is integrated with the physical crime scene so that physical evidence can be collected. The object to connect a suspect to certain digital activity.

12.2.5 Enhanced Integrated Digital Investigation Process (EIDIP) (2004)

The Enhanced Integrated Digital Investigation Process model (Baryamureeba and Tushabe 2004) redefines the forensic process and its progression through various stages. The authors suggested a variant of Carrier and Spafford's IDIP. In the EIDIP model, the authors add two extra phases: *traceback* and *dynamite*. These additional phases separate an investigation into a primary crime scene, *traceback* (the computing device); and a secondary crime scene, *dynamite* (the physical crime scene). The objective of these additional steps is to reconstruct two crime scenes with the objective of avoiding inconsistencies. A key component of this model is that it addresses data-protection issues and also highlights the reconstruction of the events that led to a particular incident.

12.2.6 Discussion

In order for digital evidence to be accepted in court, it must be precise and accurate (Schut et al. 2015). Its integrity should not be compromised by negligence due to poor procedures. The primary function of digital forensic models is to assist digital forensic practitioners in following a predefined set of steps during investigations. These models are required due to the complexity and various facets of digital forensic investigation. The frameworks ensure that safeguards are in place to enable digital evidence to be easily elucidated, examined, and processed. The digital forensics framework models described in this section lack the identification of data that may be stored in cloud-based environments. However, fundamental steps can be drawn from these models and utilized in our approach as well as future approaches.

12.3 Cloud Forensics Process and Model

Cloud computing brings fundamental changes to the way organizations manage their computing needs by enabling them to harness the flexibility of the Cloud while reducing overall ICT running costs. (Ruan et al. 2011) stated that cloud computing has the potential to become one of the most transformative computing technologies, following in the footsteps of mainframes, tablet computers, personal computers, the World Wide Web, and smartphones.

With increasing adoption rates and access to a wide variety of cloud solutions, cloud computing is greatly impacting the way digital forensic investigations are conducted. (Ruan et al. 2011) recognize that cloud computing operates in a computing environment that is different from traditional on-site client application environments. The additional complexity for digital forensic investigations in cloud-based environments arises from the various types of cloud models that exist, such as Software-as-a-Service (SaaS), Infrastructure-as-a-Service (IaaS), and Platform-as-a-Service (PaaS). Despite significant research in the field of digital forensics, little has been written about how digital forensics processes can be applied to a cloud-based environment. Performing investigations within a cloud-based environment has gained momentum in the digital forensic community during the past couple of years. The majority of research concerning cloud computing is focused on defining the challenges of performing digital forensic investigations within physical a cloud computing environment (Birk, 2011; Reilly et al. 2011; Ruan et al. 2011). Cloud forensics is a new field of digital forensics that brings new challenges (Reilly et al. 2011), such as evidence identification, legal issues, data acquisition, and the suitability of traditional digital forensic tools to acquire data from the Cloud. These challenges not only exacerbate the problems of digital forensics within a cloud environment but also create a new front for digital forensic investigations. (Barbara 2009) highlights the important issue of data identification in the Cloud, stating that "with the huge amount of potential data flowing in and out of a cloud, how do you identify individual users of individual services provided by a transient host image, particularly when they make expert efforts to cover their tracks?" Hence, it is clear that digital forensic practitioners will need to adapt their processes and tools in order to conduct investigations in cloud environments. According to (Frowen 2009), there is no foolproof, universal method of extracting evidence in an admissible fashion from the Cloud, and in some cases, very little evidence is available to extract. As such, cloud computing represents just one of the fast-paced technological developments presenting ongoing challenges to legislators, law enforcement officials, and computer forensic analysts. Cloud computing is the most difficult area when it comes to satisfying guidelines mentioned by the Association of Chief Police Officers (ACPO) related to searching and seizing evidence, due to the remoteness of cloud data centers (http://www.digital-detective.net/acpo-good-practice-guide-for-digital-evidence). (Reilly et al. 2011) state that certain aspects of computer forensic processes can be applied to cloud computing, but the main stumbling block is the fact that it may be impractical or legally impossible for digital forensic investigators to seize physical devices likely to contain digital evidence. (Dykstra and Sherman 2012) state that discovery and acquisition of evidence in remote, elastic, provider-controlled cloud computing platforms differ from traditional digital forensics, and examiners lack the proper tools to conduct these tasks. Criminals that target or use cloud computing will undoubtedly emerge in this landscape, and investigators will continue to rely on their existing expertise and tools like Guidance Software's Encase or Access Data's Forensic Tool Kit unless alternative tools or techniques are developed (Richard and Roussev 2006). Several researchers have pointed out that evidence acquisition is a forefront issue with cloud forensics (Dykstra and Sherman 2012; Taylor et al. 2011). In addition, (Ruan et al. 2011) identified the main peripheral challenges posed by cloud adoption and digital investigations within cloud-based environments:

- Data jurisdictional issues
- Lack of international collaboration and legislative mechanisms
- Lack of laws and regulations
- Decreased access to and control over data

(Birk 2011) states that technical challenges for cloud forensics investigations arise due to the various types of cloud computing environments and uncertainty about how to conduct investigations in these environments. (Garfinkel 2010) suggests that "cloud computing in particular may make it impossible to perform basic forensic steps of data preservation and isolation of forensic data/systems of interest." (Lillard et al. 2010) see cloud computing as a subject that must be approached as a matter of network forensics combined with remote disk forensics. However, there are other considerations for law enforcement officers to contemplate when conducting investigations in the Cloud, such as time-dependent issues, extracting large volumes of data, lack of access to data due to the absence of passwords or a lack of expertise, and procedures and appropriate tools during the execution of search warrants. These issues have not been considered fully by Burk and others (Dykstra and Sherman 2012; Ruan et al. 2011; Taylor et al. 2011). In addition, in cloud computing platforms, law enforcement investigators do not have physical control over the data or the data centers in which it resides. Many users access cloud platforms with data that resides locally and/or is synced (Boucher and Le-Khac 2018). How does law enforcement seize only that portion of artifacts where the evidence may exist? How will they know if they have gotten everything they will need during the analysis, interpretation, documentation, and presentation of evidence? According to the results of a survey conducted by (Ruan et al. 2011) of 156 forensics experts and practitioners worldwide, more than half of the respondents agreed that the establishment of a new foundation of standards and policies for digital forensics in cloud-based environments is an opportunity. Indeed, 88.89% agreed or strongly agreed that designing forensic architectures for the Cloud is a valuable research direction for cloud forensics. The need for digital investigations in cloud environments will increase as the adoption of cloud services continues to grow. This will compel law enforcement agencies to adapt their digital forensic procedures when conducting investigations in cloud environments. The extent to which law enforcement agencies have changed from traditional digital forensics processes to meet the challenges posed by cloud forensics could not be established through this research. The challenges in relation to cloud-based forensics are not only technical; there are many legal challenges associated with data recording, privacy, and access issues (Cushman et al. 2016). In addition, the manner in which access is provided to digital forensic practitioners and the process of acquiring evidential material also pose legal concerns. These concerns are extremely important, especially in relation to cloud environments being ubiquitous, multinational, and widely distributed. However, these issues do not fully address the intricacies law enforcement investigators are faced with when executing search warrants within cloud environments. In another survey conducted by (Ruan et al. 2011), of 72 respondents who were asked what the challenges are in cloud forensics, 90.14% agreed or strongly agreed that jurisdiction issues were a key challenge and 82.94% agreed or strongly agreed that the lack of laws/regulations was also a challenge. This is further complicated if cloud resources are distributed across international boundaries. (Ruan et al. 2011) stated that traditional digital forensic professionals identify multijurisdictional and multi-tenancy challenges as the top legal concern. Performing forensics in the cloud exacerbates these challenges. To summarize, we can say that cloud forensics is in its infancy, although a number of important papers have been published in this area that give insight into the more theoretical side. The research did identify that cloud adoption is high and, as a result, the number of cloud-based investigations will rise. These high adoption rates pose a new set of challenges for law enforcement agencies. However, a number of authors have identified critical points regarding cloud forensics and the issues that law enforcement agencies will face. A digital forensic framework model applicable to cloud forensics is required. In addition, many researchers have stated that the current set of digital forensic tools cannot be fully applied to acquisitions in cloud environments. A number of authors agree that the difficulties posed by cloud forensics are complex, given the various forms of cloud computing services that exist. In addition, there are large implications when acquiring data from a cloud environment that may spread over multiple jurisdictions. Researchers have explored the challenges and proposed some solutions to mitigate these challenges. These solutions may be practical during incident response or civil investigations. However, solutions put forward by some researchers could not be utilized by law enforcement agencies in criminal investigations. These issues illustrate the requirement to develop a digital forensic framework for cloud-based investigations supported by appropriate digital forensic tools. This would assist both law enforcement agencies and non-law enforcement bodies conducting criminal investigations in the Cloud.

12.4 Toward a New Cloud Forensics Model

Another objective of our research is how to build a new digital forensic process for investigators to identify and extract data from cloud systems, and how to address associated problems. To do so, we launched a study on how the proliferation of cloud computing is affecting investigators, including the depth of knowledge of cloud computing, digital forensic approaches, and views on moving away from the traditional digital forensic approach. We learned the following from our study:

- Investigating cloud environments is very challenging. In addition, the growth of social media is adding to the challenges faced by investigators when conducting investigations in the Cloud.
- Using traditional approaches to digital forensics may ultimately lead to the loss of evidential material if employed during the execution of search warrants. The reason is that computer forensic practitioners may only establish that a cloud-based solution was used by a suspect during the review of the seized evidence. This can lead to the destruction of evidence in the Cloud by a suspect.

Due to the limitations of traditional forensics, an alternative digital forensic model is required, supported by a robust framework to identify and extract data from cloud environments. Our new model was initially presented in (Plunkett et al. 2015). In this chapter, we continue to detail and complete it with a comprehensive study and evaluation. This model is described as a framework that enables an investigator to identify and extract specific data relating to a given case in the most efficient manner. In addition, we also propose a number of digital forensics tools that support the extraction of evidential material from a cloud system. Usually, these tools have been fully accepted by the courts. There are different ways to launch a cloud investigation. However, we conducted research and found that investigators need to be specific about the data volumes they identify and acquire. This applies to organizations or individuals that may be under investigation. It is neither practical for investigators to seize entire virtual machines running on cloud systems nor practical to seize entire physical servers of data centers. Hence, our approach has been developed by being cognizant of the factors mentioned previously while also ensuring that the following considerations are addressed: (i) time on site and (ii) large data extraction. First, when officers investigate a suspect location under a search warrant, the time spent on site is a critical factor. They need to identify, document, and acquire evidential material in a reasonable timeframe that does not impact greatly the suspect organization or individual. Second, during the execution of a search warrant, investigators can be faced with very large volumes of data. Extracting all the potentially useful data during the execution of a search warrant can cause a number of issues.

12.4.1 Model

This is a digital forensic framework model consists of three main components coupled with the use of dedicated software and hardware, outlined as follows: (i) pre-search preparation; (ii) search; (iii) post-search investigation. Each of these components has a number of tasks that must be completed prior to the next component being utilized. A diagram illustrating these steps is provided in Figure 12.1.

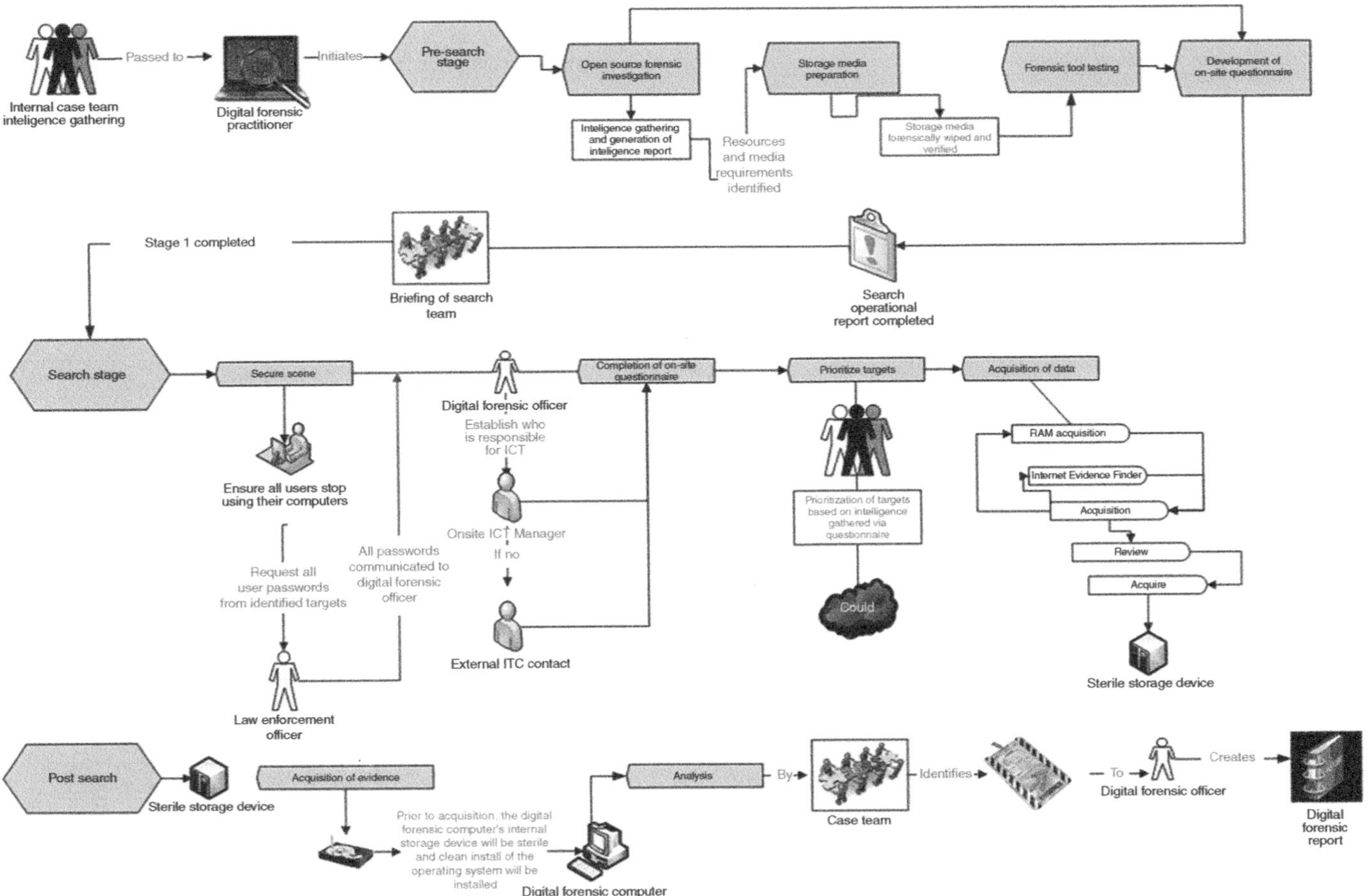

Figure 12.1 Proposed cloud forensic model.

12.4.2 Pre-Search

The pre-search stage has five tasks that must be completed prior to the execution of a search:

i) Gather all publicly available information regarding suspect individuals or organizations. Particular focus during this stage is on trying to identify the IT environment within the target location. Open source intelligence gathering can identify whether a cloud-based environment may be encountered during the execution of a search warrant. This task focuses on gathering all relevant intelligence regarding the suspect organization, its target employees, or an individual. The intake and orientation; strategy, search, store; technical capabilities, tactical applications; analysis; refine, recycle, and reporting (ISTAR) method (Doodeman 2017) can be used as a means of intelligence gathering while ensuring that the correct steps are taken during this stage.
ii) Ensure that all digital forensic tools used in the extraction of evidence are forensically sound and function correctly prior to use. This task ensures that during the execution of a search warrant, all digital forensic tools used to acquire digital evidence are used in a forensically sound manner. The tool used to wipe all sectors on the storage devices needs to be rigorously tested and documented to ensure that it is correctly functioning prior to conducting the wiping of storage devices.
iii) Ensure that all storage media used to store evidential material is sterile. It is vital that all storage media used to store evidential material is forensically wiped to ensure that no cross contamination of evidence can occur. Each storage device must be forensically wiped and verified to ensure that no data resides on the device.
iv) Build a picture of the ICT infrastructure of the target location, and identify whether cloud-based infrastructures exist. This task deals with the development of an on-site ICT infrastructure questionnaire. The objective of the questionnaire is to develop a picture of the ICT environment during the execution of a search warrant. The questionnaire will assist digital forensic practitioners in ascertaining whether cloud-based solutions are being utilized. Vital information will be recorded during this phase of the search, including information such as passwords used to access any cloud-based environments, the type of encryption solutions that may be employed within the organization, the identification and recording of the security controls in place, and establishing how access to data is controlled within the organization.
v) Ensure that all search team members are aware of the intelligence gathered and the proposed operational plan. This step ensures that all members of the investigation and search team are briefed on all intelligence gathered and the approach to be employed by the digital forensic practitioners. It is important that search team members are briefed prior to the execution of a search warrant because each team member will be responsible for securing the scene and ensuring that no digital evidence can be destroyed during the initial stages of the execution of the search warrant.

12.4.3 Search Stage

The search stage focuses on the execution of the search warrant and the identification and acquisition of digital evidence. The stage comprises four phases: (i) secure the scene; (ii) identify IT personnel and complete the on-site infrastructural questionnaire; (iii) prioritization of targets and devices; (iv) RAM and internet acquisition, and identified cloud and local acquisition.

Phase 1: Secure the scene

The main objectives of this phase are to secure scene, identify target individuals, and obtain access passwords. In addition, it is important to ensure that no suspect personnel delete any electronic data. Each search team member should have been briefed and trained on how to secure the scene and search site prior to the execution of the search warrant. In addition, each team member will be assigned a high-priority target identified in pre-search task 1 (as discussed in the previous section.

It is also vital that each team member acquire the username and password in order to maintain access to the computing devices associated with individual targets. However, this depends on the legislation of each country or region as discussed in our previous research (Ryder and Le-Khac 2016). For example, during the execution of a search warrant, Irish law enforcement officers have the right to request all passwords to access any systems they believe may contain evidential material. The Criminal Justice Bill, 2011 and the Competition Act, 2002 have provisions and associated sanctions for non-cooperation.

Phase 2: Identify IT personnel and complete the on-site infrastructural questionnaire

The purpose of this phase is to gain an understanding of the ICT infrastructure in order to facilitate the acquisition of specific target data and the prioritization of target individuals who utilize cloud systems. When using our model, it is the responsibility of the lead investigator to identify the individual responsible for the maintenance of the ICT environment during the execution of the search warrant. If the ICT is managed externally, the next step is to request that the external ICT support organization assist the lead investigator in establishing the ICT environment of the suspect organization. If no assistance can be given to the lead investigator, the warrant holder will be informed, because the prioritization of targets and data may change due to the lack of access or knowledge of the ICT infrastructure in question. Once completed, the ICT infrastructure questionnaire should provide the investigator with a detailed view as to how the ICT infrastructure of the target location is constructed.

Phase 3: Prioritization of targets and devices

The infrastructure questionnaire focuses on identifying whether any cloud-based systems are being utilized by the organization or individual. Once the questionnaire is completed, the investigator will communicate with the warrant holder to establish whether any further targets have been identified. The warrant holder will also communicate any additional passwords identified by the other team members during phase 1. If no additional targets have been identified, the lead investigator will begin the process of prioritizing the target individuals and will acquire specific digital evidence. The acquisition of data will be prioritized based on targets that can access cloud systems.

Phase 4: RAM and internet acquisition, and identified cloud and local acquisition

These steps ensure that the most effective approach is applied to acquiring digital evidence stored either on the Cloud or on a local device. This stage has a number of predefined steps that must be carried out in a certain order:

i) Acquisition of volatile data is required in order to ensure that any passwords running in random access memory (RAM) can be acquired if not voluntarily disclosed to a search team member.
ii) Acquisition of all internet-related evidence.

iii) Analyzing of data. This stage focuses on reviewing the two datasets acquired previously to identify whether any cloud-based applications have been utilized on the suspect machine. If identified, further information may be required from the user of the suspect machine. Once a detailed picture of the suspect device is established, along with how the user operates this device, the process of acquiring the digital evidence can commence. If the acquisition relates to data in cloud-based environments, then a specific approach will need to be applied, depending on the type of cloud models or cloud services.
iv) Acquisition of the registry. This is an important step in establishing detailed information regarding the suspect device such as application install dates, internet and application most-recently used lists, and username/password access. This evidence is vital to link the user of a computer to digital evidence found.
v) Investigation of the user-access control within the local or network environment. Using tools such as AccessEnum (Russinovich 2006) will assist digital forensic practitioners, post-search, in constructing a picture of who had access to particular electronic evidence.

12.4.4 Post-Search Investigation Stage

The post-search investigation stage focuses on the acquisition of the evidence seized and analysis of this evidence. This stage is composed of three phases.

Phase 1: Acquisition

All evidence seized from the suspect organization or individual will be acquired from the sterile media as discussed in the pre-search stage. Best practice techniques state that a digital forensic practitioner should never work on original evidence; therefore, all evidence seized will be copied to a digital forensic workstation (http://www.digital-detective.net/acpo-good-practice-guide-for-digital-evidence). A forensic workstation will be used to conduct analysis of all data acquired during an investigation. The forensic workstation will also utilize sterile disks and will not be connected to any networked environments. This is to ensure the integrity of the evidence being analyzed. Once the data is acquired, it is verified against the original evidence; the original evidence is then given to the case exhibits officer to ensure the continuity of this evidence.

Phase 2: Analysis

Once all the evidential material is acquired to the forensic workstation, the analysis can begin. An important aspect of this analysis is to ensure that all data seized from the target organization or individual is made available to the case team. The pertinent evidence is identified by the case team and communicated to the forensic practitioner. The forensic practitioner will identify the evidence from the original acquisition images and will attempt to establish, through document metadata, the report, and intelligence gathered through the onsite infrastructural questionnaire, who was the creator and editor of the identified evidential files.

Phase 3: Reporting

A forensic report will be created by the forensic practitioner. The on-site infrastructural questionnaire is a key component for the generation of the forensic report because it forms the initial foundations of how and why evidence was identified and acquired. The onsite infrastructural questionnaire will also detail who had access to cloud-based systems, how they were used, and what files were acquired from the Cloud. This information, coupled with the registry analysis and the report, will try to link suspect individuals to vital pieces of evidence. The report will consist of an overview of the case and a summary of where the evidence was found, the forensic analysis that was conducted, and the findings based on the evidential material.

12.5 Evaluation and Analysis

To evaluate the proposed approach, we consider the following scenario. In a country, the Authority was established following the enactment of the Competition Act, 1991. The function of the Authority is to promote competition in all sectors of the economy by tackling anticompetitive practices and by increasing awareness of such practices. Where there is evidence of businesses engaging in anti-competitive practices – whether through price-fixing or abusing their dominant position – the Authority can intervene through the enforcement of competition law. Under Section 45 of the Competition Act 2002, the Authority has the power to enter any premises to seize and retain any books, documents, and records. The application of the proposed model was utilized by the Authority's digital forensics practitioners in conjunction with traditional forensic techniques during the execution of three search warrants on organizations alleged to be engaged in cartel behavior. Prior to the implementation of our approach, the Authority utilized traditional digital forensic methods. The Authority's Cartels division is responsible for investigating alleged hard-core criminal Cartels. The information outlined here does not refer directly to the industry in which the investigation took place, the organizations that were under investigation, or the people involved in the alleged behavior. The organization, for referral purposes, will be called Organization A. The Cartels division received intelligence regarding cartel behavior in a particular industry, and, as a result, further evidence was required to progress the investigation. This evidence would be gathered through the execution of two search warrants on the suspected organizations. In this evaluation, we focus on the search stage and post-search investigation.

12.5.1 Search Stage

12.5.1.1 Secure the Scene/Onsite Infrastructural Questionnaire

The search warrant was executed, and the search scene was secured by the search team members. The lead digital forensic practitioner assigned to the search site requested access to the IT manager to ascertain the IT infrastructure of the organization.

The organization in question did not have an IT manager on site; however, the organization utilized in IT support company. The lead digital forensic practitioner made contact with the IT support company and acquired the administration passwords to access the servers and computers of Organization A.

Further information regarding the IT infrastructure of Organization A was supplied to the lead investigator, enabling them to complete the on-site infrastructural questionnaire. The infrastructural questionnaire identified that Organization A utilized Gmail as its primary e-mail application. Two users had sole access to the account. These users had previously been identified as target individuals. No other target individuals were identified within Organization A.

The lead investigator requested the Gmail passwords from the target individuals; these were voluntarily disclosed and documented in the on-site questionnaire. The lead investigator commenced the acquisition of the two targets identified in accordance with the search stage, phase 4: RAM and internet acquisition, review, identify cloud and local acquisition. The acquisition of RAM of both target devices was conducted, and Internet Evidence Finder was run on both target devices; it revealed that no other cloud-based systems were being utilized by these target individuals. The lead investigator then employed EnCase Portable and configured an Enscript to search each of the suspect devices for any locally stored e-mail files and to report on any documentary files that had been deleted from the system within a specific timeframe. No e-mail files were found; however, a number of suspect files were identified as having been deleted.

12.5.1.2 Acquisition of the Gmail Account

No locally stored e-mail applications were installed on either target device; therefore, Microsoft Outlook 2010 was required to be installed on one of the target devices. This process was documented by the lead digital forensic practitioner. Once installed, the Post Office Protocol (POP) accounts with the usernames and passwords were configured in Microsoft Outlook 2010, and a local .pst file was generated and acquired to the forensic storage device.

12.5.1.3 Acquisition of Pertinent Network Data

Both targets identified previously accessed a single shared network share that contained evidential material. The network share was located on a server within the target premises. The share name was directly related to the nature of the alleged offense, and all data within this share was deemed to be of high importance. The acquisition of the entire share was made using FTK Imager. The acquired forensic image was generated and written to the forensic storage device. Using AccessEnum, a report was generated on the security and access control of this share. This report was placed on the sterile storage device.

12.5.1.4 Seizure of Devices

During the initial stages of the analysis of both target devices, it was established that a number of suspect files had been deleted from both target machines that might hold evidential material. It was therefore recommended to the warrant holder by the lead investigator that both devices should be seized. The lead investigator powered off both target devices and seized them.

12.5.2 Results/Report

If traditional digital forensic techniques had been used in this investigation, vital information such as the cloud application Gmail and data stored on encrypted drives would not have been identified, and thus vital evidential material might have been overlooked. Using our proposed model enabled the lead investigator and the search team to work together to identify targets and evidential material prior to the execution of a search warrant. The use of the onsite questionnaire and the systematic approach enabled the investigator to identify whether cloud systems were being utilized within the target organization.

Using EnCase Portable to search various network drives for particular keywords enabled the investigator to acquire relevant data, thus reducing the size of the evidential material. All data was acquired using digital forensic tools. These tools also verified the acquisition of any data and provided the investigation team with the best evidence possible. The final stage of our approach has not been applied to this investigation because it is a live case and has not proceeded to this stage as yet.

12.6 Conclusion

In this chapter, the challenges of cloud forensics have been discussed in conjunction with examining current digital forensic tools and frameworks. The utilization of digital forensic tools that have the ability to systematically search digital devices, whether in the Cloud or locally stored, is critical to conducting effective forensic investigations. Current research efforts suggest that cloud forensics is still in its infancy. Numerous challenges have been identified and incorporated into our proposed cloud forensic model. The proposed model successfully identified and extracted data from a cloud computing system. Acquiring evidence from the Cloud is complex but can be simplified and accomplished in an organized and systematic way by utilizing an appropriate digital forensic framework. The proposed approach attempts to improve upon existing digital frameworks through the amalgamation of standard techniques. The proposed model also advocates a systematic approach supported by digital forensic tools, which reduces the risks associated with the acquisition of digital evidence.

The growth of smart mobile devices and their integration with cloud systems is a new area and requires further research. Computing devices such as laptops and PCs will soon be overtaken by smart mobile devices. This opens a new set of challenges for cloud forensics and will require fundamentally different tools and supporting frameworks (Faheem et al. 2015; Faheem et al. 2016). The current generation of digital forensics tools is limited in use when acquiring data from a cloud system. These tools have been overtaken by the advances of cloud-based solutions and the intense growth of information. Research regarding the next generation of digital forensic tools for law enforcement agencies is required to meet future advancements of cloud technologies.

References

Barbara, J.J. (2009). Cloud computing: another digital forensic challenge. Forensic Magazine. https://www.forensicmag.com/article/2009/10/cloud-computing-another-digital-forensic-challenge (accessed December 2016).

Baryamureeba, V. and Tushabe, F. (2004). The enhanced digital investigation process model. In: Proceedings of the Fourth Digital Forensic Research Workshop, 1–9.

Birk, D. (2011). Technical challenges of forensic investigations in Cloud. http://www.zurich.ibm.com/~cca/csc2011/submissions/birk.pdf (accessed December 2016).

Boucher, J. and Le-Khac, N.-A. (2018). Forensic framework to identify local vs synced artefacts. *Digital Investigation* 24 (1): 2018.

Carrier, B. and Spafford, E.H. (2003). Getting physical with the digital investigation process. *International Journal of Digital Evidence* 2 (2).

Cushman, I., Chen, L., Rawat, D. et al. (2016). Designing hybrid cloud using OpenStack for supporting multimedia with security and privacy concerns. 9th EAI International Conference on Mobile Multimedia Communications, Xi'an, China, June 18–19, 2016.

Doodeman, M. (2017). ISTAR model. Dutch National Police Agency.

Dykstra, J. and Sherman, A.T. (2012). Acquiring forensic evidence from infrastructure-as-a-service cloud computing: exploring and evaluating tools, trust, and techniques. *Digital Investigation* 9: S90–S98.

Emison, J.M. 2013. Research: (2013) State of cloud computing. Federal-CIO-Council. 2011. Guidelines for Secure Use of Cloud Computing by Federal Departments and Agencies.

Faheem, M., Kechadi, M.-T., and Le-Khac, N.-A. (2015). The state of the art forensic techniques in mobile cloud environment: a survey, challenges and current trend. *International Journal of Digital Crime and Forensics* 7 (2): 1–19.

Faheem, M., Kechadi, M-T., Le-Khac, N-A. (2016) 'Toward a new mobile cloud forensic framework'. IEEE Sixth International Conference on Innovative Computing Technology (INTECH), Dublin, Ireland, 24–26 Aug. 2016.

Frowen, A. (2009). Cloud computing and computer forensics. http://www.artipot.com/articles/384511/coud-computing-and-computer-forensics.htm (accessed December 2016).

Garfinkel, S.L. (2010). Digital forensics research: the next 10 years. *Digital Investigation* 2010 (7): S64–S73.

Hayes, D. (2014). *A Practical Guide to Computer Forensics Investigations*. Pearson IT Certification.

Kolenbrander F., Le-Khac N-A., and Kechadi M-T. (2016). Forensic analysis of ARES GALAXY peer-to-peer network. 11th annual ADFSL Conference on Digital Forensics, Security and Law, Florida, USA, May 2016.

Lessing, M. and Von Solms, SH. (2008). Live forensic acquisition as alternative to traditional forensic processes. 4th International Conference on IT Incident Management & IT Forensics.

Lillard, T.V., Garrison, C.P., Schiller, C.A. et al. (2010). *Digital Forensics for Network, Internet, and Cloud Computing*. Syngress Media.

Plunkett, J., Le-Khac N-A., and Kechadi M-T. (2015). Digital forensic investigations in the Cloud: a proposed approach for Irish law enforcement. 11th Annual IFIP WG 11.9 International Conference on Digital Forensics (IFIP119 2015), Orlando, Florida, United States, 26–28 January 2015.

Pollitt, M.M. (1995). Computer forensics: An approach to evidence in cyberspace. In: Proceeding of the National Information Systems Security Conference, Baltimore, vol. II, 487-491.

Reilly, D., Wren, C., and Berry, T. (2011). Cloud computing: pros and cons for computer forensic investigations. *International Journal Multimedia and Image Processing* 1 (1): 26–34.

Reith, M., Carr, C., and Gunsch, G. (2002). An examination of digital forensic models. *International Journal of Digital Evidence* 1 (3).

Richard, I.I.I. and Roussev, V. (2006). Digital forensic tools: the next generation. In: *Digital Crime and Forensic Science in Cyberspace*, 75–90. IGI Global.

Ruan, K., Carthy, J., Kechadi, T. et al. (2011). Cloud forensics, advances in digital forensics VII. *IFIP Advances in Information and Communication Technology* 361: 35–46.

Russinovich, M. (2006). AccessEnum v1.32. https://docs.microsoft.com/en-us/sysinternals/downloads/accessenum (accessed December 2016).

Ryder, S. and Le-Khac N-A. (2016), The end of effective law enforcement in the Cloud? To encrypt, or not to encrypt The 9th IEEE International Conference on Cloud Computing, San Francisco, CA USA, June 2016.

Schut H., Farina J., Scanlon M. et al. (2015). Towards the forensic identification and investigation of cloud hosted servers through noninvasive wiretaps. The 10th International Workshop on Frontiers in Availability, Reliability and Security FARES 2015, Toulouse, France, August 24–28, 2015.

Taylor, M., Gresty, D., and Lamb, D. (2011). Forensic investigation of cloud computing systems. *Journal Network Security* 2011 (3): 4–10.

13

Data Acquisition in the Cloud

Nhien-An Le-Khac[1], Michel Mollema[2], Robert Craig[3], Steven Ryder[4], and Lei Chen[5]

[1]*University College Dublin, Dublin, Ireland*
[2]*Dutch National High Tech Crime Unit, Driebergen-Rijsenburg, The Netherlands*
[3]*Walworth County Sheriff's Office, Elkhorn, WI, USA*
[4]*Europol, The Hague, The Netherlands*
[5]*Georgia Southern University, Statesboro, GA, USA*

13.1 Introduction

The Cloud can be considered "a shared pool of configurable computing resources (e.g. networks, servers, storage, applications, and services)" (Mell and Grance 2011). In the context of digital forensics, this could mean that, for example, a given collection of illicit material is stored on the servers of a cloud provider or across multiple cloud providers. Bear in mind that the cloud provider's country of operation does not necessarily allow conclusions about the geographic location of one or more of its servers, which could be hosted in multiple countries – not to mention that the original cloud provider may have subcontracted its services to other providers (Nishawala 2013). This means in practical terms that the illicit material stored by the suspect is literally scattered in the clouds, for all intents and purposes regarding gaining access to it. It may as well be, from the perspective of law enforcement, which may possibly be required to identify the various locations, issue specific and separate requests for mutual legal assistance, and then hope for a swift response from the various jurisdictions contacted (Dykstra 2013).

The challenges include, in order of the discovery of a suspect/suspected activity, first the identification of the use of cloud services for storage. This could be something obvious, such as a Dropbox account that is prominent on the desktop, or a Google Drive icon, even though provided by the manufacturer of the device; but it could also be a less obvious solution that is not immediately considered, such as using an e-mail account to store data in, for example, unsent messages or drafts. If the use of cloud storage is suspected and a specific provider is identified, the next challenge is the location of any stored material and its identification. If the suspect does not cooperate, the challenges increase – to such an extent that non-cooperation by a suspect as regards the provision of passwords has been made a criminal offense in a very pragmatic manner in some locations.

Security, Privacy, and Digital Forensics in the Cloud, First Edition. Edited by Lei Chen, Hassan Takabi, and Nhien-An Le-Khac.

Basically, if or when the cloud provider has been identified, the need for cooperation from the provider is essential. This may involve a non-judicial means such as a simple request for information: some providers are open to this, while others require – and even pride themselves in not divulging any information about suspected clients in the absence of – a court order to do so. Cloud providers often overwrite their own data, or may remove it without involving law enforcement if it breaches their own terms and conditions, so speed is of the essence in the identification of suspected cloud storage – which as a first step would be followed by a preservation order, forbidding the provider to delete or remove any content. As a follow-up or at the same time, an order is issued for the production of information regarding all activity of the client, together with a request for access to or provision of the material stored by the suspect.

During cybercrime investigations in a data-dense environment such as the Cloud, investigators are frequently sent to data centers to collect evidence from computer hosts located within these data centers. In an increasing number of cases, it is becoming difficult to locate the data center where the computer host the investigator is interested in is running. While it is common to reach out to the hosting provider and ask for the data center's address, there are situations in which it is not possible to contact the hosting provider ahead of time. There are also several reasons why a hosting provider cannot be trusted with the details of the involved computer host. For instance, an Internet service provider (ISP) could inform the user of the computer host prior to the investigator's arrival. The user could then alter or remove evidence before the investigator collects or intercepts it. These so-called *non-law-enforcement-friendly ISPs* require a different approach.

So far, most of the research on cloud forensics has focused on challenges, theory models, forensic services, and process or forensic frameworks (Plunkett et al. 2015). There is very little research on data acquisition in the Cloud. Therefore, in this chapter, we tackle challenges related to forensic acquisition and analysis of artifacts in the Cloud. We first discuss different legal perspectives related to cloud service providers and data storage. Next, we describe how to locate the data center where the computer host the investigator is interested in is running. We also propose an efficient approach to tackling this challenge: a new three-phase guideline that builds on known techniques and combines them with investigative techniques. Finally, we show the forensic acquisition and analysis of a popular cloud storage platform: Amazon Web Service S3. The preliminary result is promising and provides useful suggestions.

13.2 Background

13.2.1 Inside the Internet

A typical website such as cnn.com provides world news to its audience. Technically, a website like cnn.com has an Internet-connected host behind it to provide its content to the Internet. Cnn.com is a domain name with an owner; this domain name is linked to the Internet Protocol (IP) address of the Internet-connected host using the Domain Name System (DNS). DNS translates an easy-to-remember domain name into the IP address, which is more difficult to remember. The Internet-connected host of cnn.com also has an owner, but not necessarily the same owner as that of the domain name cnn.

com. The Internet connection, and the location (data center) of the host, can be owned by different entities.

Many hosting providers are very transparent in advertising their whereabouts. They enter the correct data in the regional Internet registry (RIR) database (https://www.nro.net/about/rirs) and provide contact and network details on their websites. They will disclose the correct subscriber information if they receive a court order. Other providers take less care in providing their host locations to the RIR database and have fewer details on their websites. This could be due to lack of proper administration and to save on costs. For instance, a small hosting company can save money by not having to answer phone calls, so it only allows contact via e-mail. It may still disclose the correct information if it receives a court order. Finally, there are so-called *bulletproof hosts*. These hosts advertise to their customers that they will not respond to abuse requests and law-enforcement requests. They do not keep extensive logs about their customers, and they put incorrect data on their whereabouts in the RIR database. Usually they do not mention details about their data center locations on their websites. Some do not even have a website; they get new customers by word of mouth or by advertising in the cyber underground.

13.2.2 Law Enforcement Interventions in Cybercrime

Law enforcement investigators look at the Internet from a different perspective than normal users. They try to see where traces of evidence can be found. After this, physically locating and gathering the evidence is one of the most important steps the investigators are interested in. Law enforcement and other public cybersecurity organizations and private companies around the world conduct investigations on cyber-related matters. For instance, these could be investigations into e-mail spam by a security company, or into vulnerabilities on Internet-connected devices. Usually cybercrimes are investigated by law enforcement organizations. Normally, the cybercrime investigation unit of the law enforcement agency is responsible for investigating the highest level of high-tech criminal investigations. Typically, a perpetrator uses many server hosts to perform crimes. Within cyber investigations, all types of hosting companies are encountered. The strategy for locating data centers depends on the type of hosting company encountered, as mentioned earlier.

13.3 Data Center as a Source of Evidence

Investigators often find themselves on their way to data centers to collect relevant forensic evidence on Internet-connected hosts. Based on the IP address, many of these hosts can be pinpointed to a data centers' physical address (Nicolls et al. 2016). Contacting the involved hosting provider is usually enough to get the address details of the data center. Data centers are facilities where computer systems are housed and data is stored. Governments, universities, and large businesses typically have their own data centers. Commercial data centers provide hosting of websites and storage of large quantities of data. Nowadays, data centers are also used to provide cloud services, such as cloud storage or cloud computing. A data center can be as big as a large factory. A large data center consumes as much energy as a small town (Mittal 2014).

Data centers are complex facilities. Since they need power, cooling, and connectivity, a lot of infrastructure needs to be in place. Modern data centers allow for redundancy on all these aspects. Furthermore, a typical computer system in a data center is no typical desktop PC; most of the time, it is a 19-inch-wide server system. These server systems can have server-specific hardware like SAS-hard drives. A server can be connected to the power grid by one or more power supplies; it connects to the Internet or network with one or more network cables. Servers can host one operating system or several at the same time. Servers can also be interconnected to form clusters. These interconnected server systems can also connect to each other across the Internet to share resources for cloud services. The server systems are located in racks, which can hold over 40 server systems each.

Not every hosting provider can be trusted. These non-law-enforcement-friendly ISPs cannot be contacted ahead of time. This could mean that the hosting company is not yet known to law enforcement, and therefore no objective assessment is available based on experience with the hosting company. After a first encounter with such a hosting company, it may be considered a trusted hosting provider from then on. Sometimes the hosting provider is the subject of the investigation or is thought to inform customers about law enforcement contacting the hosting provider about a specific host. This poses the risk of the customer being able to alter or remove evidence from the involved host. Such bulletproof hosts are non-law enforcement Friendly ISPs and require a different approach by law enforcement. They cannot be contacted ahead of time because of the chance they will contact their customers prior to the arrival of law enforcement officials. Investigators tend to use other methods like traceroute and WHOIS queries to find the location of the data center involved, but these have proven to be less accurate than required.

The term *non-law-enforcement-friendly ISP* is sometimes used in combination with the term *bulletproof host* (BPH) (Bernaards et al. 2012). These BPH companies willingly provide services to Internet criminals to facilitate activities like hosting child pornography, e-mail spamming, and distribution of malware. The term *non-law enforcement friendly ISP* can also mean to a law enforcement officer that there is no knowledge yet about how cooperative the ISP is. So, it doesn't necessarily mean that the ISP is willingly facilitating criminals. A different example of a non-law enforcement friendly ISP is when an ISP is very hesitant to cooperate with law enforcement and insists on informing customers if law enforcement asks questions about them. This could be due to a transparency policy, or out of political motivations. Sometimes the term *non-law-enforcement-friendly ISP* is used for one specific occurrence, like WikiLeaks. The same ISP may be considered law enforcement friendly during other encounters.

13.4 Cloud Service Providers: Essential Requirements, Governance, and Challenges

We need to establish the status of cloud providers and the circumstances in which they operate. Equally relevant is the constantly changing nature of their operating environment, the changes that are ongoing as well as those that are coming, and the varying legislation they face. Once we have fully understood the scope and strategies in which cloud providers operate, we can then assess the similar environment for law enforcement – which will then lead to an analysis of where there are joint needs as well as competing ones. We then try to assess which needs will prevail.

13.4.1 Business Model

The business models used by providers of cloud services vary and are hard to summarize due to the vast services they provide. In general, they mainly provide Infrastructure-as-a-Service (IaaS), Software-as-a-Service (SaaS), and Platform-as-a-Service (PaaS) (Grispos et al. 2012). For the purposes of this chapter, the focus will be on storage providers, which fall under the general concept of IaaS and specifically, in this respect, the consumer market, rather than commercial or business-oriented solutions. With regard to law enforcement activity, currently the majority of suspects using cloud services do so in a private capacity, rather than through business-oriented solutions. Specifically, the major providers of personal cloud storage are on a global level, such as Apple, Dropbox, Amazon, Google, and Microsoft.

Cloud storage is a massive business area. The biggest difference, compared to traditional data storage services, is the scale to which providers outsource their own services and act more as intermediaries, rather than full-service providers using their own infrastructure. This brings with it a number of specific challenges, when taking into account the need or ability for private companies to preserve or access their own logs or infrastructure for forensic purposes. In addition, due to heightened public awareness concerning data retention and collection, companies are protecting themselves by being unable to provide logs or forensic evidence to law enforcement.

13.4.2 Legal Environment of Operations

The legal governance of cloud providers is a very new challenge (Ryder and Le-Khac 2016). The field is nearly unique in its overlap with and often contradiction of legal compliance, interwoven with and dependent on various judicial jurisdictions. An assessment will be made of the specific areas of law that present unique challenges and the consequences these may have on the operations of a cloud provider.

13.4.2.1 Jurisdictional Issues

As already stated, and as is often accepted, cloud storage by definition is not bound by geographical boundaries. The client that uploads data has very little control over where the data is ultimately stored, either in its entirety or in parts. Until recently, this has not concerned consumers much – until the Snowden revelations, which are ongoing. Since then, entire markets have arisen, from making a feature of and letting consumers choose the geographical place of storage, and therefore the applicable jurisdiction from a legal perspective, to new offers such as hybrid-cloud storage systems (http://www.fujitsu.com/global/services/hybrid-cloud).

While most clients have been generally unaware of the differences in legal regimes that may apply to their data, depending on its storage location in a physical sense, the differences, especially as regards privacy and in that sense data protection (not from a security perspective, but from a personal data protection point of view) are vast.

Overall, the primary cloud storage providers are based in and/or storing their data in the EU, in the United States, or in other countries. Where a number of locations are chosen or available to a provider, as is the case for a significant number of them, the choice of location for the following analysis will follow the weakest-link concept – depending, naturally, on whose perspective it is viewed from. Based on the applicability of US law, companies that operate in the US are under an obligation to comply with US-issued court orders and warrants for all data under their control. In that sense, a reliance on the fact that other legislation is applicable to their other data centers may be a valid point, albeit a mute one, as it will not overrule US law and the obligation of the provider to supply the data ordered (In Re Grand Jury Proceedings the Bank of Nova Scotia 1984).

Further, a contrast between the EU and the US is based not only on the question of market distribution, but also on a comparison of the EU with the US. Fundamental differences exist as regards the balance of powers between law enforcement and data protection or privacy rights, with the EU taking a stronger stance on privacy, at the cost of law enforcement; the reverse is true for the US, mainly as a result of the events of September 11, 2001 (Fuchs 2013). For the purposes of the following evaluation and comparison, we can place countries in three groups, while taking into account EU legislation, US legislation, and that of other countries.

The EU can be placed in one group, as the majority of legislation applicable is of an EU nature and consequently is applicable across the EU. The same applies to data-transfer agreements with third states, which are concluded between the EU and a third state, and are binding on all of the EU's member states – just like, for example, mutual legal assistance agreements or extradition agreements, or any other agreement the EU concludes. These are all binding in their entirety on each of the individual Member States. Therefore, a specific examination per country is superfluous. The only exception, as far as EU legislation concerning law enforcement cooperation, and law enforcement specifically, is the United Kingdom; as applicable, it will be highlighted separately, along with other deviations of interest (Ryder and Le-Khac 2016).

The second group, the US, is even more homogenous as regards its legislation and specifically as regards its law enforcement powers. This includes the perceived ability to have US courts issue US law enforcement near-global mandates, regardless of the physical location of whichever virtual object or concrete physical device for storage or other use they desire to interact with or remove – as long as there is some connection to the United States (Hiller 2015).

The third group, the generically titled *third states*, is a catch-all for assorted countries based on their lack of law enforcement actions and cooperation, for practical purposes. They are in essence bulletproof hosting providers, and may even specifically market themselves as being locations renowned for lack of cooperation – be it due to the lack of will of law enforcement, lack of ability, or even cooperation or tacit acceptance by the host state. On the one hand, this speaks for strong privacy guarantees. In practical terms, however, such providers will often be used purely for criminal activities, such as botnets, child abuse material and its dissemination, or open terrorism propaganda – all safe in the knowledge that the reach of law enforcement does not stretch to them or their users (Goncharov 2015).

As concerns data protection and the ability to outsource/subcontract cloud storage, users have the greatest control if they choose a company within the EU. This will prohibit outsourcing of storage and ensure that data stays outside of the physical jurisdiction of the US, which seems to be one of the major privacy concerns of the public at present. The trend can equally be observed in the number of EU-based cloud storage providers promoting themselves equally to US or other non-EU based citizens, as well as EU citizens, with slogans such as "It's Better in Europe," or moving their headquarters to the EU to avoid association with US law enforcement. This also applies to a number of US headquartered firms moving data centers to the EU to address concerns of data sovereignty, such as IBM, Google, Amazon, and VMWare (Ryder and Le-Khac 2016).

To avoid the perceived overreach of the US onto data stored in the cloud, a solely EU-based cloud storage company, using its own infrastructure, is a definitive safeguard. As this includes not only criminal activities or considerations, but also those of businesses and corporations, we will most likely see the trend moving toward the EU being the preferred option for cloud storage; while boosting the market in the EU, this will have a detrimental impact on that of the US.

13.4.2.2 Permissibility of Encryption and Expectation of Privacy

The central aspect of this thesis as regards the likelihood of service providers moving to encryption naturally depends heavily on the legal permissibility of doing so. As argued earlier and further later in this chapter as regards possible countermeasures, outlawing encryption is an option that could be considered; but we believe it is a nonstarter based simply on the dramatic impact this would have on a civil transparent society – which would be made transparent by legislation. Equally, encryption is one of the essential manners in which businesses protect themselves against criminal activity. It is of specific relevance and interest to assess the current manner in which, from a law enforcement perspective, legislation exists to hinder, deter, or deal with the question of permissibility of encryption.

From a contextual practical perspective, encryption not only hinders swift law enforcement examination of seized media and online accounts or storage, but it also links to a need to gain access to e-mails, media devices, etc. that are protected by passwords, especially when dealing with live systems. Pragmatic approaches exist most notably in the EU in the United Kingdom, but in general the consequence of the seizure of encrypted devices leads to frustration, resignation, and dramatic delays in the forensic and evidential analysis of seized media, or to clear clashes with the basic right against self-incrimination.

13.4.2.3 Summary

The needs, requirements, and terms of operation of a cloud service provider, especially as regards the storage of data, can be simplified easily from the previous analysis and descriptions. They will also form the basis for benchmarking against proposals made to address the problem of law enforcement needs compared with those of cloud providers.

The first realization, as just discussed, is the fact that cloud services will continue to increase. The manner in which they increase will require a basis of security for providers to operate, which – based on the previous discussion and elaborated further later – is the need for clarity about the expectations providers can have about cooperation and demands from law enforcement, as well as the legal framework applicable to them.

13.5 Cloud Storage Forensics

(Quick et al. 2014) describe their research on forensic analysis of different cloud storage providers such as Dropbox, Google Drive, and Microsoft Skybox. They used Windows-based virtual machines (VM) as their test machines and examined the random access memory (RAM) using the VM's memory file instead of live acquisitions of memory. They also used a control VM as a base. The researchers downloaded client-side apps to interface with the cloud storage. These apps are designed to interact with the cloud storage and would leave artifacts such as registry entries, specific log files, and folders created on the computers. The research showed artifacts left by the client software. There were also artifacts of cloud storage activity found in the user folder AppData. Authors also examined Internet history. They used the Internet Explorer, Mozilla Firefox, and Google Chrome web browsers when they did not use a client-side app. Information about the use of cloud storage was found in the index.dat files and temporary Internet files. URLs were located, referencing transactions of cloud storage. Unencrypted passwords were located in the RAM analysis of Skybox. The authors found that crucial evidence might be stored in a cloud storage account that is not available on the computer itself. They addressed collecting evidence from cloud storage directly. Their first step is to understand the focus of the investigation. The second step is to have determined legal authority to gain access to the cloud storage in question. The third step is to identify the cloud storage account, such as Dropbox. The fourth step is the actual collection of the evidence. They discuss using a VM on a host machine with Internet access, to protect any host from any malware. Using a packet-capture tool such as Wireshark captures traffic between the VM and server. They suggest using a screen-capture tool to video-record the process. Then, download the files onto the VM, and pause the VM. In step five, the researchers conduct the analysis of the VM and packet captures. Step six reports the findings. The seventh step is to complete the backup files and reports.

(Roussev et al. 2016) discussed the traditional acquisition of data on a client-side computer. They acknowledge that using only client-side data could leave out critical data. Their research used an alternative approach of acquiring evidence on the cloud storage side by using an application program interface (API). They indicate that APIs are well documented and used by many application developers. They created a prototype called Kummodd, with a command-line tool and a graphical user interface (GUI) mode. The user's credentials (username and password) are still required to gain access to the cloud storage. A Python script uses the API to communicate with the cloud storage drive. Directly accessing the cloud storage drive gives access to the metadata to ascertain the contents by downloading them. The tool will also show revisions of files and download them. The authors acknowledge that this is a logical acquisition of files. Roussev et al. 2016 believe that this is a forensically acceptable way to acquire evidence without physical acquisition and is justified by the current storage developments. The cloud side could have data divided up onto different servers or, with the invention of solid-state drives (SSDs), use wear leveling (overwriting unallocated space) that makes recovering deleted data difficult.

Hale (2013) did research on Amazon Cloud Drive (ACD). Note that ACD is a different service than Amazon Simple Storage Service (AS3). AWS is a storage service for the

Internet that provides a web services interface so that users can store files and access them, whereas ACD is a consumer frontend that the user needs an Amazon account to access; there is also a pricing difference (Head in the Cloud 2014). ACD is closer to cloud storage, similar to Dropbox. Hale's research was done using a web-based interface and the desktop application for ACD. ACD is marketed as an online MP3 player and storage system. An Amazon account is created, and the account credentials are used to access the storage. According to (Hale 2013), the browsing history files were the most forensically rewarding and left artifacts showing how the user interacted with the web-based interface. Hale found within the web browser cache a specific file with useful information. The cache files that are the server response to `getInfoById` are issued after an upload or delete operation. The content of the cache files begins with the text *getInfoByIdResponse*, followed by a number of fields: File Name, Object ID, Amazon Customer ID, File Creation Date, File Last Updated Date, Cloud Path, File Size, and MD5. Hale's findings show that artifacts are left from a web-based interface and can show dates and times of file transfers. As would be expected, numerous persistent artifacts were located when the desktop application was used. Artifacts were found in the registry and the application-specific file AdriveNativeClientService.log.

13.6 Case Study 1: Finding Data Centers on the Internet in Data-Dense Environments

During investigations in a data-dense environment such as cloud computing, cybercrime investigators are frequently sent to data centers to collect evidence from computer hosts located in those data centers. It is becoming increasingly difficult to locate the data center where the computer host of the interest is running. While is it common to reach out to the involved hosting provider to ask for the data center's address, there are situations in which it is not possible to contact the hosting provider ahead of time.

Law enforcement investigators are known for their experience with wiretaps to collect evidence. Although wiretapping could be an option, successfully wiretapping a server in a data center cannot be done without cooperation of the entity and access to the data center.

There are several reasons why a hosting provider might not be trusted with details of the involved computer host. For instance, an ISP might inform the user of the involved computer host prior to the investigator's arrival. This user could then alter or remove evidence before the investigator could collect or intercept it.

Non-law enforcement friendly ISPs require a different approach. Typically, an investigator will try to perform an online query like a WHOIS and/or a traceroute to find information about the host's physical location. These techniques have a relatively low rate of success. To address this problem of finding the (geo)location (Tillekens et al. 2016) of the involved data center, this chapter will propose a method for law enforcement members that increases the success rate of finding the correct data center location significantly, up to 80%.

During the research, the techniques currently used were evaluated, together with other techniques found during the research. The evaluation focuses on several indicators, including accuracy and usability for law enforcement. Data analytics are performed on the results of both a questionnaire as well as the geolocation techniques currently used by European law enforcement.

Based on the results, a new three-phase guideline is introduced, which builds on known techniques and combines them with investigative techniques. The preliminary result is promising and provides useful suggestions for when the data center cannot be accurately pinpointed. The recommended three-phase guideline is more accurate and tailored for law enforcement purposes.

The following approach is used:

1) To allow for better insight in the techniques used by law enforcement, a questionnaire is completed by the digital investigators.
2) The results of this questionnaire are combined with the results of the literature survey to formulate an overall state of the art of the most promising geolocation techniques for law enforcement.
3) The most promising techniques are then reviewed using mostly publicly available tools and resources. The review is done using the target IPs from a test set. The test set contains IPs that are already geographically located by their owners.
4) A new procedure is proposed and tested using the same method involving the combination of the most accurate techniques.

13.6.1 Traditional Techniques

Normalizing the results of the questionnaire and the literature survey generates an overall state of the art. It gives us an overview of the most promising techniques. The techniques were selected based on the number of times the respondents and literature mentioned the technique as useful. The level of accuracy of the technique was also used to make this selection. An overview of the greatest number of times the technique was used and the highest level of accuracy per technique helped to formulate the top five most promising techniques. Relevant techniques used in this case study in comparison with our three-phase guideline are described in the following subsections: (i) traceroute analysis; (ii) WHOIS analysis; (iii) open source intelligence; (iv) routing analysis; (v) hop analysis; and (vi) previous data reported.

13.6.1.1 Traceroute

In a wide sense, we can see a traceroute from a single location, multiple traceroutes from different locations, and traceroutes from geolocated locations (landmarks). A traceroute provides several things: number of hops to connect to the target, the round trip time (RTT) from each hop to the target, and the fully qualified domain name (FQDN) of each hop. Delays (RTT) can help provide insight into how distant the target is from the hops.

13.6.1.2 WHOIS Analysis

In an EU country, the RIPE database (https://www.ripe.net/manage-ips-and-asns/db) stores the details of whom IP addresses are assigned to. This is also called a *network WHOIS*. It should typically provide the autonomous system (AS) number, name, address, e-mail, and phone number of the entity to which the IP address is assigned.

13.6.1.3 Open Source Intelligence

Open source intelligence is a technique of gathering as much knowledge on a specific target as possible. It involves extensive use of Internet search engines like Google. Normally, it is combined with a WHOIS to determine the entity the IP address is assigned to. It also involves visiting websites known to be closely tied to the targets. Relevant, previously unknown, online databases can also be part of this technique.

13.6.1.4 Routing Analysis

A routing analysis provides information about how IP address blocks (autonomous system numbers) are announced to the Internet. It also involves analysis of the peers of these IP blocks. Adjacent IP addresses in the same block typically are geolocated in the same datacenter, so it might be relevant to analyze them as well.

13.6.1.5 Hop Analysis

Hop analysis analyzes the FQDN domain names connected to the target IP address, or the IP addresses on its route to the target. Part of this technique is also the last-known-hop approach. The hops (almost) neighboring the target are considered to be physically very close to the target and are thus interesting subjects for geolocation as well. Analyzing DNS records is also considered part of this technique.

13.6.1.6 Previous Data Reported

This approach queries police systems. Since law enforcement investigations are showing an increase in the use of digital evidence, the chances of finding relevant information on the target IP address's location are increasing, as well. In addition, relevant information, like Chamber of Commerce records, can be obtained through police systems.

13.6.2 Three-Phase Approach

In this section, we introduce a new procedure. It uses combinations of the techniques just reviewed and tries to minimize the amount of data that must be gathered. Overall, this new method should be faster and easier to deploy than gathering all the data from the six techniques just described and combining them into an end result. It is a three-phase guideline involving: (i) data gathering; (ii) answering questions based on the gathered results; and (iii) making choices.

13.6.2.1 Phase One: Data Gathering

The gathering of the required data is performed first. To avoid unnecessary online queries, first a check is performed to see if the target IP has been queried before. The following steps are performed:

1) Query the RIPE stat web page or RIPE API to collect this info: country, autonomous system number (ASN), AS-name, prefix, Inetnum: netname, Inetnum: descry, Reverse DNS: PTR record, BGPlay: AS-numbers closest to target ASN (up to three), and Registry browser: tech-c (https://stat.ripe.net).
2) Query police databases for the following: target IP address location, target IP block location(s), if available the corresponding date time(s), and if available the connected entity and its address details.

3) Perform RIPE Atlas measurements using the web page or API for traceroute. Try to use probes of the same of target ASN or its closest peers, probe(s) that uses the minimum number of hops to the target, a probe that has the minimum RTT to the target, geocoordinates of these probes, the FQDN of the penultimate hop, and the ASN of the penultimate hop.
4) Perform hop-naming analysis to obtain the domain name of the host and hints in the FQDN referring to the location of the hops.
5) Query peeringDB.com to obtain routing information for finding the web page of the ASN and extract peer facilities of the target ASN.
6) Perform online open source intelligence (OSINT) queries to obtain the following: hits on "AS-name" and "data center" and information on the hop hints found. Visit the website of the entity of the last-known hop for the data center location info, visit the website of the host used by the target for data-center location information, and visit the website running on the target IP (anonymously) for data-center location information.
7) Analyze all results, including looking for same or similar address records; mark them as validated where applicable, converting found addresses to geocoordinates where necessary, compare found geocoordinates, and plot them on a map, for instance using Google Maps.
8) Compare the results with online records of data from different online sources such as http://www.datacentrumgids.nl/overzicht/nederland, www.datacentermap.com, http://www.telewiki.nl/Lijst_van_datacentra_in_Nederland_op_volgorde_van_plaatsnaam, http://map.ring.nlnog.net, Google Maps, and Yellow Pages.
9) Generate an overview of obtained results, including target IP, owning entity including contact details, country of the target IP, police records, top-*x* list of most-probable locations of data centers including validation scores, and the degree of separation between the target IP and the suggested data center.

13.6.2.2 Phase Two: Answering Questions Based on the Gathered Results

By answering four questions, this guideline aims to help the user make the right decisions in phase three of the guideline (Figure 13.1). The answers are specifically relevant to law enforcement to do the following:

- Help to determine if they can claim jurisdiction.
- Shed light on previous encounters with law enforcement.
- Find multiple validations of the result, which is preferred. It tells us that when different sources/techniques come up with the same result, the result is of a higher level of accuracy than if the result was provided by one source.
- Provide insight into whether further research or action is required to locate the target.

With the obtained data, the following questions need to be answered:

1) Is the target IP located in this country?
2) Was the target IP visited before by law enforcement?
3) Is the location of the target IP validated?
4) Need extra options to locate host?

13.6.2.3 Phase Three: Making Choices About What to Do Next

Depending on the outcome of the previously answered questions, decisions can be made:

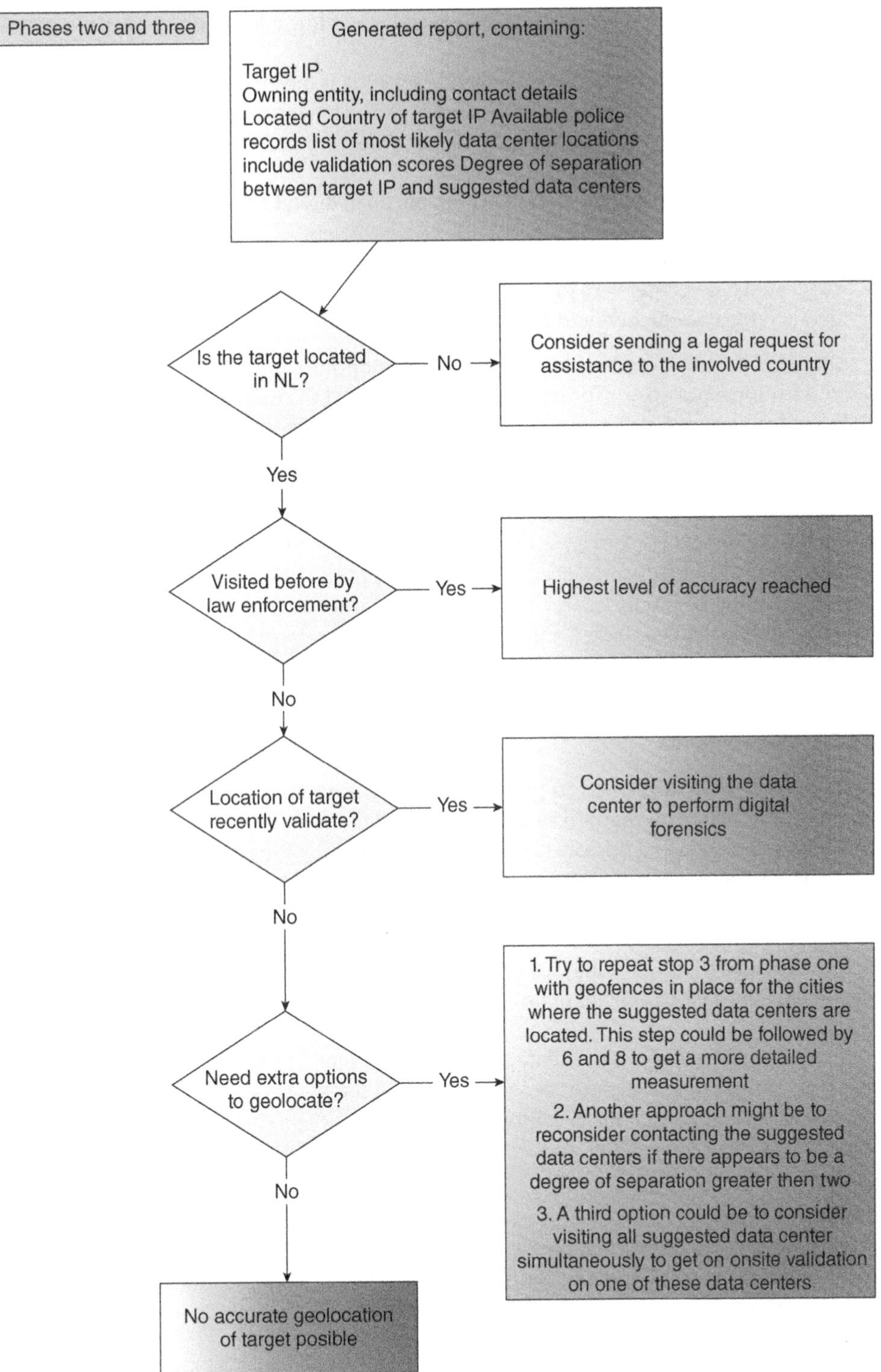

Figure 13.1 Flowchart of phases two and three of the three-phase guideline.

1) If Yes, proceed with question 2. If No, consider sending a legal request for assistance to the involved country.
2) If Yes, this gives the highest level of validation. See if the location was visited recently and what the level of cooperation was. This knowledge could also change the status from non-law enforcement friendly to law enforcement friendly. If No, proceed to question 3.
3) If Yes, consider visiting the data center to perform digital forensics. If No, proceed to question 4.
4) If Yes, the best option is to try to repeat step 3 from phase one for the cities where the suggested data centers are located. Redoing steps 6 and 8 of phase one to get a more detailed measurement could follow this step.

Although this new method is not flawless in pinpointing a single data center, it can serve additional purposes. For instance, if it cannot tell the exact location of the needed data center, it could still reduce the number of possible data centers to a workable amount. This could mean that digital investigators could visit two or three data centers at the same time to allow for control over the possible loss of evidence. This method could also give investigators indicators of which entity to contact for more information about the target IP. For instance, if the IP belongs to a client of a shady reseller, this reseller has most likely rented servers from a third party. This third party, an ISP, has its servers running in a data center belonging to another entity. The owner of this data center could be then contacted and asked for more information on the IP range, without revealing the target IP itself.

13.6.3 Experiments

A method is to be developed to pinpoint the location of data centers based on the IP address of a host. The method needs to be usable in data-dense environments. Since this research is focusing on non-law enforcement friendly ISPs, the method needs to be as undetectable as possible. The solution needs to be as accurate as possible; less than or equal to 10 km is considered to be accurate. The solution needs be easy to use and must work when there is a limited time frame available. It needs to be applicable for law enforcement so that its results can be used for court purposes. This means it should be repeatable and easy to explain in both reports and court, preferably by the investigators themselves.

A suitable test set of hosts at data centers needs to be available to review the known available techniques. It was not possible to obtain a test set of target IP addresses that are known to belong to non-law enforcement friendly ISPs. This is due to the confidentiality of police records. Thus another, more neutral test set was found.

13.6.3.1 Platform

A suitable test set of hosts at data centers needs to be available to review the known techniques. It was not possible to obtain a test set of target IP addresses known to belong to non-law enforcement friendly ISPs, due to the confidentiality of police records. Another, more neutral test set was found.

The Netherlands Network Operators Group (NLNOG) Ring is a network of hosts distributed over 51 countries. It has a total of 418 nodes, of which 72 are located in The

Netherlands. All of them are tagged with geocoordinates. The main purpose of the NLNOG Ring is to give network operators remote shell access on all these nodes, to allow for network testing.

In this chapter, the PlanetLab test bed was used. PlanetLab basically has both a global-based and a EU-based platform. The global-based platform has 1,353 nodes at 717 sites. The EU-based platform is part of this global test bed and has 288 nodes, only 7 of which are based in The Netherlands.

RIPE Atlas (https://atlas.ripe.net/about) is a global network of hardware devices called *probes* and *anchors* that actively measure Internet connectivity. Anyone can access this data via Internet traffic maps, streaming data visualizations, and an API. RIPE Atlas users can also perform customized measurements to gain valuable data about their own networks. Probe owners collect credits by hosting a probe; they can share or use these credits to perform their own measurements. RIPE also has other options for obtaining these credits. RIPE Atlas has 925 probes in The Netherlands. Due to privacy concerns, the exact location of each probe is obfuscated to 1 km away. The probes are deployed in data centers as well as in domestic and business locations. This platform was chosen for several reasons, mainly because it has many probes in the Netherlands, but also because it has an API. It also allows for generating results in a computer-readable format. Hence, it allows for automated tasks. Since the platform is open to anyone, law enforcement is also allowed to use it. Due to its public nature, RIPE Atlas also makes the results of every measurement public. After a measurement has been performed, it can be set to private.

RIPEstat (https://stat.ripe.net/index/about-ripestat) is a web-based interface that provides information on the IP address space, ASNs, and related information for host-names and countries. It uses several sources, including the RIPE database (WHOIS), databases of other RIRs, RIPE Atlas, and MaxMind. Since it can output in a computer-readable format and has an API, it will be easier to automate these tasks.

The rest of the testing, which did not have to rely on delay measurements and real-time telemetry, was performed on a regular computer with an Internet connection. For instance, a browser was used to perform the Google queries and to visit websites for OSINT purposes. Where necessary, a virtual private network (VPN) or Tor connection was invoked to allow for anonymization. Command-line tools were also used on this computer.

13.6.3.2 Findings and Analysis

13.6.3.2.1 Traceroute

The minimum hop counts in this test were between one and eight. 80% of the tested targets have a hop count greater than four. The lowest measured RTTs to the targets are between .459 and 5.48 ms. Two out of 10 targets show a hop count of less than three when tested. Target ID5 has a hop count of one. In addition, Target ID10 has a hop count of two. So although the NLNOG test set is handled by a different entity than the RIPE Atlas test bed, it appears that target ID5 and the RIPE Atlas probe are the exact same host. Interestingly, this probe reports a mean latency (RTT) of 3535 ms, which correspond to a distance of 176 km between the target and the probe.

Approaching the results from the perspective that all probes are landmarked, the distances from the probes to the targets are between 0.5 and 123.4 km. The two probes with the lowest hop count, for targets ID5 and ID10, have the lowest distance between probe and target, respectively 0.5 and 4.7 km. Considering the privacy obfuscation of up to 1 km for each probe, these two results are considered accurate enough for further investigative actions. Target ID3 has a distance to the probe of 14.3 km. Depending on the location in The Netherlands, for instance in a rural area with few data centers, this might be accurate enough. The mentioned Randstad area, where the target is actually located, has a need for better accuracy.

Although this technique is widely used by academia and the digital investigators of the LE agency, it does not prove to be highly accurate. This is where the variable of the data-dense environment pops up. The Dutch infrastructure is fast and complex at the same time. Even when we know that both the targets and probes are located in The Netherlands, the minimum hop count is sometimes still eight hops. And although the minimum RTT times are quite low, its corresponding distances are still between 18.3 and 273.8 km. Overall, among the tested traceroute techniques, the landmark-based tracerouting is the most accurate, with 20% of the results proven usable.

13.6.3.2.2 WHOIS Queries

The second-most-used technique of digital investigators has a higher success rate: 50% of the targets are geolocated based on the RIPE database entries. This level of accuracy can be debated, though. Because of the nature of the test set, they all need to be geolocated before they can be added to the NLNOG Ring. It is assumed that the owning entities have also paid extra attention to entering the correct details in the RIPE database. Results from the questionnaire state that in 30% of their encounters with non-law enforcement friendly ISPs, the respondents had to deal with bad RIPE database records. This was the second-most-common difficulty the investigators mentioned. Overall, the WHOIS technique can provide accurate data up to 50% of the time; taking into consideration the nature of non-law enforcement friendly ISPs, this percentage might drop.

13.6.3.2.3 OSINT

Since gathering WHOIS data, which could also be part of the OSINT process, was already done, the possible location obtained from WHOIS records were omitted. For 90% of the targets, locations of possible data centers were found. The number of possible locations found averaged between one and four per target. Five of the targets (50%) had the correct data center location in the results. Two of the targets (20%) had information in the results that was not exactly geolocated, but within 4 km. One target (10%) had enough hints in the results to come up with an entity that has more than one data center in The Netherlands. The OSINT technique was more difficult to review; this is why the proposed method for OSINT in subsection 4.4.3 used limited queries to allow for better reviewing.

Open source gathering of intelligence is almost limitless in its options. There is no guideline available for an OSINT process for finding data centers belonging to target hosts. Every investigator uses their own set of OSINT sources to query, based on personal experience. Overall, the OSINT technique can provide accurate data up to 50% of the time; results depend on the OSINT skills of the investigator.

13.6.3.2.4 Hop Analysis

Hop analysis showed relevant hints in the results for 30% of the targets. The FQDN of the last hop before the target, the penultimate hop, was the source for these results. The hints were not sufficient to provide hard evidence. An example is 80ge.br3-cr1.smartdc.rtd.i3d.net, where two hints – "smartdc" and "rtd" – were extracted. "rtd" could be short for the city of Rotterdam and "smartdc" for the SmartDC company that owns two data-center facilities, one of which is located in Rotterdam. The last hop (the target) and the antepenultimate hop did not provide hints on the location in the FQDN. Overall, the hop-analysis technique can provide indicative data, but typically not 100% accurate data.

13.6.3.2.5 Routing Information

One (10%) target could be accurately pinpointed to a data center using routing information from peeringdb.com. Indeed, 30% of the targets could be located down to a few options, including the correct one, using the peeringdb.com source. 20% of the targets did not have data entered in the peeringdb.com database, so no geolocation was possible using this resource. 40% had results, but the correct data center was not among them. Overall, the routing technique provided accurate data up to 10% of the time.

13.6.3.2.6 Previous Data Reported

None of the target IP addresses appeared in police databases. But 30% of the target classless inter-domain routing (CIDR) prefixes appeared in police systems. Unfortunately, none of them had a report about a visit to the involved data center. Nor was there any reporting of contact with the entity the IP block belonged to. During an assessment of the overall trustworthiness of this entity, no relevant data was found in police systems about the target. This could be due to the fact that the test set did not consist of known non-law enforcement friendly ISPs. This technique can be proven successful in the future, though. Police systems can be queried more extensively: for instance, Europol databases can be added to these queries. It is a basically a circle: if police officers report all encounters with an IP address correctly into police databases, eventually more hits will be generated when the geolocation of an IP is queried. If better reporting on previous geolocation efforts is done in police systems, including the results of visits to data centers, this technique may show better result when investigating real non-law enforcement friendly ISPs.

13.6.3.2.7 Three-Phase Approach

Using the three-phase guideline, 80% of the targets can be accurately located to a specific data center. The two added techniques in phase one (comparison with online databases with data center locations) and phase three (using new measurements from RIPE Atlas probes) are responsible for the improvement. The remaining 20% of the targets, ID4 and ID10, did get more suggestions about which data center(s) to look at. Interestingly, the most difficult target appears to be ID10. Based on the techniques used, it appears to be located in a data center 4.7 km from the real location provide by the NLNOG Ring test-set host. The real NLNOG Ring test-set location corresponds with the headquarters of the target ID10. The RIPE Atlas probe, which appears to be geographically closest to target ID10, is owned by the same entity as the target host, but located at a university at the given distance. This could mean the measurement is not correct, but it could also mean the entered location of ID10 is not correct (anymore). ID4 gets two suggestions for its data center location; they are geographically close to each other, about 4 km. In this scenario, an option could be to simultaneously visit both data centers. This allows the investigators to look for the exact location of the target

Table 13.1 Accuracy of reviewed techniques/methods.

Technique reviewed	Accuracy (%)
Traceroute	20%
WHOIS queries	50%
OSINT	50%
Hop analysis	N/A
Routing information	10%
Previous data reported	N/A
Toward proposal, combinations	70%
Three-phase guideline	80%

host. By visiting the data centers at the same moment, the investigators have control over the possible altering or removal of evidence, by keeping an eye on the personnel of the data centers and not allowing them to communicate with customers about investigators' presence. The guideline helps investigators remember which data to gather and helps to avoid errors while gathering data.

Both the state of the art and the review of available techniques show that combining techniques is the best approach to pinpoint data centers. Only one of the researched six techniques provided no results. This was the previous-data-reported technique. Querying police systems did not give the desired results. The other five techniques combined provide accuracy up to 70%. This included at least one validation. The three-phase guideline helps investigators with a workflow for gathering all the data necessary to obtain at least the previously mentioned 80% accuracy. The guideline prevents investigators from forgetting relevant steps. It also helps to avoid unnecessary steps during the geolocation process and guides investigators through a decision process to suggest possible next steps. The guideline is easy to use and not necessarily meant for digital investigators alone. Regular investigators with some knowledge of online investigations will be able to pinpoint data centers as well, with this guideline in hand. The guideline can also be used to pinpoint geographically dispersed data centers of cloud service providers. This could be relevant to a broader audience with interest in where their data resides (Table 13.1).

13.7 Case Study 2: Cloud Forensics for the Amazon Simple Storage Service

Cloud storage services are often free to customers. The customer just needs to sign up with an e-mail and will receive a limited amount of available storage space on the Cloud. This is considered cloud computing. *Cloud computing* is a shared collection of configurable network resources, such as networks, serves, storage, applications, and services. Customers can log in to the cloud service via a web browser and upload or download files. Customers can also increase storage space. The cloud service providers (CSPs) provide servers and storage space. To ensure service, CSPs maintain data centers around the world (Ruan et al. 2011). Data may not necessarily be located in just one place; and the location of the company headquarters does not necessarily mean data is stored there. This adds a level of jurisdiction. In the United States, for example, one state's law enforcement agency may have to have a federal law enforcement agency produce a subpoena or search warrant because the "data" resides across state lines.

In a cloud investigation, there is the client side, the CSP side, and the matter of law (whether the investigator / digital forensic examiner [DFE] has the right to search and seize). The client side is the traditional type of computer/digital forensics, where the investigator has access to the suspect's computer or mobile device (Faheem et al. 2015). The device is at a physical location, and jurisdiction is relatively easy to show. The device in question contains artifacts. This client approach has worked well in the past, but files are no longer in a persistent state on the client side and have shifted to being web-app based and leaving little trace (Roussev and McCulley 2016). Jurisdiction needs to be addressed. This is not an attempt to give legal advice in any form; it merely reflects the difficulties of multi-jurisdiction investigations and difficulties encountered when dealing with cloud computing. As mentioned before, CSPs use servers and data centers not centrally located or confined to one location.

An example of this difficulty is seen with Amazon Web Services (AWS). With AWS, the user can select where they would like their data stored. The corporate headquarters may not necessarily be the location of the data. CSPs intentionally hide the location of the data from customers to facilitate movement and replication.

Another scenario would be for the investigator to connect to the Cloud and download files with the user's credentials. This lends a question of legal authority. If the user gives consent freely and willingly to search the account, then the investigator can connect and download the contents. However, if the user does not give consent, then the investigator would need some kind of legal authority to connect to the cloud storage/account with the user's credentials and download data.

There is also the possibility the owner of the cloud account will cooperate and give full authority for a search. If the investigator can gain access to an account in their jurisdiction, they can intercept the communication.

13.7.1 Approach and Experiments

The examination began with the client side (user side). The focus of this research was Amazon S3 (AS3). A search was conducted for any logs, images, and Internet history left from user activity, both in a persistent state and in volatile memory (RAM). Using a non-test computer, an AS3 account was set up. This is a computer not used as a base machine or in testing. The account with contents is already established and accessed by a different computer. AS3 uses buckets to store files. These *buckets* are similar to file folders. For the experiment, the buckets were created and the region set as Sao Palo, Brazil. A region outside the US was used for storage to see what artifacts, if any, could be seen and to show that the files were actually stored outside the US. The ease of accessing and viewing the files contained in the bucket was also examined. The main target bucket was named minionswi. Images of the well-known cartoon Minions were used as substitutes for contraband images or files. The username was the e-mail address **********@gmail.com (redacted).

Some initial testing using the bucket something1 was done, downloading and renaming files stored in the bucket. Once the files were in the bucket, AS3 provided information on the files. AS3 showed that Amazon uses an ETag. This ETag is a MD5 hash value. AWS references the use of MD5 hash values. According to Amazon, the ETag may or may not be an MD5 hash value, depending on how the file was created, such as a file that is a multipart upload (http://docs.aws.amazon.com/AmazonS3/latest/API/RESTCommonResponseHeaders.html. The online reference provided by AWS says the AS3 compares the returned ETag with the MD5 hash value. Using a hash calculator, HashCalc v2.02, downloaded hash values were calculated. The hash values remained the same after download and upload. A verification was done, comparing the original file on the computer, and the hash stayed the same. Also, changing the name in AS3 did not change the hash or ETag. For the client-side part of the investigation, VMs were used for testing. The VMs were created using VM Workstation Player 12.1.0. These VMs simulated what would typically be found in a home computer. The VM RAM file, *.vmem, was used for RAM analysis.

FTK Imager v 3.4.26 was used to create an evidence file from the test VMs. The evidence file was analyzed in Autopsy 4. For collection on the cloud service side, we used CloudBerry Drive. This program was used because it will mount cloud storage as a network drive. The drive can be mounted as read only.

There are some considerations with this method. AWS uses a security key for the individual. The key needs to be known. For the investigator to access AS3, it is necessary to know the credentials and password and log in to the AWS console. Then access the security key through the user console, and there is an option to download an access-key file. A user may store this key file on the computer. If a preservation order has been sent to Amazon for the account, and Amazon blocks the user, it is likely the investigator/DFE cannot access the account by this method using the user's credentials. The security key is needed for CloudBerry Drive to connect.

13.7.2 Findings and Analysis

The first VM started with the base VM clone. IE 11 was used to search for images or videos of Minions. A video of the *Minions* movie trailer was downloaded to the desktop of the first VM. Images of Minions were downloaded to the desktop of the first VM. IE11 was used to log in to the AS3 account. Four image files and the .mp4 file were uploaded to the AS3 bucket minionswi.

When examining the first VM, it was clear the Minion files had been saved onto the VM desktop. Temporary Internet files contained the images in question. The Internet history showed a connection to AS3. IE changed after the introduction of IE 10; prior to IE 10, history resided in the index.dat file. The biggest change was that now IE used an extensible storage engine (ESE) named WebCacheV01.dat and the folder WebCache, plus other files (transaction logs) that work together (Malmstrom and Teveldal 2013). When using a web browser to access AS3, there is a web page for the login credentials.

Information regarding files was located in a WebCache log in the V01.log (path: Users/RCRAIG/AppData/Local/Microsoft/Windows/WebCache/V01.log). The ETag (md5Hash) of the Minion files was recorded. The temporary Internet files of the Minions could have been created by the Google search for such images, normal web-browsing activity, and may not have been directly related to the AS3 account. Links were found with the Etag, filename, and file path pointing to the AS3 web URL. There was also a reference to the date and time in this artifact.

The second VM would give a better idea what was created just by viewing the files using IE 11 but never downloading the images of Minions. Using Autopsy 4, artifacts were indeed found from viewing through the web browser. V01.logs correlated with the Minion images.

To begin the activity of the user on the second VM, we went to the AS3 console using IE 11, on 15 June 2016 at 4:31 p.m. (UTC-5). Once logged in, minionswi was opened. The video in the bucket, 518752464_2.mp4, was opened. It automatically downloaded and was opened in the default player, Windows Media Player. At 4:38 p.m. (UTC-5), each file in the bucket was opened to view. All the viewing was done through the web browser. The files were viewed in this order: Beefeater.jpg, cornerpicture.jpg, download.jpg, napoleanic.jpg, th2P068ZMZ.jpg, th4Z9C28AE.jpg, thCA0PWCAL.jpg, and thCaS1V76V.jpg. The file napoleonic.jpg was downloaded to the desktop. Analysis of the second VM showed activity in the V01.log. A record of the V01.log is shown in Figure 13.2.

```
https://s3-sa-east-1.amazonaws.com/minionswi/napoleanic.jpg?X-Amz-
Date=20160615T213913Z&X-Amz-Expires=300&X-Amz-Algorithm=AWS4-HMAC-
SHA256&X-Amz-
Signature=2147b53c2d9e463260e22134f693d12e02a81f97089671d0795ac7be4ffaa
cd7&X-Amz-Credential=ASIAIL43XAV6HH7KGXTQ/20160615/sa-east-
1/s3/aws4_request&X-Amz-SignedHeaders=Host&x-amz-security-
token=FQoDYXdzEJf//////////wEaDEKGljhlfRZTCs3F8iLHASP2dljsxfF3vTKM0niMI
5nQxwQ5rMbTS7/5%2BKDXi4Q9Wf9O30ZScQbhvf0zms4GUviuhXg2I6v/TrhJdpal4e9%2B
JS9aD4f8mHhI8QFV2vOJ/MJprNpF4%2Bki6DRvEhOcHIX4/HZjD76u095VdbHb2BVs5w9Wk
uTaHP%2BJ6xng26irjpeGvxtno86rWQLEm31JgOM8klVBgXKzS0FRts4PGVk
%2B0zRfcUa7idbkkLkTRZ4F02Z%2B/q4%2BVlgtTkU5Vr32YvsB2Abm2vIo4pKHuwU%3D

napoleanic[1].jpg

HTTP/1.1 200 OK

x-amz-id-2:
Iyh/XSsF/xDYQ9WGzA5WGI8Nenql5SGIeo4vAEqh96lhopbHeBsV+n9CWE0hbQRvbBNT4IL
S+Sc=

x-amz-request-id: 698CC193A548728D

ETag: "

83e1eb35f13ebe144b8d42133280a466"

Content-Type: image/jpeg

Content-Length: 7555

Visited:                                       RCRAIG@https://s3-sa-east-
1.amazonaws.com/minionswi/napoleanic.jpg?X-Amz-Date=20160615T213913Z&X-
Amz-Expires=300&X-Amz-Algorithm=AWS4-HMAC-SHA256&X-Amz-
Signature=2147b53c2d9e463260e22134f693d12e02a81f97089671d0795ac7be4ffaa
cd7&X-Amz-Credential=ASIAIL43XAV6HH7KGXTQ/20160615/sa-east-
1/s3/aws4_request&X-Amz-SignedHeaders=Host&x-amz-security-
token=FQoDYXdzEJf//////////wEaDEKGljhlfRZTCs3F8iLHASP2dljsxfF3vTKM0niMI
5nQxwQ5rMbTS7/5%2BKDXi4Q9Wf9O30ZScQbhvf0zms4GUviuhXg2I6v/TrhJdpal4e9%2B
JS9aD4f8mHhI8QFV2vOJ/MJprNpF4%2Bki6DRvEhOcHIX4/HZjD76u095VdbHb2BVs5w9Wk
uTaHP%2BJ6xng26irjpeGvxtno86rWQLEm31JgOM8klVBgXKzS0FRts4PGVk
%2B0zRfcUa7idbkkLkTRZ4F02Z%2B/q4%2BVlgtTkU5Vr32YvsB2Abm2vIo4pKHuwU%3D

1SPS
```

Figure 13.2 V01.log.

This record correlates with the viewing of the image napoleanic.jpg. The relevant portions are highlighted. Note the URL path is the same as the link in the bucket. The blue highlighted data is an actual link to the file. This was compared to the download link in AS3 in an open browser. The paths of the bucket were the same, but when the link was created, the date and time indicate when the link is created in view/open or download. To make it clearer, when a user wants to view a file or download a file, they need to right-click the file. The user can choose to open the file or download it. When they choose Open, the link is created and opens in a new window of the browser. When Download is chosen, the user needs to Save Link As and select where to save the file. There is reference to a date and time, 20160615T213912Z. This time appears to be in UTC-0. The viewing of this image correlates with the time period 15 June 2016 at 4:38 p.m. (UTC-5). There is also a reference to the ETag, and it is the correct ETag for that file. This record also corresponds to the creation of the temporary Internet file napoleanic.jpg. Even the MD5 hash value is the same as the ETag. The image is viewed and is cached in the temporary Internet files. The RAM file was searched for the MD5 hash value in text. Records were found in the RAM that appear to be the same as found in the V01.log (Figure 13.2). Similar findings were located that detail the same information regarding viewing of the other files in question. The napoleonic.jpg file was also downloaded onto the desktop. A link file also shows it located on the desktop. The file in question was downloaded at the approximate modified, accessed, created (MAC) date and times.

The /AppData/Roaming/Microsoft/Windows/IEDownloadHistory/container.dat file did not contain information regarding the download.

A third VM was created, called Browse_Deleted. In this scenario, a user logged in to the AS3 using the web browser and viewed the files bunchofminions.jpg, th2P068ZMZ.jpg, and twominions.jpg in the bucket "minions." The web-browser history was also deleted. This activity was done to see what artifacts were left. The three files viewed were located in unallocated space. The files th2P068ZMZ.jpg, bunchofminions.jpg, and twominions.jpg had the original MD5 hash values. Shown in Figure 13.3 is the file information of the files located in unallocated space. Since the three files were found in unallocated space, there was no filename.

Even though there was an attempt to delete the Internet history, references were found in the WebCache folder in a log. This was consistent with a previous test that

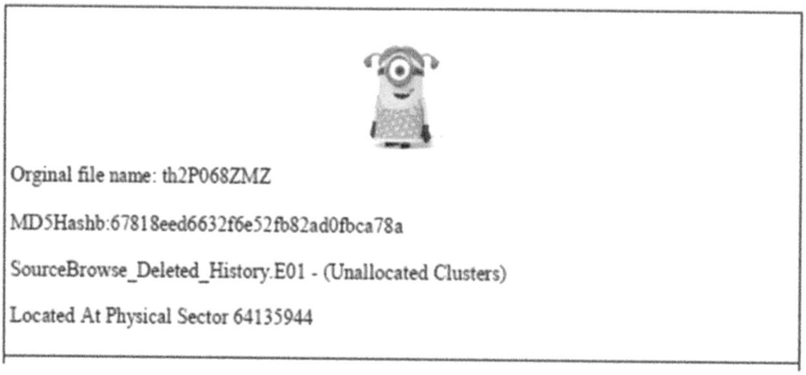

Orginal file name: th2P068ZMZ

MD5Hashb:67818eed6632f6e52fb82ad0fbca78a

SourceBrowse_Deleted_History.E01 - (Unallocated Clusters)

Located At Physical Sector 64135944

Figure 13.3 Example of file information for the files located in unallocated space.

showed viewing of a file through AS3 using the web browser. Looking closely, the file length listed for the entries is the correct file size.

13.7.2.1 Collecting Evidence via Internet

CloudBerry Drive is able to mount an AS3 account as a read-only network drive. To do this, an investigator/examiner must have the user's credentials (username and password). Using CloudBerry Drive also requires the access key and secret access key to be known. With these keys, anyone can log in to the buckets, so a user could share buckets with others. Logging in to the AS3 account with the users credentials, an investigator could find the access key but not a secret access key. This creates a problem. A user can only have two access keys at one time. In order to gain access, a new access key and secret access key will need to be created. If only one set is made, an additional one can be created. If two are made, the oldest key could be deleted and a new set created. This is all done through the web browser and is located in the AWS console (Figure 13.4).

For testing, CloudBerry v2.0.1.6 was installed on an examination computer with Internet access. The evidence file was verified successfully. MD5 hash values were compared with the files in minionswi, and the hashes were the same. One thing of note that has not been mentioned is that AS3 has the option to turn on or off versions of files. If a file is deleted, AS3 does save an older version. When the option is on, deleted files can be viewed when using the web browser interface. CloudBerry Drive did not see these older versions when the option was on or off. That could be important if the user of the account has tried to delete evidence.

13.7.3 Discussion

AS3 is ideal for web service providers, but anybody can create a free account and have storage. If the person wants to expand their storage, they can always purchase more.

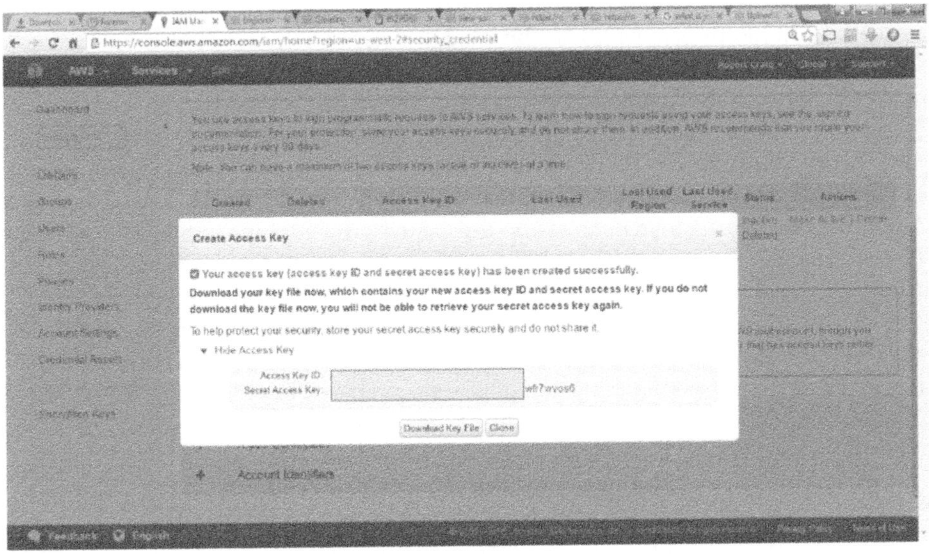

Figure 13.4 Access key.

If the person is sharing files, they could give out the access keys and share with other users. The user does not have to download a desktop application to view, download, or upload files. All the person needs is a computer with an Internet connection and a web browser.

The first hurdle in investigating a suspect is the legal authority to seize evidence that is stored on cloud storage. This is not just a problem in the United States, but also in other countries such as the UK. One way to seize evidence stored on cloud storage would be to obtain a search warrant and serve the CSP. This could be an issue because the CSP may be in a foreign country and may not recognize the courts of another country. This was the scenarios during testing, when the buckets were owned by Amazon, but the files were located in the region of Sao Palo, Brazil. This process relies on the CSP to provide the evidence. It is important that the search warrant also asks for the right files. One thing found in the research is that AS3 and other CSPs keep older versions of files (Roussev et al. 2016). The older versions actually contained delete files. Any warrant served should contain language such as, "all versions of files attached to the account."

The person the account belongs to could give permission, but they will need to provide certain credentials to access the account. The person also has to freely consent to such a search.

Cloud storage accounts can be anywhere in the world. During an investigation, credential information might be located, such as a key file. Files can be considered electronic communication. If the target files are located in another jurisdiction, and the investigator could obtain authorization for a wiretap, they could log in to the target account and acquire data.

Testing showed that AS3 uses an ETag that is an MD5 hash. There are numerous references to the ETag in the Internet history, and a specific URL that details the date and time, the file path being viewed, and the file length. Files that were located in the bucket and were not viewed did not create URLs and ETag references. The image itself is stored in the Internet temporary files. When the image is hashed in the temporary Internet files, it has the same hash as the ETag. A user viewing a contraband image will leave artifacts. Finding a contraband image in unallocated space usually has no reference. In the case of a suspect using AS3, taking the MD5 hash value of the contraband image found in unallocated space and doing a keyword search can give reference to that contraband image. The Internet history, or even whether the AS3 URLs are located in RAM or unallocated space, can tell an investigator the time and date viewed, and the bucket file path. This activity shows the user actively opened individual files to view. This information at a minimum could be used to obtain a search warrant for the AS3 account. If no contraband images were found, the investigator could still do a keyword search with known "bad" MD5 hash values and get results indicating viewing of contraband images through the URLs. This would point to the AS3 account and the likelihood that it contains contraband. Using an application such as CloudBerry Drive has some limitations. The user credentials are a must, and the user may refuse to cooperate, even if there is a court order. The access keys are needed and may not be accessible. Deleting one of the sets of keys to get new ones may be outside legal authority. Connecting to cloud storage and acquiring the data maintains chain of custody and does not rely on the CSP. However, some files could be missed, such as older versions. Client-side forensic examination of the suspect's computer yields useful information and direct correlation of evidence with activity. It can be said with a high degree of certainty that a user viewed a contraband image when the URL, WebCache log files, ETag, date and time, and image MD5 hash values are all connected.

13.8 Conclusion

The usage of cloud storage for criminal purposes is well known and will most likely not end. The eradication of crime is a noble cause, yet not one that seems to be a realistic prospect, without any intention of entering into a philosophical discourse on human nature and societies. The fact that criminals and crime and their methods will continue to evolve in pace with and take advantage of technological development and innovations is equally acknowledged. In this chapter, we discussed aspects related to data acquisition in cloud computing platforms. We also showed an efficient approach to locate the data center where the computer host of interest to investigators is running. In addition, we described a forensic acquisition and analysis of Amazon Web Service, one of the most popular cloud storage platforms.

Obtaining data stored on cloud storage is problematic. The cross-jurisdictional nature of the CSP creates issues, and no specific laws deal with cloud storage. Existing laws are used and may not be the most useful. There is still a dependency on the CSP complying and providing the contents of cloud storage. Further research would have to be done on how a folder is treated when it is uploaded to AS3. In addition, the number of non-law enforcement friendly ISPs is increasing over time. Further research into this phenomena is advised, including the advice to better report encounters with non-law enforcement friendly ISPs. In addition, more intrusive methods can be explored: for example, wiretaps on upstream connections (Schut et al. 2015), not for content, but only for IP addresses, might also help to improve on results.

References

Bernaards, F., Monsma, E., and Zinn, P. (2012). *Hightech Crime: Crime Image Analysis.* Driebergen: Korps Landelijke Politiediensten.

Dykstra, J. (2013). Seizing electronic evidence from cloud computing environments. In: *Cybercrime and Cloud Forensics: Applications for Investigation Processes* (ed. K. Ruan), 156–185. Hershey: IGI Global.

Faheem, M., Kechadi, M.-T., and Le-Khac, N.-A. (2015). The state of the art forensic techniques in mobile cloud environment: a survey, challenges and current trend. *International Journal of Digital Crime and Forensics* 7 (2): 1–19.

Fuchs, C. (2013). Privacy and security in Europe. The Privacy & Security Research Paper Series, No. 6.

Goncharov, M. (2015). *Criminal Hideouts for Lease: Bulletproof Hosting Services.* Irving: TrendLabs.

Grispos, G., Storer, T., and Glisson, W.B. (2012). Calm before the storm: the challenges of cloud computing in digital forensics. *International Journal of Digital Crime and Forensics* 4 (2): 28–48.

Hale, J.S. (2013). Amazon Cloud Drive forensic analysis. *The International Journal of Digital Forensics & Incident Response* 10 (3): 259–265.

Hiller, J. (2015). Civil Cyberconflict: Microsoft, cybercrime and botnets. *Sanata Clara High Technology Law Journal* 31 (2): 163–214.

In Re Grand Jury Proceedings the Bank of Nova Scotia. (1984). United States of America, Plaintiff-appellee, v. the Bank of Nova Scotia, Defendant-appellant, 740 F.2d 817 (11th Cir.).

Head in the Cloud (2014). Amazon S3 and Amazon Cloud Drive: what's the difference? https://web.archive.org/web/20140608040735/http://www.headinthecloudstorage.com/amazon-ec2-and-s3-whats-the-difference.

Malmstrom, B. and Teveldal, P. (2013). Forensic analysis of the ESE database in Internet Explorer 10. Bachelors thesis: School of Information Science, Computer and Electrical Engineering, Halmstad, Sweden.

Mell, P. and Grance, T. (2011). The NIST definition of cloud computing. National Institute of Standards and Technology.

Mittal, S. (2014). Power management techniques for data centers: a survey. Technical report. https://pdfs.semanticscholar.org/c389/9a699ecd188e658374c861b3b21e80c364e4.pdf (accessed July 2017).

Nicolls, V., Le-Khac, N-A., Chen, L. et al. (2016). IPv6 security and forensics. The 6th IEEE International Conference on Innovative Computing Technology, Dublin, Ireland, August 2016.

Nishawala, V.N. (2013). Subcontracting in the Cloud. Pillsbury Global Sourcing. http://www.sourcingspeak.com/2013/06/subcontracting-in-the-cloud.html (accessed May 2017).

Plunkett J., Le-Khac N-A., and Kechadi, M-T. (2015). Digital forensic investigations in the Cloud: a proposed approach for Irish law enforcement. 11th Annual IFIP WG 11.9 International Conference on Digital Forensics (IFIP119 2015), Orlando, Florida, 26–28 January 2015.

Quick, D., Martini, B., and Choo, K.R. (2014). *Cloud Storage Forensics*. Waltham, MA: Syngress.

Roussev, V. and McCulley, S. (2016). Forensic analysis of cloud-native artifacts. *The International Journal of Digitl Forensics & Incident Response.*

Roussev, V., Barreto, A., and Ahmed, I. (2016). Forensic acquisition of cloud drives. In: *Advances in Digital Forensics XII* (ed. G. Peterson and S. Shenoi), 5–8. Springer.

Ruan, K., Carthy, J., Kechadi, T. et al. (2011). Cloud forensics. *IFIP Advances in Information and Communication Technology* 361: 35–46.

Ryder, Steven and Le-Khac, N-A. (2016). The end of effective law enforcement in the cloud? To encrypt, or not to encrypt. The 9th IEEE International Conference on Cloud Computing, San Francisco, CA USA, June 2016.

Schut, H., Farina, J., Scanlon, M. et al. (2015). Towards the forensic identification and investigation of cloud hosted servers through noninvasive wiretaps. The 10th International Workshop on Frontiers in Availability, Reliability and Security (FARES 2015), Toulouse, France, August 24–28, 2015.

Tillekens, A., Le-Khac, N-A., and Pham-Thi, T-T. (2016). A bespoke forensics GIS tool. IEEE International Symposium on Mobile Computing, Wireless Networks, and Security, Nevada, USA, Dec 2016.

14

Digital Evidence Management, Presentation, and Court Preparation in the Cloud

A Forensic Readiness Approach

Lucia De Marco, Nhien-An Le-Khac, and M-Tahar Kechadi

University College Dublin, Dublin, Ireland

14.1 Introduction

In the modern IT era, computation capability is delivered through computing services. This name became popular with the public when the Service Oriented Architecture and Web Services (SOA-WS) spread in the 1990s (Alonso et al. 2004). The concept of delivering IT and computation capabilities through a network dates back to the late 1960s. In 1969, J.C.R. Licklider, who contributed to the development of the Advanced Research Projects Agency Network (ARPANET), promoted the concept of an intergalactic computer network (Lee et al. 1992). Such a scientist had a vision and a hope that in the future every individual would have access to data and applications from anywhere. In 1961, the computer pioneer John McCarthy predicted that computation may someday be organized as a public utility (Foster et al. 2008).

Cloud computing service architecture is designed to provide a computing environment that utilizes virtual resources that dynamically allocate the underlying physical resources. The result is to balance the load and to scale resource provisioning up and down in order to guarantee some services execution that satisfy the needs of the end users. Cloud services can be seen as an evolution of SOA-WS services; the Cloud is taking their advantages to build its service architecture.

However, the ease of access to such resources is exploited by criminals who design more sophisticated and targeted methods to hack any type of digital device, or to exploit existing computing platforms for illegal activities. Hence, cloud forensics (CF) (Ruan et al. 2011a) deals with the management of crimes committed on cloud platforms or that used the Cloud as means to commit crimes. Cloud architecture novelties lead forensic practitioners to deal with a computing infrastructure that cannot be investigated with traditional forensic tools and procedures. Nevertheless, practitioners are required to manage cloud evidence respecting the admissibility and reliability principles of digital evidence (Casey 2011). Some cloud features have been used to build a cube model for CF (Ruan et al. 2011a), which is composed of technical, organizational, and legal dimensions. The technical dimension deals with tools and procedures for performing forensic investigations; the organizational dimension is concerned with the

Security, Privacy, and Digital Forensics in the Cloud, First Edition. Edited by Lei Chen, Hassan Takabi, and Nhien-An Le-Khac.

manner of establishing a forensic capability; e.g., the roles and the responsibilities to assign to a cloud organization. Finally, the legal dimension covers issues of multi-jurisdiction, multitenancy, and service-level agreement (SLA) policies.

Recently, cloud architectures have generated some challenges for law enforcement (Birk and Wegener 2011; Plunkett et al. 2015) due to the lack of aforementioned and efficient models and processes in terms of digital evidence management, presentation, and court preparation. Research scientists have proposed the idea of providing a computing infrastructure with a capability to make it ready and prepared for forensic investigations and procedures, called digital forensic readiness (DFR) (Tan 2001). The principal aim of a dedicated system is identifying, collecting, and storing critical data coming from the underlying computing infrastructure, which is the potential evidence. Hence, in this chapter, we present the capability of using forensics readiness for cloud computing.

14.2 Cloud Forensics and Challenges

14.2.1 Technical

Cloud services are elastic, meaning they are provisioned and released based on users' scaling demands. The services run on a cloud infrastructure composed of multiple machines located potentially in different geographical zones without precise routing information; the resources are virtualized by using virtual machine managers (VMMs) (Mell and Grance 2011). From a forensic perspective, these features result in a reduced access to data, because providers intentionally hide data locations to facilitate ubiquitous access and replicas. Furthermore, physical control of the architecture components is lacking; it varies for the three services models, becoming larger when a customer moves to the bottom of the architecture. Another issue of cloud architectures concerns the heterogeneity of log files: because there is no standard format; each provider can customize their own log type. There is no timestamp synchronization among data centers and servers under a single provider scope or among different providers' components.

14.2.2 Organizational

Conducting a forensic investigation in the Cloud might involve data and service information belonging to both providers and customers. There might also be situations where cloud providers outsource some services from third parties, and thus the scope of an investigation becomes wider. Moreover, such outsourced services can be based on a cloud architecture; hence all the issues related to the replication of data on multiple data centers located potentially under different physical jurisdictions escalates. The lack of legal expertise specific to these features determines that there is considerable uncertainty about the measures to undertake in case of cross-providers or third-party suppliers of resources.

14.2.3 Legal

Cloud physical resources are virtualized to be used by multiple consumers via a multi-tenant model; they are also dynamically assigned according to demand. The principal issue is the trade-off between multitenancy and tenants' data privacy, i.e. what the correct trade-off is to guarantee multitenancy and at the same time preserve tenants' data privacy. Another side effect of on-demand elasticity is the spread of customers' and providers' data under different jurisdictions; in most cases, the SLAs also do not include information about the manner for determining data ownership or what jurisdiction to consider: the one related to the physical location of the customer, or to providers' machines, and which provider; in this case, contracts might be tailored to include proper constraints. Few proposals exist in the literature discussing and addressing this issue (Orton et al. 2012; Ryder and Le-Khac 2016).

14.3 Digital Forensics Readiness

In digital forensics, some scientists proposed the idea of providing a computing infrastructure with a capability to make it ready and prepared for forensic investigations when required. Such a capability is called digital forensic readiness (DFR), and it was introduced by (Tan 2001). The author defined DFR as "the ability of an organization to maximize its potential to collect digital evidence and minimizing the costs of an investigation." In order to prepare computing architectures for forensics, a readiness capability must be imagined as the provisioning of an information system communicating with such architectures.

A crime may happen; thus, the pure sense of such a capability is to render a digital context proactively for something that can theoretically never take place. This consideration may lead the reader to doubt about the effectiveness of DFR: specifically, if such a capability is dedicated to performing activities whose output might never be utilized. What the incentive is for spending effort to design and implement a dedicated system is a legitimate question. Positive side effects of DFR are to provide an approach for addressing some issues of digital forensics and enhancing some security and privacy issues of a computing environment. In 2004, a few years after DFR was introduced, (Rowlingson 2004) proposed a 10-step process designed for organizations willing to implement DFR. The process includes some key activities necessary for gathering potential digital evidence complying with the admissibility and reliability principles for court cases. It places emphasis on the features that a forensics readiness system needs to be effective.

An interesting approach for managing forensics readiness is discussed in (Reddy and Venter 2013). The examined issues deal with human, technical, and departmental management problems for implementing a DFRS in large organizations. The examination leads the authors to propose a solution composed of frameworks rather than ad hoc systems. Such a novel architecture is provided for assisting the realization of an optimal level for managing DFR. It is composed of detailed functional requirements determined by a literature survey, and it is also supported by an early proof-of-concept prototype system to demonstrate that it is feasible. Other work stressed the importance of a DFR capability in order to enhance the internal security of an organization. (Grobler and Louwrens 2007) examined the overlap between the DF and some information security (IS) best practices. The consideration made is that some DF aspects can be considered as IS best practices missing event-prosecution procedures. These best practices excluded the requirements for the preservation of digital evidence necessary for investigations. Organizations adopting the actual best practices cannot prosecute events and information related to security controls. In the authors' opinion, DFR is the solution for implementing and respecting the legal admissibility guidelines of evidence gathered during investigation procedures. A dedicated system can enrich the security strategies of an organization; this is justified by the main feature of providing a way to prepare the existing computing infrastructure for incident handling by collecting potential digital evidence. Thus, DFR is a good candidate to become a component of the IS best practices, demonstrating that protecting valuable company information resources is critical. (Endicott-Povsky and Frinckle 2007) discussed several network forensics aspects. The authors analyzed some situations when cyber targets are powerless with respect to attackers and intruders exploiting and disrupting networks. The authors affirmed that forensics readiness for network infrastructures can be a valuable solution in order to decrease the power of such attacks. Thus, a theoretical framework to implement network forensics readiness in enterprise contexts is proposed. (Danielsson and Tjostheim 2004) discussed the availability of digital evidence. It must be collected in a proper and proactive manner in order to make the investigations effective and successful. For this purpose, a DFR capability must be implemented in an organization, and it must follow a structured approach. Its implementation includes several features regarding national and international legislation, together with their constraints and requirements about data collection and preservation, and user data privacy protection. Such an approach aims to proactively seek the sources of digital evidence and to configure the existing computing infrastructure for collecting and preserving potential evidence. The proposal takes into account relevant and established standards and best practices; nevertheless, it considers some existing organizational routines, such as data-collection operations performed for purposes different from forensics, which can record events related to potential crimes. Finally, it provides guidance for reporting incidents to law enforcement, including the content, the format, the criteria for the report, and the manner in which the interaction between law enforcement and the affected parties is regulated. Again, the impact of DFR on a corporate context was analyzed by (Pangalos et al. 2010), where some positive aspects were highlighted, e.g. the enhancement of the security strategy of an organization, the reduction of security incidents, the availability of evidence, and the derived effectiveness of an investigation. (Mouton and Venter 2011) discussed another proposal for implementing forensics readiness capability that concerns wireless sensor networks. A dedicated prototype was designed as an additional layer to the existing infrastructure in order to avoid modifying the original architecture of an existing IEEE 802.15.4 network. The prototype was designed according to a list of requirements that have not been tested in real wireless sensor network scenarios. Thus, the requirements' usability has been tested through a prototype implemented as an additional layer of the network architecture. A DFR capability is considered crucial and necessary to be provided also to cloud computing architectures through a dedicated system (Ruan et al. 2013). It is responsible to perform proactive forensic investigations activities; doing so offers positive side effects, such as increased security and control over data access.

(Valjarevic and Venter 2011) discussed a forensics readiness capability for Public Key Infrastructure (PKI). A PKI system is a set of hardware, software, people, policies, and procedures necessary to create, manage, store, distribute, and revoke digital certificates. These systems are used to implement information system security services such as authentication and confidentiality. The authors investigated a set of policies, guidelines, and procedures, together with a model for implementing a forensics readiness framework for such systems. Some requirements for either preserving or improving information security and at the same time not altering the existing business processes of such PKI systems is the analyzed and addressed issue.

A DFR capability is shaped as an information system communicating with a computing architecture. The main aim is collecting and monitoring sensitive and critical information potentially related to digital crimes before they happen, leading to savings of time and money for the investigations. Data is closely related to the system artifacts and logging tools available. The collected data should be encrypted in order to guarantee more protection and stored in a place accessible by appropriate subjects.

The reason to shape a capability with an information system is driven by the necessity to represent something abstract, as a capability is, with something else that can be seen, as an information system is (Sommerville and Sawyer 1997). Nevertheless, with the execution of a process, some output can be generated; they are related to proactive forensic tasks aimed to prepare an infrastructure for possible investigations.

Such outputs are the mere operations of the capability: they compute input data collected from the monitored infrastructure. This information is composed of log files and additional system artifacts related to them, because they can hide facts related to digital crimes, or close to their happening. The relation of this data to crimes will be defined in the following. The reason data must be encrypted and stored in a place different from where it is gathered relies on forensic best practices described in (ACPO 2012), which provides details about evidence-admissibility principles, among other procedures. Finally, as mentioned in (De Marco et al. 2013), the provided definition for DFR is considered general and adaptable to every computing infrastructure; hence it is valid for both the past and the future, as well as for the mentioned cloud infrastructures.

14.4 Cloud Forensics Readiness

A forensics readiness capability must be provided to cloud computing architectures because, due to their escalating popularity, they can be the object of several attacks; thus, a way to conduct forensic investigations effectively, e.g. saving time, money, and resources, must be designed. A result of a recent survey conducted by (Ruan et al. 2011b) can corroborate these needs; indeed, almost 90% of the interviewees familiar with digital forensics stated that "a procedure and a set of tool-kits to proactively collect forensic-relevant data in the cloud is important." (Dykstra and Sherman 2012) analyzed some existing forensic tools such as EnCase in a cloud context; the result confirmed that the data collected by those tools is unreliable, because some cloud features require more effort for performing forensics than simply tailoring existing tools and procedures. The reason for this need is that new technical requirements must be managed for complying with the legal principles required for digital evidence. The same authors proposed a proper remote forensic acquisition suite of tools for an open source cloud environment (Dykstra and Sherman 2013). This suite, named FROST, provides a forensic capability for the Internet-as-a-Service (IaaS) level of OpenStack, an open source cloud computing platform. FROST performs data collection from provider machines and from the host operating system, and makes the data available to users, because it is assumed that customers are cooperative during investigations. The data collected in FROST include VM images, logs coming from application programming interface (API) requests, and OpenStack firewall logs. This suite is considered by the authors as a way to enhance forensics readiness in the Cloud because it performs the necessary investigation-preparation activities, such as data collection. Also, in (Trenwith and Venter 2013), a means of achieving DFR in the Cloud is described. It is composed of a remote and central logging facility for accelerating the acquisition of data; the model was also prototyped for Windows platforms.

14.4.1 Reference Architecture for a Cloud Forensics Readiness System: An Attempt

A reference architecture provides a general approach and understanding about the necessary operations that a cloud forensics readiness system (CFRS) must perform at a higher level of abstraction. Its main advantage resides in its design, which is not constrained by any specific and/or technical configuration; rather, it is flexible and customizable, and it can be considered a template for most organizations and cloud service providers that will implement a forensics readiness capability. The forensics readiness system is designed to communicate with an existing cloud infrastructure without altering the original components. It includes two main subsystems; the first is a *forensic database*, dedicated to the collection of cloud services information (the potential evidence). Such data is classified depending on the type; the possible types are monitored data, services' artifacts, and forensic logs; dedicated subsystems are included in the architecture design. The *monitored data subsystem* refers to information coming from cloud facilities dedicated to data monitoring and control (https://cloudsecurityalliance.org/guidance/csaguide.v3.0.pdf.); e.g. database- and file-activity monitoring, URL filtering, data-loss prevention, digital rights management system, and content discovery system. The database- and file-activity monitoring tools are capable of recognizing whenever a huge amount of data is pushed into the Cloud or replicated, thus indicating a data migration. The data-loss prevention facility is used for monitoring data in motion; it also manages policies and rights. URL filtering controls customers' connections to cloud services, thus it can be used during the reconstruction of a case timeline. The digital rights management system implements and monitors customers' rights and restrictions with regard to data, as stated by the SLAs and terms-of-use contractual clauses cosigned by providers and customers; the content-discovery system includes tools and processes aimed to identify sensitive information in storage components of a cloud architecture, and hence their output can allow the identification of some data violations or misuses. The *forensics artifacts subsystem* is dedicated to the storage of a significant quantity of artifacts gathered from the provider side, i.e. from Software-as-a-Service (SaaS), VM images, and single sign-on logs; from Platform-as-a-Service (PaaS), system states, and application logs; and from IaaS, snapshots, and the running system memory. Cloud auditor and error logs coming from VM hypervisors are instead collected by the forensic log; both of them are relevant for incident-response procedures and crime investigations. Also, some information from the cloud carrier has to be considered in the forensic log module. A cloud carrier is an intermediate between customers and providers, responsible for providing connectivity and transport of services to customers through the network and other access devices (Ruan and Carthy 2012).

Therefore, some information suitable for forensic investigations includes network logs, activity logs, access record facility logs, hypervisor event logs, and virtual images. The second main component of the cloud forensics readiness system is the *readiness core module*, which performs different activities on the gathered data, executed by dedicated subsystems. The collected data is encrypted and stored by dedicated subcomponents, i.e. data encryption and data storage, respectively. The data-management module performs forensic analysis and knowledge extraction with the purpose of reconstructing a correct and reliable event timeline about the recorded information. Finally, the chain-of-custody report necessary for case resolution is performed by the *chain-of-custody subsystem*. A communication and data-exchange channel is necessary between the cloud infrastructure and the forensics readiness system, and also among the several subsystems. For this purpose, the Open Virtualization Format (OVF) standard language (http://www.dmtf.org/standards/ovf) is considered suitable for the design and the distribution of the system. This standard language is capable of creating and distributing software applications to be executed on different VMs, independently from the hypervisors and from the CPU architectures. Moreover, it exploits the XML standard to establish the configuration and installation parameters; it can be extended for future VM hypervisor developments and is thus considered extremely flexible and adaptable for future versions of a forensics readiness system. In the reference architecture, the OVF communication channel between the Cloud and the system can be used to convert data formats into a specific target one, in order to render the necessary information readable and usable by the system.

14.4.2 Operations in a CFRS

The initial activity of a cloud forensics readiness system is data collection. The valuable forensic data includes cloud service artifacts and output from some existing cloud monitoring tools (Cloud Security Alliance 2011). Data is gathered from the Cloud and manipulated outside the architecture. In order to accomplish the UK (ACPO 2012) guideline, for example, concerning the preservation of potential digital evidence, the collected data has to be copied and secured to avoid tampering. This is performed by dedicated data-storage and -encryption subsystems, where proper digital signature and data-securing routines are implemented. This step is necessary for preserving the original copies when forensic activities are performed. The entire system's activities and modules are constantly running and collecting the most up-to-date data. All this information is fed into the intrusion detection subsystem, which is responsible for relating the available information, in order to detect suspicious behaviors. This subsystem has to consider the cosigned SLAs clauses (Mell and Grance 2011) necessary for correctly detecting contractual violations. The intrusion detection system component communicates with the event-alerting subsystem, as it generates alarms as soon as suspicious behaviors and contractual violations are detected. Such alarms might be different depending on the type of events, but this is out of the scope of a forensics readiness capability. The data-mining module is responsible for extracting hidden knowledge necessary to generate the incident-related evidence, and to relate the data and the sequence of events that have happened and are happening, leading to the construction of a correct and reliable timeline. The evidence must be treated considering guidelines, best practices, and laws used in court admissibility for case prosecutions. For this purpose, proper and dedicated policies and routines are implemented in the preservation-of-digital-evidence module. Some information related to them, e.g. location, treatment, date, time, time zone, and system component, must be recorded (Boucher and Le-Khac 2018) in order to maintain a reliable chain of custody necessary for prosecution purposes, which is performed by the chain of custody subsystem. The CFRS has to be communicative with the possible competent bodies involved in criminal case management, which can mean transmitting necessary information related to the detected case, such as a contractual violation. The competent bodies can be private or public incident responses; thus, dedicated communication interfaces with their information systems become necessary where the competent bodies are incident responses and law enforcement.

14.4.3 Forensics Readiness System Constraints

In order to benefit the most from the presented FR system, some constraints must be verified. Initially, the cloud infrastructure to be furnished with such a capability must provide the necessary monitoring tools to gather the data, considered common components to most cloud providers (Cloud Security Alliance 2011), and therefore, their presence should be verified. These are as follows:

- Components dedicated to the monitoring of both databases and files, necessary for detecting data migrations.
- Tools for filtering URLs, aimed to verify the connections made by different IP addresses.
- Tools with the purpose of controlling policies and rights established by the cosigned contracts.

High importance is also assigned to potential evidence data sources. This encompasses several logs generated by appropriate logging facilities present in cloud architectures, as well as system images gathered through dedicated tools. Another requirement concerns the capability of installing the necessary OVF communication channels, responsible for data transmission. From both an organizational and legal perspective, these communication channels should require authorization for data exchange. In this manner, the involved cloud actors will be warned, and eventual privacy violation threats can be managed.

14.4.4 CFRS Advantages

The implementation and use of a forensics readiness system for cloud computing architectures are very important for multiple purposes. Implicitly, the first aim is making a cloud infrastructure ready for digital forensics by executing the operations described. One of the system side effects is the enhancement of cloud customers' data privacy, together with major internal security; this can happen because wider control and monitoring will be performed by the system to protect critical and sensitive information (De Marco et al. 2013). Nevertheless, the reconstruction of a case's timeline accompanied by a related chain-of-custody document is the biggest contribution of such added value. A cloud organization or provider might realize that being prepared to manage crimes or incidents can be vital for both the reliability and the reputation of the offered services;

indeed, a proactive gathering of digital evidence minimizes the impact of a forensic investigation on a cloud organization's routines and performance (Rowlingson 2004). The detection of SLA clause violations can be managed by a CFRS. The subsystem dedicated to event reconstruction should be capable of determining a source of attack or the exact time when a customer data violation happened, relating them to specific service levels described in an SLA. The implementation of a CFRS can also be helpful to address cloud challenges for forensics as described earlier. A means of aligning multiple log file formats and synchronizing several machines' timestamps should be implemented; such a solution can lead to a correct, reliable reconstruction of event timelines, not necessarily related to crimes, but also to process executions. From a cloud forensics organizational perspective, the use of such a system can be the means to assign roles and responsibilities necessary for managing cloud incidents, such as investigator or incident handler; the people trained for the system can be responsible of some system modules and the manner in which data is managed in the cloud organization. Finally, from a legal point of view, a CFRS can highlight the main issues regarding jurisdiction borders; it can become the instrument for alerting proper governmental institutions, helping to address a more general problem.

14.5 Forensics Readiness in Evidence Management, Presentation, and Court Preparation

A digital forensics investigation (DFI) is defined as a process of collecting, identifying, preserving, analyzing, and presenting digital evidence in a manner that is legally acceptable (McKemmish 1999). The best-known and most-used DFI definitions have been proposed by the National Institute of Standards (NIST) (Kent et al. 2006). The main phases of such DFI processes are collection, examination, analysis, and reporting of media and digital evidence. Since a standard for DFI processes does not exist, several models have been proposed in the literature during the last few years (Agarwal et al. 2011; Alharbi et al. 2011; Baryamureeba and Tushabe 2004; Pollitt 2007; Yusoff et al. 2011). Each of them consists of a number of phases and subphases.

From the analysis viewpoint, few characteristics can be derived from the proposed DFI models. First, the computer architecture is not a mandatory feature for designing a new DFI, but it would be preferable for this to be expressed, in order to have a reliable basis for specific computing environments. Moreover, it would be more complete to also include the actors/stakeholders in order to assign responsibilities and to schedule the investigation phases in the most appropriate way and without overlapping. The common features discussed in the previous section should be considered in future models. The manner in which forensics readiness is conceived is very close to a preparation activity, present in 13 process models, by including preventive data-collection operations from the target computing architectures.

14.5.1 SLA in Cloud Forensics Readiness

14.5.1.1 Service Level Agreements

Information systems and computing capabilities are delivered through the Internet in the form of services; they are regulated by a SLA contract (Ford 1996) cosigned by a generic application service provider (ASP) and the end user(s), as happens for instance in the Cloud (Mell and Grance 2011). In such a contract, several clauses are established; they concern the level of services guaranteed, also known as quality of service (QoS) parameters, and the penalties to apply in case the requirements are not met during the SLA validity time, among others. SLA contracts are written in natural language and may be personalized by idioms, so that a different lingual version may exist for each of them. An SLA's validity begins when a customer is looking for a particular (set of) service(s), and it finishes when such provisioning is terminated. During this time period, both parties are responsible for respecting the clauses, due to the legal value of the document (Baset 2012). Therefore, a dedicated contract-management facility should be part of the service provisioning because of the contractual importance and contents (Cloud Security Alliance 2013). Some effort has been made in the literature to address this challenge, as discussed in the following sections. In particular, different metrics are exploited to measure specific contractual constraints concerning nonfunctional requirements of services, such as availability or performance indicators included in the contracts.

14.5.1.2 Service Level Agreement Interaction

In the Cloud, SLAs are cosigned between a provider and a customer that subscribes to a service. Additional SLAs can exist in other circumstances: for example, SLAs cosigned among different providers for hardware and software outsourcing, or SLAs involving third parties. Usually, customers are unaware of the complete data flow among different subproviders; this is because the chain of subservices necessary to accomplish an activity and the related SLAs are not disclosed to unconcerned parties.

An SLA is composed of a set of clauses, which describe all the constraints, behaviors, and duties of the cosigner parties in order to guarantee the level of the predefined services. For instance, some clauses concern the metrics necessary for measuring the described service-level attributes, such as latency or average transmission error rate. In this chapter, an analysis of the SLA's contents is discussed, together with a classification of some contractual contents in a cloud forensics readiness context.

14.5.1.3 Contractual Constraints

The structure of an SLA may differ from one cloud service provider to another. However, such a contract is composed of several sections. Among these sections, an SLA can be structured as a set of service-level objectives (SLOs). In a European Union guideline document (European Commission 2014), SLOs are catalogued based on the following factors:

- Performance
- Security
- Data management
- Personal data management

The focus of this section is to outline the SLOs necessary for DFR. The approach undertaken is composed of a number of steps. Initially, the presence of the SLOs mentioned in (European Commission 2014) has been verified in most public cloud service providers that have accessible SLAs. The annual list of the 100 most important cloud providers published by the top news source CRN has been utilized for this purpose.

After the selection has been made, as described later, the resulting SLOs are matched with the cloud threats discussed in a CSA report (https://cloudsecurityalliance.org/group/top-threats/#_overview).

14.5.1.4 SLO Selection

The annual list of the 100 most important cloud providers (CRN 2015) is composed of providers in every cloud service model. The model categorization utilized in this document includes IaaS, PaaS, SaaS, storage, and security. Moreover, there are 20 providers for each model. After an initial screening of the document, some included providers are still open projects and are therefore excluded from the SLO selection study because they did not provide the necessary information. The whole set of analyzed providers is composed of 76 elements. Unfortunately, only half of the selected elements provide a public SLA, mostly as providers of infrastructure model services. All the analyzed SLOs are described in (De Marco et al. 2013), depending on what category they belong to: the description is composed of their name, together with a definition and the percentage of their presence in the analyzed 38 SLAs.

14.5.1.5 SLO and Security Threats

According to the CSA document mentioned previously, the main threats for cloud service security are the following:

- *Data breach/loss:* A customer can lose control of their data; there can be several causes, such as multitenancy, provider vulnerabilities, and network misuse.
- *Hijacking:* Attackers can gain access to customer credentials to manipulate data, return false information, or redirect navigation to illegitimate sites. In addition, the power of a cloud provider can be used to launch subsequent attacks. Cloud vulnerabilities permitting hijacking attacks include mash-up authorization, the transitive nature of the Cloud, and authentication and authorization vulnerabilities.
- *Insecure APIs*: Attackers can be aware of the service architecture and design details; providers should select what to make publicly available through encryption, abstraction, or encapsulation mechanisms.
- *DoS and DDoS:* Denial of service (DoS) and distributed denial of service (DDoS) attacks prevent users from accessing their data or applications.

Not much effort has been expended do defend service platforms from such threats:

- *Malicious insiders:* An attacker can have access to sensitive information. Even with the use of encryption techniques, the system is still vulnerable to malicious insiders.
- *Abuse of services:* Attackers use cloud platforms to address their attacks and to host illegal materials. Nevertheless, providers allow quick and easy service subscriptions; this makes it harder to detect an offender's identity.
- *Lack of transparency:* Cloud organizations promise cost reduction together with operational and security improvements; several risks and issues can then arise, which are not disclosed to enterprises and organizations moving to cloud services.
- *Shared technology:* Multitenancy architectures and shared resources represent key points of elastic scalability guaranteed by cloud organizations; unfortunately, these features introduce vulnerabilities. A compromised component shared in the architecture can represent a threat for the entire system.

In order to prevent security threats with a forensics readiness capability, some cloud parameters need to be measured. The measurement constraints to be guaranteed are identified in the SLOs, but not in all of them; thus, according to their relation to the main cloud threats, they can be classified as primary, optional, or unnecessary SLOs.

14.5.1.6 Court Presentation

Evidence to be collected during a forensic investigation has to fulfill court-admissibility guidelines (ACPO 2012). In some cases, such guidelines can be in contrast with SLA constraints expressing jurisdictional principles. For instance, let us assume that SaaS cloud service provider X is responding to the European Jurisdiction. It can outsource additional services from storage cloud service provider Y, which responds to Asian or Middle Eastern laws. The SLA regulating the relationships between X and Y includes clauses that do not allow the collection of evidence, such as network logs or database transaction logs, and that regulate data access depending on other jurisdictions. Let us also assume that a customer of X accessing the service from the US is victim of a data-breach crime, and law enforcement has to conduct an investigation. Very likely, depending on both the SLAs regulating the relationships between the customer and X, and X and Y, respectively, such an investigation cannot be finalized due to the presence of the clauses denying access to the potential evidence. The hypothetical investigation can collect evidence-related data belonging to communications between the customer and service provider X; moreover, the logs from both the customer and provider sides can be utilized, as well as performance indicators and the values of the used metrics to evaluate the resource parameters. However, once the investigation has to deal with the infrastructure of service provider Y, depending on the expressed constraints, access to the necessary information can be denied to law enforcement.

14.5.2 Formal Model

Introducing a formal model representing the forensics readiness capability for cloud computing is of high priority. Such a model utilizes such formalisms as set theory, tuples, and functions in order to represent and relate the concept abstractions involved in it, such as SLAs and cloud logs. Moreover, some constraints among these concepts are represented in the form of theorems, and some specific definitions are designed.

A forensics readiness system for the Cloud is meant to observe and record information from the underlying computing architecture to make it forensically ready. Such information concerns operations happening in the Cloud to be related to SLA constraints. The capability output includes important investigative details about the recorded information and the detection of contractual clause violations.

Contractual monitoring is a topic actively investigated in the recent past in different contexts. Moreover, researchers provide customized ways to structure and represent SLA contents. The most effective representation is the adoption of formalisms. Natural-language-based SLA clauses have been structured via formal specification methods.

For instance, (Czajkowski et al. 2002) focus on the design of a protocol for negotiating SLAs among several actors. Different types of SLAs are defined, and some formalisms are utilized, such as tuples for describing an SLA. Also, some definitions concerning the metrics to use for services are provided. (Skene et al. 2007) formalize SLAs by using set theory for defining the concepts of actions, actors, events, parties, actions, and requirements. The purpose is to determine the possible SLA degree of monitoring in the context of service provisioning through the Internet. In (Paschke and Bichler 2008), a framework called Contract Log for monitoring SLAs is presented, which uses several formalisms. The SLAs are categorized depending on the purpose they are written for. Their contractual contents are formalized with different kinds of rules, such as derivation rules, reaction rules, integrity rules, and deontic rules; all of them are included in a homogeneous syntax and knowledge base. Finally, the conceptual framework is evaluated by a tool running specific test suites. In (Unger et al. 2008), the concepts of parties, SLA parameters, and SLOs are used to formalize SLAs in order to provide a way to aggregate more SLAs in a single business process. In this formal model, several formalisms are utilized, such as tuples, logic predicates, Boolean algebra, and normal forms. In (Ghosh and Ghosh 2012) the contracts are decomposed into the concepts of services parameters, SLOs, and key performance indicators; all these entities are formalized via tuples. The SLAs concern a storage-as-a-service facility where a design model for a dedicated monitoring system is provided. Formal specifications are used by (Ishakian et al. 2011) to represent and transform SLAs in order to address the issue of verifying efficient workload colocation of real-time applications. The approach allows transforming the SLAs whenever they do not meet the workload efficiency requirements, into an equivalent SLA that respects the same QoS. The proposal includes a reasoning tool used by the transformation process that comprehends inference rules based on a database of concepts, propositions, and syntactic idioms.

A cloud forensic readiness for SLA management (SLACFR) formal model is aimed to provide a theoretical approach to structure the management of SLA contracts for cloud computing services in the context of a forensics readiness capability. Its principal purpose is to record information about cloud behavior with respect to SLAs. This information is structured as a set of comparisons between an attribute of a cloud entity and a (set of) constraint(s) on that attribute at a specific time.

The capability recognizes suspicious information in real time: it represents a violation of a contractual constraint, such that preinvestigative activities are executed. The input of forensics readiness is composed of both information about cloud attributes and SLA constraints, all represented with formal rules. The execution begins on the availability of the contract(s) to monitor. The text is properly parsed via information-extraction techniques (Grishman 1997) and transformed into a set of formal rules. The approach used to build this formal model follows a bottom-up strategy: the contents of the SLAs are decomposed and structured to represent a constraint on a cloud entity. The cloud information is gathered from service logs; they represent resource information and are used to compute the actual value of a specific entity. For information coming from the cloud logs, a bottom-up approach is followed: the contents of the logs are decomposed and structured to represent individual cloud entities and the operations changing their values.

14.6 Conclusion

The adaptation of existing forensic procedures to computing novelties is a constant and challenging task; moreover, the provisioning of a forensics readiness capability to computing infrastructure is becoming more and more complicated. FR is conceived as the provisioning of an information system communicating with an underlying computing architecture with the purpose of identifying, collecting, and storing critical data coming from them, representing potential evidence. This FR capability must be provided to cloud computing architectures due to their escalating popularity, because they can be the object of several attacks. Thus, a way to conduct forensic investigations effectively, saving time, money, and resources, must be designed. A DFR capability for the Cloud is meant to observe and record changes concerning the operations happening in the Cloud with respect to SLA constraints related to potential crimes. The capability output includes important investigative details about the recorded information and the detection of contractual clause violations. Moreover, a reference architecture for the implementation of an FR system for the Cloud is designed and illustrated, together with constraints and advantages. A means for implementing such a DFR capability in the Cloud includes a representation of the information to monitor. The most effective representation is the adoption of formalisms. Then, natural-language-based SLA clauses, cloud logs, and several entities necessary to output a comparison between them, have been structured via formal specifications. The formal model utilizes tuples, set theory, and functions to represent the necessary entities.

The formal model can be enriched with information from a forensics readiness capability. For instance, some principle formal representations can be added to the existing ones, paying attention to not altering the relations among them. Case studies involving conflicting SLAs can be the drivers for this extension. Moreover, the SLACFR formal model and its prototype actually increase some security aspects of a cloud provider. Finally, a very important extension of this capability can be driven by the availability of historical data: cloud log files. Such a large dataset can allow reasoning, knowledge extraction, and prediction information useful to foresee SLA violations. Also, the design of a cyber-attack prediction metric can be a possible application of this data availability. We are also looking at applying this model for mobile cloud forensics (Faheem et al. 2015).

References

ACPO. (2012). Good practice guide for computer based electronic evidence. http://www.digital-detective.net/digital-forensics-documents/ACPO_Good_Practice_Guide_for_Digital_Evidence_v5.pdf.

Agarwal, A. et al. (2011). Systematic digital forensic investigation model. *International Journal of Computer Science and Security* 5 (1): 118–131.

Alharbi, S., Weber-Jahnke, J., Traore, I. et al. (2011). The proactive and reactive digital forensics investigation process: a systematic literature review. *Communications in Computer and Information Science* 200: 87–100.

Alonso, G., Casati, F., Kuno, H. et al. (2004). *Web Services*, 123–149. Berlin Heidelberg: Springer.

Baryamureeba, V. and Tushabe, F. (2004). The enhanced digital investigation process model. In: Proceedings of the DFRWS Workshop, 1–9.

Baset, S.A. (2012). Cloud SLAs: present and future. *ACM SIGOPS Operating Systems Review* 46 (2): 57–66.

Birk, D. and Wegener, C. (2011). Technical issues of forensic investigations in cloud computing environments. In: Proceedings of the IEEE 6th International Workshop on Systematic Approaches to DF Engineering, 110. IEEE.

Boucher, J. and Le-Khac, N.-A. (2018). Forensic framework to identify local vs synced artefacts. *Digital Investigation* 24 (1): 2018.
Casey, E. (2011). *Digital Evidence and Computer Crime*, 3e. Academic Press, Elsevier Science.
Cloud Security Alliance. (2011). Security guidance for critical areas of focus in cloud computing v 3.0. https://cloudsecurityalliance.org/guidance/csaguide.v3.0.pdf.
Cloud Security Alliance. (2013). Mapping the forensic standard ISO IEC 27037 to cloud computing.
CRN. (2015). The 100 coolest cloud computing vendors of 2015. http://www.crn.com/news/cloud/300075525/the-100-coolest-cloud-computing-vendors-of-2015.htm.
Czajkowski, K., Foster, I., Kesselman, C. et al. (2002). SNAP: A protocol for negotiating service level agreements and coordinating resource management in distributed systems. In: *Workshop on Job Scheduling Strategies for Parallel Processing*, 153–183. Springer.
Danielsson, J. and Tjostheim, I. (2004). The need for a structured approach to digital forensic readiness. In: Proceedings of the International Conference on Digital Forensic Readiness and E-commerce (IADIS), 417–421.
De Marco, L., Kechadi, M-T., Ferrucci, F. et al. (2013). Cloud forensic readiness: foundations. In: Proceedings of the 5th International Conference on DF & Cyber Crime (ICDF2C), LNICST series, 132: 237–244. Springer International Publishing.
Dykstra, J. and Sherman, A.T. (2012). Acquiring forensic evidence from Infrastructure-as-a-Service cloud computing: exploring and evaluating tools, trust, and techniques. In: Proceedings of the 12th Annual DF Research Conference, DFRWS, Digital Investigation, 9: 9098.
Dykstra, J., Sherman, A.T. (2013). Design and Implementation of FROST: Digital Forensic Tools for the OpenStack Cloud Computing Platform, preprint submitted to the 13th Annual DFRWS Conference, 2013.
Endicott-Povsky, B. and Frinckle, D.A. (2007). A theoretical framework for organizational network forensic readiness. *Journal of Computers* 2 (3): 111.
European Commission. (2014). Cloud service level agreement standardisation guidelines. https://ec.europa.eu/digital-agenda/en/news/cloud-service-level-agreement-standardisation-guidelines.
Faheem, M., Kechadi, M.-T., and Le-Khac, N.-A. (2015). The state of the art forensic techniques in mobile cloud environment: a survey, challenges and current trend. *International Journal of Digital Crime and Forensics* 7 (2): 1–19.
Ford, G. (1996). Service level agreements. *New Review of Academic Librarianship* 2 (1): 49–58.
Foster, I., Zhao, Y., Raicu, I. et al. (2008). Cloud computing and grid computing 360-degree compared. In: *Grid Computing Environments Workshops*, 1–10. IEEE.
Ghosh, N. and Ghosh, S.K. (2012). An approach to identify and monitor SLA parameters for Storage-as-a-Service cloud delivery model. In: *Grid Computing Environments Workshops*, 724–729. IEEE.
Grishman, R. (1997). Information extraction: techniques and challenges. In: *Information Extraction: A Multidisciplinary Approach to an Emerging Information Technology* (ed. M.T. Pazienza), 10–27. Springer.
Grobler, T. and Louwrens, B. (2007). Digital forensic readiness as a component of information security best practice. In: Proceedings of New Approaches for Security, Privacy and Trust in Complex Environments, IFIP TC- 11, 22nd International Information Security Conference, 232: 13–24.

Ishakian, V., Lapets, A., Bestavros, A. et al. (2011). A formal verification of SLA transformations. In: Proceedings of the IEEE World Congress on Services, 540–547. IEEE.

Kent, K., Grance, T., Chevalier, S. et al. (2006). *Guide to Integrating Forensic Techniques into Incident Response*, Special Publication 800-86. Gaithersburg, Maryland: National Institute of Standards and Technology (NIST).

Lee, J., NcCarthy, J., Licklider, J.C.R. et al. (1992). The beginnings at MIT. *IEEE Annuals of the History of Computing* 14 (1): 18–30.

McKemmish, R. (1999). *What Is Forensic Computing?* Trends and issues in crime and criminal justice. Canberra: Australian Institute of Criminology.

Mell, P. and Grance, T. (2011). The NIST definition of cloud computing. http://csrc.nist.gov/publications/nistpubs/800-145/SP800-145.pdf.

Mouton, F. and Venter, H.S. (2011). *A Prototype for Achieving Digital Forensic Readiness on Wireless Sensor Networks*, 16. AFRICON.

Orton, I., Alva, A., Endicott-Popovsky, B. et al. (2012). Legal process and requirements for cloud forensic investigations. In: *Cybercrime and Cloud Forensics: Applications for Investigation Processes* (ed. K. Ruan), 332–375. IGI Global.

Pangalos, G., Ilioudis, C., Pagkalos, I. et al. (2010). The importance of corporate forensic readiness in the information security framework. In: 19th IEEE International Workshop on Enabling Technologies: Infrastructures for Collaborative Enterprises (WETICE), 1216.

Paschke, A. and Bichler, M. (2008). Knowledge representation concepts for automated SLA management. *Decision Support Systems* 46 (1): 187–205.

Plunkett, J., Le-Khac, N-A., and Kechadi, M-T. (2015). Digital forensic investigations in the Cloud: a proposed approach for Irish law enforcement. 11th Annual IFIP WG 11.9 International Conference on Digital Forensics (IFIP119 2015), Orlando, Florida, United States, 26–28, January 2015.

Pollitt, M. (2007). An ad hoc review of digital forensic models. In: Second International Workshop on Systematic Approaches to Digital Forensic Engineering, 43–54.

Reddy, K. and Venter, H.S. (2013). The architecture of a digital forensic readiness management system. *Computers & Security* 32: 73–89.

Rowlingson, R. (2004). A ten step process for forensic readiness. *International Journal of Digital Evidence* 2 (3): 1–28.

Ruan K., Baggili, I., Carthy, J. et al. (2011b). Survey on cloud forensics and critical criteria for cloud forensic capability: a preliminary analysis. In: Proceedings of the 6th Annual Conference on Digital Forensics, Security and Law.

Ruan, K. and Carthy, J. (2012). Cloud computing reference architecture and its forensic implications: a preliminary analysis. In: Proceedings of the 4th International Conference on Digital Forensics & Cyber Crime (ICDF2C), 114: 1–21.

Ruan K., Carthy, J., Kechadi, M-T. et al. (2011a). Cloud forensics: an overview. Advances in Digital Forensics VII.

Ruan, K., Carthy, J., Kechadi, M.-T. et al. (2013). Cloud forensics definitions and critical criteria for cloud forensic capability: an overview of survey results. *Digital Investigation* 10 (1): 34–43.

Ryder, Steven and Le-Khac N-A. (2016). The end of effective law enforcement in the Cloud? To encrypt, or not to encrypt. The 9th IEEE International Conference on Cloud Computing, San Francisco, CA USA, June 2016.

Skene, J., Skene, A., Crampton, J. et al. (2007). The monitorability of service-level agreements for application-service provision. In: Proceedings of the International Workshop on Software and Performance, 3–14.

Sommerville, I. and Sawyer, P. (1997). *Requirements Engineering: A Good Practice Guide.* John Wiley and Sons, Inc.

Tan, J. (2001). Forensic readiness, Technical report. @Stake Organization. http://isis.poly.edu/kulesh/forensics/forensicreadiness.pdf.

Trenwith, P. M. and Venter, H.S. (2013). Digital forensic readiness in the Cloud. In: Proceedings of Information Security for South Africa, 1–5.

Unger, T., Leymann, F., Mauchart, S. et al. (2008). Aggregation of service level agreements in the context of business processes. In: Proceedings of the ICEDOC Conference, 43–52.

Valjarevic, A. and Venter, H.S. (2011). Towards a digital forensic readiness framework for Public Key Infrastructure systems. In: Proceedings of Information Security South Africa (ISSA), 1–10.

Yusoff, Y., Ismail, R., Hassan, Z. et al. (2011). Common phases of computer forensics investigation models. *International Journal of Computer Science & Information Technology* 3 (3): 17–31.

15

Analysis of Cloud Digital Evidence

Irfan Ahmed and Vassil Roussev

University of New Orleans, New Orleans, LA, USA

15.1 Introduction

Analysis of digital evidence acquired from cloud computing deployments, which we refer to as *cloud evidence* analysis, is in its very early stages of development. It is still in its exploration and experimentation phase where new, ad hoc solutions are developed on a per-case basis; efforts are made to map problems in the cloud domain to prior solutions; and, most of all, ideas for the future are put forward. In other words, the state of knowledge is quite immature, and that is well illustrated by the steady stream of recommendations – primarily from academia – on what *should* be done by providers and clients to make cloud forensics easier and better (for the existing toolset).

The goal of this chapter is to present a broad framework for reasoning about cloud forensics architectures and scenarios, and for the type of evidence they provide. We use this framework to classify and summarize the current state of knowledge, as well as to identify the blank spots and likely future direction of cloud forensics research and development.

15.1.1 Cloud Forensics as a Reactive Technology

Since our discussion is primarily focused on the technical aspects of analyzing cloud evidence (and not on legal concerns), we adopt the following technical definition of digital forensics (Roussev 2016):

> *Digital forensics is the process of reconstructing the relevant sequence of events that have led to the currently observable state of a target IT system or (digital) artifacts.*

The notion of *relevance* is inherently case-specific, and a big part of a forensic analyst's expertise is the ability to identify case-relevant evidence. Frequently, a critical component of the forensic analysis is the causal *attribution* of an event sequence to specific human actors of the system (such as users and administrators). When used in legal

Security, Privacy, and Digital Forensics in the Cloud, First Edition. Edited by Lei Chen, Hassan Takabi, and Nhien-An Le-Khac.

proceedings, the *provenance, reliability*, and *integrity* of the data used as evidence are of primary importance.In other words, we view all efforts to perform system or artifact analysis after the fact as a form of forensics. This includes common activities such as incident response and internal investigations, which almost never result in any legal actions. On balance, only a tiny fraction of forensic analyses make it to the courtroom as formal evidence.

Digital forensics is fundamentally reactive in nature – we cannot investigate systems and artifacts that do not exist; we cannot have *best practices* before an experimental period during which different technical approaches are tried, (court-)tested, and validated. This means there is always a lag between the introduction of a piece of information technology and the time an adequate corresponding forensic capability is in place. The evolution of the IT infrastructure is driven by economics and technology; forensics merely identifies and follows the digital breadcrumbs left behind.

It follows that forensic *research* is also inherently reactive and should focus primarily on understanding and adapting to the predominant IT landscape, as opposed to trying to shape it in any significant fashion. Throughout the rest of this chapter, we will make the case that the Cloud presents a new type of challenge for digital forensics and that it requires an entirely different toolset, as the existing one becomes quickly and increasingly inadequate.

Twelve years have elapsed since the introduction in 2006 of public cloud services by Amazon under the Amazon Web Services (AWS) brand. As of 2015, according to RightScale's *State of the Cloud Report* (RightScale 2015), cloud adoption has become ubiquitous: 93% of businesses are at least experimenting with cloud deployments, with 82% adopting a *hybrid* strategy, which combines the use of multiple providers (usually in a public-private configuration). However, much of the technology transition is still ahead as 68% of enterprises have less than 20% of their application portfolio running in a cloud setup. Similarly, (Gartner 2014) predicts another two to five years will be needed before cloud computing reaches the "plateau of productivity," which marks mass mainstream adoption and widespread productivity gains.

Unsurprisingly, cloud forensics is still in its infancy despite dozens of articles in the literature over the last five years; there is a notable dearth of *practical* technical solutions on the analysis of cloud evidence. Thus, much of our discussion will necessarily tilt toward identifying new challenges and general approaches as opposed to summarizing existing experiences, of which there are few.

15.1.2 The New Forensics Landscape

Most cloud forensics discussions start with the false premise that, unless the current model of digital forensic processing is *directly* and faithfully reconstructed with respect to the Cloud, then we are bound to lose all notions of completeness and integrity. The root of this misunderstanding is the use of traditional desktop-centric computational model that emerged in the 1990s as the point of reference. (This approach has been subsequently tweaked to work for successive generations of ever-more-mobile client devices.)

The key attribute of this model is that practically all computations take place on the device itself. Applications are monolithic, self-contained pieces of code that have immediate access to user input and consume it instantly with (almost) no trace left behind;

periodically, the current state is saved to stable storage. Since a big part of forensics is attributing the observed state of the system to user-triggered events, we (forensic researchers and tool developers) have obsessively focused on two driving problems: discover every little piece of log/timestamp information, and extract every last bit of discarded data that applications and the operating system (OS) leave behind, either for performance reasons, or just plain sloppiness. Courtesy of countless hours spent on painstaking reverse engineering, we have become quite good at these tasks.

Indeed, our existing toolset is almost exclusively built to feast upon the leftovers of computations – an approach that is becoming more challenging even in traditional (non-cloud) cases. For example, *file carving* of acquired media (Richard and Roussev 2005) only exists because it is highly inefficient for the OS to sanitize the media. However, for solid state disk (SSD) devices, the opposite is true – they *need* to be prepared before reuse. The result: deleted data is sanitized, and there is little left to carve (King and Vidas 2011).

The very notion of low-level *physical* acquisition is reaching its expiration date even from a purely technological perspective – the current generation of high-capacity hard disk drives (HDDs) (8 TB+) use a *track-shingling* technique and have their very own Acorn RISC Machine (ARM) based processor, which is tasked with identifying hot and cold data, and choosing appropriate physical representation for it. The HDD device exposes an object store interface (not unlike key-value databases) that effectively makes physical acquisition, in a traditional sense, impossible – legacy block-level access is still supported, but the block identifiers and physical layout are no longer coupled as they were in prior generations of devices. By extension, the feasibility of most current data-recovery efforts, such as file carving, will rapidly diminish.

Mass hardware disk encryption is another problem worth mentioning, as it is becoming increasingly *necessary* and *routine* in IT procedures. This is driven both by the fact that there is no observable performance penalty, and by the need to effectively sanitize ever-larger and -slower HDDs. The only practical solution to the latter is to always encrypt and dispose of the key when the disk needs to be reclaimed.

In sum, the whole concept of acquiring a *physical* image of the storage medium is increasingly technically infeasible and is progressively less relevant because interpreting the physical image requires understanding of the (proprietary) internals of the device's data structures and algorithms. The inevitable conclusion is that forensic tools will have to increasingly rely on the logical view of the data presented by the device.

Logical evidence acquisition and processing will also be the norm in most cloud investigations, and it will be performed at an even higher level of abstraction via software-defined interfaces. Conceptually, the main difference between cloud computing and client-side computing is that *most* of the computation and, more importantly, the application logic executes on the server, with the client effectively becoming a remote terminal for collecting user input (and environment information) and for displaying the results of the computation.

Another consequential trend is the way cloud-based software is developed and organized. Instead of one monolithic piece of code, the application logic is almost always decomposed into several layers and modules that interact with each other over well-defined service interfaces. Once the software components and their communication are formalized, it becomes quite easy to organize extensive logging of all aspects of the system. Indeed, it becomes *necessary* to have this information just to be able to test, debug, and monitor cloud-based applications and services. Eventually, this will end up helping forensics tremendously as important stages of computation are routinely logged, with user input being both the single most important source of events and the least demanding to store and process.

Returning to our driving problem of analyzing cloud artifacts, it should be clear that – in principle – our task of forensically reconstructing prior events should be becoming *easier* over time as a growing fraction of the relevant information is being *explicitly* recorded. As an example, consider that with a modest reverse-protocol engineering effort, (Somers 2014), later expanded by (Roussev and McCulley 2016), was able to demonstrate that Google Docs timestamps and logs every single user keystroke. The entire history of a document can be replayed with a simple piece of JavaScript code; in fact, the log is the primary representation of the document, and the current (or prior) state of the document is computed on the fly by replaying (part of) the history. From a forensics perspective, this is a time-travel machine and is practically everything we could ask for in terms of evidence collection, with every user event recorded with microsecond accuracy.

15.1.3 Adapting to the New Landscape

According to (Ruan et al. 2013), more forensic examiners see cloud computing as making forensics harder (46%) than easier (37%). However, the more revealing answers come from analyzing the reasoning behind these responses. The most frequent justifications for the *harder* answer fall into two categories: (i) restricted access to data (due to lack of jurisdiction and/or cooperation from the cloud provider), and (ii) inability to physically control the process of evidence acquisition/recovery, and to apply currently standard processing techniques. While data access is primarily a nontechnical issue – to be solved by appropriate legal and contractual means – the natural inclination to attempt to apply legacy techniques will take some time and new tools to resolve.

All of these concerns merely emphasize that we are in a transitional period during which requirements, procedures, and tools are still being fleshed out. From a technical perspective, the simplest way to appreciate why forensics professionals lack any *cloud-specific* tools is to consider the current dearth of tools that support the investigation of server deployments. Practically all integrated forensic environments, both commercial and open source, focus on the client and the local execution model discussed earlier. However, a server-side inquiry is an exercise in tracking down and correlating the available logs – a task that, today, is accomplished largely in an ad hoc manner using custom scripts and other "homegrown" solutions. Investigating a cloud application is not unlike performing a server-side investigation, with a lot more log data and more complex data relationships.

From a research perspective, it may appear that log analysis does not present a very exciting prospect for the future. However, the real challenge will come from the sheer volume and variety of logs and the need to develop ever-more-intelligent tools to process and understand them. The long-term upside – and, likely, necessity – is that we can, for the first time, see a plausible path toward *substantially higher levels of automation* in forensics. At present, the process of extracting bits and pieces of artifacts and putting them together in a coherent story is too circuitous and vaguely defined for it to be further automated to a meaningful degree. Once log data becomes the primary source of evidence, it is conceivable that a substantial number of forensic questions could be formalized as data queries to be automatically answered, complete with formal statistical error estimates.

The transition from artifact-centric to log-centric forensics will take some time – artifact-analysis methods will always be needed, but they will be applied much more selectively. Nevertheless, it is a relatively safe prediction that, within a decade, this transition will fundamentally change forensic computing and the nature of investigative work.

15.1.4 Summary

Cloud computing presents a qualitatively new challenge for the existing set of forensic tools, which are focused on analyzing leftover artifacts on local client devices. Cloud services are inherently distributed and server-centric, which renders ineffective large parts of our present acquisition and analysis toolchain. In this transitional period, forensic analysts are struggling to bridge the gap using excess manual technical and legal effort to fit the new data sources into the existing pipeline.

Over the medium-to-long term, the field requires an entirely new set of cloud-native forensic capabilities that work in unison with cloud services. Once such tools are developed and established, this will open up the opportunity to define more formally legal and contractual requirements that providers can satisfy at a reasonable cost. As soon as technical and legal issues are worked out, we will face the unprecedented opportunity of automating and scaling up forensic analysis to a degree that is currently not possible.

The rest of this chapter is organized as follows: Section 15.1 presents necessary background of cloud computing service models, followed by Section 15.2 discussing the current approaches for each model. Section 15.3 presents potential approaches and solutions as a way forward to address forensics in cloud computing. Sections 15.4 and 15.6 present a detailed discussion and conclusion, respectively.

15.2 Background

Cloud computing services are commonly classified into one of three canonical models – *Software-as-a-Service* (SaaS), *Platform-as-a-Service* (PaaS), and *Infrastructure-as-a-Service* (IaaS) – and we use this split as a starting point in our discussion. We should note, however, that practical distinctions are often less clear-cut, and a real IT cloud solution (and a potential investigative target) can incorporate elements of all of these. As illustrated on Figure 15.1, it is useful to break down cloud computing environments into a stack of layers (from lower to higher): *hardware* such as storage and networking, *virtualization* consisting of a hypervisor allowing the installation of virtual machines (VMs), *operating system* installed on each VM, *middleware* and *runtime* environment, and *application* and *data*.

In a private (cloud) deployment, the entire stack is hosted by the owner, and the overall forensic picture is very similar to the problem of investigating a non-cloud IT target. Data ownership is clear, as is the legal and procedural path to obtain it; indeed, the very use of the term *cloud* is mostly immaterial to forensics; therefore, we will not discuss this case any further.

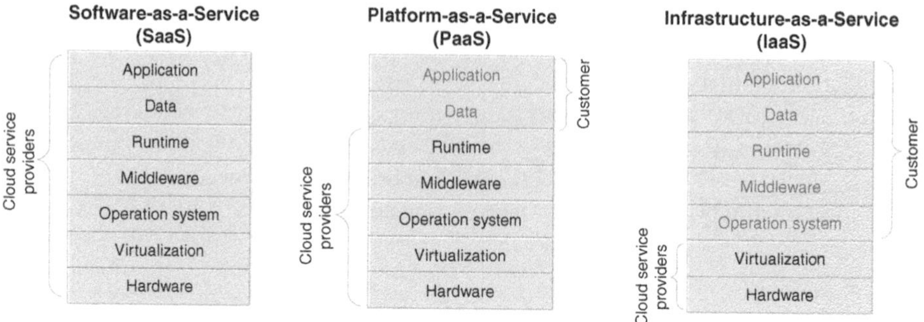

Figure 15.1 Layers of the cloud computing environment owned by the customer and cloud service provider on three service models: IaaS, PaaS, and SaaS (public cloud).

Table 15.1 Examples of some popular commercial products based on the cloud service models: Software-as-a-Service, Platform-as-a-Service, and Infrastructure-as-a-Service.

Software-as-a-Service	Platform-as-a-Service	Infrastructure-as-a-Service
Google Gmail	Apprenda	Amazon Web Service
Microsoft 365	Google App Engine	Microsoft Azure
Salesforce		Google Compute Engine
Citrix GoToMeeting		
Cisco WebEx		

In a public deployment, the SaaS/PaaS/IaaS classification becomes important as it indicates the ownership of data and service responsibilities. Figure 15.1 shows the typical ownership of layers by customer and service provider on different service models; Table 15.1 presents the examples of commercial products of the cloud service models.

In hybrid deployments, layer ownership can be split between the customer and the provider and/or across multiple providers. Further, it can change over time as, for example, the customer may handle the base load on owned infrastructure, but *burst* to the public cloud to handle peak demand or system failures.

15.2.1 Software-as-a-Service (SaaS)

In this model, cloud service providers (CSPs) own all the layers including the application layer that runs the software offered as a service to customers. In other words, the customer has only indirect and incomplete control (if any) over the underlying operating infrastructure and applications (in the form of policies). However, since the CSP manages the infrastructure (including the application), maintenance costs on the customer side are substantially reduced. Google Gmail/Docs, Microsoft 365, Salesforce, Citrix GoToMeeting, and Cisco WebEx are popular examples of SaaS, which run directly from the web browser without downloading and installing any software. Their desktop and smartphone versions are also available to run on the client machine. The applications have a varying but limited presence on the client machine, making the client an incomplete source of evidence; therefore, investigators need access to server-side logs to paint a complete picture.

SaaS applications log extensively, especially when it comes to user-initiated events. For instance, Google Docs records every insert, update, and delete operation of characters performed by the user along with timestamps, which makes it possible to identify specific changes made by different users in a document (Somers 2014). Clearly, such information is a treasure trove for a forensic analyst and is a much more detailed and direct account of prior events than is typically recoverable from a client device.

15.2.2 Platform-as-a-Service (PaaS)

In the PaaS service model, customers develop their applications using software components built into middleware. Apprenda (https://apprenda.com) and Google App Engine (https://cloud.google.com/appengine/pricing) are popular examples of PaaS, offering quick and cost-effective solutions for developing, testing, and deploying customer applications. In this case, the cloud infrastructure hosts customer-developed applications and provides high-level services that simplify the development process. PaaS provides full control to customers on the application layer including interaction of applications with dependencies (such as databases, storage, etc.) and enabling customers to perform extensive logging for forensics and security purposes.

15.2.3 Infrastructure-as-a-Service (IaaS)

In IaaS, the CSP is the party managing the VMs; however, this is done in direct response to customer requests. Customers then install the OS and applications within the machine without any interference from the service providers. AWS, Microsoft Azure, and Google Compute Engine (GCE) are popular examples of IaaS. IaaS provides capabilities to take snapshots of the disk and physical memory of VMs, which has significant forensic value for quick acquisition of disk and memory. Since VMs support the same data interfaces as physical machines, the traditional forensic tools for data acquisition and analysis can also be used inside the VMs as remote investigation of a physical machine is performed. Furthermore, VM introspection provided by a hypervisor enables CSPs to examine live memory and disk data, and perform instant data acquisition and analysis. However, since the functionality is supported at the hypervisor level, customers cannot take advantage of this functionality.

In summary, we can expect SaaS and PaaS investigations to have a high dependency on logs, since disk and memory image acquisition is difficult to perform due to lack of control on middleware, OSs, and lower layers. In IaaS, the costumer has control over the OS and upper layers, which makes it possible to acquire disk and memory images, and perform traditional forensic investigations.

15.3 Current Approaches

The different architectural models shown in Figure 15.1 imply the need for a differentiated approach to building forensic tools for each of them. An additional dimension to this challenge is that implementations of the same class of service (e.g. IaaS) can vary substantially across providers. Moreover, providers could be using and/or reselling other providers' services, making the task of physically acquiring the source data impractically complicated, or even intractable.

Over time, we can expect the large (and still growing) number of cloud service types and implementations to naturally coalesce into a smaller set of de facto standards, which may eventually provide some needed visibility into the provider's operations. In the meantime, cloud forensics research is likely best served by focusing on the information available at the subscriber-provider boundary interface. The key observation is that providers *must* collect and retain substantial amounts of log information for accounting and operational purposes. For example, an IaaS provider must have detailed records of VM operations (launch, shutdown, CPU/network/disk usage), assignment of IP addresses, changes to firewall rules, long-term data storage requests, and so on. Such data should be readily available, segregated by subscriber, and, therefore, readily obtainable via the legal process. However, invasive requests for physical media and information that cut to the core of a provider's operation are highly unlikely to succeed in the general case.

15.3.1 SaaS Forensics

Cloud customers access SaaS applications such as Google Gmail, Google Docs, and Microsoft 365 through a web interface or desktop application from their personal computing devices such as laptop/desktop computers and smartphones. The applications maintain a detailed history/log of user inputs that is accessible to customers and has forensic value. Since applications are accessed from a client machine, remnants of digital artifacts pertaining to user activities in the applications are usually present and can be forensically retrieved and analyzed from the hard disk of the machine.

15.3.1.1 Cloud-Native Application Forensics

Perhaps the very first *cloud-native* tool with forensics applications is *Draftback* (https://draftback.com): a browser extension created by the writer and programmer James Somers, which can replay the complete history of a Google Docs document (Somers 2014). The primary intent of the code is to give writers the ability to look over their own shoulder and analyze how they write. Coincidentally, this is precisely what a forensic investigator would like to be able to do – rewind to any point in the life of a document, right to the very beginning.

In addition to providing in-browser playback of all the editing actions – in either fast-forward or real-time mode – Draftback provides an analytical interface that maps the time of editing sessions to locations in the document (Figure 15.2). This can be used to narrow down the scope of inquiry for long-lived documents.

Somers's work, although not motivated by forensics, is probably the single best example of SaaS analysis that does *not* rely on trace data resident on the client – all results are produced solely by reverse engineering the web application's simple data protocol. Assuming that an investigator is in possession of valid user credentials (or such are provided by Google under legal order), the examination can be performed on the spot: any spot with a browser and an Internet connection.

The most profound forensic development here is that, as far as Google Docs is concerned, there is no such thing as deletion of data; every user editing action is recorded

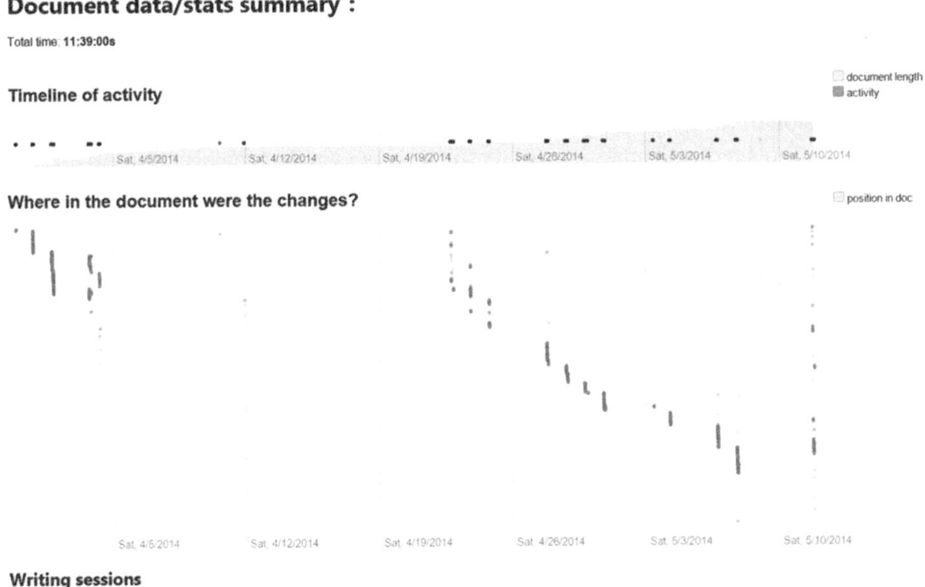

Figure 15.2 Draftback analytical interface.

and timestamped. Indeed, even the investigator cannot spoil the evidence because any actions on the document will simply be added to the editing history with the appropriate timestamp. This setup is likely to be sufficient for most informal/internal scenarios, however, in order to make it to the courtroom, some additional tooling and procedures will need to be developed.

Clearly, the *acquisition* and long-term *preservation* of the evidence is yet to be addressed. The data component is the low-hanging fruit because the existing replay code can be modified to produce a log of the desired format. The challenging part is preserving the application logic that interprets the log; unlike client-side applications, a web app's code is split between the client and the server, and there is no practical way to acquire an archival copy of the execution environment as of a particular date. Since the data protocol is internal, there is no guarantee that a log acquired now could be replayed years later.

One possible solution is to produce a screencast video of the entire replayed user session. The downside here is that most documents are bigger than a single screen, so the video would have to be accompanied by periodic snapshots of the actual document (e.g. in PDF). Another approach would be to create a reference text-editor playback application in which the logs could be replayed. This would require extra effort and faces questions of how closely the investigated application can be emulated by the reference one.

The next logical question is, how common is fine-grain user logging among cloud applications? As one would expect, a number of other editing applications from Google's Apps for Work suite – such as Sheets, Slides, and Sites – use a very similar model and provide scrupulously detailed history (Slides advertises "unlimited revision history";

https://www.google.com/work/apps/business/products/slides). A deeper look reveals that the particular history available for a document depends on the age of the file and/or the size of the revisions, as revisions may be merged to save storage space (https://support.google.com/docs/answer/95902). In other words, Google starts out with a detailed version of the history; over time, an active document's history may be trimmed and partially replaced with snapshots of its state. It appears that the process is primarily driven by technical and usability considerations, not policy.

Microsoft's Office 365 service also maintains detailed revisions based on edits in part because, like Google, it supports real-time collaboration. Zoho is another business suite of online apps that supports detailed history via a shared track-changes feature similar to Microsoft Word's feature. Most cloud drive services offer generic file-revision history; however, the available data is more limited because it is stored as simple snapshots.

15.3.1.2 Cloud Drive Forensics

Cloud users access their cloud storage through personal computing devices such as laptop/desktop computers and smartphones. (Chung et al. 2012) suggest that the traces of services present in client devices can be helpful to investigate criminal cases, particularly when CSPs do not provide the cloud server logs to protect their client's privacy. Investigation on cloud storage identifies user activities from subscription to the service until the end of using the service. They authors analyze four cloud storage services (i.e. Amazon S3, Google Docs, Dropbox, and Evernote) and report that the services may create different artifacts depending on specific features of the services. The authors proposed a process model for forensic investigation of cloud storage services. The model combines the collection and analysis of artifacts of cloud storage services from both personal computer and smartphones. The model suggests acquiring volatile data from personal (Mac/Windows) computers (if possible) and then gathering data from the Internet history, log files, files, and directories. In Android phones, rooting is performed to gather data; iTunes data is gathered from iPhones, and the backup iTunes files from personal computers. The analysis checks for the traces of a cloud storage service that exist in the collected data.

(Hale 2013) discusses the digital artifacts left behind after an Amazon Cloud Drive has been accessed or manipulated from a computer. Amazon's cloud storage service allows users to upload and download files from any location, without having a specific folder on a local hard drive to sync with the cloud drive. The user uses a desktop application or online web interface to transfer selected files or folders to/from the cloud drive. The online interface is similar in appearance to Windows Explorer, with Upload, Download and Delete buttons to perform actions on files and folders. The desktop application also provides a drag-and-drop facility. Hale analyzes the cloud drive by accessing and manipulating the drive's content via the desktop application and online web interface. He found artifacts of the interface in the web browser history and cache files. The desktop application had artifacts on the Windows registry, application installation files on the default location, and a SQLite database used by the application to hold transfer tasks (i.e. upload/download) while the task's status was pending.

(Quick and Choo 2013) discuss the digital artifacts of Dropbox after a user has accessed and manipulated Dropbox content. Dropbox is a file-hosting service enabling users to store and share files and folders it is accessed through a web browser or client software. The authors use hash analysis and keyword searches to determine if Dropbox client software has been used. They determine the Dropbox username from the browser history (of Mozilla Firefox, Google Chrome, or Microsoft Internet Explorer) and the use of Dropbox through several avenues such as directory listings, prefetch files, link files, thumbnails, the registry, the browser history, and memory captures.

(Martini and Choo 2013) discuss the digital artifacts of ownCloud on both the server and client side. ownCloud is a file-sync and file-share software application configured and hosted on the server. It provides client software and a web interface to access files on the server. The authors recover artifacts including sync and file-management metadata (such as logging, database, and configuration data), cached files describing files the user has stored on the client device and uploaded to the cloud environment or vice versa, and browser artifacts.

15.3.1.3 Building New Tools for SaaS Forensics

As our review of existing work demonstrates, research and development efforts have been focused on the traditional approach of finding local artifacts on the client. This is an inherently limited and inefficient approach requiring substantial reverse-engineering effort; the future of SaaS forensics lies in working *with* the web infrastructure the way web applications do: through application programming interfaces (APIs).

Practically all user-facing cloud services strive to be platforms (i.e. they provide an API) in order to attract third-party developers who build apps and extensions enhancing the base product. The most relevant example is the wide availability of backup products, such as those provided by EMC's Spanning (http://spanning.com/products), which provides scheduled cloud-to-cloud backup services on multiple platforms – Google Apps, Salesforce, and Office 365. Otixo (www.otixo.com) is another service that provides single sign-on and data-transfer capability across more than 20 different SaaS platforms.

The latter provides a clear demonstration that the systematic acquisition of SaaS data can be readily accomplished via the provided APIs. At present, the amount of data in cloud storage is small relative to the size of local storage – free services offer only up to 15GB. However, as businesses and consumers get comfortable with the services, and more willing to pay for them, we can expect a fast and substantial increase in volume. For example, Google Drive currently offers up to 30TB at $10/month per terabyte.

This development is likely to blur the line between acquisition and analysis. As full acquisition becomes too burdensome and impractically slow, one logical development would be to use the *search* interface offered by cloud service APIs to narrow down the scope of the acquisition. Procedurally, this aligns well with what already takes place during e-discovery procedures.

Looking further ahead, as cloud storage grows, it will be increasingly infeasible to acquire data by downloading it over the Internet. This will bring a new impetus to the development of *forensics-as-a-service* (FaaS), because the only practical means to perform the processing in a reasonable amount of time would be to collocate the data and the forensic computation in the same data center. Clearly, the practical use of FaaS is some years away, and a nontrivial number of legal and regulatory issues would have to be addressed beforehand. Nonetheless, the fact that storage-capacity growth constantly outpaces network-bandwidth growth inexorably leads to the need to move the computation close to the data. Forensic computation will be no exception, and procedures will have to be adjusted to account for technological realities.

15.3.2 PaaS/IaaS Forensics

PaaS packages middleware platforms on top of the OS. Commercial products on PaaS are available, such as Google App Engine. However, the forensic research community did not pay much attention to PaaS, which is evident from the lack of research papers on this topic. On the other hand, IaaS has received attention because of the close resemblance among service models to traditional computing infrastructure. It has VMs running contemporary OSs and software, similar to physical machines. The conventional forensic tools for data acquisition and analysis, such as WinDD, Forensic Toolkit (FTK), and EnCase, can be used on VMs. Furthermore, IaaS offers unique features such as VM snapshotting for quick physical memory and HDD acquisition.

(Dykstra and Sherman 2012) evaluated the effectiveness of EnCase, FTK, and three physical-memory acquisition tools (i.e. HBGary's FastDump, Mandiant's Memoryze, and FTK Imager) in a cloud computing environment. They remotely acquired geographically dispersed forensic evidence over the Internet and tested their success at gathering evidence, the time to do so, and the trust required. They used a public cloud (Elastic Compute Cloud [EC2] from AWS) for their experiments and concluded that forensic tools are technically capable of remote data acquisition. They illustrated IaaS in six layers (from lowest to highest): network, physical hardware, host OS, virtualization, guest OS, and guest application/data. Each layer (except the last) has to trust all the lower layers. Given the trust requirements, the authors mention that technology alone is insufficient to produce trustworthy data and solve the cloud forensics acquisition problem. They recommend a management plane enabling consumers to manage and control virtual assets through an out-of-band channel interfacing with the cloud infrastructure, such as that provided by AWS: AWS Management Console. The management plane interfaces with the provider's underlying file system and hypervisor, and is used to provision, start, and stop VMs.

(Dykstra and Sherman 2013) developed a tool called *FROST*, which integrates forensic capabilities with OpenStack. FROST uses a management plane through a website and APIs, and collects data from the host OS level outside the guest VMs, assuming that the hardware, host OS, hypervisor, and cloud employees are trusted. OpenStack creates a directory on the host OS containing the virtual disk, RAMdisk, and other host-specific files. FROST retrieves the files from the host and transforms the virtual disk format to raw using the available utilities. For instance, QEMU provides utilities to convert QEMU QCOW2 images to raw format.

15.4 Proposed Comprehensive Approaches

At present, there are no dedicated deployable solutions that can handle cloud forensics tasks and evidence at the same level of comprehensiveness as the current integrated forensic suites already discussed. The key reasons are of a procedural and technical nature. In many respects, evidence procedures have been – until now – relatively easy to establish, because the physical location and ownership of the hardware, software, and data were closely tied and readily accessible. In turn, this allowed many legal evidence procedures to be directly translated to the digital world without having to rethink the rules.

Cloud services break this model and will, eventually, require that legal procedures evolve to catch up with technology development. Technical challenges arise from the overall shift from client-centric to server-centric computation, which breaks many of the assumptions of traditional digital forensics and makes applying the currently prevalent processing workflow problematic.

Thus, efforts to address the challenges posed by cloud forensics in a general way have taken one of two approaches. Work coming from digital forensics researchers tends to heavily favor the procedural approach, which assumes that we need (primarily) new acquisition processes, but the toolset and investigative process will mostly remain the same. Often, it is assumed that new legal obligations will be placed on service providers and/or tenants.

The alternative is to look for new technical solutions; these need not be strictly forensics in origin, but may address related problems in auditing, security, and privacy. In essence, this would acknowledge the concept that cloud-based software works differently, and that we need a completely new toolset to perform effective and efficient forensic analysis on cloud systems.

15.4.1 Procedural Expansion of Existing Forensic Practices

(Martini and Choo 2012) is a representative example of the approach embraced in the digital forensics literature – it seeks to identify the problems but has little in the way of technical detail. The focus is on minor refinements of the accepted procedural models of forensics, such as (McKemmish 1999) and (Kent et al. 2006). Further, the authors prescribe a six-step process to get the final version of the new framework: *conceptual framework, explication interviews, technical experiments, framework refinement, validation interviews, finalized framework.*

It is entirely possible that digital forensics researchers and practitioners, as a community, will adopt such a deliberate, time-consuming process to solve the problem; however, looking at the history of digital forensics, this seems highly unlikely. Experience tells us that the way new practices get established is much more improvised during disruptive technological transitions. Once enough experience, understanding, and acceptance of the new forensic techniques are gained, practices and procedures undergo revisions to account for the new development.

An instructive example in that regard is main-memory forensics. As recently as 10 years ago, best practices widely prescribed pulling the plug (literally) on any computer found running during search and seizure operations. This was not entirely unreasonable, because dedicated memory forensics tools did not exist, so there was no extra evidence to be gained. Today, we have highly sophisticated tools to acquire and analyze memory images (Ligh et al. 2014), and they are the only key to solving many investigative scenarios. Accordingly, training and field manuals have been rewritten to point to the new state of knowledge.

To summarize, by their very nature, *standards lag technical development* and merely incorporate the successful innovations into the canon of best practices. In our view, it is critically important to understand that we *need* new technical solutions, and no amount of procedural framework enhancement will bring them about. Technical advances are achieved by extensive and deliberate research and experimentation and often borrow and adapt methods from other fields.

15.4.2 API-Centric Acquisition and Processing

In traditional forensic models, the investigator works with physical evidence carriers, such as storage media or integrated computing devices. Thus, it is possible to identify the computer performing the computations and the media that store (traces of) processing, and to physically collect, preserve, and analyze information content. Because of this, research has focused on discovering and acquiring every little piece of log and timestamp information, and extracting every last bit of discarded data that applications and the OS have left behind.

Conceptually, cloud computing breaks this model in two major ways. First, resources – CPU cycles, RAM, storage, etc. – are first pooled (e.g. Redundant Array of Independent Disks [RAID] storage) and then allocated at a fine granularity. This results in physical media potentially containing data owned by many users, and to data relevant to a single case being spread among numerous providers. Applying the conventional model creates a long list of procedural, legal, and technical problems that are unlikely to have an efficient solution in the general case. Second, both computations and storage contain a much more ephemeral record because VM instances are created and destroyed with regularity and working storage is sanitized.

As we discussed in the prior section, current work on cloud storage forensics has treated the problem as just another instance of application forensics. It applies basic differential analysis techniques to gain a basic understanding of the artifacts left on client devices by taking before and after snapshots of the target compute system, and deducing relevant cause-and-effect relationships. During an actual investigation, the analyst would be interpreting the state of the system based on these known relationships.

Unfortunately, there are several serious problems with this extension of existing client-side methods:

- *Completeness:* The reliance on client-side data can leave out critical case data. One example is older versions of files, which most services provide; another is cloud-only data, such as a Google Docs document, which literally has no serialized local representation other than a link. Some services, such as a variety of personal information management apps, live only in the browser, so a flush of the cache would make them go away.
- *Reproducibility:* Because cloud storage apps are updated on a regular basis and versions have a relatively short life-span, it becomes harder to maintain the reproducibility of the analysis and may require frequent repetition of the original procedure.
- *Scalability:* As a continuation of the prior point, manual client-side analysis is burdensome and simply does not scale with the rapid growth of the variety of services and their versions.

We have performed some initial work using an alternative approach for the acquisition of evidence data from cloud storage providers: one that uses the official APIs provided by the services. Such an approach addresses most of the shortcomings just described:

- *Correctness:* APIs are well-documented, official interfaces through which cloud apps on the client communicate with the service. They tend to change slowly, and changes are clearly marked – only new features need to be incrementally incorporated into the acquisition tool.

- *Completeness/reproducibility:* It is easy to demonstrate completeness (based on the API specification), and reproducibility becomes straightforward.
- *Scalability:* There is no need to reverse-engineer the application logic. Web APIs tend to follow patterns, which makes it possible to adapt existing code to a new (similar) service with modest effort. It is often feasible to write an acquisition tool for a completely new service from scratch in a short time.

We have developed a proof-of-concept prototype called *kumodd* (Roussev et al. 2016) that can perform complete (or partial) acquisition of a cloud storage account's data. It works with four popular services – Dropbox, Box, Google Drive, and Microsoft's OneDrive – and supports the acquisition of revisions and cloud-only documents. The prototype is written in Python and offers both command-line and web-based user interfaces.

15.4.3 Audit-Centric Forensic Services

The move to cloud computing raises a number of security, privacy, and audit problems among the parties involved – tenants, (multiple) cloud providers, and cloud brokers. The only practical means to address them is for all to have a trustworthy history – a *log* – of all the relevant events in the computation. Such logs are created on the boundary between clients and servers, as well as during the normal operation of services, typically in response to client requests.

For example, a tenant providing SaaS for medical professionals will need to convince itself and its auditors that it is complying with all relevant privacy and audit regulations. Since the computation executes on the provider's platform, the tenant needs the assurances of a third party, such as a trusted logging service.

In many cases, the same log information collected for other purposes can directly answer forensic queries, such as the history of user input over time. It is also likely to provide much greater detail than is currently unavailable on the client. For example, Google Cloud Storage (https://cloud.google.com/storage/docs/access-logs) maintains access logs in comma-separated values (CSV) format containing information about the access requests made on the cloud storage area allocated to the user. Tables 15.2 and 15.3 present the list of fields and their descriptions maintained in the log files on Google Cloud Storage and AWS.

(Zavou et al. 2013) developed Cloudopsy: a visualization tool to address privacy concerns of a cloud customer about the third-party service/infrastructure providers handling customer data properly. The tool offers a user-friendly interface to the customers of cloud-hosted services to independently monitor the handling of sensitive data by third party. Cloudopsy's mechanism is divided into three main components: (i) the generation of audit trails, (ii) the transformation of the audit logs for efficient processing, and (iii) the visualization of the resulting audit trails. Cloudopsy uses the Circos visualization tool to generate graphs that enable users with no technical background to get a better understanding of the management of their data by third-party cloud services.

(Pappas et al. 2013) proposed CloudFence, which is a data flow-tracking framework for cloud-based applications. CloudFence provides APIs for integrating data-flow

Table 15.2 List of fields (with their data types and descriptions) used in Google storage access log format.

Field	Type	Description
time_micros	Integer	Time taken by a request to complete, in microseconds
c_ip	String	The IP address of the client system from which the request is made
c_ip_type	Integer	The version of IP used, i.e. either IPv4 or IPv6
cs_method	String	The HTTP method of the request from client to server
cs_uri	String	URI of the request
sc_status	Integer	HTTP status code sent from server to client
cs_bytes	Integer	Number of bytes sent in an HTTP request message from client to server
sc_bytes	Integer	Number of bytes sent in an HTTP response message from server to client
time_taken_micros	Integer	The time it took to serve the request by the server, in microseconds
cs_object	String	The object specified in the request
cs_operation	String	The Google Cloud Storage operation, such as GET_Object

Table 15.3 List of fields (and their descriptions) used in amazon web services server access log format.

Field	Description
Time	The time at which the request was received
Remote IP	IP address of the requester
Requester	Canonical user ID of the requester
Request ID	A string generated by Amazon S3 to uniquely identify each request
Operation	Such as SOAP.*operation* and REST. *HTTP_method*
Request-URI	URI in the HTTP request message
HTTP status	HTTP status code in the response message
Error Code	Amazon S3 error code
Bytes Sent	Number of bytes sent in the response message
Object Size	Total size of the object requested
Total Time	Number of milliseconds the request was in flight from the server's perspective
Turn-Around Time	Number of milliseconds that Amazon S3 spent processing the request

tracking in cloud services, marking sensitive user data to monitor data propagation for protection. The authors implemented a prototype of CloudFence using Intel's Pin (Luk et al. 2005), a dynamic binary instrumentation toolkit without modifying applications. CloudFence can protect against information-disclosure attacks with modest performance overhead.

15.5 Discussion

Clearly, the discussed work in other relevant domains may not perfectly align with the typical needs of forensics. Nonetheless, it is representative of the *kind* of data that is likely to be available for forensic purposes. This can provide critical help in both building new analytical tools and in defining *reasonable* additional data-retention and provenance requirements for different cloud actors. In our view, one likely outcome is the emergence of *secure logging* services (SecLaaS) such as the ones proposed by (Zawoad 2013).

Another bright spot for the future is the fact that logging is central to *all* aspects of the functioning of a cloud system, and most of the forensic concerns related to investigating logs (Ruan et al. 2013, Zawoad and Hasan 2013)), such as cleanup, time synchronization, data correlation, and timeline analysis, are quite generic. Therefore, a robust log-management infrastructure will be available to the right forensic tools (Marty 2011).

Even as digital forensics practitioners struggle to come to terms with the current state of cloud computing, an even bigger wave of challenges is on the horizon. Indeed, the very definition of cloud forensics is likely to expand to include much of mobile device forensics (as more of the computation and logged data remain in the Cloud) and the emerging concept of automated *machine-to-machine* interaction (a.k.a. the Internet of Things [IoT]). The latter is poised to dramatically escalate the amount of data generated as the current limiting factor – the human operator – is removed from the loop. In other words, the number of possible machine-to-machine interactions will no longer be tied to the number of humans and can readily grow at an exponential rate.

15.6 Conclusions

In this chapter, we argued that the acquisition and analysis of cloud artifacts is in its infancy, and that current-generation tools are ill-suited to the task. Specifically, the continued focus on analyzing client-side artifacts is a direct extension of existing procedural approaches that, in the cloud context, fail to deliver on two critical forensic requirements: completeness and reproducibility. We have shown that SaaS cloud services routinely provide versioning and use cloud-native artifacts, which demands a new API-centric approach to discovery, acquisition, and analysis.

Another major point of our analysis is that we are in the very early stages of a paradigm shift from artifact-centric to log-centric forensics. That is, the current focus on extracting snapshots in time of OS and application data structures (primarily out of the file system) will have wide applicability *only* to IaaS investigative scenarios. For PaaS/SaaS situations – which will be increasingly common – the natural approach is to work with the existing log data. In some cases, such as Google Docs, such data can provide a *complete* chronology of user edits since the creation of the document.

Finally, although data growth was identified as a primary concern for forensic tool design over a decade ago (Roussev and Richard 2004), we are facing an even steeper curve because the IoT – built on automated machine-to-machine interaction – will escalate the amount of data available that (potentially) needs to be examined. This implies that the drive for ever-higher levels of automated processing will no longer be just an issue of efficiency, but a clear and present necessity. On the bright side, we note that logical (API-based) acquisition will *enable* higher levels of automated processing by eliminating tedious, low-level device acquisition and interpretation; the acquired data will have known a structure and semantics, thereby eliminating much of the need for manual reverse engineering.

It is important to recognize that, in forensics, technical experimentation and development have always led the way, with best practices and legal scrutiny following suit. At present, we are at the starting point of a major technology transition, which naturally leads to a moment of confusion, hesitation, and efforts to tweak old tools to a new purpose. There seems to be some conviction that, more than ever, we need a multidisciplinary effort to cloud forensics (NIST 2014); that is, we should attempt to solve *all* problems – technical and nontechnical – at the same time.

It is worth remembering that the current state of digital forensics is the result of some 30 years of research, development, and practice, all on client devices. We face a moment of disruption with the weight (and history) of computations shifting to the server environment. This is a substantial change, and "big project" approaches almost never succeed in managing such an abrupt transition. What *does* succeed is small-scale technical experimentation, followed by tool development and field use. The legal and procedural framework can only be meaningfully developed once a critical amount of experience is accumulated.

References

Chung, H., Park, J., Lee, S., and Kang, C. (2012). Digital forensic investigation of cloud storage services. *Journal of Digital Investigation* 9 (2): 81–95. https://doi.org/10.1016/j.diin.2012.05.015.

Dykstra, J. and Sherman, A.T. (2012). Acquiring forensic evidence from infrastructure-as-a-service cloud computing: Exploring and evaluating tools, trust, and techniques. *Proceedings of the Twelfth Annual Digital Forensic Research Conference (DFRWS)* S90–S98. doi:10.1016/j.diin.2012.05.001.

Dykstra, J. and Sherman, A.T. (2013). Design and implementation of FROST: digital forensic tools for the OpenStack cloud computing platform. *Journal of Digital Investigation* 10 (Supplement): S87–S95. https://doi.org/10.1016/j.diin.2013.06.010.

Gartner. (2014). Gartner's 2014 hype cycle of emerging technologies maps. http://www.gartner.com/newsroom/id/2819918.

Hale, J.S. (2013). Amazon cloud drive forensic analysis. *Journal of Digital Investigation* 10 (3): 259–265. https://doi.org/10.1016/j.diin.2013.04.006.

Kent K., Chevalier S., Grance T. et al. (2006). Guide to integrating forensic techniques into incident response. SP800–86. Gaithersburg: U.S. Department of Commerce.

King, C. and Vidas, T. (2011). Empirical analysis of solid state disk data retention when used with contemporary operating systems. *Journal of Digital Investigation* 8: S111–S117. https://doi.org/10.1016/j.diin.2011.05.013.

Ligh, M.H., Case, A., Levy, J., and Walters, A. (2014). *The Art of Memory Forensics: Detecting Malware and Threats in Windows, Linux, and Mac Memory*. Wiley. ISBN: 978-1118825099.

Luk, C.K., Cohn, R., Muth, R. et al. (2005). Pin: building customized program analysis tools with dynamic instrumentation. In: Proceedings of PLDI, 190–200.

Martini, B. and Choo, K.R. (2012). An integrated conceptual digital forensic framework for cloud computing. *Journal of Digital Investigation* 9 (2): 71–80. https://doi.org/10.1016/j.diin.2012.07.001.

Martini, B. and Choo, K.R. (2013). Cloud storage forensics: *ownCloud* as a case study. *Journal of Digital Investigation* 10 (4): 287–299. https://doi.org/10.1016/j.diin.2013.08.005.

Marty, R. (2011). Cloud application logging for forensics. In: Proceedings of the 2011 ACM Symposium on Applied Computing (SAC '11), 178–184. ACM. http://doi.acm.org/10.1145/1982185.1982226.

McKemmish, R. (1999). What is forensic computing? *Trends & Issues in Crime and Criminal Justice* 118: 1–6.

NIST. (2014). NIST cloud computing forensic science challenges. (draft NISTIR 8006). NIST Cloud Computing Forensic Science Working Group. http://csrc.nist.gov/publications/drafts/nistir-8006/draft_nistir_8006.pdf.

Pappas, V., Kemerlis, V.P., Zavou, A. et al. 2013. CloudFence: data flow tracking as a cloud service. In: 16th International Symposium, RAID 2013, 411–431

Quick, D. and Choo, K.R. (2013). Dropbox analysis: data remnants on user machines. *Journal of Digital Investigation* 10 (1): 3–18. https://doi.org/10.1016/j.diin.2013.02.003.

Richard, G. and Roussev, V. (2005). Scalpel: a frugal, high-performance file carver. In: *Proceedings of the 2005 Digital Forensics Research Conference (DFRWS)*. New Orleans, LA.

RightScale. (2015). RightScale 2015 state of the Cloud report. http://assets.rightscale.com/uploads/pdfs/RightScale-2015-State-of-the-Cloud-Report.pdf.

Roussev, V. (2016). *Digital Forensic Science: Issues, Methods, and Challenges*. Morgan & Claypool.

Roussev, V. and McCulley, S. (2016). Forensic analysis of cloud-native artifacts. 3rd Annual Digital Forensic Research Conference Europe (DFRWS-EU), Geneva, Switzerland. https://doi.org/10.1016/j.diin.2016.01.013.

Roussev, V. and Richard, G. (2004). Breaking the performance wall: the case for distributed digital forensics. In: *Proceedings of the 2004 Digital Forensics Research Workshop (DFRWS)*. Baltimore, MD.

Roussev, V., Barreto, A., and Ahmed, I. (2016). API-based forensic acquisition of cloud drives. In: *Research Advances in Digital Forensics XII* (ed. G. Peterson and S. Shenoi), 213–235. Springer doi:10.1007/978-3-319-46279-0_11.

Ruan, K., Carthy, J., Kechadi, T., and Baggili, I. (2013). Cloud forensics definitions and critical criteria for cloud forensic capability: an overview of survey results. *Journal of Digital Investigation* 10 (1): 34–43. https://doi.org/10.1016/j.diin.2013.02.004.

Somers, J. (2014). How I reverse engineered Google Docs to play back any document's keystrokes. http://features.jsomers.net/how-i-reverse-engineered-google-docs (accessed 20 December 20 2014).

Zavou, A., Pappas, V., Kemerlis, V.P. et al. (2013). Cloudopsy: an autopsy of data flows in the Cloud. *HCI* (27): 366–375.

Zawoad, S. and Hasan, R. (2013). Cloud forensics: a meta-study of challenges, approaches, and open problems. https://arxiv.org/abs/1302.6312.

16

Forensics-as-a-Service (FaaS) in the State-of-the-Art Cloud

Avinash Srinivasan[1] *and Frank Ferrese*[2]

[1] *Computer and Information Sciences, Temple University, Philadelphia, PA, USA*
[2] *Electrical and Computer Engineering, Temple University, Philadelphia, PA, USA*

16.1 Introduction

Advances and fundamental changes in the computing and communications industries have resulted in significant challenges to current *digital forensic analysis* practices, policies, and regulations. Consequently, the forensic analysis process is suffering from significant roadblocks not only from unclear cyberlaws and regulations, but also as a result of significant technology challenges. Integrity is the key requirement in the forensic analysis process. To further complicate matters, computer forensic analysis is fundamentally a serial process. Therefore, inherent scalability challenges exist. Most importantly, the ability to withstand the Daubert test during the trial is pivotal to designing parallel and distributed forensic analysis tools (Ball 2017). In light of this web of challenges, case backlogs are growing at an increasing rate. As noted in (Hitchcock et al. 2016), the backlog is commonly in the order of 6–18 months, but can reach significantly higher numbers in some jurisdictions.

One instance of a key paradigm shift in the computing industry is the advent of *cloud computing*. In recent years, cloud computing capabilities have advanced significantly and evolved from a mere plausible concept to hard reality of survival for many industries. It has brought along numerous business opportunities; and everyone, from start-ups and small industries to Fortune 100 companies, is embracing cloud computing, though perhaps from different viewpoints and varying business needs. Some of the attractive benefits of cloud computing include a reduced in-house infrastructure burden, minimized maintenance and update pressures, and the ability to quickly scale as computing needs increase. A 2013 Gartner report predicted that the cloud-based security services market, which includes secure e-mail and web gateways, identity and access management (IAM), remote vulnerability assessment, security information, and event management would surpass $4 billion by 2017 (Messmer 2013).

Security, Privacy, and Digital Forensics in the Cloud, First Edition. Edited by Lei Chen, Hassan Takabi, and Nhien-An Le-Khac.

16.1.1 Current State of Cloud Computing

Cloud computing is undoubtedly one of the most significant technology advances of twenty-first century computing technology. The dawn of the cloud computing paradigm had three service delivery models: *Software-as-a-Service (SaaS)*, *Platform-as-a-Service (PaaS)*, and *Infrastructure-as-a-Service (IaaS)*. However, innovation and advancement fueled by growing consumer and business needs led to the birth of numerous other delivery models, *Scanning-as-a-Service* (Gionta et al. 2014) and *Monitoring-as-a-Service* (Alhamazani et al. 2015).

On the flip side, the cloud computing platform presents some very serious security and privacy concerns. The vast resource pool it offers has been and continues to be exploited by malicious actors. An adversary can easily exploit resources in real time for malicious reasons. This situation has transformed matters from bad to worse for *law enforcement* (LE) and the *intelligence community* (IC). Some potential threats from the cloud computing platform can be evidenced from services such as Cybercrime-as-a-Service (CaaS) (Robinson 2016), Malware-as-a-Service (Drozhzhin 2016), Attacks-as-a-Service (Lemos 2010), Crimeware-as-a-Service (CaaS) (Sood and Enbody 2013), and Exploit-as-a-Service (Grier et al. 2012). Today's cloud computing architectures, though very popular, are not designed to meet some of the stringent digital forensics requirements for electronic evidence. The most important requirements that are impacted by cloud computing are chain of custody and data provenance.

Numerous works have focused in this area, including (Reilly et al. 2010; Birk and Wegener 2011; Marty 2011; Taylor et al. 2011; Dykstra and Sherman 2012; Sibiya et al. 2012; Zawoad and Hasan 2012; Grispos et al. 2013; Zawoad et al. 2013; Zawoad and Hasan 2013b). Of particular relevance is (Zawoad and Hasan 2013a), which notes that many of the assumptions of digital forensics with regard to tools and techniques are not valid in cloud computing. In (Chen et al. 2013), the authors evaluate the implementation of a cloud-based security center for network security forensic analysis to process stored network traffic using cloud computing platforms to find malicious attacks.

16.1.2 What Is This Chapter About?

The chapter's primary focus solving the ever-increasing number of both criminal and civil cases that involve electronic evidence, increasing data and storage device sizes, and devices connected to the Internet of Things (IoT) that have been and continue to be foot soldiers for geographically remote cybercriminals and nation states. Some in the forensics community – LE and IC agencies, researchers, and practitioners – have turned toward parallel and distributed computing paradigms in the hope of overcoming the seemingly unsurmountable case backlog. One specific direction of interest is cloud computing. It is now clear that utilization of cloud resources to accelerate the turnaround times for forensics investigations is inevitable, and the its adoption of massive scale is both imminent and impending. Some of the early works toward this aim include (Wei 2004; Richard and Roussev 2006a; Richard and Roussev 2006b; Beebe and Clark 2007; Liebrock et al. 2007; Marziale et al. 2007; Ayers 2009; Roussev et al. 2009; Reilly et al. 2010).

16.1.3 Chapter Road Map

The remainder of this chapter is organized as follows. In Section 16.2, we discuss relevant background and present the necessary preliminaries of this chapter. Then, in Section 16.3, we review existing state-of-the-art work focusing on parallel and distributed digital forensic analysis, followed by a discussion of the limitations in this work in Section 16.3.2. In Section 16.3.3, we present some of the key requirements to offering cloud-based FaaS. Finally, in Section 16.3.4, we conclude the chapter with future research directions.

16.2 Background and Motivation

16.2.1 Limitations of Traditional Computer Forensics – Now and Forever

Today, it is not uncommon for laptops and desktops to be equipped with terabyte-sized storage. Similarly, in contrast to a decade ago, digital forensic analysts today deal not only with significantly larger average disk size, but also with an extremely large variety of devices. Consequently, the amount of data that needs to be processed can run into tens of terabytes. Adding to this problem is the number of cases today that require computer forensic analysis. As witnessed in recent crimes, attackers' level of sophistication has significantly advanced from the days of the Rabbit virus "fork bomb" and the Morris worm (Chen and Robert 2004) to state-of-the-art Petya and Mirai. Even widely used commercial forensics suites such as EnCase (www.guidancesoftware.com) and Forensic Toolkit (FTK; accessdata.com) are not keeping pace with the increased complexity and data volumes of modern investigations. The growing burden on computer forensic analysts is evident from the reports published by the FBI Regional Computer Forensics Laboratories (RCFLs) and Computer Analysis Response Team (CART). According to the 2010 RCFL annual report (RCFL 2011), a total of 6564 examinations were conducted, requiring processing of 3086TB data, with an average case size of 0.4TB. In its 2011 annual report (RCFL 2012), the RCFL reported a total of 7629 examinations by analyzing 4263TB of data. During fiscal year 2012, the FBI CART supported nearly 10 400 investigations, with over 13 300 computer forensic examinations, processing data volumes in excess of 10 500 TB (FBI-CART 2013).

Numerous works in recent years have tested the limits of traditional computer forensic tools and techniques to deal with evolving technology. Conventional wisdom may seem to be that computer systems should make investigations much faster simply by virtue of being able to perform billions of operations per second. In reality, however, the ever-increasing drive sizes necessitate significant (pre)processing times that far outweigh the benefits of those billions of operations per second.

Limitations of first-generation computer forensic tools are presented in (Ayers 2009) along with metrics for measuring the efficacy and performance of good tools. The author further lays out a broad set of requirements for second-generation tools and presents a high-level work-in-progress design for a second-generation computer forensic analysis system. The goal is to implement and test the prototype using two different processing architectures: (i) *Beowulf cluster*, and (ii) *IBM BlueGene/L supercomputer*.

A *forensic cloud* is a framework for a forensic index-based search application presented in (Lee and Hong 2011). While it takes substantial effort to construct an index database, the authors argue that searching the indexed database returns a query response in a fraction of the time the same query would take without indexing. Later, (Lee and Un 2012) present a case study supporting forensic indexed search as a service along with a work-in-progress model.

In their experiments, they achieve significantly better performance (≈56MB/s^{-1}) when the target data to be processed is more than 56GB. When a 1TB drive is analyzed with *bigrams*, their system takes ≈2 hours. Their system can also retrieve results from compressed text document formats at an average of ≈25MB/s^{-1} for a single query. Processing this query against a 1.27TB target took the authors ≈13 hours. However, they argue that this performance indeed outperforms existing forensic bitwise search methods by a significant margin. Further, the authors note that forensic bitwise search methods take ≈18.5 hours to perform a single keyword search on a 1TB drive.

This conclusion is supported further in (Roussev and Richard 2004), where the authors argue that a large part of the processing time is the "think" time, i.e. time needed for the human investigator to analyze the data. While it may be possible for a system to accumulate experience and reduce this time through Machine Learning, they are confident that the processing time needed by the system to execute investigator-issued queries is largely dependent on the quality of the construction of the query.

In summary, the limitations of current forensic tools and techniques are deeply rooted in the following: (i) data diversity and abstraction, (ii) input/output (I/O) and processing speed, (iii) I/O-intensive tasks, (iv) lack of automation, (v) inability to scale, and (vi) potential open source tools that aren't yet approved.

16.2.2 Potential of Looking Up to the Cloud – Forensics-as-a-Service

Cyberspace is highly dynamic and will not cease to evolve in its applications, sophistication, and reach. Consequently, the LE community will continue to work against the odds, making forensic analysis ever-more challenging. (Marziale et al. 2007) presents compelling real-world use cases justifying the need for more advanced tools. Their use cases clearly demonstrate the inadequate capacity of traditional forensic investigation tools executing on a single workstation.

The time has come for a paradigm shift in computer forensic analysis. We require an adaptive, widely available, priority-driven parallel and distributed computing architecture. While the Cloud is inherently a distributed computing paradigm, its resourcefulness as a parallel computing paradigm has also been established (Ekanayake and Fox 2009). This migration to the Ccloud is necessary to both clear current backlogs as well as make the backlog manageable in the future.

The Advanced Forensics Format (AFF) was proposed as an alternative to proprietary disk image formats. AFF is an open and extensible format for storing images of hard disks and other kinds of storage devices (Stevens et al. 2006). The authors also present AFFLIB, an open source library that implements AFF. This work also proposes *Advanced Imager* (AIMAGE), which is a new disk-image-acquisition program that compares favorably with existing alternatives. (Cohen et al. 2009) later redesigned this as AFF4 with backward compatibility. The redesigned AFF4 format built on the well-supported ZIP file format specification, making it simple to implement. Furthermore, the AFF4 implementation has downward comparability with existing AFF files.

16.3 State of the Art in Parallel and Distributed Forensic Analysis

16.3.1 GPU-Based Distributed Forensic Analysis

(Gao et al. 2004) discuss user and software engineering requirements for on-the-spot digital forensics tools to overcome time-consuming, in-depth forensic examinations. They present their *Bluepipe* architecture (shown in Figure 16.1) for on-the-spot investigation along with the remote forensics protocol they have developed.

The feasibility of using *graphics processing units* (GPUs) for accelerating the traditional digital forensic analysis process is explored in (Marziale et al. 2007). They note that the current generation of GPUs contains a large number of general-purpose processors, in sharp contrast to previous generations of designs, where special-purpose hardware units such as texture and vertex shaders were commonly used. This fact, combined with the prevalence of multicore general-purpose *central processing units* (CPUs) in modern workstations, suggests that performance-critical software such as digital forensics tools should be "massively" threaded to take advantage of all available computational resources.

Results from a number of experiments that evaluate the effectiveness of offloading processing common to digital forensics tools to a GPU, using "massive" numbers of threads to parallelize the computation, are presented in (Marziale et al. 2007). These results are compared to speedups obtainable by simple threading schemes appropriate for multicore CPUs, indicating that in many cases, the use of GPUs can substantially increase the performance of digital forensics tools.

(Roussev and Richard 2004) present the impact of evidence data size on analysis turnaround time. They evaluate the performance of the very popular commercial tool FTK by opening a case containing an old 6GB hard disk using the default options of the tool. During their study, FTK took approximately 2 hours to just open the case with the 6GB image. Using this time as the baseline, with a conservative assumption that the processing time grows linearly as a function of size, the authors conclude that it would take the state-of-the-art commercial tool approximately 60 hours to simply open a case with a 200GB disk image. However, in reality, when they tested their estimation on an 80GB image, it took FTK over 4 days (96+ hours) just to open the image. Therefore, there are indications that the tool does not scale linearly with increasing sizes of disk images.

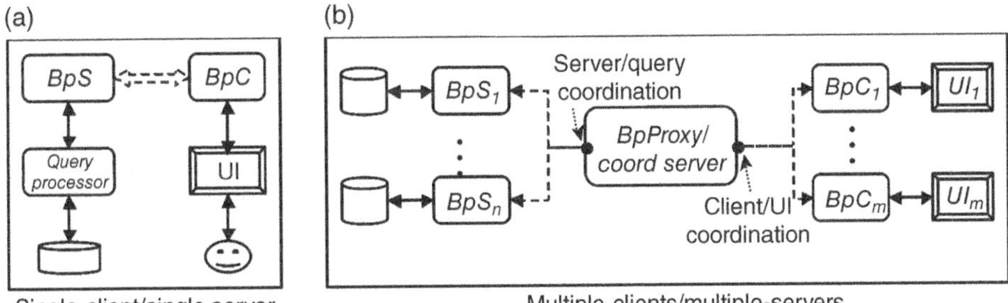

Figure 16.1 Bluepipe architecture (Gao et al. 2004).

Finally, (Roussev and Richard 2004) weigh in on the long-standing debate on whether to adopt a *generic distributed framework* (GDF) for distributed digital forensics (DDF) purposes or to develop a more specialized solution. They conclude that a specialized solution is a better approach for the following reasons. First, specialized solutions are more amenable to optimization for any specific purpose and, hence, can achieve better performance with less overhead. Second, specialized solutions minimize requirements for preinstalled infrastructure on machines. This enables regular users to run the system with ease and minimal administrative overhead. Finally, specialized solutions are better because GDFs have specialized programming interfaces requiring effort and experience for the operator to use them.

In summary, the conclusion of their work was that the fundamental resource constraints on workstation-class systems have been pushed to their processing and performance limits. Consequently, efforts focusing on task and resource optimizations will only result in marginal improvements, if any, on execution time.

16.3.1.1 XML Information Retrieval Approach to Digital Forensics (XIRAF)

(Alink et al. 2006) propose XIRAF, a prototype system for forensic analysis that is an Extensible Markup Language (XML) based implementation aimed at managing and querying forensic traces extracted from digital evidence. XIRAF systematically applies forensic analysis tools to evidence files. Each forensic analysis tool that is used produces an output consisting of structured XML annotations capable of referring to regions in the corresponding evidence file. Furthermore, such annotations are stored in a persistent back end such as an XML database (DB) that can be queried at a later time. To query XIRAF's XML database, the authors have developed *XQuery*, which is a custom query tool.

XIRAF's XML-based forensic analysis platform provides the forensic investigator with a powerful, feature-rich query environment in which browsing, searching, and predefined query templates are all expressed as XQuery queries – XML DB queries. The authors address two key data-processing problems that occur during the feature-extraction and analysis phases of a computer system investigation:

- *Evidence quantity:* Modern computer systems are routinely equipped with hundreds of gigabytes of storage, and a large investigation will often involve multiple systems, so the amount of data to process can run into terabytes. The amount of time available for processing this data is often limited (e.g. because of legal limitations). Also, the probability that a forensic investigator will miss important traces increases every day because there are simply too many objects to keep track of.
- *Evidence diversity:* A disk image contains a plethora of programs and file formats. This complicates processing and analysis and has led to a large number of special-purpose forensic analysis tools such as *browser history analyzers, file carvers, file-system analyzers, Internet relay chat (IRC) analysis tools, registry analysis tools,* etc. While it is clear that the output of different tools can and should be combined in meaningful ways, it is difficult today to obtain an integrated view of the output from different tools. Furthermore, even if proprietary and commercial tools are approved and acceptable, it is highly unlikely that any forensic investigator would have the time and the knowledge to apply the relevant tools to the case and evidence at hand. Hence the authors propose their XIRAF framework, which has the following key

properties: (i) clean separation between feature extraction and analysis; (ii) single, XML-based output format for all forensic analysis tools; (iii) XML DB for storing the XML annotations; and (iv) custom query tool XQuery for querying analysis tools' XML output.

Since December 2010, the Netherlands Forensic Institute has been using XIRAF – a service-based approach for processing and investigating high volumes of seized digital material. Service-based XIRAF has over the years evolved significantly and become a standard for hundreds of criminal cases and over a thousand investigators, both in the Netherlands and in other parts of the world. The authors note the impact of the XIRAF system and the paradigm shift it is causing, having processed over a petabyte of data with the XIRAF system.

XIRAF was originally primarily aimed at identifying and developing techniques for automating (parts of) the data analysis process for forensics investigations. It was never meant to be an operational system for processing large volumes of data, and most definitely not data volumes in petabytes. Consequently, design considerations made during the development of XIRAF leave significant room for improvement.

16.3.1.2 Hansken: Digital Forensics as a Service (DFaaS) Successor to XIRAF

Hansken was well defined and designed from its inception and has a proof of concept (PoC) based on the new principles and ideas and a production version to replace XIRAF (Alink et al. 2006). The forensic drivers behind the design and development of Hansken have been to provide a service that processes high volumes of digital material in a forensic context. In addition, it provides easy and secure access to the processed results. The Hansken forensics framework is designed to focus on the following three drivers: (i) minimization of case lead time, (ii) maximization of trace coverage, and (iii) specialization of people involved (Van Beek et al. 2015).

Processing seized material must be automated to provide the investigations team access to critical data. This impacts the way digital material is handled (Van Baar et al. 2014). Furthermore, the results of this automated process must be made available to the investigation team directly, not to specialized digital investigators. To further speed up the investigation, analysts should be able to annotate or tag interesting traces such as those that need further analysis, or those that are not clear to the investigator who tagged them. Such annotation/tagging should be available to other analysts so that the case can be solved through collaborative analysis.

The design of Hansken (Figure 16.2) supports distributed extraction of traces from images. XIRAF, the precursor to Hansken, applies multiple tools to a forensic image on a single machine. This is iterative in nature and hence does not scale well. Most importantly, the design of XIRAF means taking data to the tools, since tools are applied sequentially, with each tool having dedicated access to the image. To overcome this limitation of sequential processing, Hansken's design was driven toward taking the tools to the data. Hansken uses distributed technology, making it possible to process one forensic image using multiple machines. Consequently, as soon as the data is read from the image, it is kept in memory, and all tools are applied. Once a trace is fully processed, the results are stored in a database so it can be queried while other traces are still being extracted. This makes the first trace available in minutes, with more traces available for querying, mitigating idle time.

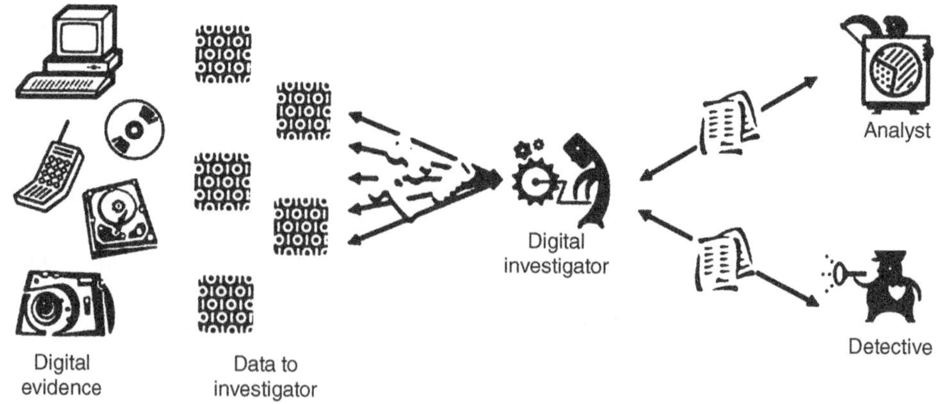

Figure 16.2 Hansken architecture (Van Beek et al. 2015).

Another key feature of Hansken is its *data-driven acquisition*, such that analysts can start the process of extracting traces from a forensic image as soon as the first bits of a device are uploaded to the central system. To support this feature, the authors have designed an image format that splits the image data into encrypted blocks. Such a format supports processing unordered blocks, which makes it possible to implement *dynamic pipelining* where the extraction process influences the imaging process by asking for certain blocks of data to become available with priority.

16.3.1.3 MPI MapReduce (MMR)

(Roussev et al. 2009) present three possible alternative approaches for augmenting forensics data processing in a fixed amount of time. The first is through the development of improved algorithms and tools for better and more efficient use of available machine resources. The second approach is the use of additional hardware resources to deploy additional machine resources. The third alternative is to facilitate human collaboration, taking advantage of human expertise in problem solving. All three approaches are mutually independent and support large-scale forensics in complementary ways.

The authors propose an open implementation of the *MapReduce* processing model that they call *MPI MapReduce* (MMR). The proposed MMR falls under the second category since it supports the use of additional hardware in the form of commodity distributed computational resources to speed up forensic investigations.

MMR's performance has been evaluated through a proof-of-concept implementation using two key technologies. The first is the *Phoenix shared-memory implementation* of MapReduce. The second is the *Message Passing Interface* (MPI) distributed communication standard. In summary, MMR provides linear scaling for CPU-intensive processing and super-linear scaling for indexing-related workloads.

16.3.1.4 GRR Rapid Response Framework

(Cohen et al. 2011) present GRR Rapid Response Framework (GRR), a new multiplatform, open source tool for enterprise forensic investigations. A key feature of GRR is its ability to support remote raw disk and memory access. GRR is designed to be scalable and is a distributed approach for remote live access. However, it is not a cloud-based solution; instead, it is a live forensics tool geared toward preserving volatile evidence. Yet another remote-access technique utilized is presented in (Cohen 2005). The advantage of this technique is that the client side is very simple, while the server side performs the complex forensic analysis.

A key challenge to automating analysis is that it may require executing many sequential steps. Current solutions create a dedicated console process that waits for the client to complete each step before issuing the next step. This limits scalability because the server needs to allocate resources for each client and wait until the entire analysis is complete. In GRR, the authors use state serialization to suspend execution for analysis processes for each client. These serialized forms are then stored dormant on disk until the client responds. Consequently, this approach resolves the problem of a resource drain imposed on servers. In GRR, such constructions are referred to as *flows*. A flow is simply a state machine with well-defined serialization points where it is possible to suspend its execution.

The architecture of GRR addresses auditing and privacy issues by allowing for nonintrusive automated analysis with audited access to retrieved data. However, it strives to achieve a balance between protecting access to user data and warranted forensically sound analysis. It also provides a secure and scalable platform to facilitate employing a variety of forensic analysis solutions. The authors support the usefulness and practicality of their proposed GRR through the following four case studies: (i) Investigation of intellectual property leaks, (ii) Isolation of a targeted malware attack, (iii) discovery request compliance, and iv) periodic snapshots of system states.

16.3.1.5 A Scalable File-Based Data Store for Forensic Analysis

(Cruz et al. 2015) present a specific implementation of the *GRR Rapid Response* (GRR) framework (Cohen et al. 2011). (Cruz et al. 2015) present a new data store back end (Figure 16.3) that can be used as a storage layer for the AFF4 Resolver. GRR's AFF4 Resolver stores AFF4 objects permanently in a *NoSQL* data store, enabling the application to only deal with high-level objects. The proposed GRR's distributed data store partitions data into database files that can be accessed independently, enabling scalable distributed forensic analysis. Furthermore, the authors discuss utilizing the software reference database *National Software Reference Library* (NSRL) in tandem with their distributed data store to avoid wasting resources when collecting/processing benign files. The following two functionalities must be implemented by the data store in order to support an AFF4 Resolver.

- *Single-object access:* Simplifies the partitioning of data because operations never deal with multiple objects. GRR systems require synchronous operations to guarantee globally deterministic ordering.
- *Support for synchronous and asynchronous operations:* Synchronous operations will block until the data store returns the results, while asynchronous operations will be scheduled to be performed at some point in the future. Asynchronous operations improve program concurrency and provide a huge performance advantage, and hence are heavily used by GRR systems.

Originally, the SQLite data store provided by GRR exhibits two limitations: (i) the capacity of each individual worker degrades as new workers are added to the GRR system due to contention at the data store, which limits its *horizontal scaling*; and (ii) since

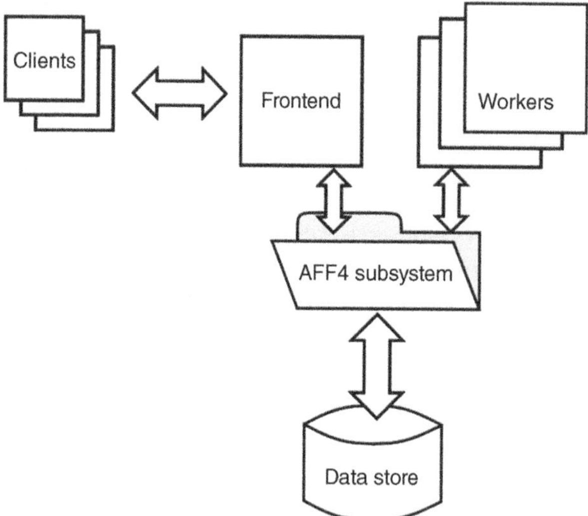

Figure 16.3 GRR architecture (Cruz et al. 2015).

existing data stores rely on a central database server, increasing storage demands on a single server are only possible to a certain extent, which limits *storage scaling*.

(Cruz et al. 2015) reason that these limitations are due to file-lock contention at the central server. Therefore, they work to resolve this problem by completely dividing the AFF4 namespace into independent storage files. This helps mitigate the file-lock contention problems. The benefits of their approach can be witnessed in their validation results.

16.3.1.6 Forensics-as-a-Service

(Wen et al. 2013) propose a domain-specific cloud environment that can use the emerging trends of service-based computing for supporting forensic applications. The proposed cloud-based forensics framework (Figure 16.4) is specifically designed for dealing with large volumes of forensic data. Furthermore, their approach has the ability to enable the sharing of interoperable forensic software and provides tools for forensic investigators to create and customize forensic data-processing workflows. The authors have conducted experiments using their forensic cloud framework with Amazon's Elastic Compute Cloud (EC2) service.

The experimental infrastructure is based on Hadoop 0.20 and HBase 0.20 and is managed by *Cloudera* (www.cloudera.com). For evaluations, the workloads are parallelized, and the results show that their approach can reduce forensic data analysis time considerably. They also argue that the overhead for investigators to design and configure complex forensic workflows is greatly minimized. Finally, they claim their proposed workflow management solution can save up to 87% of analysis time in the tested scenarios.

16.3.1.7 Data Deduplication Driven Acceleration of Forensic Analysis

(Scanlon 2016; Wolahan et al. 2016) present a unique perspective to combat the digital forensic backlog. The proposed method explores a data deduplication framework to

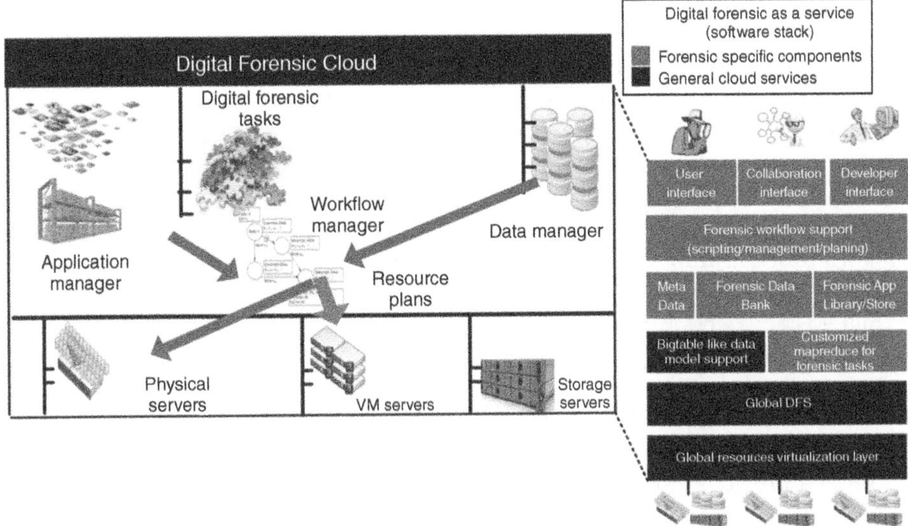

Figure 16.4 Digital forensic-as-a-service software stack (Wen et al. 2013).

eliminate redundancy in reacquisition, storage, and analysis of previously processed data. The primary objective of the authors in this case is to design a system that can alleviate some of the backlog by minimizing duplicated effort, while providing a number of enhancements to the functionality available with the traditional alternative. (Wolahan et al. 2016) explore alternatives to the traditional evidence-acquisition model by using a forensic data deduplication system. This work also presents the advantages of a deduplicated approach along with some preliminary results of a prototype implementation.

16.3.2 Limitations in State-of-the-Art Research and Tools

The speed of digital forensic evidence acquisition is traditionally limited by two main factors: (i) the *read speed* of the storage device being acquired and (ii) the *write speed* of the system the evidence is being acquired to. None of key research discussed here in distributed and parallel forensic analysis has addressed this issue. The researchers are assuming that the data used is collected from different sources in a distributed way, including using the Cloud during acquisition. This is not a realistic assumption.

Typically, first responders collect and image all of the evidence, and then it is uploaded to the Cloud. Unless multiple systems are being imaged, using the Cloud for acquiring evidence images does not yield better results due to the system I/O limitations noted previously. Additionally, the authors have not tested their frameworks on disk images without ground truth. Only knowing the ground truth of an image and then processing it with tailored workflow management will yield good results. Therefore, the process efficiency and increased-speed claims are questionable.

In (Cohen et al. 2011), the proposed system provisions remote access to networked systems. However, the tool is specifically designed for remote live forensics of the networked systems. In (Wen et al. 2013), the authors note that the data they use for experiments is collected from different sources in a distributed way using the Cloud. They further note that the forensic data manager provides support for uploading evidence files to the Cloud. However, the upload time for evidence files is not considered when evaluating the performance of their framework. Therefore, the increased speed they report in their results does not truly reflect the actual increase in speed, since uploading the evidence files is one of the most time-consuming steps in forensic analysis.

Another key area that has not been addressed is the difficulty in merging analysis results from various tools into a single case report. Note that frameworks (Van Beek et al. 2015) that facilitate execution of various tools on the evidence images need a streamlined approach for consolidating the output into a meaningful analysis report.

16.3.3 Cloud-Based Forensics-as-a-Service (FaaS)

16.3.3.1 Security and Privacy Requirements

FaaS service providers must assure all stakeholders – suspects, victims, judge, and jury – that their implementation and the operations of FaaS meet the regulatory standards for security and privacy of data and the integrity requirements of the forensics processes. A FaaS service provider is expected to assure its stakeholders of the three core security requirements – confidentiality, integrity, and availability – with regard to case and evidence data security and privacy. The service provider must ensure that resource pooling in a multitenant environment does not risk the fundamental requirements of the security triad.

Confidentiality of case-relevant information and evidence data is a key requirement. The service provider must ensure that appropriate control mechanisms (Figure 16.5) are in place to prevent accidental or intentional data disclosure, unauthorized access, or accidental/intentional data leaks either during or after the case analysis is complete. Furthermore, any potential user confidentiality violations can potentially have a domino effect, resulting in secondary violations of the *Health Insurance Portability and Accountability Act* (HIPAA), *Family Educational Rights and Privacy Act* (FERPA), etc. Similarly, third-party tools must be thoroughly vetted to detect any potential data leaks.

The integrity of case-relevant data is of even greater significance in the realm of computer forensic analysis. The FaaS provider mush have well-established and tested

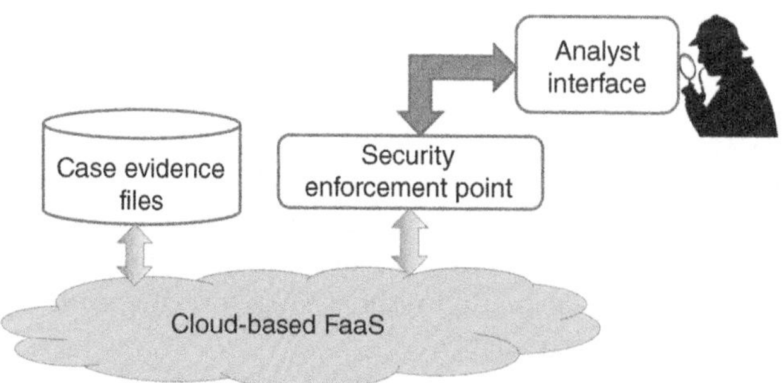

Figure 16.5 Security enforcement in FaaS.

integrity controls enforced to counter any potential risk of accidental or intentional alterations to case information and, more importantly, evidence data. Failure to implement strong integrity-preserving security mechanisms can be catastrophic to digital investigations, with the potential of rendering all evidence data inadmissible.

Finally, case information and evidence data should be available whenever authorized users need access. Though non-availability is not a critical security concern to the investigation, it can impact the investigation indirectly due to downtime resulting in delayed analysis. This can cascade to the discovery of information that could warrant additional seizures, which may already have been destroyed irreversibly. Also, at the completion of the analysis, there must be proper procedures for backup and archiving to ensure the availability of case-relevant data in the future for (re)appeals or other legal purposes.

16.3.3.2 Regulatory and Legal Requirements

Compliance in the realm of information security is a fundamental requirement. A majority of enterprise forensics investigations include noncompliant matters involving employees or the employer. Forensics investigations can span the whole spectrum of possibilities – from enterprise policy violations to insider threats, harassing e-mails to cyberstalking, robbery to vandalism, and suicide to homicide. Digital forensics investigations should comply with key regulations:

- There must be strict control over the cloud infrastructure and resources, ensuring consistency in jurisdiction and applicable laws of the FaaS platform.
- The FaaS platform and the entire process of analysis are monitored and logged at appropriate granularity, enabling audits by a neutral, trusted third party. The logs are themselves secured such that the neutral, trusted third party's auditing will not have access to any sensitive information such as personally identifiable information (PII) during the course of the audit.
- All methods, tools, and techniques must be validated and approved by appropriate government authorities. One of the key approvals often comes from the National Institute of Standards and Technology (NIST) *Computer Forensics Tool Testing* (CFTT) program. Failure to prove the integrity and reproducibility of the process would render all efforts futile in a court of law.

16.3.3.3 Design Requirements

Some of the key requirements for designing a parallel, distributed digital forensics toolkit framework are delineated next:

- *Modular:* Since the entire forensic analysis is a complex process, a modular design facilitates a systematic breakdown of the complex process. Subsequently, tools and techniques can be developed for smaller tasks at a level of granularity and abstraction that supports the case hypothesis. A modular design enables flexibility and extensibility, two key requirements to cope with an evolving technology and threat landscape. It also enables rapid development of newer tools and their easy integration into the master tool framework.
- *Scalable:* The architecture of the FaaS should be capable of scaling well with increasing numbers and sizes of cases and associated evidence. An increasing workload

should not compromise resource allocation and execution capabilities. A digital forensic analysis process is scalable if it can keep the average time per investigation constant in the face of growing target sizes and diversity (Roussev and Quates 2012).
- *Platform independent:* FaaS should be able to handle forensics tools independent of the tools' needs for a specific hardware/software platform. Furthermore, for the FaaS framework, it should be possible to pool the machine resources of a group of investigators working on the same case, to speed up the processing of critical evidence (Roussev and Richard 2004).
- *Extensible:* Cloud-based FaaS frameworks should be devoid of vendor-locked functionality and capability expansions. This is a critical requirement for enhancing FaaS relevance and capabilities so they are current with evolving technology needs and caseloads. Note that this is a standard software engineering requirement and mandates that it should be easy to add new or replace existing functions (Roussev and Richard 2004).

16.3.3.4 Benefits of Provisioning Cloud-Based Forensics-as-a-Service

By migrating the computer forensic analysis process to the cloud, the digital forensic science discipline will experience a broad spectrum of benefits. The first and foremost benefit will be more efficient utilization of limited manpower with required skills. This would also mean improved consistency in results from forensic analysis. Since the Cloud already offers metered services, migrating the forensic analysis process to the cloud will result in improved resource utilization while minimizing costs. Since the Cloud as a computing platform is ubiquitous and widely accessible, it enables better interagency and intra-agency information and resource sharing. Furthermore, FaaS will offer consistent analysis platforms and resource allocation through an established baseline. Finally, the most important benefit of FaaS will be provisioning accreditation and certification bodies with convenient access to tools and processes for validation and certification.

16.4 Conclusion and Future Research Direction

Current trends in computing and communications technologies are putting vast amounts of disk storage and abundant bandwidth in the hands of ordinary computer users. These trends have long surpassed the capabilities of traditional workstation-based platforms for computer forensics. There is plenty of evidence in the existing body of work, which addresses the limitations of the current generation of tools and technologies from different perspectives. However, timely processing of digital data is still fundamental to computer forensic analysis. Consequently, large-scale distributed computing resources coupled with the flexibility to customize forensics processing is critical.

There have been some initial attempts to use parallel and distributed computing paradigms to address a plethora of challenges faced by computer forensics analysts. (Roussev et al. 2009) have developed MPI MapReduce (MMR) as an alternative to Hadoop and demonstrated that the basic building blocks of many forensic tools can be efficiently realized using the MapReduce framework. Nonetheless, the true power of cloud computing is yet to be fully explored by providing a ubiquitous Forensics-as-a-Service platform. The future for accelerating digital forensic analysis to keep pace with the ever-evolving technology and complexities in computer forensic analysis is inevitably in the direction of parallel and distributed computing. In particular, the ubiquitous and plentiful resources available in the Cloud are the most promising option to alleviate most – if not all – of the problems currently faced.

References

Alhamazani, K., Ranjan, R., Jayaraman, P.P. et al. (2015). Cross-layer multi-cloud real-time application qos monitoring and benchmarking as-a-service framework. arXiv preprint arXiv:1502.00206.

Alink, W., Bhoedjang, R., Boncz, P.A., and de Vries, A.P. (2006). Xiraf–xml-based indexing and querying for digital forensics. *Digital Investigation* 3: 50–58.

Ayers, D. (2009). A second generation computer forensic analysis system. *Digital Investigation* 6: S34–S42.

Beebe, N.L. and Clark, J.G. (2007). Digital forensic text string searching: improving information retrieval effectiveness by thematically clustering search results. *Digital investigation* 4: 49–54.

Birk, D. and Wegener, C. (2011). Technical issues of forensic investigations in cloud computing environments. In: 2011 IEEE Sixth International Workshop on Systematic Approaches to Digital Forensic Engineering (SADFE), 1–10. IEEE.

Ball, C.E. (2017). Swaying the jury: the effect of expert witness testimony on jury verdicts in rape trials. Senior Capstone thesis. Arcadia University.

Chen, T. and Robert, J.-M. (2004). The evolution of viruses and worms.

Chen, Z., Han, F., Cao, J. et al. (2013). Cloud computing-based forensic analysis for collaborative network security management system. *Tsinghua Science and Technology* 18 (1): 40–50.

Cohen, M. (2005). Hooking io calls for multi-format image support. http://www.sleuthkit.org/informer/sleuthkit-informer-19.txt.

Cohen, M., Bilby, D., and Caronni, G. (2011). Distributed forensics and incident response in the enterprise. *Digital Investigation* 8: S101–S110.

Cohen, M., Garfinkel, S., and Schatz, B. (2009). Extending the advanced forensic format to accommodate multiple data sources, logical evidence, arbitrary information and forensic workflow. *Digital Investigation* 6: S57–S68.

Cruz, F., Moser, A., and Cohen, M. (2015). A scalable file based data store for forensic analysis. *Digital Investigation* 12: S90–S101.

Drozhzhin, A. (2016). Adwind malware-as-a-service hits more than 400,000 users globally. Kaspersky Lab.

Dykstra, J. and Sherman, A.T. (2012). Acquiring forensic evidence from infrastructure-as-a-service cloud computing: exploring and evaluating tools, trust, and techniques. *Digital Investigation* 9: S90–S98.

Ekanayake, J. and Fox, G. (2009). High performance parallel computing with clouds and cloud technologies. In: *International Conference on Cloud Computing*, 20–38. Springer.

FBI-CART (2013). Piecing together digital evidence – the computer analysis response team. http://www.fbi.gov/news/stories/2013/january/piecing-together-digital-evidence.

Gao, Y., Richard, G.G., and Roussev, V. (2004). Bluepipe: A scalable architecture for on-the-spot digital forensics. *International Journal of Digital Evidence (IJDE)* 3.

Gionta, J., Azab, A., Enck, W. et al. (2014). Seer: practical memory virus scanning as a service. In: Proceedings of the 30th Annual Computer Security Applications Conference, 186–195. ACM.

Grier, C., Ballard, L., Caballero, J. et al. (2012). Manufacturing compromise: the emergence of exploit-as-a-service. In: Proceedings of the 2012 ACM Conference on Computer and Communications Security, 821–832. ACM.

Grispos, G., Storer, T., and Glisson, W.B. (2012). Calm before the storm: the challenges of cloud computing in digital forensics. *International Journal of Digital Crime and Forensics (IJDCF)* 4 (2): 28–48. https://arxiv.org/pdf/1410.2123.pdf.

Hitchcock, B., Le-Khac, N.-A., and Scanlon, M. (2016). Tiered forensic methodology model for digital field triage by non-digital evidence specialists. *Digital investigation* 16: S75–S85.

Lee, J. and Hong, D. (2011). Pervasive forensic analysis based on mobile cloud computing. In: 2011 Third International Conference on Multimedia Information Networking and Security (MINES), 572–576. IEEE.

Lee, J. and Un, S. (2012). Digital forensics as a service: A case study of forensic indexed search. In: 2012 International Conference on ICT Convergence (ICTC), 499–503.

Lemos, R. (2010). Criminals 'go cloud' with attacks-as-a-service. Technical report, University of Zurich, Department of Informatics.

Liebrock, L.M., Marrero, N., Burton, D.P. et al. (2007). A preliminary design for digital forensics analysis of terabyte size data sets. In: Proceedings of the 2007 ACM Symposium on Applied Computing, 190–191. ACM.

Marty, R. (2011). Cloud application logging for forensics. In: Proceedings of the 2011 ACM Symposium on Applied Computing, 178–184. ACM.

Marziale, L., Richard, G.G., and Roussev, V. (2007). Massive threading: using GPUs to increase the performance of digital forensics tools. *Digital Investigation* 4: 73–81.

Messmer, E. (October 2013). Calm before the storm: The challenges of cloud computing in digital forensics. *Network World.*

RCFL (2011). Annual report for fiscal year 2010.

RCFL (2012). Annual report for fiscal year 2011.

Reilly, D., Wren, C., and Berry, T. (2010). Cloud computing: Forensic challenges for law enforcement. In: 2010 International Conference for Internet Technology and Secured Transactions (ICITST), 1–7. IEEE.

Richard, G.G. and Roussev, V. (2006a). Digital forensics tools: the next generation. In: *Digital Crime and Forensic Science in Cyberspace*, 75–90. IGI Global.

Richard, G.G. and Roussev, V. (2006b). Next-generation digital forensics. *Communications of the ACM* 49 (2): 76–80.

Robinson, R.M. (2016). Cybercrime-as-a-service poses a growing challenge. https://securityintelligence.com/cybercrime-as-a-service-poses-a-growing-challenge.

Roussev, V. and Quates, C. (2012). Content triage with similarity digests: the m57 case study. *Digital Investigation* 9: S60–S68.

Roussev, V. and Richard, G.G. (2004). Breaking the performance wall: The case for distributed digital forensics. In: Proceedings of the 2004 Digital Forensics Research Workshop (DFRWS) 94.

Roussev, V., Wang, L., Richard, G., and Marziale, L. (2009). *A Cloud Computing Platform for Large-Scale Forensic Computing*, 201–214. Berlin, Heidelberg: Springer Berlin Heidelberg.

Scanlon, M. (2016). Battling the digital forensic backlog through data deduplication. In: *2016 Sixth International Conference on Innovative Computing Technology (INTECH)*, 10–14. IEEE.

Sibiya, G., Venter, H.S., and Fogwill, T. (2012). Digital forensic framework for a cloud environment. IST-Africa 2012.

Sood, A.K. and Enbody, R.J. (2013). Crimeware-as-a-service – a survey of commoditized crimeware in the underground market. *International Journal of Critical Infrastructure Protection* 6 (1): 28–38.

Stevens, C., Malan, D., Garfinkel, S. et al. (2006). Advanced forensic format: An open, extensible format for disk imaging. In: *Advances in Digital Forensics II*, 13–27. Springer.

Taylor, M., Haggerty, J., Gresty, D., and Lamb, D. (2011). Forensic investigation of cloud computing systems. *Network Security* 2011 (3): 4–10.

Van Baar, R., Van Beek, H., and van Eijk, E. (2014). Digital forensics as a service: a game changer. *Digital Investigation* 11: S54–S62.

Van Beek, H., Van Eijk, E., Van Baar, R. et al. (2015). Digital forensics as a service: game on. *Digital Investigation* 15: 20–38.

Wei, R. (2004). A framework of distributed agent-based network forensics system. In: Digital Forensic Research Workshop (DFRWS), 11–13.

Wen, Y., Man, X., Le, K. et al. (2013). Forensics-as-a-service (FaaS): computer forensic workflow management and processing using cloud. In: Fifth International Conferences on Pervasive Patterns and Applications, 1–7.

Wolahan, H., Lorenzo, C. C., Bou-Harb, E. et al. (2016). Towards the leveraging of data deduplication to break the disk acquisition speed limit. In: 2016 8th IFIP International Conference on New Technologies, Mobility and Security (NTMS), 1–5.

Zawoad, S., Dutta, A. K., and Hasan, R. (2013). SecLaaS: secure logging-as-a-service for cloud forensics. In: Proceedings of the 8th ACM SIGSAC Symposium on Information, Computer and Communications Security, 219–230. ACM.

Zawoad, S. and Hasan, R. (2012). I have the proof: providing proofs of past data possession in cloud forensics. In: 2012 International Conference on Cyber Security (CyberSecurity), 75–82. IEEE.

Zawoad, S. and Hasan, R. (2013a). Cloud forensics: A meta-study of challenges, approaches, and open problems. arXiv preprint arXiv:1302.6312.

Zawoad, S. and Hasan, R. (2013b). Digital forensics in the cloud. Technical report, Defense Technical Information Center DTIC document. http://www.dtic.mil/dtic/tr/fulltext/u2/a590911.pdf.

Index

Security, Privacy, and Digital Forensics in the Cloud, First Edition. Edited by Lei Chen, Hassan Takabi, and Nhien-An Le-Khac.